GEORGE WASHINGTON'S PROVIDENCE

Raymond G. Lorber

DEDICATION

To Kay
My Guiding Light

To Mrs. Littaur

Congratulation on furthering
the study of God and
the founding of our
Country! Please
continue your calling.
God's blessing!
Elaine Meier
2014

CONTENTS

LIST OF MAPS

LIST OF TIMELINES

ACKNOWLEDGMENTS

With a project that takes over ten years, there are many who need to be recognized. Carolyn Lenert is the primary person whose help brought about the completion of my work. I thank her for the many months of editing and review that enabled me to bring my manuscript to the publisher's desk. Her friendship and dedication will always be valued.

I thank Joan Baker for her initial edit and Barbara Piquet for her guidance and advice on the manuscript's structure. I also express my appreciation for the assistance provided by the University of Virginia Press and the Ladies of Mount Vernon. By generously sharing their knowledge of the literature on George Washington, they enabled me to effectively focus my research.

I express my heartfelt appreciation to Dick Seashore who encouraged me to write this book. For Leo and the staff at The Redwood Café, I thank you for allowing me to spend my mornings reading and researching, while enjoying a cup (or two) of your excellent coffee, in preparation for my afternoons of writing. And I thank my many friends for their continual encouragement and support during these challenging ten years.

CHAPTER TIMELINE

Chapter	Event	Date	Age
1	George Washington is born	Feb. 22, 1732	
1	GW's father, Gus, dies at age 48	1743	11
1	GW contracts malaria	1749	17
1	GW accompanies Lawrence to Barbados and contracts smallpox	1751	19
1	George Washington contracts TB	1752	20
2	George Washington survives Indian assassination attempt	Dec. 27, 1753	21
2	George Washington nearly drowns crossing the Allegheny River	Dec. 29, 1753	21
3	George Washington experiences his first battle at Jumonville Glen	May 23, 1754	22
3	GW surrenders Fort Necessity	July 3, 1754	22
4	GW survives General Braddock's Battle of the Wilderness	July 12, 1755	23
5	During General Forbes's march to Fort Duquesne, GW halts a friendly firefight	Nov.12, 1758	26
	George Washington marries Martha	Jan. 6, 1759	26
6	George Washington appointed commander in chief	July 16, 1775	43
6	General Howe evacuates Boston	Mar. 17, 1776	44
6	Declaration of Independence signed	July 4, 1776	44
6	General Howe returns to America and defeats GW on Long Island	Aug. 27, 1776	44
7	Battle of Princeton – GW leads Americans against the British	Jan. 3, 1777	45
8	Battle of Monmouth – GW leads Americans against the British	June 28, 1778	46
	George Washington dies	Dec. 14, 1799	67

INTRODUCTION

Against all odds, George Washington lived to fulfill his belief that with a protecting and guiding Providence he would realize his destiny of greatness. At a time when the median age was sixteen, Washington lived to the advanced age of sixty-seven. His longevity is remarkable given that he experienced a life filled with numerous close calls from disease and enemy fire. His belief that, with the protection of Providence, he would live to accomplish greatness, proved prescient. Although he experienced countless life-threatening episodes, he lived to foster the world's first modern democracy and became renowned as the "Father of our Country." The following chapters depict the notable moments in Washington's life when his trust in Divine Providence gave him the strength and courage to face imminent peril from disease and combat.

Washington's lifelong hardiness was amazing—not only in battle but also in his frequent bouts with fatal infections. Therefore, the first chapter is committed to the little-known but horrendous struggles against the many typically fatal illnesses that Washington endured. Chapter one reviews Washington's battles with lethal diseases that began in his teenage years and continued until his final episode at the age of sixty-seven. Research for this chapter was very challenging because the eighteenth-century medical community did not retain comprehensive medical records. Not having access to proper documentation, historians and authors have frequently reported incorrectly on the state of Washington's health. To provide a credible account, only illnesses described by Washington himself and his correspondents who had firsthand knowledge are included.

The second chapter details Washington's close calls with death while on an expedition in the wilderness in the winter of 1753–54. In the service of his country at the age of twenty-one, he heroically undertook a wilderness expedition of over one thousand miles to deliver Virginia's Lieutenant Governor Dinwiddie's diplomatic letter to the invading French commandant. While returning from the meeting with the French commandant, he survived a point-blank assassination attempt by his

French Indian guide. And then, while escaping from further attack, he nearly drowned in a rafting accident in the frigid Allegheny.

Chapter three portrays the first two of Washington's potentially life-ending battlefield experiences. After completing his wilderness expedition, he was sent back into the wilds to block the French incursion into the Ohio country. His first live firefight occurred at Jumonville Glen where he attacked a small French encampment. The French retaliated by attacking Washington's Fort Necessity (near modern-day Farmington, PA). Washington's attack on the French forces at Jumonville Glen is considered by many historians to be the confrontation that initiated the French and Indian War. The colonial army suffered heavy losses during these battles but Washington emerged unscathed.

General Braddock's doomed expedition to drive the French out of the Ohio territory in the spring of 1755 is covered in chapter four. Braddock's campaign was slow and arduous, and Washington became ill with the bloody flux (dysentery). Before he fully recovered, he joined Braddock and participated in the battle that became a massacre of the British forces. Washington had two horses shot from under him and received four bullet holes in his coat, but he was not wounded. When his patron, William Fairfax, next wrote to George, he expressed confidence and gratitude that Providence was looking after the young man.[1]

Brigadier General John Forbes's 1758 effort to conquer Fort Duquesne is described in chapter five. During this third and final attempt to remove the French from Fort Duquesne, Washington risked his life to save the lives of his men. He stepped between the two American scouting parties who were mistakenly firing upon each other and encouraged them to cease firing. Again Washington took extreme risks and remained unscathed.

Chapter six describes Washington's initial battles as commander in chief of the American army during the Revolutionary War. It details the difficult but successful siege of the city of Boston and his subsequent defeat at Long Island. While crossing the East River during his retreat, he was saved by an unexpectedly heavy fog that prevented the British from observing his movements.

Washington faced death while turning the retreating American forces in the battle at Princeton, New Jersey, in January 1777. Chapter seven depicts the confusion and disarray that he found among his troops as the British were forming lines. George Washington rode between the opposing forces within range of the British units and ordered the American troops to charge.

Chapter eight portrays Washington again taking a stand against the hard-charging British and reversing the flow of battle. In the battle at Monmouth, New Jersey, in June 1778, Washington rallied General Lee's retreating American forces by confronting a blazing British barrage and forcing the British to yield the battlefield. By defeating the best of the British army in America, conflict in the northern states ceased.

Throughout the volumes of literature on the life of George Washington, there is extensive commentary on his survivability. Many of these reports are questionable. To maintain accuracy, only first-person accounts of events in which Washington surprisingly survived are included in this review. Consequently, not all of the reported episodes that could have ended the life of Washington are included in these chapters. For example, in *The Life of Washington*, Parson Mason Weems wrote that he knew of an Indian who swore "Washington was not born to be killed by a bullet! For, I had seventeen fair fires at him with my rifle, and after all could not bring him to the ground!"[2] According to the editor, Marcus Cunliffe, Weems's book provided a long list of questionable inclusions. In summary, he wrote, "In a word, the objection to Weems is that he was slapdash and even fraudulent; and that he forced upon the world a false and repellent picture of George Washington."[3]

The research supporting the information revealed in this document strengthens the observation that George Washington miraculously survived numerous life-threatening events and that he believed it was Providence's protection that enabled him to live to fulfill a grander purpose. History has shown that he was the one and only leader in the late eighteenth century with the requisite military and political skills to lead America out of a world of monarchy and colonialism and into the new reality of constitutional freedom.

GEORGE WASHINGTON'S CLOSE ENCOUNTERS WITH DEATH TIMELINE

Year	Life-threatening Close Encounter	Age	Non-medical Close Encounters
1749	Contracted malaria	17	
1751	Contracted smallpox	19	
1752	Contracted tuberculosis	20	
1753	Survived Indian attack	21	Shot at by his French Indian guide
1753	Survived near drowning	21	Knocked off his raft into Allegheny River
1754	Survived enemy fire	22	Jumonville Glen
1754	Survived enemy fire	22	Fort Necessity
1755	Suffered tuberculosis and survived enemy fire	23	Campaign with General Braddock
1757	Suffered tuberculosis	25	
1758	Survived friendly firefight	26	Campaign with General Forbes
1761	Suffered tuberculosis	29	
1776	Survived enemy fire	44	Battle of Trenton
1777	Survived enemy fire	45	Battle of Princeton
1778	Survived enemy fire	46	Battle of Monmouth
1786	Suffered malaria	54	
1789	Suffered malignant tumor	57	
1790	Suffered violent attack of peripneumony	58	
1799	Died from a throat infection	67	

THE GRIM KING
February 22, 1732–December 14, 1799

"I once thought the grim King would certainly master my utmost efforts and that I must sink in spite of a noble struggle but thank God I have now got the better of the disorder..."

– George Washington – October 20, 1761

THROUGHOUT HIS LIFE GEORGE WASHINGTON suffered through the disease and illness that took many of his countrymen during the eighteenth century. His survivability was amazing and is difficult to comprehend. Although it is a challenge to understand how he survived, George Washington understood that his being was in the hands of Providence and that he was saved to achieve greatness.

On February 22, 1732, George Washington was born into the world when medical care was primitive. Medical treatment frequently was more hazardous than the disease. Eighteenth-century medical practitioners believed that the best way to rid the body of disease was by drawing and leeching while mistakenly assuming that blood would be restored in the body within a few hours. With today's highly trained medical specialists, sterile operating rooms, and Federal Drug Administration-approved prescription medicines, we wonder how anyone could have survived these rudimentary eighteenth-century medical procedures.

With such dire medical assistance, the hand of death was always present. Infectious diseases (yellow fever, smallpox, diphtheria, malaria, typhoid, cholera, tuberculosis, bubonic plague, influenza, etc.) spread rapidly and destroyed whole communities. The median age in the eighteenth century was about sixteen. Being exposed to so many health hazards, few expected to see the golden years of their lives.

Research for this chapter was very challenging because the eighteenth-century medical community did not value comprehensive medical records. Various historians and authors have accordingly incorrectly reported Washington's illnesses. To provide a credible report, included are only the illnesses described by Washington in his correspondence and in correspondence from those with firsthand knowledge.

Many of the symptoms described by Washington and his doctors are not included in today's terminology, and this made it more difficult in my effort to accurately identify Washington's life-threatening illnesses. For example, bloody flux, stitches, and violent pleuretic pains and pleurisy leave today's reader wondering just how today's medical community would describe these symptoms. Was Washington's reference to pleurisy really the illness that we recognize with this name or was it a symptom of tuberculosis? My identification of an illness is based upon the symptoms described in the correspondence and therefore may not always be correct. Sometimes, with the description offered, it was difficult to identify whether Washington was suffering from tuberculosis or malaria. Although it was not always clear what disease Washington was suffering from, included in this chapter is the episode believing that whatever the illness may have been it was clearly life threatening.

Washington's male legacy endowed him with great physical strength and athletic ability but diminished his expectations for longevity. George

Washington's great-grandfather John Washington, who immigrated to Virginia in 1657 from Great Britain, died at the age of forty-six. His grandfather, Lawrence Washington, died at the age of thirty-nine. His father, Augustine (Gus) Washington, died at the age of forty-eight. With the limited lifespan of his male ancestry, George Washington expected his life too would be short lived.

Living with this eighteenth-century limited life expectancy, a spouse usually remarried soon after the death of his or her partner. Augustine (Gus) Washington, father of George Washington, initially married Jane Butler. She died at the age of twenty-nine. Sixteen months later Gus married twenty-three-year-old Mary Ball. Gus Washington and Jane Butler had four children. Their two sons, Lawrence and Augustine (Austin), grew to manhood. George Washington was the first of Gus and Mary Ball's six children. All but one daughter survived to adulthood.

Lawrence Washington, George Washington's half brother, married fifteen-year-old Anne Fairfax. Lawrence and Anne conceived four children. All four children died of tuberculosis in their childhood. Lawrence died of tuberculosis at the age of thirty-four. Upon his death Anne Fairfax remarried within six months. Anne died of tuberculosis at the age of thirty-three.

George Washington expected that he too would follow the Washington male legacy and have a short life, but having lived to the age of sixty-seven he outlived his forefathers, his two half brothers, and his three brothers. His half brother Augustine (Austin) Washington lived to age forty-two. His brothers died at the following ages: Samuel Washington at age forty-seven, John Washington at age fifty-one, and Charles Washington, his youngest brother, at age sixty-two.

Teenage Years (1748–1752):

With Lawrence, Washington's half brother, having married into the Fairfax family, George enjoyed visiting Belvoir, the Fairfax plantation. William Fairfax became George Washington's patron and provided him with the support that guided him through his teenage years. George William Fairfax, William's son, and George Washington developed a close friendship that lasted until the demise of George William in 1787.

As a youth, Washington displayed a rugged strength. At the age of sixteen, he joined George William Fairfax on a surveying expedition in the mountains of Virginia's western frontier and along the South Branch of the Potomac River. This very strenuous journey required great stamina. In March 1748 he wrote in his diary:[1]

> *Tuesday 15th.   We set out early with Intent to Run round the sd. Land but being taken in a Rain & it Increasing very fast obliged us to return. It clearing about one oClock & our time being too Precious to Loose we a second time ventured out & Worked hard till Night & then returnd…*
>
> *Friday 18th.   We Travell'd up about 35 Miles to Thomas Barwicks on Potomack here we found the River so excessively high by Reason of the Great Rains that had fallen up about the Allegany Mountains as they told us which was then bringing down the melted Snow & that it would not be fordable for severall Days it was then above Six foot Higher than usual & was Rising.*
>
> *Monday 21st.   We went over in a Canoe & Travell'd up Maryland side all the Day in a Continued Rain to Collo. Cresaps right against the Mouth of the South Branch about 40 Miles from Polks I believe the worst Road that ever was trod by Man or Beast.*

The following year he received his commission and became a surveyor for Culpeper County. Throughout the summer he traveled vast distances surveying the wilderness of western Virginia, once again demonstrating his considerable strength and endurance while working this rugged mountainous frontier.

At the age of seventeen, while working the frontier, he contracted malaria. In the autumn of 1749, he wrote to his sister-in-law Anne Fairfax Washington that he was unable to visit because of his illness.[2]

[September—November 1749]

I heartily Congratulate you on the happy News of my Brothers safe arrival in health in England and am joy'd to hear that his stay is likely to be so short I hope you'l make Use of your Natural Resolution and contendness as they are the only Remedys to spend the time with ease & pleasure to yourself. I am deprived of the pleasure of waiting on you (as I expected) by Aguee and Feaver which I have had to Extremety since I left which has occasioned my Return D[own].

His half brother Lawrence Washington suffered from tuberculosis and in an attempt to arrest the illness traveled to Barbados in the autumn of 1751. Nineteen-year-old George Washington accompanied Lawrence on this journey, and while in Barbados he contracted smallpox. He suffered painfully for three weeks and described the seriousness of his illness in his diary on November 17.[3]

Saturday 17th. Was strongly attacked with the small Pox: sent for Dr. Lanahan whose attendance was very constant till my recovery, and going out which was not 'till thursday the 12th of December

At the age of twenty, shortly after his return from Barbados, he contracted tuberculosis while living with Lawrence Washington's family in Mount Vernon.

Lawrence died in 1752, the same year that George Washington contracted tuberculosis. Tuberculosis was the primary cause of death in the eighteenth century and took the lives of millions. But again George Washington survived a disease that had proven fatal to many others.

In a letter to William Fauntleroy on May 20, 1752, he wrote that his illness prevented him from visiting.[4]

Sir   May 20th 1752

I shou'd have been down long before this but my business in Frederick detain'd me somewhat longer than I expected and imediately upon my return from thence I was taken with a Violent Pleurisie which has reduced me very low but purpose as soon as I recover my strength to wait on Miss Betcy, in hopes of a revocation of the former, cruel sentence, and see if I can meet with ⟨any alter⟩ation in my favour. I have inclos'd a letter to her which i shou'd be much obligd to you for the delivery of it. I have nothing to add but my best respects to your good Lady and Family and that I am Sir Yr most Obedient Hble Servt

G. Washington

It appears that he may have been infatuated with William Fauntleroy's daughter, Elizabeth Fauntleroy.

Following three years of suffering from the debilitating illnesses of malaria, smallpox, and tuberculosis, Washington amazingly had the strength to trek over a thousand miles of wilderness during the winter of 1753–1754 to deliver a message from Dinwiddie to the French commandant requesting the French cease their construction of forts in British territory. The challenges that he endured during this trek are described in detail in chapter two. Surviving such devastating illnesses evidently provided Washington with the drive and ambition to excel in this incredibly physical trek.

French and Indian War Years (1754–1763):

In his twenty-third year, while campaigning with General Braddock, he suffered again from an acute attack of malaria.

George Washington left Mount Vernon on April 23, 1755, to join General Braddock's campaign against Fort Duquesne.[5] Upon his arrival at Fort Cumberland, the general sent Washington to Williamsburg to acquire funds for the campaign. On May 15, he set out from Fort Cumberland. Upon reaching Clairborne's Ferry on May 22, about twenty-seven miles from Williamsburg, he wrote to Robert Orme, General Braddock's aide-de-camp, that the extensive riding had exhausted him.[6]

As I am fatigued and a good deal disorderd by constant riding (in a droughth that has almost destroyd this part of the Country) I shall proceed more slowly back, unless I am fortunate enough, contrary to expectation, to receive the money, in that case I shall hurry with the utmost dispatch.

He returned to Fort Cumberland on June 7, and in a letter to Sarah Fairfax Carlyle, he again mentioned his fatigue from the long journey:[7] *"I arrivd here in tolerable health tho something fatiegued with the journey…"*

On June 7, he also wrote to his brother John Augustine Washington. In his letter he mentioned that several soldiers became sick and died while they were camped at Fort Cumberland.[8]

A Captn of Sir Peter's Regimt with several of the common Soldiers of the different Corps have died since our Incampmt here, and many others are now sick with a kind of Bloody Flux.

Around June 18, 1755, Washington began to experience the effects from another attack of malaria. Captain Roger Morris, General Braddock's other aide-de-camp, wrote to Washington on June 23 to express the general's concerns and to encourage Washington to follow the doctor's advice.[9]

Dear Washington   *[Squaw's Fort, Pa., 23 June 1755]*
   I am desird by the General, to let you know that he marches, to morrow, & next day, but that he shall halt, at the Meadows two or three days, It is the Desire of every particular in the Family, & the Generals positive Commands to you, not to stirr, but by the Advice of the Person under whose Care you are, till you are better, which we all hope will be very soon—This I can personally assure you, that you may follow the Advice of Dr Murdoch Surgeon to Col: Dunbarr, to whom I know you are recommended as a proper Man, by Dr. Stephen. yours &c.
                                          Roger Morris
Camp at this Side of the Youghangany—Monday five o'Clock in the Afternoon.

While experiencing violent headaches and fever (symptoms of malaria), George Washington wrote to his half brother John Augustine Washington on June 28.[10]

[Great Crossing of the Youghiogheny, Pa.,
28 June–2 July 1755]

Mount Vernon

To Mr Jno. Auge Washington

Dear Brother

Immediately upon our leavg the C. at Geors. Ck the 14th Inst. (from whe I wrote to yo.) I was siezd wt violt Fevers & Pns in my hd wch con[tinue]d wtout Intermisn till the 23 follg when I was reliev'd by the Genls absolty ordering the Phyns to give me Doctr Jas Powders; (one of the most excelt mede in the W.) for it gave me immee ease, and removed my Fevrs & othr Compts in 4 Days time. My illness was too violent to suffer me to ride, therefore I was indebted to a coverd Waggon for some part of my Transpn; but even in this I cd not conte far for the joltg was so gt that I was left upon the Road with a Guard and necessys, to wait the Arrl of Colo. Dunbars Detacht, whh was 2 days M. behind us. The Genl giving me his wd of honr that I shd be brought up before he reachd the French Fort; this promise, and the Doctrs threats that if I perseverd in my attempts to get on, in the Condn I was, my Life, wd be endangered, determind me to halt for the above Detacht.

Washington, resting under the care of physicians, remained behind the main body of troops as they marched to Fort Duquesne. On July 9, 1755, as the troops were advancing to attack Fort Duquesne, he joined them. Although still very ill, he participated in the disastrous Battle of Monongahela fighting alongside General Braddock. Chapter three provides a detailed description of George Washington's incredible struggle in this disastrous battle.

Ten days after the battle he wrote to his brother John Augustine Washington explaining that he had not been injured during the battle, but was still suffering from the illness.[11]

A Weak, and Feeble State of Health, obliges me to halt here for 2 or 3 days, to recover a little strength, that I may thereby be enabled to proceed homewards with more ease…

On the same day he also wrote to his mother, Mary Ball Washington.[12]

I was not half recoverd from a violent illness that had confin'd me to my Bed, and a Waggon, for above 10 Days; I am still in a weak and Feeble condn which induces me to halt here 2 or 3 Days in hopes of recovg a little Strength, to enable me to proceed homewards; from whence, I fear I shall not be able to stir till towards Sepr, so that I shall not have the pleasure of seeing you till then, unless it be in Fairfax…

On July 26, to facilitate his rehabilitation, Washington returned to Mount Vernon.

Lieutenant Governor Dinwiddie, having learned of General Braddock's defeat, requested that the Virginia General Assembly increase the colony's forces. There was strong support to appoint George Washington as colonel of the reconstituted Virginia regiment.

Augustine Washington, a member of the House of Burgesses, had encouraged Washington to travel to Williamsburg to promote his interest in being assigned to command the Virginia regiment. Washington, still suffering from his bout with malaria and concerned about further impairing his health, declined to travel to Williamsburg. On August 2nd, he wrote,.[13]

[Mount Vernon, 2 August 1755]
prest at Williamsburgh

To Colo. Auge Washington,
Dear Brothr

The pleasure of your Company at Mount-Vernon always did, & always will, afford me infinite satisfaction but as this time I am too sensible how needful the Country is of the assistance of all its Members, to have a wish to hear that any are absent from the assembly. I most sincerely wish that Unanimity may prevail in all your Councils, and that a happy issue may attend your deliberations at this importt crises.

I am not able, were I ever so willing, to meet you in Town; for I assure you it is with some difficulty and much fatiegue that I visit my Plantation's in the Neck, so much has a sickness of five weeks continuance reduced me: but tho. it is not in my power to meet you there, I can nevertheless assure you, and other's (whom it may concern, to borrow a phrase from Govr Innes) that I am so little dispirited at what has happen'd, that I am always ready, and always willing to render my Country any Services that I am capable off; but never upon the Terms I have done, having suffer'd much in my private fortune beside impairing one of the best Constitution's.

By late August, he had fully recovered from this bout with malaria. On September 1, 1755, Colonel Washington returned to the mountainous western frontier to defend the colony against the incursions of the French and Indians as commander of the First Virginia Regiment.

Washington described this arduous and dangerous assignment in a letter to Richard Washington, a London merchant, on April 15, 1757.[14]

I have been posted then for twenty Months past upon our cold and Barren Frontiers, to perform I think I may say impossibilitys that is, to protect from the cruel Incursions of a Crafty Savage Enemy a line of Inhabitants of more than 350 Miles extent with a force inadequate to the taske, by this mean I am become in a manner an exile and Seldom informd of those oppertunitys which I might otherwise embrase of corrisponding with my friends.

Later in the year, while leading the campaign along the frontier, he suffered from another violent attack of tuberculosis. Following doctors' orders, he returned to Mount Vernon to seek refuge.

On November 9, Captain Robert Stewart wrote to Lieutenant Governor Dinwiddie from Fort Loudoun (Washington's command post) describing Washington's latest episode with malaria.[15]

Honble Sir   *Fort Loudoun Novr 9th 1757*

For upwards of three Months past Colo. Washington has labour'd under a Bloody Flux, about a week ago his Disorder greatly increas'd attended with bad Fevers, the day before yesterday he was seiz'd with Stitches & violent Pleuretick Pains upon which the Docr Bled him and yesterday he twice repeated the same operation. This Complication of Disorders greatly perplexes the Doctr as what is good for him in one respect hurts him in another, the Docr has strongly Recommended his immediately changing his air and going to some place where he can be kept quiet (a thing impossible here) being the best chance that now remains for his Recovery, the Colo. objected to following this advice before he could procure Yr Honrs Liberty but the Docr gave him such reasons as convinc'd him it might then be too late and he has at length with reluctance agreed to it, therefore has Directed me to acquaint Yr Honr (as he's not in condition to write himself) of his resolution of leaving this immediatly and of his reasons for doing it which I have now the honor to do.

Upon arriving at Mount Vernon, Washington wrote to Sarah Cary Fairfax and requested some medications to combat his illnesses.[16]

Dear Madam   *Mount Vernon 15th Novr 1757.*

I have lingerd under an Indisposition for more than three Months; and finding no relief above, on the contrary, that I daily grew worse, I have followd ⟨*m*⟩

y Surgeons advice to leave the place, & try what effects ⟨f⟩resh Air and Water may have upon my disorder.

On Sunday last I arrivd here, and on Yesterday Mr Green was so kind to favour me with a visit & prescribd to me. He forbids the use of Meats, and substitures Jelly's and such kind of Food for a constancy: now, as my Sister is from home and I have no Person that has been usd to making these kind of things; and no directions; I find my self under a necessity of applying to you for yr rec⟨eip⟩t Book for a little while, and indeed for such materials to make Jellys as you think I may not just at this time have. for I cant get Hartshorn Shavings any where. I must also beg the favour of you to lend me a Pound, or a smaller quantity if you can't spare that, of Hyson Tea. I am quite out & cannot get a supply any where in these parts. please also to lend me a bottle or two of Mountain, or Canary Wine Mr Green directs me to drink a Glass or two of this every day mixd with Water of Gum Arabic.

Pray make my Compliments acceptable to the Young Ladies of Your Family, and believe me to be Dr Madam Yr Most Obedt Servt

Go: Washington

Lieutenant Governor Dinwiddie, upon learning about Washington's latest illness, wrote to Captain Stewart via a courier named Jenkins to express his concern on November 15.[17]

Sir   Williamsburg Novr 15th 1757

I recd Your Letter by Jenkins last Night — The violent Complaint Colo: Washington labors under gives me great Concern, it was unknown to me or he shou'd have had Leave of Absence sooner, & I am very glad he did not delay following the Doctr's Advice, to try a change of Air, I sincerely wish him a speedy Recovery.

Captain Stewart then wrote to Colonel John Stanwix, commander of the British forces in the southern colonies, on November 24 describing Washington's latest malaria attack.[18]

Sir   *Fort Loudoun November 24th 1757*

For near Four Months past Colo. Washington has Labour'd under a Bloudy Flux which till of late he did not conceive could be productive of those bad consequences it now too probably will terminate in, at least he would not be prevail'd upon in any Degree to abate the exertion of that steady Zeal for the Interest of the Service he in so emenent a manner has always been remarkable for, however about two weeks ago his Disorder greatly encreas'd and at same time was Seiz'd with Stitches & violent Plueretick Pains under that Complication of Disorders his Strength & viguour diminish'd so fast that in a few days he was hardly able to Walk and was (by the Docr) at length prevail'd upon to leave this place as change of air & quietness (which he could not possibly enjoy here) was the best chance that remain'd for his Recovery he is now retir'd to his Seat on Potomack River (about 90 Miles from hence[)] his Physicians give him no room to hope for his speedy Recovery. I heard from him yesterday he expresses much concern for his omission of not giving you previous Notice of the necessity he was under of leaving this place and as he's not in condition to write himself desires me to inform you of the reasons of it which I have now the honr to do & begs leave to subscribe myself Very respectfully Sir &ca

                                         Robert Stewart

On November 25, Dr. James Craik, an officer and surgeon in Washington's Virginia regiment, wrote to Washington that he was hoping that Washington would recuperate quickly.[19]

Dear Sir   *Fort Loudoun Novr 25th 1757*

The dissagreeable news I recd by Jenkins, of the Increase of your disorder, is real concern to me—I had been flatering my self with the Pleasant hope of seeing you here again soon—thinking that the change of Air, with the quiet Situation of Mount Vernon—would have been a Speedy means of your recovery—however as your disorder hath been of long Standing, and hath corrupted the whole mass of Blood—it will require some time for to remove the cause—And I hope by the Assistance of God and the requesite care, that will be taken of you, where you now are: that tho. your disorder may reduce you to the lowest ebb; yet you will in a short time get the better of it—And render your friends here happy, by having the honour of serving once more under your Command—As nothing is more conducive to a Speedy recovery, than a tranquill easy mind, Accompanied with a good flow of Spirits—I would beg of you; not, as a Physician; but as a real friend who has your Speedy recovery Sincerely at heart; that you will keep up your Spirits, and not allow your mind to be disturbed, with any part of Publick bussiness; that perhaps may not be going on so well, as your concern for the Publick could wish—Any little step of this kind, that might happen, would be triffling to the Neglect of yourself—The fate of your Friends and Country are in a manner dependent upon your recover—And as I am sensible of the regard you have for both, I make no doubt, but that you will use every endeavour that will be in the least conducive to your recovery so that both may still rejoice in the Enjoyment of you—I am very much Surprised at Doctr Browns Neglect in not coming to see you, I cannot see how he can Account for it—I wish Doctr Jameson could be got, I have a great oppinion of his judgement and I realy beleive he would be of Service to you.

*　Collo. Stanwix I am inform'd is to continue in Winter Quarters at Lancaster—If it is agreeable to you, I should be glad of your permission to go there, in order to see my Cousin Captn Stewart—The Sick in the Hospitall are very few at present, which emboldens me to apply for leave—As reading & writing must be very troublesome to you in your present Circumstance, I shall only Pray God, who is the best of all Physicians, that he in his infinite mercy, may restore you, to your wonted health, and preserve you in the Command which is so agreeable to many, and none more so, than to him, who has the honour, to subscribe himself with the greatest Duty & Esteem Dr Sir Your Most Affe & Devoted huml. Sert*

Jas Craik

P.S. Please hint to me in a few lines, if your disorder hath yet taken a turn for the better.

Upon Robert Dinwiddie's departure for England on January 12, 1758, John Blair became acting lieutenant governor. With this change in leadership, George Washington wrote to Blair on January 30 that he had been sick and had taken leave from the service in order to recover from his illness. He requested leave to travel to Williamsburg to settle his accounts and receive money for frontier command expenses.[20]

[Fredericksburg, 30 January 1758]

To The Honble John Blair, Esquire

Honble Sir,

    Hearing of the Governors' departure for England; I think it a duty incumbent on me to inform your Honor, that I lingered a long time under an illness which obliged me to retire from my command (by the Surgeons advice, and with the Governors approbation;) and that I am yet but imperfectly recovered from it: which is the cause that detains me from my Duty.

    I have many accompts to settle with the country committee, and should be glad to obtain leave to come down for that purpose now. This being the proper season, as our Frontiers are quiet.

    I also want to receive money, for contingent Expenses, before I return to Winchester; as there are several demands of the Public, that I shou'd be glad to be provided against. And further—I shall, at that time, have an opportunity of laying before your Honor, a state of the frontier Settlements; a matter worthy of great attention; as the well-being of the people depends upon seasonable and well-concerted measures for their defence!

    If your Honor has any Orders for the Troops, under my command, please to favour me with them, and they shall be forwarded up; while I come down myself, for the purposes aforesaid. I am, with great Esteem, Your Honors most obedient, Hble Servant,

G: W.

Fredericksburgh: January 30th 1758.

In February 1758, Washington, believing that he had sufficiently recovered from his illness, set out for Williamsburg to settle his accounts. But after having traveled only a short distance, he again began to suffer and returned to Mount Vernon. He wrote to John Blair, president of the House of Burgesses, on the twentieth of February.[21]

To The President
Honble Sir,　　　　　　　　　　　Mount—Vernon, the 20th February, 1758.
　I set out for Williamsburg the day after the date of my letter by Jenkins; but found I was unable to proceed, my fever and pain encreasing upon me to an high degree, and the Physicians assured me, that I might endanger my life in prosecuting the journey. In consequence of this advice, I returned back to this place again, and informed your Honor of the reason of my detention by the Post, whom I met with on the road, and who I have since understood, never lodged my letter in the Post-Office at Fredericksburgh; which is the cause of my writing this second one to the same purport. Whenever I shall be sufficiently able to attempt the journey again, I can not say: but shall delay no time after I am in a condition to perform it. I am your Honor's &c.

　　　　　　　　　　　　　　　　　　　　　　　　　　　　G:W.

A few weeks later and still severely ill, he wrote to his commanding officer, Colonel John Stanwix, on March 4 expressing his thoughts of resigning.[22]

　I have never been able to return to my Command since I wrote to you last—my disorder at times returning obstinately upon me in spight of the efforts of all the Esculapion Tribe I have yet had an oppertunity of trying—At times I have been reducd to great extremity, and have now some Reason to apprehend an approaching Decay being visited with several Symptoms of that Disorder—I am under a strict Regimen, and shall set of to morrow for Williamsburg to receive the Advice of the best Physicians. My Constitution I believe has receivd great Injury, and as nothing can retrieve it but the greatest care, & most circumspect Conduct—As I now see no prospect of preferment in a Military Life—and as I despair of rendering that immediate Service which this Colony may require of the Person Commanding their Troops, I have some thoughts of quitting my

Command & retiring from all Publick Business, leaving my Post to be filld by others more Capable of the Task; and who may perhaps, have their Endeavours crownd with better success than mine has been. Wherever I go, or whatever becomes of me I shall always feel the sincerest, & most affecte regard for you— and am Dr Sir Yr most Obedt & Obligd Hble Servt

Go: Washington

Exhausted by ten months of suffering with malaria, Colonel Washington set out for Williamsburg on March 5 to consult with doctors. There he met with John Amson, a highly respected physician, and learned that his ailments were not terminal. While in Williamsburg he learned of General Forbes's upcoming campaign to capture Fort Duquesne. Washington also heard about the wealthy widow Martha Dandridge Custis during his stay in Williamsburg. Washington arranged a meeting with her and she shortly thereafter expressed an interest in him. He soon recovered and went back to Mount Vernon, arriving on April 1 in time to resume command of the Virginia regiment.

In the autumn of 1758, Washington participated in General Forbes's march across Pennsylvania's mountainous frontier to successfully recapture Fort Duquesne. Upon completion of this strenuous and exhausting campaign, Washington once more succumbed to his illness.

Although not feeling well, he agreed to travel to Williamsburg and deliver General Forbes's request for additional provisions to Lieutenant Governor Francis Fauquier. On December 9, while resting in Winchester, he wrote to Fauquier.[23]

To The Honble Governor Fauquer.

Sir.   *Winchester, the 9th Dec. 1758*

I arrived at this place last night, and was just setting out (tho' very much indisposed) for my own House, when I was honored with your obliging favour of the 3rd instant....

If I easily get the better of my present Disorder, I shall hope for the honor of kissing your hand, about the 25th instant.

Dr. James Craik wrote to Washington on December 20 expressing his concern for Washington's health.[24]

I am extremely sorry to hear your bad state of health remain'd with you when here—However I flatter my self with the hopes that you are well—And that as the fatigues of war are now mostly over, you will recover dayly.

Upon reaching Williamsburg in late December, Washington delivered General Forbes's request for supplies to Lieutenant Governor Fauquier and submitted his resignation from the service.

On January 6, 1759, he married the very nurturing widow Martha Dandridge Custis. The newly wedded couple moved into Mount Vernon, where George rested and received the medical attention required to regain his health.

In May 1761, while campaigning for reelection in the House of Burgesses, he became dangerously ill with another attack of tuberculosis. On July 14, he wrote to Richard Washington, his London agent, explaining that he had been ill or he would have responded earlier.[25]

Dear Sir,   *Mount Vernon July 14th 1761*
Since my last by Mr Fairfax I have had the pleasure of receiving your obliging favours of the 16th October and first of January following. A Mixture of bad Health and Indolence together; has kept me from paying that due respect to your Letters which I am sure they much merited at my hands, till this time,…

In a July 27 letter to Andrew Burnaby, a British clergyman, Washington informed him that he would travel to his plantation as soon as his health would allow. In this letter, he provided a poignant description of his distressing condition.[26]

and this journey I propose to undertake as soon as my health will permit, which at present is in a very declining way, and has been so in spite of all the Esculapian tribe ever since the middle of May, occasioned by a violent cold I then got in a tour to Manchester, etc. I have found so little benefit from any advice yet received that I am more than half of the mind to take a trip to England for the recovery of that invaluable blessing—health.

His reference to Manchester should have stated Winchester, where he had gone to campaign for reelection to the House of Burgesses.

This attack turned out to be his worst. Searching for some relief, he traveled to Warm Springs in western Virginia. On August 26, he wrote to Dr. Green describing the difficult journey and the condition of his health.[27]

Revd Sir   The Warm Springs [Va.] 26th[–30] Augt 1761.

I shoud think myself very inexcusable were I to omit so good an oppertunity as Mr Douglass's return from these Springs, of giving you some Account of the place, and of Our Approaches to it.

To begin then—We arrivd here yesterday, and our Journey (as you may imagine) was not of the most agreable sort, through such Weather & such Roads as we had to encounter; these last for 20 or 25 Miles from hence are almost impassable for Carriages; not so much from the Mountainous Country (but this in fact is very rugged) as from Trees that have fallen across the Road, and renderd the ways intolerable.

We found of both sexes about 2⟨5⟩0 People at this place, full of all manner of diseases & Complaints; some of which are much benefitted, while others find no relief from the Water's—two or three Doctors are here, but whether attending as Physicians or to Drink of the Waters I know not—It is thought the Springs will soon begin to loose there Virtues, and the Weather get too cold for People, not well provided, to remain here—They are situated very badly on the East side of a steep Mountain, and Inclosed by Hills on all Sides, so that the Afternoon's

Sun is hid by 4 Oclock and the Fogs hang over us till 9 or 10 to wch occasion's great Damps and the Mornings and Evenings to be cool.

The Place I am told, and indeed have found it so already, is supplyed with Provisions of all kinds—good Beef & venison, fine Veal, Lamb, Fowls &ca may be bought at almost any time; but Lodgings can be had on no Terms but building for them, and I am of opinion that numbers get more hurt by there manner of lying, than the Waters can do them good—had we not succeeded in getting a Tent & marquee from Winchester we shoud have been in a most miserable situation here.

In regard to myself I must beg leave to say, that I was much overcome with the fatigue of the Ride & Weather together—however I think my Fevers are a good deal abated, althô my Pains grow rather worse, & my sleep equally disturbd; what effect the Waters may have upon me I cant say at present, but I expect Nothing from the Air—this certainly must be unwholesome—I purpose to stay here a fortnight & longer if benefitted.

Lieutenant Colonel Robert Stewart, Washington's commanding officer, discussed Washington's condition with the Virginia regiment physician, Dr. John Stewart. Dr. John Stewart reviewed Washington's condition with Dr. Laughlin Macleane, a University of Edinburgh graduate and the physician assigned to the Thirty-eighth Regiment. Lieutenant Colonel Stewart wrote to Washington on September 17, and provided him with the doctors' opinions.[28]

My dear Sir   *Philadelphia Sepr 17th 1761*
I arrived here last Saturday in Compy with Doctor Stuart who laid a State of your case before Doctor Macleane and now send you their opinions But as the changes to which your Disorder are Subject and the distance of Time and Place may probably in some measure destroy the efficacy of what they prescribe I would earnestly beg leave to recommend your coming here as soon as the circumstances of your affairs can possibly permit for when I consider the advantages you must derive from being under the immediate care of the most eminent and universally

acknowledg'd ablest Physician on the Continent in a place where you could enjoy variety of agreeable Compy &Ca as well as from change of air I cannot help again repeating my entreaties of your loosing none of that valuable Time requisite to re-establish your Health with which no Bussiness however important ought to be put in competition.

After successful treatment at Warm Springs, Washington wrote on September 23 to another London agent, Robert Cary & Co., an explanation as to why he had not responded sooner.[29]

Gentn,   *Mount Vernon 23d Septr 1761*
   An Indisposition which I have been under 3 or 4 Months inducd me to take a trip Northward to try the effects of Exercise and our Mountain Air upon my disorder—I find some benefit from the Journey—…

In October, Washington felt healthier and was expecting to completely recover. He wrote to Richard Washington on October 20 explaining how extremely ill he had been and that he felt Providence had saved him from the "grim King."[30]

Dear Sir,   *Mount Vernon October the 20th 1761.*
   Since my last of the 14th July I have in appearance been very near my last gasp—The Indisposition then spoken of Increasd upon me and I fell into a very low and dangerous State—I once thought the grim King would certainly master my utmost efforts and that I must sink in spite of a noble struggle but thank God I have now got the better of the disorder and shall soon be restord I hope to perfect health again.

George William Fairfax received a letter from Washington written in July of that year and wrote back from Great Britain on October 30 expressing his concern for Washington's health.[31]

Dear Sir   30 October 1761

Your favors of the 2d of Decr 6th of March 3d of Apl 27th of July and the first of Augt came very safe to hand. In that of July I am sorry to find that you were in such a bad state of health, and that neither Mr Greens nor Hamiltons prescriptions had then the desired effect. The latters it seems you had but just begun and consequently could not expect an immediate cure, but I hope long before this you are perfectly restored. If not probabilly change of Air might be of service and if you had any particular business, or even fancy to see England we shall be extreamly glad to see you at York, or at our little retreat not many Miles from it. But I hope a bad state of Health will not oblige you to cross the terrible western Ocean, tho' if better advice should be really necessary the sooner it is taken the better, and not delay it so long as our deceased friend—…

Since he was feeling stronger, Washington went to Williamsburg on November 2, 1761, to attend the current session of the House of Burgesses. But he soon became ill yet again and was unable to continue his activities there. On November 9, Washington wrote to Peter Stover, a resident of Frederick County that,[32]

…—this Bill was to have come into the House on Saturday but whether it did or not I can't certainly say, as I was too sick to attend the whole day, notwithstanding I went there for that purpose;…

My Indisposition continuing upon me puts it out of my power to attend the House—…

On December 16, Andrew Burnaby wrote to George Washington from Leicestershire expressing his concern for Washington's health.[33]

Asfordby near Melton—Mowbray

Dear Sir,   Leicestershire Decr 16th 1761

I received the favour of Your letter dated the 27th of July, some time ago; which would have given me much greater pleasure had it brought me a better account of

Your health; I hope however You are perfectly recovered, and that if You come to England, which I can assure Dear Sir would be greatly to my wish, it will be upon some much better Errand than ill health.

In March 1762, Washington ventured from his home to attend his half brother Augustine Washington's funeral in Westmorland County. After the funeral he returned to Williamsburg for a meeting of the House of Burgesses.[34]

On May 28, he was finally well enough to manage his accounts with his British brokers. He responded to the many letters Robert Cary & Company had sent to him throughout the previous year.[35]

Gentlemen,   *Mount Vernon 28th May 1762*
Your unacknowledged favours of the 26th June 10th Augt 16 & 19th Septr and the 19th of Octr following now lye before—...

This bout of tuberculosis had lasted a year and was nearly fatal, but he suffered no further significant illnesses for the next quarter century.

From these dreadful experiences, Washington had developed a stronger belief in Providence. He felt he was protected and being prepared for some future purpose. He demonstrated this in a letter he wrote to Burwell Bassett (Martha's brother-in-law) wherein he chided Bassett for writing a letter on the Sabbath and for not attending church.[36]

Dear Sir   *Mount Vernon, 28th August 1762*
I was favoured with your Epistle wrote on a certain 25th of July when you ought to have been at Church, praying as becomes every good Christian Man who has as much to answer for as you have—strange it is that you will be so blind to truth that the enlightening sounds of the Gospel cannot reach your Ear, nor no Examples awaken you to a sense of Goodness—could you but behold with what religious zeal I hye me to Church on every Lords day, it would do your heart good, and fill it I hope with equal fervency—...

This counsel to Bassett is from one of George Washington's few surviving personal letters. It exposes a very dedicated and committed believer. This view of George Washington was seldom revealed to the public.

Revolutionary War Years (1776–1783):

During the eighteenth century, smallpox was rampant and significantly impacted the colonial army's effectiveness during the Revolutionary War. Washington had contracted smallpox while visiting Barbados in 1751 and therefore was immune. Hundreds had died from smallpox during the Siege of Boston in 1774. Smallpox was also widespread among the troops in the Quebec campaign in 1776 and was the main cause for its failure. The British endeavored to use germ warfare by releasing persons suffering from smallpox into the camps of the American troops at Boston and again at Jamestown. To minimize this hazard to his troops, Washington commanded that the Continental army be inoculated. This is the first time in history that an entire army was immunized to prevent the spread of a disease. This effort began during the winter of 1777 while he was encamped in Morristown, NJ. Before allowing a large number of new troops from the south to join his forces, he instructed that they be inoculated.

Dr. William Shippen Jr., chief physician of the flying camp, provided General Washington with his plan to inoculate all the troops as they passed through Philadelphia in his letter written on January 25, 1777.[37]

I found a great number of your troops here in a miserable situation, which I have the pleasure to inform you are now in a comfortable situation. The small-pox rases & it is the opinion of the committee of Congress & the generals that inoculation should take place immediately in such a manner as that those who pass & repass hereafter, may not be liable to receive the infection unless circum-

stances may make it proper. It is 3 to 1 that all in town have taken the infection
& will carry it to the Army unless inoculated.

W. Sn

On February 6, in the following letter responding to Dr. Shippen's proposal, Washington directed the implementation of Shippen's plan.[38]

Dear Sir   Head Qurs Morristown February 6th 1777.
   Finding the Small pox to be spreading much and fearing that no precaution can prevent it from running through the whole of our Army, I have determined that the troops shall be inoculated. This Expedient may be attended with some inconveniences and some disadvantages, but yet I trust in its consequences will have the most happy effects. Necessity not only authorizes but seems to require the measure, for should the disorder infect the Army in the natural way and rage with its usual virulence we should have more to dread from it than from the Sword of the Enemy. Under these circumstances I have directed Doctr Bond to prepare immediately for inoculating in this Quarter, keeping the matter as secret as possible, and request that you will without delay inoculate All the Continental Troops that are in philadelphia and those that shall come in as fast as they arrive. You will spare no pains to carry them through the disorder with the utmost expedition, and to have them cleansed from the infection when recovered, that they may proceed to Camp with as little injury as possible to the Country through which they pass. If the business is immediately begun and favoured with the common success, I would fain hope they will be soon fit for duty, and that in a short space of time we shale have an Army not subject to this the greatest of all calamities that can befall it when taken in the natural way.

As a result of his successful plan, on April 11, 1777, Congress unanimously elected Dr. William Shippen Jr. the director general of all military hospitals.

At Jamestown (the last major battle of the war) the British again tried using germ warfare. They infected the slaves who had joined the British army with hopes of gaining their freedom and then released them into the American encampments. Since the colonial army had already been immunized, this had no deleterious effect upon the troops. Washington's efforts to immunize the whole army proved completely successful. Historians have identified this mass immunization as one of the most significant and successful campaigns in the war.

While serving as commander in chief of the Continental army, George Washington remained in relatively good health except for one serious occasion that caused great concern. While in winter encampment in March 1777, he suffered a severe attack of quinsy (a painful abscess located in the throat and accompanied with a severe sore throat and fever). He suffered so severely from this illness that he was unable to attend to the affairs of the commander in chief. For several days his staff executed the command functions for him.

On March 10, Alexander Hamilton, as aide-de-camp to the commander in chief, responded to Brigadier General Alexander McDougall's letter of March 7, 1777, in which McDougall expressed his concern that the British might attack upstate New York.[39]

Your letter of the 7th instant to his Excellency fell into my hands—He has been very much indisposed for three or four days past, insomuch that his attention to business is pronounced by the Doctors to be very improper; and we have made a point of keeping all from him which was not indispensably necessary. I detained your express a day in hopes of a convenient opportunity to communicate your letter to him; but though he has grown considerably better than he was, I find he is so much pestered with matters which cannot be avoided, that I am obliged to refrain from troubling him on the occasion; especially as I conceive the only answer he would give, may be given by myself.

On March 11, Washington's secretary, Tench Tilghman, also commented on the seriousness of Washington's condition while responding to a March 8 letter from William Livingston, the governor of New

Jersey:[40] "His Excellency being much indisposed commands me to acknowledge the honor of yours of the 8th Currt."

Washington recovered in about ten days and resumed command of the army. Joseph Reed, a private citizen awaiting the command of the Light Horse, wrote on March 22 to express his anxiety over Washington's illness and his desire that Providence look after him.[41]

> *I most sincerely congratulate you on your Recovery from an Illness which gave a very sensible Alarm to every one, but more particularly to those who feel a particular Attachment to your Excelly & have been favoured with Marks of your Regard. Besides the common Interest we have in your Health & Comfort as Members of the great Community—The Feelings of Gratitude & Friendship were added to the general Concern & the Pleasure we feel on your Recovery can only be equalled by the Fears & Anxiety excited by your Indisposition.*
>
> *May Heaven long preserve you my dear General, a Blessing & Ornament to your Country as well as the Delight of your particular Friends—...*

Domestic Years at Mount Vernon (1783–1787):

Washington returned to Mount Vernon when the Revolutionary War ended in December 1783 and began rebuilding his devastated plantation.

In late August 1786, Washington suffered from another malarial attack. He wrote in his diary on Thursday, August 31, that he was suffering from a fever and had sent for Dr. Craik.[42]

> *Thursday, 31st. Siezed with an ague before six Oclock this morning after having laboured under a fever all night.*
>
> *Sent for Doctr. Craik, who arrived just as we were setting down to dinner; who, when he thought my fever sufficiently abated, gave me a cathartick and directed the Bark to be applied in the Morning.*

Washington's reference to the "Bark" was the "Jesuit's Bark," a quinine treatment for malaria.

A meeting of the Potomac Company's board of directors was scheduled for a few days later, on September 4, 1786, but Washington was suffering too intensely to attend. On September 1, he wrote letters to the directors of the Potomac Company, Colonels George Gilpin and John Fitzgerald, to explain why he would be absent.[43]

> *Gentn,*   *Mount Vernon 1st Septr 1786.*
>
> *Nothing but sickness would have prevented my attendance at the Seneca Falls on Monday next agreeably to appointment. On sunday last (occasioned by an imprudent act) I was seized by an ague & fever. on Tuesday & yesterday they returned with great violence, with scarce any intermission of the fever. Whether the Doctors efforts will baffle them tomorrow, remains to be determined; but at any rate he thinks it would be improper for me to leave home. The fevers, moreover, have made such havock of my mouth, nose & chin that I am unable to put a razor to my face. Thus circumstanced, I have given up all idea of meeting the Board the 4th instant.*

In a letter to David Humphreys (Washington's aide-de-camp during the war) on September 1, 1786, Washington described one of his attacks of malaria.[44]

> *I write to you with a very aching head, and disordered frame, and Mr. Lear will copy the letter. Saturday last, by an imprudent act, I brought on an ague and fever on Sunday, which returned with violence Tuesday & Thursday; and if Doctor Craik's efforts are ineffectual, I shall have them again this day....*

By September 9, Washington was feeling better. In a letter to Colonel John Fitzgerald, he mentioned his improved status:[45] "I am tolerably well again, but obliged to make use of Scissars instead of a Razor, for part of my face, when shaving."

Washington continued taking quinine bark for two weeks. On September 14, he noted in his diary:[46] "Thursday, 14th. At home all day repeating dozes of Bark, of which I took 4 with an interval of 2 hours between...."

Washington, as president of the Society of the Cincinnati, issued a circular letter dated October 31, 1786, scheduling a national meeting in Philadelphia for May 1787. In the letter, he informed the members that his malarial attacks and rheumatic pain prevented him from attending the meeting.[47]

Sir,   *Mount Vernon in Virginia 31st Octo. 1786*

I take this early opportunity, in my character of President of the Cincinnati, of announcing to you, that the triennial General Meeting of the Society is to be convened at the City of Philadelphia on the first Monday of May in the year 1787.

As it will not be in my power (for reasons which I shall have the honor of immediately communicating) to attend the next General Meeting;...

The numerous applications for information, advice, or assistance which are made to me in consequence of my military command; the multiplicity of my correspondencies in this Country as well as in many parts of Europe; the variety & perplexity of my own private concerns, which, having been much deranged by my absence through the war, demand my entire & unremitting attention; the arduousness of the task, in which I have been as it were unavoidably engaged, of superintending the opening the navigation of the great rivers in this State; the natural desire of tranquility and relaxation from business, which almost every one experiences at my time of life, particularly after having acted (during a considerable period) as no idle spectator in uncommonly busy & important scenes; and the present imbecility of my health, occasioned by a violent attack of the fever & ague, succeeded by rheumatick pains (to which till of late I have been an entire stranger); will, I doubt not, be considered as reasons of sufficient validity to justify my conduct in the present instance.

The Constitutional Convention was scheduled for Philadelphia on the same dates as the meeting of the Society of the Cincinnati. The assembly of the state of Virginia selected George Washington to head up their delegation to the convention. James Madison, in a letter dated November 8, 1786, informed Washington of the assembly's intentions.[48]

> *This idea will also be pursued in the selection of characters to represent Virga in the federal Convention. You will infer our earnestness on this point from the liberty which will be used of placing your name at the head of them.*

Again Washington declined the invitation to travel to Philadelphia in May for the same reasons he had previously enumerated, and he responded to Madison on November 18.[49]

> *I presume you heard Sir, that I was first appointed & have since been rechosen President of the Society of the Cincinnati; & you may have understood also that the triennial Genl Meeting of this body is to be held in Philada the first monday in May next. Some particular reasons combining with the peculiar situation of my private concerns; the necessity of paying attention to them; a wish for retirement & relaxation from public cares, and rheumatic pains which I begin to feel very sensibly, induced me on the 31st ulto to address a circular letter to each State society informing them of my intention not to be at the next Meeting, & of my desire not to be rechosen President, the Vice President is also informed of this, that the business of the Society may not be impeded by my absence. Under these circumstances it will readily be perceived that I could not appear at the same time & place on any other occasion, with out giving offence to a very respectable & deserving part of the Community—the late officers of the American Army.*

Although feeling too unhealthy to attend the convention, Washington felt he had a civic responsibility to attend. In a letter to Henry Knox on March 8, 1787, he asked for Knox's assessment of public sentiment.[50]

A thought however has lately run through my mind, which is attended with embarrassment. It is, whether my non-attendance in this Convention will not be considered as a dereliction to republicanism—nay mor—whether other motives may not (however injuriously) be ascribed to me for not exerting myself on this occasion in support of it. Under these circumstances let me pray you, my dear Sir, to inform me confidentially, what the public expectation is on this head—that is, whether I will, or ought to be there?

On March 19, Knox strongly encouraged Washington's attendance because his presence was crucial to the success of the convention.[51]

I am persuaded that your name has had already great influence to induce the States to come into the measure—That your attendance will be grateful, and your absence chagrining—That your presence would confer on the assembly a national complexion, and that it would more than any other circumstance induce a compliance to the propositions of the convention.

On March 28, Washington submitted a letter to Edmund Randolph, governor of Virginia, conceding that, although still feeling poorly, he would try to attend the convention.[52]

However, as my friends, with a degree of sollicitude which is unusual, seem to wish my attendance on this occasion, I have come to a resolution to go if my health will permit, provided, from the lapse of time between the date of your Excellencys letter and this reply, the Executive may not—the reverse of which wd be highly pleasing to me—have turned its thoughts to some other character—for independantly of all other considerations, I have, of late, been so much afflicted with rheumatic complaint in my shoulder that at times I am hardly able to raise my hand to my head, or turn myself in bed. This, consequently, might prevent my attendance, and eventually a representation of the State; which wd afflict me more sensibly than the disorder which occasioned it.

On April 2, Washington wrote to Henry Knox to describe his reluctance to attend the convention or the society meeting because he was still greatly concerned about his health.[53]

Indeed my health is become very precarious—a Rheumatic complaint which has followed me more than Six months is frequently so bad, that it is with difficulty I can, at times, raise my hand to my head, or turn myself in bed. This, however smooth and agreeable other matters might be, might almost in the moment of my departure, prevent my attendance on either occasion.

Feeling healthier, Washington traveled to Philadelphia and attended the convention. He wrote to Arthur Lee on May 20 from Philadelphia.[54]

My Rheumatic complaint having very much abated (after I had the pleasure of seeing you at Mount Vernon) I have yielded to what appeared to be the wishes of many of my friends, and am now here as a delegate to the Convention.

George Washington was elected president of the Constitutional Convention on May 25, 1787. He did not attend the meeting of the Society of the Cincinnati but was reelected to its presidency.

The convention approved the Constitution and adjourned on September 17, 1778. The Constitution was ratified on June 21, 1788. George Washington was inaugurated president of the United States of America on April 30, 1789.

Presidential Years (1789–1797):

During the initial term of his presidency, George Washington became severely ill with life-threatening illnesses on two separate occasions. First, in June 1789, he suffered from a high fever caused by a large tumor on his thigh. Dr. Samuel Bard, a highly respected New York physician, initially diagnosed Washington as having anthrax. A friend of

Dr. Bard, Professor John McVicar, commented that Dr. Bard anticipated that Washington's illness would cause his demise.[55]

"so malignant as for several days to threaten mortification. During this period, Dr. Bard never quitted him. On one occasion, being left alone with him, General Washington...desired his candid opinion as to the probable termination of the disease....Dr. Bard's answer, though it expressed hope, acknowledged his apprehensions

Dr. Samuel Bard elected to incise and drain the tumor. On June 17, he performed the operation accompanied by his father, Dr. John Bard. Washington responded quickly to the procedure but remained bedridden for two more weeks.

On June 28, James McHenry, one of Washington's aides at Valley Forge, wrote to him expressing his great concern and encouraging him to request the attendance of Dr. James Craik.[56]

Dear Sir.   *Baltimore 28 June 1789.*

Your late indisposition which has alarmed me not a little makes me more desirous than ever that you should have some person near you who is well acquainted with your constitution and who has been accustomed to your confidence. This leads me to take the liberty to remind you of old Doctor Craik whom I well know, unless he is greatly changed cannot be very happy at a distance from you. I think you said when I suggested this subject that he had settled most of his children to his satisfaction, a circumstance which may enable him to follow his inclinations should you incline to indulge them. I have two reasons for mentioning this again to you. I know him to be an attached friend which nothing can alter, and one whom you might find useful on a variety of occasions. I know also that he is a man of skill in his profession and that from habit and opinion you would place more reliance on his advice than perhaps on any other persons. I may add also that there is no one amongst all those who are devoted to you from even the purest motives, that as far as I can judge of the human heart loves you with a more fervent friendship or would serve you with more zeal—in whatever respect either your fame or internal tranquility.

By July 3, Washington had recovered sufficiently to respond to James McHenry.[57]

my health is restored, but a feebleness still hangs upon me, and I am yet much incommoded by the incision which was made in a very large and painful tumor on the protuberance of my thigh—this prevents me from walking or sitting; however the Physicians assure me that it has had a happy effect in removing my fever, and will tend very much to the establishment of my general health....I am able to take exercise in my coach, by having it so contrived, as to extend myself the full length of it.

After six weeks, Washington returned to work, but the incised tumor continued to drain for several months. On July 27, he wrote to Bushrod Washington, his nephew.[58]

Dear Bushrod,   New York July 27th 1789.
    Among the first acts of my recommencing business (after lying six weeks on my right side) is that of writing you this letter in acknowledgement of yours of the [ ] ultimo—Not being fairly on my seat yet, or in other words not being able to sit up without feeling some uneasiness, it must be short.

Dr. James Craik wrote to Washington on August 24 expressing happiness over his recovery and encouraging exercise to maintain his health.[59]

Dear Sir   Alexandria Augt 24th 1789
    after a long and anxious solicitude on Account of your late indisposition, permit me to tender my Sincere congratulations for your happy recovery—Among your numberless Correspondents, and a time when every pen has been bussy in inquiring for your health, the Anxiety of an old friend thus expressed might have

been somewhat troublesome, as it might seem to induce the necessity of a literary reply which in your late situation could not be agreeable. Under this Idea have I hitherto submitted to the painful recital of your late tedious confinement at second hand. And have rather trusted to the friendly information of my good friend the Major than risk the possibility of intrusion—I flatter myself you will believe me sincere when I asure you that few things in this life would have given me greater pleasure than to have been in a Situation to have in the least degree ministred to your ease and recovery, and tho' every assistance has been given, which a careful attention and acknowledged abilities could insure, I have constantly felt unhappy at being at such a distance as not to have it in my power to contribute my Mite towards the restoration of your health—Although the Abcess on your Thigh has proved a painful and tedious termination of your Complaint, I flatter myself it will leave you in possession of a large Stock of future good health—Much I think will depend upon your determination at all events, to take exercise[.] The confinement of a City life, and the care and weight of business incident to your appointment, will create too great a transition from the late activity of your life, unless attention is paid to the Article of exercise—...

On August 25, Dr. Bard wrote to his daughter, Susan Bard, informing her of Washington's recovery.[60]

"the President's complaint continues to mend and I have not the least doubt of affecting a perfect and, I hope, a speedy cure. It will give you pleasure to be told that nothing can exceed the kindness and attention I receive from him."

The incision was still open on September 8, twelve weeks after the operation, when he wrote to Dr. Craik describing his condition.[61]

Dear Sir   New-York September 8th 1789.
The letter with which you favored me on the 24th ultimo came duly to hand, and for the friendly sentiments contained in it, you have my sincere and hearty thanks.
My disorder was of long and painful continuance, and though now freed from the latter, the wound given by the incision is not yet closed— Persuaded as I am

that the case has been treated with skill, and with as much tenderness as the nature of the complaint would admit, yet I confess that I often wished for your inspection of it—During the paroxysm, the distance rendered this impracticable, and after the paroxysm had passed I had no conception of being confined to a lying posture on one side six weeks—and that I should feel the remains of it more than twelve—The part affected is now reduced to the size of a barley corn, and by saturday next (which will complete the thirteenth week) I expect it will be skinned over—Upon the whole, I have more reason to be thankful that it is no worse than to repine at the confinement. The want of regular exercise, with the cares of office will I have no doubt hasten my departure for that country from whence no Traveller returns; but a faithful discharge of whatever trust I accept, as it ever has, so it always will be the primary consideration in every transaction of my life be the consequences what they may. Mrs Washington has, I think, better health than usual, and the children are well and in the way of improvement.

Then, a second life-threatening illness occurred the following spring. He developed a serious lung inflammation and was unable to perform his presidential duties for several weeks. On May 9 he wrote in his diary:[62] "Sunday, 9th. Indisposed with a bad cold, and at home all day writing letters on private business."

Subsequently, at an unknown date, he commented in his diary, still under the date of May 9, on the seriousness of his illness and explained that he had made no entries while he was ill.[63]

Sunday, 9th. Indisposeed with a bad cold, and at home all day writing letters on private business.

A severe illness with which I was seized the 10th of this month and which left me in a convalescent state for several weeks after the violence of it had passed; and little inclination to do more than what duty to the public required at my hands occasioned the suspension of the Diary.

Drs. Samuel Bard, John Charlton, and Charles McKnight attended the president, but his conditioned worsened and he developed pneumonia. On May 12, 1790, William Jackson, one of Washington's secretaries, sent an urgent message to Clement Biddle, Washington's purchasing agent in Philadelphia, requesting him to forward a letter from Dr. Bard to the highly regarded Dr. John Jones.[64]

Dear Sir,   *New York, wednesday noon, May 2nd 1790.*
   The enclosed letter, from Doctor Bard to Doctor Jones, is transmitted to you with a view to ensure secrecy, certainty, and dispatch in the delivery of it.
   To relieve you of any extraordinary personal anxiety I am happy to inform you that the symptoms which attend the President's indisposition, are not threatening—but it has been thought the part of prudence to call upon Doctor Jones, in anticipation of any unfavorable change that may arise.
   I need not repeat to you the necessity of delivering the letter with privacy, and keeping the object of it a secret from every person—even Mrs Biddle.
   Doctor Jones may want your aid to accelerate his arrival at New York—and I am persuaded you will give him every assistance in your power—The Doctor's prudence will suggest the propriety of setting out as privately as possible—perhaps it may be well to assign a personal reason for visiting new York, or going into the Country. I am, with great regard, Dear Sir, your most obedient Servant
                                                          W. Jackson.

The forwarded letter from Dr. Bard requested that Dr. Jones travel to New York to assist in Washington's treatment. Jackson believed that the president's illness should be kept secret for fear of the public's reaction. But the news of the president's dire straits traveled quickly throughout New York and Philadelphia and was quickly broadcast in the newspapers.

His health deteriorated into another near-death experience. On May 15, Senator William Maclay from Pennsylvania called upon the president and found him in imminent danger, and he wrote in his journal:[65]

Called to see the President. Every eye full of tears. His life despaired of. Dr. MacKnight told me he would trifle neither with his own character nor the public expectation; his danger was imminent, and every reason to expect that the event of his disorder would be unfortunate.

Miraculously, his fever broke the following day and he began to restore his health. On May 30, Cyrus Griffin, a federal judge, concerned that Washington's failing health would have perilous effects upon the country, wrote to the president to express his happiness upon hearing of his recovery.[66]

Richmond [Va.] May 30th 1790

pardon me, Sir, that I take the freedom to disturb your anxious moments, to congratulate you and my Country on the most happy recovery from your late Indisposition. the last mail has brought to us that pleasing and most important Intelligence, the reverse of which would have thrown this Country into despair and confusion. I hope to heaven the malady may operate as the renovation of health, and will continue the blessing unto a very distant period.

David Stuart, administrator of the Custis estate, believed that living in the city of New York and enduring the pressures of the presidency had damaged George's health. He wrote to Washington on the second of June encouraging him to return to Mount Vernon to facilitate his recovery.[67]

Dear Sir,   *Abingdon [Va.] 2nd June—1790*

The accounts of your recent illness having just reached this place on my return, I delayed writing, 'till I could again congratulate you on the reestablishment, of your health; which I now do most sincerely, both on your account, and on that of your Country—I fear much, that the great change which has been unavoidably made, in your accustomed mode of living, by your office; has been the cause of both the attacks you have so unfortunately been subject to—I have understood,

that you had some intention before your late illness, of visiting Virginia this
Summer for your health. I hope you will now think it ind⟨i⟩spensably necessary.

In early June, Washington had recovered sufficiently to respond to the letters he had received while he was indisposed. On June 3, Washington sent a letter to Henry Hill, an executor of Benjamin Franklin's will, thanking him for forwarding Franklin's walking stick. He apologized for not responding earlier, explaining that his illness had prevented him.[68]

The severe indisposition from which I am just recovering will excuse this late acknowledgement of your letter of the 7th instant, which accompanied the cane left me by the great and invaluable Dr Franklin.

On June 3, he responded to a letter from his friend the Marquis de Lafayette. In this letter, he mentioned that he had been severely ill and that the physicians had encouraged him to work less and exercise more. He also mentioned that he was thinking of spending some time at Mount Vernon while Congress was recessed for the summer.[69]

I have, a few days since, had a severe attack of the peripneumony kind: but am now recovered, except in point of strength. My Physicians advise me to more exercise and less application to business. I cannot, however, avoid persuading myself that it is essential to accomplish whatever I have undertaken (though reluctantly) to the best of my abilities. But it is thought Congress will have a recess this summer, in which case, I propose going for a while to Mount Vernon. With sentiments of the sincerest affection I am, My dear Marquis, Yours &c.
                                                                    George Washington

Richard Henry Lee, US senator from Virginia, wrote to the president on June 12 expressing his deep concern for the president's well-being and encouraging him to return to Mount Vernon for his convalescence.[70]

My dear Sir   *Stratford June 12th 1790*

We have been all again made most miserable by the accounts received of the desperate state of your health—True it is that the general gloom has been succeeded by joy in as much as we have just heard that you was safe & likely to be restored to your usual vigor.

But when I recollect that in the course of a few months you have been twice dangerously ill, & am informed by all who have seen you of the unfortunate change which your constitution seems to have undergone, I profess my mind is far from ease & quietude.

Surely sir, either you do not use your accustomed exercise of body, or the air of N. York disagrees with you.

In either or both cases a return to Mt Vernon for a few months might prove highly advantageous. The relaxation from business, as well other concurring causes would probably produce a complete recovery.

The same principles which governed you in your return to public life, commands you to pay every respect to your health.

You engaged in the arduous dutys of your present station from love of country & obedience to the will of the people—To do them permanent good was your sole object—this cannot be done in two years—therefore the conservati⟨on⟩ of your life by every possible means is a duty you owe to the community, a duty which I ardently hope you never will slight, however indifferent the philosophy of your mind may render you to the las⟨t⟩ task of mortals.

Whatever you may do, whether you come once more among us, or determine to run all risks of a life invaluable to your friends & fellow citizens, I beg leave to renew my unabated & sincere zeal for your health & happiness—a zeal which encreases with my knowledge of human nature & my reflexions on those characters whose virtues & labors in different periods of time & different quarters of the globe have stamped with the title of immortality. With the highest ⟨re⟩spect & the warmest affection I am unalterably your most ob. servt

Henry Lee

On June 15, 1790, Washington responded to David Stuart's letter of June 2 and explained that the excessive work during the initial year of his presidency had caused the two serious illnesses and expressed his doubts about surviving another serious illness.[71]

These public meetings and a dinner once a week to as many as my table will hold with the references to and from the different Departments of State, and other communications with all parts of the Union is as much, if not more, than I am able to undergo, for I have already had within less than a year, two severe attacks—the last worse than the first—a third more than probable will put me to sleep with my fathers; at what distance this may be I know not. Within the last twelve months I have undergone more, and severer sickness than thirty preceding years afflicted me with, put it altogether—I have abundant reason however to be thankful that I am so well recovered; though I still feel the remains of the violent affection of my lungs—The cough, pain in my breast, and shortness in breathing not having entirely left me. I propose in the recess of Congress to visit Mount Vernon—but when this recess will happen is beyond my ken, or the ken I believe of any of its members. I am dear Sir &ca

G. Washington

On August 30, with Congress adjourned for the summer, Washington departed New York and returned to Mount Vernon. For three months, he remained in Virginia working on his plantation and successfully regained his health. He returned to New York and resumed serving out his term. He was elected to a second term in 1793. At the age of sixty-four, Washington decided to not run for a third term.

Final Years in Retirement (1797–1799):

On March 7, 1797, Washington departed Philadelphia for Mount Vernon. His remaining days were devoted to overseeing the plantation, entertaining visitors, and managing his extensive correspondence. Albin

Rawlins was recruited by Washington to assist with the correspondence. Rawlins arrived at Mount Vernon on March 20, 1798.

On the morning of December 14, 1799, Washington awakened with a sore throat. He found it difficult to speak, and as the day wore on, it became difficult to breathe. Dr. Craik was sent for, and Washington asked Albin Rawlins to bleed him. When the doctors arrived, they tried various remedies, such as hot applications, gargles, footbaths, etc., and they also bled him again. At around 10:00 p.m., Washington passed away.[72]

Conclusion:

With the mission accomplished, Providence was no longer needed to save the life of the man who led the revolution against the world's most dominant military and guided the debates that formulated the Constitution that enabled the founding of the greatest nation ever.

Of interest, though, is that he did not suffer from a serious illness during the eight years of the American Revolutionary War even though American soldiers suffered and died from disease at a rate ten times greater than those who died from combat.[73]

Washington's bout with the eighteenth century's most killing diseases during his teenage years appear to have steeled his character to take on leadership challenges that few men would elect to pursue. Filling the shoes of his well-educated and well-connected oldest brother, Lawrence, became the initial guiding force for young George Washington. He replaced his brother as adjutant general in the Virginia militia while Lawrence lay suffering and subsequently dying from tuberculosis at Mount Vernon.[74] This assignment to the Virginia militia brought George Washington to the attention of Lieutenant Governor Dinwiddie who, after being persuaded by Washington's patron, William Fairfax, selected Major George Washington to trek a thousand miles and deliver a diplomatic letter to the French commandant. This trek established his reputation and launched his military career.

George Washington was admired for his character and physical strength. His character was forged at an early age from suffering through multiple deadly diseases and grieving the loss of his father and his older brother. Washington's strength of character enabled him to victoriously lead a ragtag bunch of vagabonds in battle against the superior forces of the British. The subsequent acclaim led to his unanimous election to the presidency of our struggling nation. His strength of character and superior physical strength yielded a leader who was dedicated to duty and was committed to serving his country.

Washington's physical strength enabled him to endure the most strenuous of assignments, and his amazing survivability empowered his belief that Providence was protecting him for future greatness. The chapters that follow will take you through the journey that was made possible by Washington's belief in his guiding savior, Providence.

THE COLD WAS SO EXTREMELY SEVERE

November 1753–January 1754

"The Indian made a stop, turned about; the Major saw him point his gun toward us and fire."

– December 27, 1753 – Christopher Gist

BRITISH CULTURE DOMINATED THE ATLANTIC colonies during the eighteenth century, influencing Washington's perspective and affecting his most critical life-altering decisions.

Washington, at the youthful age of twenty-one, was sent into the wilderness in midwinter by the British lieutenant governor of Virginia, Robert Dinwiddie, to tell the French that they were to stop building forts in British territory. During this journey he would face death on more than one occasion. This treacherous campaign demonstrated Washington's strength of character, which would gain him acclaim throughout colonial America and Great Britain. This journey would become the cornerstone for his esteem that has extended through the generations. The experience not only altered the direction of his life but also initiated his belief that Providence was protecting him and saving him for something of great importance.

During the seventeenth century, the British established colonies along the Atlantic coastline from Massachusetts to South Carolina, and the French established territories in both Canada and along the lower Mississippi River. Early in the eighteenth century, both countries reached into the heartland of America to define their domain. The French extended their territorial claims down the Ohio River from the Great Lakes to the lower Mississippi River. The English expanded their territory westward across the Allegheny Mountains. As these two nations expanded their boundaries, they began intruding upon each other's territorial claims in a region they called the Ohio Country.

To protect themselves from the foreign invaders, five Indian tribes (Cayuga, Mohawk, Oneida, Onondaga, and Seneca) joined together and founded the Five Nations of the Iroquois and in 1701 set a policy of neutrality. Almost simultaneously the Five Nations of the Iroquois met with the French in Montreal and the English in Albany, NY. The resulting arrangement was called the 1701 Grand Settlement. With the 1701 Grand Settlement, the Five Nations of the Iroquois signed conflicting agreements with the French and the English. In their agreement with the French, the Five Nations agreed to remain neutral if war were to break out between the French and English, as long as the French ceased their attacks upon the Iroquois. The French assumed that the neutral Iroquois would keep the English out of the Ohio Country. In their agreement with the English, the Iroquois were assured that the British would defend them from a French invasion. The British assumed that their agreement allowed them to move into the Ohio Country to trade with the Iroquois and protect them from the French. Neither the French nor the English knew of the other country's agreement. The struggle for control of the Ohio Country did not end with the 1701 Grand Settlement, but it did delay open warfare between the French and the English for nearly fifty years.

In 1726, with the admission of the Tuscarora Indians, the Five Nations of the Iroquois became the Six Nations of the Iroquois. The Six Nations of the Iroquois provided a buffer zone between the British and the French that extended from the Great Lakes to the Carolinas.

The Grand Settlement of 1701 began to unravel in 1744 when the Six Nations of the Iroquois negotiated a new treaty with the British at Lancaster. The British interpretation of this treaty opened the entire Ohio Valley for settlement. To capitalize on the opportunity to establish settlements in the Ohio Country, a group of Virginia statesmen formed the Ohio Company to acquire land west of the Allegheny Mountains. Robert Dinwiddie, lieutenant governor of the Virginia colony, was included in the initial investment. In 1747, the Ohio Company received a grant of two hundred thousand acres of land from King George II near the forks of the Ohio (modern-day Pittsburgh, Pennsylvania). This gateway to the Ohio Country was created with the stipulation that the Ohio Company must provide for the settlement of one hundred families.

To provide for the settlers, the English negotiated the 1752 treaty at Logstown with Tanaghrisson (known as the "Half-King"), the representative for the Six Nations of the Iroquois. The Logstown Treaty enabled the British to locate a trading post and a fort at the forks of the Ohio.

On July 1, Ange Duquesne de Menneville arrived in Canada as the new governor general with instructions from King Louis XV to extract the British from the Ohio Country. Following his orders, Duquesne initiated the building of four forts (Fort Presque Isle, Fort Le Boeuf, Fort Machault, and Fort Duquesne) extending from Lake Erie to the forks of the Ohio. The construction of Fort Presque and Fort Le Boeuf was completed in the summer of 1753.

Because both King Louis and King George instructed their forces to build forts at the forks of the Ohio, the battleground for their inevitable conflict was established and twenty-year-old George Washington's career was launched. On November 6, 1752, George Washington was appointed to the position of adjutant general of the southern district of Virginia's militia with the rank of major. Thus began a career that would propel Washington to a position of leadership among America's founding fathers.

In June 1753, Lieutenant Governor Dinwiddie reported to London headquarters that the French were building a series of forts to prevent the British from entering the Ohio Country. On August 28, King George II issued orders to Dinwiddie to ask the French to leave, and if they did not, he should dispel them.[1]

> *if You shall find, that any Number of Persons, whether Indians, or Europeans, shall presume to erect any Fort or Forts within the Limits of Our Province of Virginia,…You are to require of Them peaceably to depart, and not to persist in such unlawfull Proceedings, & if, notwithstanding Your Admonitions, They do still endeavour to carry on any such unlawfull and unjustifiable Designs, We do hereby strictly charge, & command You, to drive them off by Force of Arms.*

Major Washington learned of Dinwiddie's plans to send a messenger to the French and offered his services for the assignment. Dinwiddie, familiar with Major Washington's wilderness frontier exploits, requested that the Council of Virginia commission him for the assignment. The Council formed a committee, consisting of William Fairfax, Richard Corbin, and Philip Ludwell, to write a letter to be presented to the French commandant and the commission's instructions for Washington. William Fairfax was Washington's patron during his teenage years and knew of Washington's western Virginia frontier explorations. He was confident of his ability to execute this physically taxing assignment. The commission was approved and presented to Washington on October 31, 1753.[2]

[Williamsburg, 30 October 1753]

The Honble Robert Dinwiddie Esqr. Governor & Commander in Chief of the Colony & Dominion of Virginia[.] Chancellor & Vice Admiral of the same.

To George Washington Esqr. One of the Adjutants Genl of the Troops & Forces in the Colony of Virginia.

I reposing especial Trust & Confidence in the Ability Conduct, & Fidelity, of You the said George Washington have appointed You my express Messenger, And You are hereby authoriz'd & impower'd to proceed hence with all convenient & possible Dispatch, to that Part, or Place, on the River Ohio, where the French have lately erected a Fort, or Forts, or where the Commandant of the French Forces resides, in order to deliver my Letter & Message to Him; & after waiting not exceeding one Week for an Answer, You are to take Your Leave & return immediately back.

To this Commission I have set my Hand, & caus'd the Great Seal of this Dominion to be affix'd, at the City of Williamsburg, the Seat of my Government. this Thirtieth Day of October in the twenty-seventh Year of the Reign of His Majesty George the Second King of Great Britain &ca Annoque Domini 1753.

Lieutenant Governor Dinwiddie's letter to the French commandant explained that the objective of Major Washington's mission was to request that the French forces be withdrawn from His Majesty's colony.[3]

Sir,

The Lands upon the River Ohio, in the Western Parts of the Colony of Virginia, are so notoriously known to be in the Property of the Crown of Great Britain, that is a Matter of equal Concern and Surprize to me, to hear that a Body of French Forces are erecting Fortresses, and making Settlements upon that River, within his Majesty's Dominions.

The many and repeated Complaints: I have received of these Acts of Hostility, lay me under the Necessity of sending, in the Name of the King my Master, the Bearer hereof, George Washington, Esq; one of the Adjutants Generals of the

Forces of this Dominion, to complain to you of the Encroachments thus made, and of the Injuries done to the Subjects of Great Britain, in open Violation of the Law of Nations, and the Treaties now subsisting, between the two Crowns.

If the Facts are true, and you shall think fit to justify your Proceedings, I must desire you to acquaint me, by whose Authority and Instructions you have lately marched from Canada, with an armed Force, and invaded the King of Great Britain's Territories, in the Manner complained of; that according to the Purport and Resolution of your Answer, I may act agreeably to the Commission I am honoured with, from the King my Master.

However, Sir, In Obedience to my Instructions, it becomes my Duty to require your peaceable departure; and that you would forbear prosecuting a Purpose so interruptive of the Harmony and good Understanding, which his Majesty is desirous to continue and cultivate with the most Christian King.

I persuade myself you will receive and entertain Major Washington with the Candour and Politeness natural to your Nation; and it will give me the greatest Satisfaction, if you return him with an Answer Suitable to my Wishes for a very long and lasting Peace between us.

I have the Honour to Subscribe myself,

SIR,

Your most Obedient,

Humble servant,

Robert Dinwiddie

Williamsburg, in Virginia,

October 31st, 1753.

Dinwiddie gave George Washington instructions to utilize friendly Indians to locate the French forces and to collect strategic information about their capabilities. He also advised Washington to ask the French commandant to provide an escort to protect them from hostile Indians on their return trip. Lieutenant Governor Dinwiddie's advice proved prescient.[4]

[Williamsburg, 30 October 1753]

Instructions for George Washington Esqr.

Whereas I have receiv'd Information of a Body of French Forces being assembled in an hostile Manner on the River Ohio, intending by force of Arms to erect certain Forts on the said River, within this Territory & contrary to the Peace & Dignity of our Sovereign the King of Great Britain.

These are therefore to require & direct You the said George Washington Esqr. forthwith to repair to the Logstown on the said River Ohio; & having there inform'd YourSelf where the said French Forces have posted themselves, thereupon to proceed to such Place: & being there arriv'd to present Your Credentials, together with my Letter to the chief commanding Officer, &, in the Name of His Britanic Majesty, to demand an Answer from him thereto.

On Your Arrival at the Logstown, You are to address Yourself to the Half King, to Monacatoocha, & other the Sachems of the Six Nations; acquainting them with Your Orders to visit & deliver my Letter to the French commanding Officer; & desiring the said Chiefs to appoint You a sufficient Number of their Warriors to be Your Safeguard, as near the French as You may desire, & to wait Your further Direction.

You are diligently to enquire into the Numbers & Force of the French on the Ohio, & the adjacent Country; how they are like to be assisted from Canada; & what are the Difficulties & Conveniences of that Communication, & the Time requir'd for it.

You are to take Care to be truly inform'd what Forts the French have erected, & where; How they are Garrison'd & appointed, & what is their Distance from each other, & from Logstown: And from the best Intelligence You can procure, You are to learn what gave Occasion to this Expedition of the French. How they are like to be supported, & what their Pretentions are.

When the French Commandant has given You the requir'd & necessary Dispatches, You are to desire of him that, agreeable to the Law of Nations, he wou'd grant You a proper Guard, to protect You as far on Your Return, as You may judge for Your Safety, against any stragling Indians or Hunters that may be ignorant of Yr Character & molest You.

Wishing You good Success in Yr Negotiations & a safe & speedy return I am Sr Yr hble Sevrt

On October 31, Washington departed Williamsburg on an extremely exhausting and hazardous journey encompassing more than one thousand miles of rugged mountainous terrain in frigid winter conditions that would test his stamina and courage.

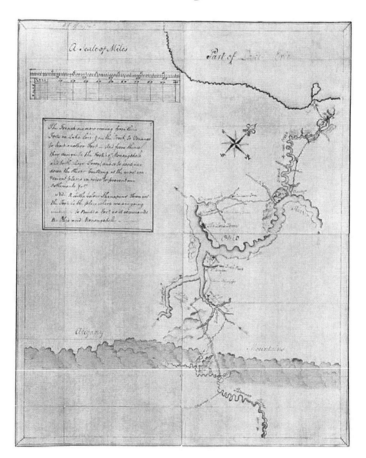

Washington's map of the Ohio Country accompanied his report to Governor Dinwiddie.[5] (Public Record Office, London. Crown Copyright)

Washington maintained a diary throughout his expedition. The initial entries identified the critical persons he recruited to fulfill his mission. First he selected Jacob Vanbraam, who had previously instructed him in fencing and basic military protocol, to be his French interpreter. He then hired Christopher Gist to be his wilderness guide. He also hired servants to assist with the baggage and traders to enable Indian negotiations.[6]

Wednesday, 31st. I was commissioned and appointed by the Honourable Robert Dinwiddie, Esq; Governor, &c., of Virginia, to visit and deliver a letter to the Commandant of the French forces on the Ohio, and set out on the intended Journey the same day: The next I arrived at Fredericksburg, and engaged Mr. Jacob Vanbraam, to be my French interpreter; and proceeded with him to Alexandria, where we provided Necessaries. From thence we went to Winchester, and got Baggage, Horses, &c; and from thence we pursued the new Road to Wills-Creek, were we arrived the 14th of November.

Here I engaged Mr. Gist to pilot us and also hired four others as Servitors, Barnaby Currin and John MacGuire, Indian Traders, Henry Steward, and William Jenkins; and in company with those persons left the Inhabitants the Day following.

Christopher Gist had acquired critical knowledge of frontier wilderness survival during his previous Ohio Country expeditions for the Ohio Company. His experience would prove life-saving when they found themselves the target of a "French Indian" ambush during their return. Gist also maintained a diary during their journey. On November 14, he wrote:[7]

Wednesday 14 November, 1753.—Then Major George Washington came to my house at Will's Creek, and delivered me a letter from the council in Virginia, requesting me to attend him up to the commandant of the French fort on the Ohio River.

The following day, Christopher Gist learned that his son was ill. But knowing the importance of the mission, Washington was unwilling to let Gist go to aid his ailing son, and they continued on their journey. In his journal, Gist wrote,

> *Thursday 15.—We set out, and at night encamped at George's Creek, about eight miles, where a messenger came with letters from my son, who was just returned from his people at the Cherokees, and lay sick at the mouth of Conegocheague. But as I found myself entered again on public business, and Major Washington and all the company unwilling I should return I wrote and sent medicines to my son, and so continued my journey, and encamped at a big hill in the forks of Youghiogany, about eighteen miles.*

For the next week they traveled approximately seventy miles in rain and heavy snow. They arrived at the Monongahela River and stayed at John Frazier's encampment. Frazier was one of the many Indian traders that the French had forced out of the Ohio Country. Washington noted:[8]

> *The excessive Rains and vast Quantity of Snow which had fallen, prevented our reaching Mr. Frazier's, an Indian Trader, at the Mouth of Turtle Creek, on Monongahela, till Thursday, the 22d.*

Washington then traveled by horseback to the forks of the Ohio, a distance of approximately ten miles. There he studied the terrain and envisioned the location for a fort at the forks.

> *The Waters were quite impassible without swimming our Horses; which obliged us to get the Loan of a Canoe from Frazier, and to send Barnaby Currin and Henry Steward down the Monongahela, with our Baggage, to meet us at the Forks of Ohio, about 10 miles, there to cross the Alighany.*

As I got down before the Canoe I spent some time in viewing the Rivers, and the Land in the Fork; which I think extremely well situated for a Fort, as it has the absolute Command of both Rivers.

After studying the forks of the Ohio, Washington traveled two more miles to meet with Shingiss, chief of the Delaware Indians.

About two Miles from this, on the South East Side of the river, at the Place where the Ohio Company intended to erect a Fort, lives Shingiss, king of the Delawares: We called upon him, to invite him to Council at the Loggstown.

Washington then traveled to Logstown, arriving there on November 24, to meet with the Indian tribes as Dinwiddie had instructed.

Shingiss attended us to the Loggs-Town, where we arrived between Sun-setting and Dark, the 25th Day after I left Williamsburg. We travelled over extreme good and bad Land, to get to this Place.—

In Logstown, Washington met also with Monakatoocha as Dinwiddie had suggested.

As soon as I came into Town, I went to Monakatoocha (as the Half-king was out at his hunting-Cabbin on little Beaver-Creek, about 15 Miles off) and informed him by John Davison, my Indian Interpreter, that I was sent a Messenger to the French General; and was ordered to call upon the Sachems of the Six Nations, to acquaint them with it—I gave him a String of Wampum, and a twist of Tobacco, and desired him to send for the Half-King; which he promised to do by a runner in the Morning, and for other Sachems,—I invited him and the other great Men present to my Tent, where they stayed about an Hour and return'd.

The following day the Half-King arrived, and Washington found out that he had met with the French commandant. Washington asked him to reiterate his discussion with the French commandant and to map the route to the commandant's fort.[9]

> *About 3 o'Clock this Evening the Half-King came to Town. I went up and invited him with Davison, privately to my Tent; and desir'd him to relate some of the Particulars of his Journey to the French Commandant, and Reception there: Also to give me an account of the Ways and Distance. He told me that the nearest and levellest Way was now impassable, by Reason of many large mirey Savannas; that we must be obliged to go to Venango, and should not get to the near Fort under 5 or 6 Nights Sleep, good Travelling. When he went to the Fort, he said he was received in a very stern Manner by the late Commander; who ask'd him very abruptly, what he had come about, and to declare his Business: Which he said he did in the following Speech:*

The Half-King had met with Jacques Legardeur de St. Pierre at Fort Le Boeuf and had requested that the French forces leave the Indian land. The Half-King based his request on the 1701 Grand Settlement with the Iroquois Nations in which the French had agreed to stop invading the Iroquois lands. The Half-King provided Washington with the substance of his speech to the French commandant. Washington included the Half-King's speech in his diary (the French referred to the Indians as their children and Indians referred to the French as their father. The English and the Indians referred to each other as their brothers).[10]

> *Fathers, I am come to tell you your own Speeches; what your own Mouths have declared. Fathers, You in former Days, set a silver Bason before us, wherein there was the Leg of a Beaver, and desir'd all the Nations to come and eat of it; to eat in Peace and Plenty, and not to be churlish to one another: and that if any such Person should be found to be a Disturber, I here lay down by the edge of the Dish a Rod, which you must scourge them with; and if I your Father, should get Foolish in my old Days, I desire you may use it upon me as well as others.*

Now Fathers, it is you who are the Disturbers in this Land, by coming and building your Towns; and taking it away unknown to us, and by Force.

Fathers, We kindled a fire a long Time ago, at a Place called Montreal, where we desired you to stay, and not to come and intrude upon our Land. I now desire you may dispatch to that Place for be it known to you, Fathers, that this is our Land, and not yours.

Fathers, I desire you may hear me in Civilness; if not, we must handle that Rod which was laid down for the Use of the abstreperous. If you had come in a peaceable Manner, like our Brothers, the English, we should not have been against your trading with us, as they do; BUT TO COME, FATHERS, AND BUILD HOUSES UPON OUR LAND, AND TO TAKE IT BY FORCE, IS WHAT WE CANNOT SUBMIT TO.

Fathers, Both you and the English are white, we live in a country between; therefore the Land belongs to neither one nor t'other; But the Great Being above allow'd it to be a place of Residence for us; so Fathers, I desire you to withdraw, as I have done our Brothers the English: For I will keep you at Arm's length. I lay this down as a Trial for both, to see which will have the greatest Regard for it, and that Side we will stand by and make equal shares with us. Our Brothers, the English, have heard this, and I come now to tell it to you; for I am not afraid to discharge you off this Land.

In response to the Half-King's request that they withdraw, the French commandant declared that the territory belonged to the French and that he would expel any who stood in his way. Washington wrote the French commandant's reply in his diary.[11]

Now my child, I have heard your Speech: you spoke first, but it is my time to speak now. Where is my Wampum that you took away, with the Marks of towns in it? This wampum I do not know, which you have discharged me off the Land with; but you need not put yourself to the Trouble of speaking, for I will not hear you. I am not afraid of Flies, or Musquitos, for Indians are such as those. I tell you, down the River I will go, and will build upon it, according to my command. If the River was block'd up, I have forces sufficient to burst it open and tread under my Feet all that Stand in Opposition, together with their Alliances; for my Force is as the Sand upon the Sea Shore; therefore, here is your Wampum, I fling it at you. Child, you talk foolish; you say this Land belongs to you, but there is not the Black of my Nail yours. I saw that Land sooner than you did, before the Shannoahs and you were at War: Lead was the Man who went down and took Possession of that River: It is my Land, and I will have it, let who will stand-up for, or say-against it. I'll buy and sell with the English (mockingly). If People will be rul'd by me, they may expect kindness, but not else.

The Half-King informed Washington that he had inquired about two Englishmen that had been captured by the French. Washington wrote the French commandant's reply in his diary.[12]

Child, you think it a very great Hardship that I made Prisoners of those two People at Venango. Don't concern yourself with it: We took and carried them to Canada, to get Intelligence of what the English were doing in Virginia.

Later in the day, Washington met with the Indians, as instructed by Dinwiddie, and described the purpose for his visit and to request that they provide guidance, support, and an escort to the French commandant's fort.[13]

26th. We met in Council at the Long-House, about 9 o'clock, where I spoke to them as follows:

Brothers, I have called you together in Council by order of your Brother, the Governor of Virginia, to acquaint you, that I am sent, with all possible Dispatch, to visit, and deliver a Letter to the French Commandant, of very great Importance to your Brothers, the English; and I dare say, to you their Friends and Allies.

I was desired, Brothers, by you Brother the Governor, to call upon you, the Sachems of the Nations, to inform you of it, and to ask your Advice and

Assistance to proceed to the nearest and best Road to the French. You see, Brothers, I have gotten thus far on my Journey.

His Honour likewise desired me to apply to you for some of your young Men, to conduct and provide Provisions for us on our Way; and be a safe-guard against those French Indians who have taken up the hatchet against us. I have spoken thus particularly to you Brothers, because his Honour our Governor treats you as good Friends and Allies; and holds you in great Esteem. To confirm what I have said, I give you this String of Wampum.

For the next four days Washington negotiated with the Half-King and the Sachems. The French had already befriended several of the tribes and they were reluctant to provide an escort. On November 30, Washington noted in his diary that they finally agreed to provide an escort of three of their chiefs and one warrior.[14]

30th. Last Night the great Men assembled to their Council-House, to consult further about this Journey, and who were to go: The Result of which was, that only three of their Chiefs, with one of their best Hunters, should be our Convoy. The Reason they gave for not sending more, after what had been proposed at Council the 26th, was, that a greater Number might give the French Suspicions of some bad Design, and cause them to be treated rudely: But I rather they could not get their Hunters in.

On November 30, with the Indian escort agreed upon, they set out for Venango. Throughout this leg of the journey they again had to endure bad weather. Washington noted in his diary:

We set out about 9 o-Clock with the Half-King, Teskakake, White Thunder, and the Hunter; and travelled on the Road to Venango, where we arrived the 4th of December, without any Thing remarkable happening but a continued Series of bad Weather.

Upon their arrival at Venango on December 4, Washington observed that the French flag was flying on John Frazier's previous home. The French had driven him out of Venango. Washington met with Captain Daniel Joncaire and learned that the French commandant was housed at Fort La Boeuf, which was located farther north. In his journal he wrote,[15]

> [4th.] *This is an old Indian Town, situated at the Mouth of French Creek on Ohio; and lies near N. about 60 Miles from the Loggs-Town, but more than 70 the way we were obliged to go.*
>
> *We found the French Colours hoisted at a House from which they had driven Mr. John Frazier, an English Subject. I immediately repaired to it, to know where the Commander resided. There were three Officers, one of whom, Capt. Joncaire, informed me, that he had the command of the Ohio; But that there was a General Officer at the near Fort, where he advised me to apply for an Answer.*

For two days they were forced to remain encamped at Venango because Captain Joncaire had liquored Washington's Indians in an effort to persuade them to stay behind. Washington finally enlisted Christopher Gist's persuasions to get the Indians to leave camp. In his diary on the seventh, he described the difficulties he experienced.[16]

> 7th. *Monsieur La Force, Commissary of the French Stores, and three other Soldiers came over to accompany us up. We found it extremely difficult to get the Indians off To-day, as every Stratagem had been used to prevent their going-up with me. I had last Night, left John Davison (the Indian Interpreter whom I brought with me from Town), and strictly charged him not to be out of their Company, as I could not get them over to my Tent; for they had some Business with Kustaloga, and chiefly to know the Reason why he did not deliver up the French Belt which he had in Keeping: But I was obliged to send Mr. Gist over To-day to fetch them; which he did with great Persuasion.*

When the Indian guides returned, they set out to call upon the commandant at Fort Le Boeuf. During this leg of the trek they had to endure extreme rain and snow yet again while struggling through frigid marshes.

At 11 o'Clock we set out for the Fort, and were prevented from arriving there till the 11th by excessive Rains, Snows, and bad Travelling, through many Mires and Swamps. These we were obliged to pass, to avoid crossing the Creek, which was impossible, either by fording or rafting, the Water was so high and rapid.

They arrived at Fort Le Boeuf on December 11. The following day, Washington presented Lieutenant Governor Dinwiddie's letter to Commander Legardeur de St. Pierre, the commandant of the French forces in America.[17]

12th. I prepared early to wait upon the Commander, and was received and conducted to him by the second Officer in Command. I acquainted him with my Business, and offered my Commission and Letter: Both of which he desired me to keep till the arrival of Monsieur Riparti Captain, at the next Fort, who was sent for and expected every Hour.

This Commander is a Knight of the military Order of St. Lewis, and named Legardeur de St. Pierre. He is an elderly Gentleman, and has much the air of a Soldier. He was sent over to take the Command immediately upon the Death of the late General, and arrived here about seven Days before me.

At 1 o'Clock the Gentleman who was sent for arrived, when I offered the Letter, &c, again; which they received, and adjourned into a private Apartment for the Captain to translate, who understood a little English. After he had done it, the Commander desired I would walk-in, and bring my Interpreter to pursue and correct it; which I did.

While awaiting the commandant's reply, Washington decided to return the horses to Venango, for they were weakened by the weather. They were to remain at Venango and wait for Washington if the river became frozen. If not they were to continue traveling south to the forks of the Ohio and Washington would canoe down the Allegheny River and rendezvous there.[18]

> *14th.   As the Snow increased very fast, and our Horses daily became weaker, I sent them off unloaded; under the Care of Barnaby Currin, and two others, to make all convenient Dispatch to Venango, and there await our Arrival, if there was a prospect of the Rivers freezing: If not, then to continue down to Shanapin's Town, at the Forks of the Ohio, and there to wait till we came to cross the Aliganey; intending myself to go down by Water, as I had the Offer of a Canoe or two.*

The Half-King and the Indian chiefs wanted to meet with the French commandant to offer Chief Shingiss's wampum. But Washington knew that the commandant would try to discourage them from joining him on their return trip and tried to persuade the Indians from meeting with the French. Washington's efforts were futile.

> *As I found many Plots concerted to retard the Indians Business, and prevent their returning with me; I endeavor'd all that lay in my Power to frustrate their Schemes, and to hurry them on to execute their intended Design. They accordingly pressed for Admittance this Evening, which at Length was granted them, privately, with the Commander and one or two other officers.*

The French commandant did not accept the Half-King's offer of the wampum, but countered with an offer to send goods to Logstown for the Indians.

> *The Half-King told me, that he offer'd the Wampum to the Commander, who evaded taking it, and made many fair Promises of Love and Friendship; said he wanted to live in Peace, and trade amicably with them, as Proof of which he would send some Goods down immediately to the Logg's-Town for them.*

Washington believed the real reason the French commandant made the offer was an excuse to send a French military escort for Washington's party on the return journey. He arrived at this conclusion after learning that the French commandant had not returned the English prisoners who had been recently captured by their French Indians.

But I rather think the Design of that is, to bring away all our straggling Traders they meet with, as I privately understood they intended to carry an Officer, &c, with them. And what rather confirms this Opinion, I was enquiring of the Commander, by what Authority he had made Prisoners of several of our English Subjects. He told me that the Country belong'd to them; that no Englishman had a Right to trade upon those Waters; and that he had Orders to make every Person Prisoner who attempted it on the Ohio, or the Waters of it.

I enquir'd of Capt. Riparti about the Boy who was carried by this Place, as it was done while the Command devolved on him, between the Death of the late General, and the Arrival of the present. He acknowledged, that a Boy had been carried past; and that the Indians had two or three white Men's Scalps (I was told by some of the Indians at Vanango Eight) but pretended to have forgotten the name of the Place the Boy came from, and all the Particular Facts, though he had question'd him for some Hours, as they were carrying him past. I likewise enquired what they had done with John Trotter and James MacClocklan, two Pensylvania Traders, whom they had taken, with all their Goods. They told me, that they had been sent to Canada, but were now returned Home.

This E—vening I received an Answer to his Honour the Governor's Letter from the Commandant.

After having Lieutenant Governor Dinwiddie's letter interpreted, the French commandant provided a response to Dinwiddie's request. The letter contained the commandant's refusal to leave the Ohio Country. Following is the English translation of the commandant's letter.[19]

Sir,

As I have the honour to Command in Chief here, Mr. Washington delivered me the letter which you wrote to the Commander of the French Troops. It would have afforded me great Pleasure, if you had given him Orders, or that he had himself been inclined to have proceeded to Canada, to see our General, to whom it belongs more properly than to me, to put in a clear Light, the Evidence and Reality of the Rights of the King my Master to the Lands situated on Belle River, and to contest the pretentions of the King of Great Britain in this Respect.

I am going to address your letter to Monsieur the Marquis Duquesne, whose answer shall be a Law to me, and if he orders me to communicate it to you, I can assure you, Sir, I will not neglect to transmit it to you, with all possible Expedition.

As to the Summons you have given me to withdraw, I do not think myself under any Obligation to submit to it; whatever your Instructions may be, I am here in Virtue of the Orders of my General, and I beseech you, Sir, not to entertain the least doubt of my constant Resolution to conform to them, with all the Exactness and Firmness becoming a better Officer.

I do not know that in the Course of this Campaign any Thing has happened, which can be construed an Act of Hostility, or contrary to the Treaties which subsist between the two Crowns, the Continuance of which concerns as much, and is as agreeable to us as to the English. If you had been pleased, Sir, upon this Occasion to have entered into a particular Detail of the Facts which are the Motives to your complaint, I should have had the Honour of answering you in the most positive Manner, and I am persuaded, that you would have had Room to have been satisfied.

I have made it a particular Duty, to receive Mr. Washington with that Distinction which is suitable to your Dignity, his own Rank and great Merit; I flatter myself that he will do me the Justice to acknowledge this to you, and that he will inform you as well as I of the profound Respect with which I am, Sir, &c.

The French provided Washington and his Indians with canoes for their journey south, but, as in Venango, they discouraged the Indians from departing with him. Washington realized that this maneuvering put the mission in great jeopardy and that his return trip would be dangerous without the protection and guidance of friendly Indians. On the fifteenth he recorded in his diary,[20]

> *15th. The Commandant ordered a plentiful Store of Liquor, Provision, &c., to be put on Board our Canoe; and appeared to be extremely complaisant, though he was exerting every Artifice which he could invent to set our own Indians at Variance with us, to prevent their going 'till after our Departure. Presents, Rewards, and every Thing which could be suggested by him or his Officers. — I can't say that ever in my Life I suffered so much Anxiety as I did in this Affair: I saw that every Stratagem which the most fruitful Brain could invent, was practised, to win the Half-King to their Interest; and that leaving him here was giving them an Opportunity they aimed at. — I went to the Half-King and press'd him in the strongest Terms to go: He told me the Commandant would not discharge him 'till the Morning. I then went to the Commandant, and desired him to do their Business; and complain'd of ill Treatment: For keeping them, as they were Part of my Company, was detaining me. This he promised not to do, but to forward my Journey as much as he could. He protested he did not keep them, but was ignorant of the Cause of their Stay; though I soon found it out: — He had promised them a present of Guns, &c, if they would wait 'till the morning.*
>
> *As I was very much press'd by the Indians, to wait this Day for them, I consented, on a Promise, That nothing should hinder them in the Morning.*

The following day the French continued to encourage the Indians to remain at Fort Le Boeuf, but the Half-King kept his word to Washington and they departed together. On December 16, Washington wrote in his diary,[21]

16th.   The French were not slack in their Inventions to keep the Indians this Day also: But as they were obligated, according to Promise, to give the Present, they then endeavored to try the Power of Liquor; which I doubt not would have prevailed at any other Time than this; But I urged and insisted with the King so closely upon his Word, that he refrained, and set off with us as he had engaged.

The return canoe trip down French Creek from Fort Le Boeuf to Venango was dangerous and fatiguing. The river at times was so swift the canoes were nearly thrown against the rocks and at times so shallow the canoes had to be ported. Washington provided in his diary the following description of the canoe trip.[22]

We had a tedious and very fatiguing Passage down the Creek. Several Times we were like to have been staved against Rocks; and many Times were obliged all Hands to get out and remain in the Water Half an Hour or more, getting over the Shoals. At one Place the Ice had lodged and made it impassable by Water; therefore we were obliged to carry our Canoe across a Neck of Land, a quarter of a Mile over. We did not reach Venango, till the 22d, where we met our Horses.

Christopher Gist also wrote a description of this hazardous leg of the journey.[23]

Friday 21. —The ice was so hard we could not break our way through, but were obliged to haul our vessels across a point of land and put them in the creek again. The Indians and three French canoes overtook us here, and the people of one French canoe that was lost, with her cargo of powder and lead. This night we encamped about twenty miles above Venango.

Saturday 22. — Set out. The creek began to be very low and we were forced to get out, to keep our canoe from oversetting, several times; the water freezing to our clothes; and we had the pleasure of seeing the French overset, and the brandy and wine floating in the creek, and run by them, and left them to shift for themselves. Came to Venango, and met with our people and horses.

At Venango, Washington elected to continue the journey over land with the horses. But the winter weather stymied their progress and he soon realized that the horses could not continue. In order to expedite his return to Williamsburg, Washington decided that he and Christopher Gist would continue the journey on foot. On the twenty-sixth, they set out without their horses and Washington described his reasoning in his diary.[24]

> *Our Horses were now so weak and feeble, and the Baggage so heavy (as we were obliged to provide all the Necessaries which the Journey would require) that we doubted much their performing it; therefore myself and others (except the Drivers, who were obliged to ride) gave up our Horses for Packs, to assist along with the Baggage. I put myself in an Indian walking Dress, and continued with them three Days, till I found there was no Probability of their getting home in any reasonable Time. The Horses grew less able to travel every Day; the Cold increased very fast; and the Roads were becoming much worse by a deep Snow, continually freezing: Therefore as I was uneasy to get back, to make Report of my Proceedings to his Honour, the Governor, I determined to prosecute my Journey the nearest Way through the Woods, on Foot.*
>
> *Accordingly I left Mr. Vanbraam in Charge of our Baggage: with Money and Directions to Provide Necessaries from Place to Place for themselves and Horses, and to make the most convenient Dispatch in Travelling.*
>
> *I took my necessary Papers; pulled off my Cloaths; and tied myself up in a Match Coat. Then with Gun in Hand and Pack at my Back, in which were my Papers and Provisions, I set-out with Mr. Gist, fitted in the same Manner, on Wednesday the 26th.*

Christopher Gist agreed to proceed without the horses although he was greatly concerned over Washington's ability to endure the rigors of cross-country wilderness trekking.[25]

Wednesday 26. — The Major desired me to set out on foot, and leave our company, as the creeks were frozen, and our horses could make but little way. Indeed, I was unwilling he should undertake such a travel, who had never been used to walking before this time. But as he insisted on it, I set out with our packs, like Indians, and travelled eighteen miles. That night we lodged at an Indian cabin, and the Major was much fatigued. It was very cold; all the small runs were frozen, that we could hardly get water to drink.

The following day, they met a French Indian at an aptly named place called Murdering-Town who agreed to show them the fastest way to the forks. The Indian betrayed them and, from point-blank range, fired at Washington. Washington briefly described the failed assassination attempt in his diary.[26]

The Day following, just after we had passed a Place called the Murdering-Town (where we intended to quit the Path, and steer across the Country for Shannapins Town) we fell in with a Party of French Indians, who had lain in Wait for us. One of them fired at Mr. Gist or me, not 15 steps off, but fortunately missed.

Christopher Gist also provided a description of the French Indian's attempt at murdering them.[27]

Thursday 27. — We rose early in the morning, and set out about two o'clock. Got to the Murthering town, on the southeast fork of Beaver creek. Here we met with an Indian, whom I thought I had seen at Joncaire's, at Venango, when on our journey up to the French fort. This fellow called me by my Indian name, and pretended to be glad to see me. He asked us several questions, as how we came to travel on foot, when we left Venango, where we parted with our horses, and when they would be there, etc. Major Washington insisted on travelling on the nearest way to forks of Alleghany. We asked the Indian if he could go with us, and show us the nearest way. The Indian seemed very glad and ready to go with us. Upon which we set out, and the Indian took the Major's pack. We travelled very brisk for eight or ten miles, when the Major's feet grew very sore, and he very weary, and the Indian steered too much north-eastwardly. The Major desired to encamp, to which the Indian asked to carry his gun. But he refused that, and then the Indian grew churlish, and pressed us to keep on, telling us that there were Ottawa Indians in these woods, and they would scalp us if we lay out; but to go to his cabin, and we should be safe. I thought very ill of the fellow, but did not care to let the Major know I mistrusted him. But he soon mistrusted him as much as I. He said he could hear a gun to his cabin, and steered us more northwardly. We grew uneasy, and then he said two whoops might be heard to his cabin. We went two miles further; then the Major said he would stay at the next water, and we desired the Indian to stop at the next water. But before we came to water, we came to a clear meadow; it was very light, and snow on the ground. The Indian made a stop, turned about; the Major saw him point his gun toward us and fire. Said the Major, "Are you shot?" "No," said I. Upon which the Indian ran forward to a big standing white oak, and to loading his gun; but we were soon with him. I would have killed him; but the Major would not suffer me to kill him. We let him charge his gun; we found he put in a ball; then we took care of him.

Washington then took the French Indian into custody. That night they released him and then continued trekking throughout the night to avoid being tracked and pursued the next day. Following is Washington's description of the experience.[28]

We took this fellow into Custody, and kept him till about 9 o'clock at Night; Then let him go, and walked all the remaining Part of the Night without making any Stop; that we might get the start, so far, as to be out of the Reach of their Pursuit the next Day, since we were well assured they would follow our Tract as soon as it was light. The next Day we continued traveling till quite dark, and got to the River about two Miles above Shannapins. We expected to have found the River frozen, but it was not, only about 50 Yards from each Shore; The Ice I suppose had broken up above, for it was driving in vast Quantities.

Christopher Gist's description of how they handled the Indian affair provided the following detail.[29]

> *The Major or I always stood by the guns; we made him make a fire for us by a little run, as if we intended to sleep there. I said to the Major, "As you will not have him killed, we must get him away, and then we must travel all night." Upon which I said to the Indian, "I suppose you were lost, and fired your gun." He said, he knew the way to his cabin, and 'twas but a little way. "Well," said I, "do you go home; and as we are much tired, we will follow your track in the morning; and here is a cake of bread for you, and you must give us meat in the morning." He was glad to get away. I followed him, and listened until he was fairly out of the way, and then we set out about half a mile, when we made a fire, set our compass, and fixed our course, and travelled all night, and in the morning we were on the head of Piney creek.*
>
> *Friday 28. —We travelled all the next day down the said creek, and just at night found some tracks where Indians had been hunting. We parted, and appointed a place a distance off, where to meet, it being then dark. We encamped, and thought ourselves safe enough to sleep.*

When Washington and Gist arrived at the Allegheny River they found it was not frozen. So they spent the day chopping down some trees with a hatchet to make a raft. While rafting across the river, a large chunk of ice hit the raft and knocked Washington into the frigid waters. After failing to recover their raft, they swam to an island where they spent the night. Gist's fingers and toes had become frozen and Washington described the whole harrowing experience in his diary.[30]

> *There was no way for getting over but on a Raft; Which we set about with but one poor Hatchet, and finished just after Sun-setting. This was a whole Day's Work. Then set off; But before we were Half Way over, we were jammed in the Ice, in such a Manner that we expected every Moment our Raft to sink, and ourselves to perish. I put-out my setting Pole to try to stop the Raft, that the Ice*

might pass by; when the Rapidity of the Stream threw it with so much Violence against the Pole, that it jerked me out into ten Feet Water: but I fortunately saved myself by catching hold of one of the Raft Logs. Notwithstanding all our efforts we could not get the Raft to either Shore; but were obliged, as we were near an Island to quit our Raft and make to it.

The Cold was so extremely severe, that Mr. Gist had all his Fingers, and some of his Toes frozen; but the water was shut up so hard, that we found no Difficulty in getting-off the Island, on the Ice, in the Morning, and went to Mr. Frazier's.

Christopher Gist's summary of their crossing was brief but still portrayed the extreme danger they encountered.[31]

Saturday 29.— We set out early, got to Alleghany, made a raft, and with much difficulty got over to an island, a little above Shannopin's town. The Major having fallen in from off the raft, and my fingers frost-bitten, and the sun down, and very cold, we contented ourselves to encamp upon that island. It was deep water between us and the shore; but the cold did us some service, for in the morning it was frozen hard enough for us to pass over on the ice.

After a short stay at Frazier's cabin, Washington set out to continue the return journey to Williamsburg. They arrived at Mr. Gist's on January 2, and on January 7 they made it back to Wills Creek. In his diary, Washington reflected on how challenging the expedition had been.[32]

This Day we arrived at Wills Creek, after as fatiguing a Journey as it is possible to conceive, rendered so by excessive bad Weather. From the first Day of December to the 15th, there was but one Day on which it did not rain or snow incessantly: and throughout the whole Journey we met with nothing but one continued Series of cold wet Weather, which occasioned very uncomfortable Lodgings: especially after we had quitted our Tent, which was some Screen from the Inclemency of it.

On January 11, Washington stopped at Mount Vernon for a day of rest and then completed his return to Williamsburg on the sixteenth.

He arrived unscathed from the many hazards he had endured and presented the French commandant's reply to Lieutenant Governor Dinwiddie. In the final journal entry, he modestly expressed the hope that the lieutenant governor would find his conduct satisfactory.[33]

> *On the 11th I got to Belvoir: where I stopped one Day to take necessary Rest; and then set out and arrived in Williamsburg the 16th; when I waited upon his Honour the Governor with the Letter I had brought from the French Commandant; and to give an Account of the Success of my Proceedings. This I beg leave to do by offering the foregoing Narrative as it contains the most remarkable Occurrences which happened in my Journey.*
>
> *I hope what has been said will be sufficient to make your Honour satisfied with my Conduct; for that was my Aim in undertaking the Journey, and chief Study throughout the Prosecution of it.*

Washington had proven the strength of his character, and Dinwiddie recognized it. He had Washington's journal printed and then personally presented it to the Virginia Council. Dinwiddie then arranged for it to be published in newspapers. Major George Washington became renowned throughout the colonies and Great Britain. His physical strength, endurance, diplomatic skills, acumen, and commitment to duty all demonstrated that Washington had the ability required to meet the challenges and lead the struggling colonies.

Washington's success demonstrated to the British leadership that he had the character and strength to endure a frontier encounter with the recalcitrant French. Lieutenant Governor Dinwiddie's decision to send George Washington on this mission effectively provided Washington with the cornerstone for a career that would enable him to become one of our greatest leaders. Lieutenant Governor Dinwiddie recognized the leadership qualities of Washington and subsequently appointed him to lead the fight to oust the French from the Ohio Country. Dinwiddie's continuing support enabled Washington to further build upon this foundation.

The thousand-mile trek was the first of many close encounters that Washington endured without ever receiving an injury. His survival and success led him to believe that he was being protected by Providence for some future great endeavor.

CHARMING SOUND

January 1754–November 1754

"I fortunately escaped without a wound, tho' the right Wing where I stood was exposed to & received all the Enemy's fire and was the part where the man was killed & the rest wounded. I can trust assure you, I heard Bullets whistle and believe me there was something charming in the sound."

– May 31, 1754 – Lieutenant Colonel George Washington

WHEN THE FRENCH COMMANDANT REFUSED TO concede to the demands of the British colonial governor, both imperial powers initiated military campaigns to control access to the Ohio Country. The domination of the Ohio Country became the strategic goal of both nations. The battle line was drawn at the forks of the Ohio, where the Allegheny and the Monongahela Rivers flow together and the Ohio River is formed.

On January 21, 1754, Lieutenant Governor Robert Dinwiddie informed the Virginia Council that the French commandant, Jacques Legardeur de Saint Pierre, refused to submit to Dinwiddie's demand.[1]

The Council responded to the commandant's rejection by advising Dinwiddie to act quickly to defend the forks of the Ohio.[2]

The Council and Lieutenant Governor Dinwiddie valued Washington's boldness, stamina, and knowledge of Virginia's western frontier, and they appointed him to lead the Virginia forces against the French incursion into the Ohio Country. This appointment launched George Washington's career in the military just days after he returned from his thousand-mile wilderness expedition.

With a strengthening belief in his ability to survive the most challenging conditions, Washington accepted the command and marched his newly formed detachment to the forks of the Ohio to confront the French. Washington's belief in the protection of Providence would become stronger as a result of his close encounters on the battlefield.

This appointment tested young Major Washington's leadership skills and strength of character. He had to recruit and train his own company of soldiers. These raw recruits had to fight the professional French army. Major Washington's corps was vastly outnumbered, undisciplined, and poorly supplied. Additional difficulties were caused by two factors. Firstly, the inherent differences between the colonial and the British command structures created endless confusion and internal conflicts. Secondly, the mission required the construction of a road through the mountainous terrain—a task relegated to the colonials. The British soldiers were excused from this exhausting task, resulting in numerous arguments between the English and colonial troops.

The Virginia Council advised Dinwiddie to promote William Trent to the rank of captain and ordered him to proceed immediately to the forks of the Ohio to begin the construction of a fort. In his orders to Captain Trent, Dinwiddie informed him that when the House of Burgesses authorized the funds, he would send an additional four hundred troops to help defend the fort.[3]

Sir:

Y'r Letter of the 6th curr't I rec'd from Maj'r Washington, from his report, informat'n and Observat's I find the French intend down the Ohio to build Forts and take Possession of the Lands of that River, w'ch I w'd very earnestly prevent. And as You think You c'd (Omission in the records) this Winter, if properly impower'd to do so, I therefore inclose You a Capt's Com'o to raise 100 Men in Augusta and in the exterior Settlem'ts of this Dom'n and a blank Com'o for You to choose a suitable Lieut. to Co-operate with You. Y'r Comp'a will be in the Pay of this Gov't agreeable to the Assembly. Maj'r Washington has a Com'o to raise 100 Men, with them he is to join You and I desire You may march Y'r Men out to the Ohio where a Fort is propos'd to be built. When You are there You are to protect and assist them in finishing the Fort and to be on Y'r Guard ag'st any Attempts of the French. I doubt not the Woodsmen You may enlist will be provided with Guns &c., I have appointed Maj'r Carlisle of Alexandria a Commiss'y of Stores and Provisions, he will supply You accordingly with what Necessaries You may want and in case of want of Guns I have sent some to his Care to be delivered to the Com'd'rs of either of these Compa's giving receipt accordingly for them. As You have a good Interest with the Ind's I doubt not You will prevail with many of them to join You in order to defeat the Designs of the French in taking their Lands from them by force of Arms. The Ho. Of Burgesses are to meet the 14th of next Mo. w'n I hope they will enable me to send out 400 more Men early in the Spring to Y'r Assistance. I wrote to the neighboring Gov'rs for their Aid and Assistance on the present Emergency and I am in hopes they will supply a good Number of men &c. I have some Cannon come in—ten I send up to the Comissary at Alexandria—they carry four Pound shot—I fear there will be a difficulty in carrying them out—as You are acquainted with the Roads, I shall be glad of Y'r Advice therein, and comunicate the same to Maj'r Carlisle. You see the Confidence and good Opinion I have of Y'r Capacity and Diligence w'ch I hope You will Exert on this Occasion by keeping a good Comand and strongly engaging our friendly Ind's to be on the Active. Provisions will be difficult to send regular Supplies. Mr. Washington says one Mr. Frazier can provide large Qu'ty of Venison, Bear, &c. I desire

You may write him to get what he can. When You have completed Y'r Comp'a send me a List thereof and the time of their enlisting and the Places of their Aboad. I wish You Health and Success in the present Expedition and am Sincerely

S'r Y'r h'ble Serv't

Dinwiddie then provided specific instructions to Washington to protect the men building the fort, to assist in its construction, and to take prisoners or to kill the intruding French.[4]

[Williamsburg, January 1754]

Instructs to be observ'd by Majr Geo. Washington on the Expeditn to the Ohio

MAJR GEO. WASHINGTON

You are forthwith to repair to the Coty of Frederick, & there to take under Yr comd 50 Men of the Militia, who will be deliver'd to You by Comdr of the sd Coty pursuant to my Orders—You are to send Yr Lieut. at the same Time to the Coty of Augusta, to receive 50 Men from the Comdr of that Coty as I have order'd, & with them he is to join you at Alexandria to which Place You are to proceed, as soon as You have recd the Men in Frederick—Having recd this Detachmt You are to train & discipline them in the best Manner You can, & for all Necessaries You are to apply YrSelf to Mr Jno. Carlisle at Alexa. who has my Orders to supply You—Having all Things in readiness, You are to use all Expedition in proceeding to the Fork of Ohio, with the Men under Yr Comd & there You are to finish & compleat in the best Manner, & as soon as You possibly can the Fort which I expect is there already begun by the Ohio Compa. You are to act on the Difensive, but in Case any Attempts are made to obstruct the Works or interrupt our Settlemts by any Persons whatsoever, You are to restrain all such Offenders, & in Case of resistance to make Prisoners of or kill & destroy them. For the rest You are to conduct Yrself as the Circumsts. of the Service shall require, & to act as You shall find best for the Furtherence of His Majesty's Service, & Good of the Domn.

Wishing You Health & Success I bid You Farewell

On February 23, the House of Burgesses appropriated £10,000 for the expedition, and Lieutenant Governor Dinwiddie prorogued the Assembly to meet in April.[5]

Gent. Of the Council, Mr. Speaker and Gent. of the Ho. Of Burgesses:

The Business of the Session being concluded, I shall detain You no longer, Y'n to thank You for the Supply You have granted, w'ch I will endeavour to make effective of the good Purposes for w'ch it is given. I have tho't fit to prorogue this Assembly to the third Thursday in Apr. next, and You are accordingly prorogu'd to y't Time.

Dinwiddie now had the funds to raise six additional companies and to wage the campaign against the French. On March 1, Dinwiddie wrote to Colonel Joshua Fry and informed him that he was appointed commander in chief of the Virginia regiment and placed him in command of all the forces in the campaign. He instructed Fry to proceed to Alexandria, take charge of the forces there, and march them to Wills Creek (present-day Cumberland, MD) and then to the forks of the Ohio. Colonel Fry was instructed to build an additional fort along the Monongahela River. Dinwiddie also advised Colonel Fry that he anticipated support of the friendly Indians from numerous tribes.[6]

Mar. 1754.

Sir:

The Forces under Y'r Com'd are rais'd to protect our frontier Settlements from the incursions of the French and the Ind's in F'dship with them. I therefore desire You will with all possible Expedition repair to Alexandria on the Head of the Poto. River, and there take upon You the com'd of the Forces accordingly; w'ch I Expect will be at that Town the Middle of next Mo. You are to march them to Wills's Creek, above the Falls of Poto. from thence with the Great Guns, Amunit'n and Provisions You are to proceed to Monongahela, when arriv'd there, You are to make Choice of the best Place to erect a Fort for mounting y'r

Cannon and ascertain'g His M'y the King of G. B's undoubt'd right to those Lands. My Orders to You is to be on the Defensive and if any foreign Force sh'd come to annoy You or interrupt Y'r quiet Settlem't, and building the Fort as afores'd, You are in that Case to represent to them the Powers and Orders You have from me, and I desire they w'd imediately retire and not to prevent You in the discharge of your Duty. If they sh'd continue to be obstinate after your desire to retire, You are then to repell Force by Force. I expect a Number of the Southern Indians will join You on this Expedit'n, w'ch with the Indians on the Ohio, I desire You will cultivate a good Understanding and Correspondence with, supplying them with what Provisions and other Necessaries You can spare; and write to Maj'r Carlyle w'n You want Provisions, who has my Orders to purchase and Keep in proper Magazine for Your dem'ds. Keep up a good Com'd and regular Discipline, inculcate morality and Courage in Y'r Soldiers that they may answer the Views on w'ch they are rais'd. You are to constitute a Court Martial of the Chief of You Officers, with whom You are to advise and consult on all Affairs of Consequence; and as the Fate of the Expedition greatly depends on You, from the Opinion I have of Your good Sense and Conduct, I refer the Management of the whole to You with the Advice of the Court Martial. Sincerely recommending You to the Protect'n of God, wishing Success to our just Designs' I heartily wish You farewell.

In addition, His Majesty ordered three more independent companies, two from New York and one from South Carolina, to join in the expedition to drive the French from the Ohio Country under the lieutenant governor's command. The independent companies were provided by the king while Washington's Virginia regiment was authorized by the Assembly. One of the problems with this arrangement was that the officer rankings within the independent companies were superior to the ranks of the officers provided by the Virginia Assembly. Therefore, a British regular army captain outranked a major in the colonial forces. This proved to be a constant irritant and cause of confusion during the campaign.

With the addition of the independent companies, Dinwiddie believed that he would have five companies of men reporting to Commander in Chief Colonel Fry, a force that he thought would be of sufficient size to battle the French. On March 15, Lieutenant Governor Dinwiddie learned that the French were on the move and wrote to Major Washington instructing him to depart Alexandria immediately, ahead of Colonel Fry, and to march to the forks of the Ohio. In the letter, he informed Washington that he was promoted to lieutenant colonel.[7]

Sir   *Mar. 15th 1754*

Yr two Letters of the 3d & 7th Currt I recd & the enclos'd from Messrs Trent & Cresap. I am surpriz'd from their Letters that the French are so early expected down the Ohio; which I think makes it necessary for You to march what Soldiers You have enlisted immediately to the Ohio, & escort some Waggons, with the necessary Provisions; Colo. Fry to march wth the others as soon as possible. I shall send three Sloops with Recruits from York, James River, & the Eastern Shoar, so that I hope the Number of Men will be fully Compleated. By the First of these Sloops, I shall send 24 more Tents, which is all that's to be had here. Picks, Cutlasses, or Halberts, none in the Magazine; so the Officers must head their Comps. with small Arms.

I have no Objection to the Soldiers being in an uniform Dress, on the Head You propose, but I am perswaded You have not Time to get them made, unless to be sent after You; in that Case, Care shd be taken of buying the Cloth at the cheapest rate—The Soldiers are to be pd from the Day they were enlisted, 'til the Day they march, after that every two Mos. to be pd by Mr Carlyle at Alexa. on producing a Certificate from the Comdg Officer & their Capt. which Certificate will be a Voucher to Mr Carlyle, & he will be supplied accordingly. Mr Muse was with me this Day, & will soon be at Alexa. I have appointed him Majr at 10/per Day; & enclos'd You have a Como. for Lieut. Colo. pay 12/per Day, without any Trouble of Comanding a Compa.—I have sent to the Treasurer for Money, if he disappoints me, I shall nevertheless send You some immediately, which You may expect in 24 Hours after this Messenger. I recommend to You

Dispatch to be with Capt. Trent if possible before the French come down the river; send a Runner before You for Intelligence that You may not meet with any Surprize. I hope the Colonies to the Nowd will assist Us.

His M[ajest]y has order'd two Independt Comps. From NY: & one from Carolina, to come here to be under my Comd—I have sent Expres[se]s for their immediate coming here, wn they arrive I propose sending them out to the Ohio. I wd gladly hope, as Capt. Trent has begun to build a Fort at Allegany, that the French will not immediately disturb us there; & wn our Forces are properly collected we shall be able to keep Possession, & drive the French from the Ohio. I hope the Cherokees and Catawbas are there by this Time. I intreat You to be diligent in Yr March, take wt Officers You see proper that are at Alexa., & keep up a good, Dicipline, 'till Colo. Fry joins You: He has Orders to choose a Court Martial, to peruse the Articles of War, & select from them such the Court may think proper for the Dicipline of the Men.

Pray God preserve You, & grant Success to our just Designs. I am most Sincerely Sr Yr Friend & hble Servt

In his diary, Washington noted that he had been promoted to lieutenant colonel and had received instructions to march immediately to the forks of the Ohio to protect His Majesty's property from the anticipated French attack.[8]

On the 31st March I received from his Honour a Lieutenant Colonel's Commission of the Virginia Regiment whereof Joshua Fry, Esquire, was Colonel, dated the 15th, with Orders to take the troops, which were at that time quartered at Alexandria under my command, and to march with them towards the Ohio, there to aid Captain Trent in building Forts, and in defending the possessions of his Majesty against the attempts and hostilities of the French.

Lieutenant Governor Dinwiddie expected to receive support from the friendly Indians. He wrote to Governor James DeLancey of New York on March 21, advising him that he was planning to meet with the different Indian tribes in Winchester and to provide them with the appropriate wampum in order to gain their support.[9]

I hope to see at least two of the Chiefs of the Five Nations at Winchester in May, as the Design of that Meeting is to make a Peace between the Northern and Southern Ind's, after which to make a strict Alliance between them and the whole British Subjects on the Cont't.

Dinwiddie also wrote to Governor James Hamilton of Pennsylvania on March 21, informing him of the intended meeting with the Indians and the plan to erect two forts at the forks of the Ohio.[10]

I have wrote the Catawbas and Cherokees to join our Forces on the Ohio in April next. I promis'd them a Present from their Father, the King, next Year. They must have Provision and Arms, but I did not engage them any Clothing, the Messenger I sent to them is not yet ret'd. I shall be glad if we can, this Sumer, erect two Forts, w'ch if effected, I propose leaving the three Independ't Compa's to remain in them all Winter.

Washington departed Alexandria on April 2, leading two companies totaling more than 150 men. In his diary, he wrote,[11]

April the 2nd. Every Thing being ready, we began our march according to our Orders, the 2nd of April, with two Companies of Foot, commanded by Captain Peter Hog and Lieutenant Jacob Van Braam, five subalterns, two Sergeants, six Corporals, one Drummer, and one hundred and twenty Soldiers, one Surgeon, one Swedish Gentleman, who was a volunteer, two wagons guarded by one Lieutenant, Sergeant, Corporal and twenty-five Soldiers. We left Alexandria on Tuesday Noon and pitched our tents about four miles from Cameron having marched six miles.

On April 15, Dinwiddie sent a letter to Governor James Glen of South Carolina thanking him for dispatching a company of eighty men to the forks. He also informed Glen that he was expecting to meet with the Indians at Winchester.[12]

> *I am obliged to You for the Care You have taken in ordering the Independ't Compa. here, w'ch I daily expect, tho' not yet arriv'd, and am glad of the Acc't You give of them. It is impossible for me as yet to describe to You the different Tribes of Ind's or their Number of Gun-men, but after the Meeting at Win. I hope to be able to give You a particular Acc't. My Invitat'n is to the Six Nat's, the different Tribes of Ind's on the Ohio River, The Twightwees, a large Nat'n of Ind's to the So'w'd, that inhabit between the Ohio and Lake Erie, The Cherokees, Catawbas, and Chickasaws, and if we meet and come to a proper Treaty, I shall be very glad to include the Creeks and all other Ind'n Nat's in Fr'dship with Britain and these Colonies.*

Captain William Trent and Lieutenant John Fraser departed the site of the fort at the forks of the Ohio in search of supplies and left Ensign Ward in command. However, on April 17, the French arrived at the forks with a force of nearly a thousand troops. Ensign Edward Ward commanded only thirty-three men and readily surrendered control of the fort's construction site.[13]

On April 19, Washington received a message from Captain Trent advising him that the French were approaching their construction site and he needed Washington to expedite his reinforcements. Washington noted in his diary that he had forwarded the information to Colonel Fry, who had not yet marched from Alexandria.[14]

> *April 19th. Met an Express who had letters from Captain Trent, at the Ohio, demanding a reenforcement with all possible speed, as he hourly expected a body of eight hundred French. I tarried at Job Pearsall's for the arrival of the troops, where they came the next day. When I received the above Express, I dispatched a messenger to Colonel Fry, to give him notice of it.*

Washington sent a letter to Dinwiddie on April 25 informing him that the French had captured the forks of the Ohio.[15]

Honble Sir,   25th April 1754 Wills Creek [Md.]

Captain Trents Ensign Mr Ward this Day arrived from the Forks of Monongehele, and brings the disagreeable account that the Fort on the Seventeenth Instant was surrender'd at the summons of Captain Contrecour to a Body of French consisting of upwards of one Thousand Men, who came from Vena[n]go with Eighteen pieces of Cannon, Sixty Battoes, and three Hundred Canoes: they gave him liberty to bring off all his men and working Tools, which he accordingly did the same Day.

Dinwiddie forwarded a letter to Colonel Joshua Fry on May 4 expressing his surprise that Fry had not yet arrived at Wills Creek and his disappointment that the French had captured the fort at the forks of the Ohio (the French named it after their minister, Fort Duquesne). Dinwiddie informed Fry that the independent companies from South Carolina had arrived at Hampton and that Fry should rendezvous all his forces at Redstone Creek. Dinwiddie also gave instructions for the court-martial of both Trent and Fraser for abandoning the forks of the Ohio when they anticipated the imminent arrival of the French.[16]

You will allow me to be surpriz'd, on receiving Y'r Let'r dated at Alex'a the 31st of Apr. last, w'n I perswaded myself You must be near Wills's Creek. It is a great Misfortune that the active French outdo Us by their timely Vigilance and Applicat'n. We must now exert our Utmost to dispossess the French of their present Possession of the Fort of Monongahela. The Independ't Compa. from So. Car. Is arriv'd at Hampton, is compleat of 100 Private Men, will re-embark on Monday for Alex'a, thence proceed imediately to follow You to the Mouth of red Stone Creek, the Place recommended for the rendezvous 'till You can be joined by the Forces from N. Car. and the other Colonies, w'n Y'r own Council will best direct Y'r further proceedings. I am advis'd that Capt. Trent, and his Lieut., Fraser, have been long absent from their duty, leaving Ensign Ward with ab't 23 Men only, to guard the Workmen whilst preparing Materials to erect the Fort begun, and who was oblig'd to surrender, on the Sumons of the French Com'd'r; Which Conduct and Behaviour I require and expect You will enquire into at a Court Martial, and give Sentence accordingly.

Washington, with the concurrence of Dinwiddie, elected to continue marching to the forks of the Ohio and challenge the French. He found that the route was difficult to traverse because there was no road and his men had to cut down trees to enable the wagons to get through. In a letter to Dinwiddie on May 9, he described the challenges he was encountering and noted that he had only progressed as far as the Great Meadows (about fifty miles from Wills Creek and approximately halfway to the forks of the Ohio). He also reported to Dinwiddie that the Indian Half-King was marching with fifty warriors to meet them.[17]

Honble Sir   Little Meadows [Md.] 9th of May 1754
  I acquainted your Honour by Mr Ward with the determination's, which we prosecuted in 4 Days after his Departure, as soon as Waggons arrived to convey our Provisions. The want of proper Conveyances has much retarded this Expedition, and at this time, unfortunately delay'd the Detachment I have the Honour to command—Even when we came to Wills Ck my disappointments were not less than before, for there I expected to have found a sufficient number of pack Horses provided by Captn Trent conformable to his Promise, Majr Carlyles Letter's and my own (that I might prosecute my first intention with light expeditious Marches) but instd of tht, there was none in readiness, nor any in expectation, that I could perceive, which reducd me to the necessity of waitg till Waggon's cd be procur'd from the Branch (40 Miles distant) However in the mean time I detach'd a party of 60 Men to make and amend the Road, which party since the 25th of Apl, and the main body since the 1st Instt have been laboriously employ'd, and have got no further than these Meadows abt 20 Miles from the new Store; where we have been two Days making a Bridge across and are not gone yet: The great

difficulty and labour that it requires to amend and alter the Roads, prevents our Marchg above 2, 3, or 4 Miles a Day, and I fear (thô no diligen⟨ce⟩ shall be neglected) we shall be detained some considerable time before it can be made good for the Carriage⟨s⟩ of the Artillery with Colo. Fry.

We Daily receive Intelligence from Ohio by one or other of the Trader's that are continually retreating to the Inhabitants with their Effects; they all concur, that the French are reinforced with 800 Men; and this Day by one Kalender I receiv'd an acct which he sets forth as certain, that there is 600 Men building at the Falls of Ohio, from whence they intd to move up to the lower Shawno Town at the Mouth of Sciodo Ck to Erect other Fortresses—He likewise says that these forces at the Fork's are Erectg their works with their whole Force, and as he was coming met at Mr Gists new settlemt Monsieur La-Force with 4 Soldrs who under the specious pretence of hunting Deserters were reconnoitreg and discovering the Country. He also brings the agreeable news that the Half King has receiv'd, & is much pleas'd with the speech I sent them, and is now upon their March with 50 Men to meet us.

The French down the River are sending presents and invitations to all the neighboring Indians, and practiseing every means to influence in their Interest.

We have heard nothing from the Cawtaba's or any of the Southern Indians thô this is the time we mostly need their assistance I have not above 160 Effective Men with me since Captn Trent⟨s⟩ have left us, who I discharg'd from this Detacht & order'd them to wait your Honour's Comds at Captn Trents for I found them rather injurious to the other Men than Serviceable to the Expn till they could be upon the same Establisht with us and come under the rigr of the Martial Law. I am Honble Sir with the most profound respect yr Honour's most Obt & most Hbe Servt

Go: Washington

In mid-May, Lieutenant Governor Dinwiddie traveled to Winchester, VA, intending to have a meeting with the Indians and to encourage them to assist in the battle against the French. Dinwiddie asked Washington to inform the Half-King and the other chiefs that he wanted to meet, and Washington immediately did so.

In his diary entry on May 24, Washington noted that the Half-King had forwarded a message informing him that the French were marching from the forks and advancing toward Wills Creek. This message was reiterated by a trader who had just arrived at the Great Meadows encampment.[18]

> *May 24th. This morning an Indian arrived in company with one whom I had sent to the Half-King and brought me the following letter from him.*

> *To any of his Majesty's officers whom this may Concern. As 'tis reported that the French army is set out to meet M. George Washington, I exhort you my brethren, to guard against them, for they intend to fall on the first English they meet; They have been on their march these two days, the Half-King and other chiefs will join you within five days, to hold a council, though we know not the number we shall be. I shall say no more; but remember me to my brethren the English. Signed The Half-King.*

> *The same day at two o'clock, we arrived at the Meadows, where we saw a trader, who told us that he came this morning from Mr Gist's, where he had seen two Frenchmen the night before, and that he knew there was a strong detachment on the march, which confirmed the account we had received from the Half-King; wherefore I placed troops behind two natural entrenchments, and had our wagons put there also.*

After learning that the French were on the move, Washington decided to move his forces back to the Great Meadows and set up a defensive position. At the Great Meadows, they established a defensible perimeter by clearing the shrubbery, digging trenches, and aligning their wagons. The next day, Washington received a note from Colonel Fry informing him that Dinwiddie had arrived in Winchester and still wanted to meet with the Half-King and other chiefs of the Six Nations of the Iroquois. Washington sent out scouting parties in an effort to locate the

advancing French troops. His diary entry on May 25 described the ineffectual efforts of his scouts.[19]

> *May 25th. Detached a scouting party on horseback to go along the roads, and
> sent other small parties to scour the woods. I gave the Horse-men orders to exam-
> ine the country well, and endeavor to get some view of the French, of their forces,
> of their movements, etc. In the evening all these parties returned, without having
> discovered anything, though they had been pretty far towards the place whence it
> was said the party was coming.*

In his May 27 letter to Dinwiddie, Washington exhibited his youthful
enthusiasm and battlefield inexperience when he referred to the Great
Meadows encampment as "a charming field for an Encounter."[20]

> *Honble Sir   Gt Meadws [Pa.] 27th May 1754*
> *The 25th Ult. by an Express from Colo. Fry I receiv'd the News of your
> Honour's arrival at Winchester and desire of seeing the Half King and other
> Chiefs of the 6 Nations—I have by Sundry Speeches and messages invited
> him Monacatoocha &ca to meet me and have reason to expect he is on his
> Road as he only purposd to settle his People to planting at a place choose on the
> <u>Monongehele</u> Yaughyaughgane for that purpose but fearing something might
> have retarded this March I imediately upon the arrival of the Express dispatch'd
> a Messenger with a speech he is not return yet—abt 4 Days ago I received a
> message from the Half [King] of which the following is a copy exactly taken.*
> *"To the forist his Magesteis Commanden Offeverses to hom this meay concern.*
> *"An acct of a french armey to meat Miger Georg Wassiontton therfor my
> Brothers I deisir you to be awar of them for deisind to strike the forist English
> they see tow deays since they marchd I cannot tell what nomber the hilf King and
> the rest of the Chiefes will be with you in five dayes to Consel—no more at pres-
> ent but give my serves to my Brother's the English."*
> *"The Half King*
> *John Davison"*

This acct was seconded in the Evening by another that the French were at the xing of Yaughyaughgane abt 18 Miles—I hereupon hurried to this place as a convenient spott. We have with Natures assistance made a good Intrenchment and by clearing the Bushes out of these Meadows prepar'd a charming field for an Encounter—I detach'd imediately upon my arrival here small light partys of Horse (Wagn Horses) to reconnoitre the Enemy and discover their strength & motion who returnd Yesterday witht seeing any thing of them nevertheless we were alarmd at Night and remain under Arms from two oClock till near Sun rise we conceive it was our own Men as 6 of them Deserted but can't be certain Whether it was them or other Enemy's be it as it will they were fired at by the Centrys but I believe without damage.

This Morning Mr Gist arrivd from his place Where a Detachment of 50 Men was seen Yesterday at Noon Comd by Monsr Laforce he afterwards saw their tracks within 5 Miles of our Camp—I imediately detachd 75 Men in pursuit of them who I hope will overtake them before they get to red Stone where their Canoes Lie[.] Mr Gist being an Eye Witness of our proceedings hereupon, and waiting for this witht my knowing till just now that he intended to wait upon your Honr obliges me to refer to him for particulars—as I expect my Messenger in to Night from the half King I shall write more fully to morrow by the Express that came fm Colo. Fry.

But before I conclude I must take the Liberty of mentioning to Your Honour the gt necessity there is for having goods out here to give for Services of the Indians they all expect it and refuse to Scout or do any thing without—saying these Services are paid well by the French—I really think was 5 or 600 Pounds worth of proper goods sent it wd tend more to our Interest than so many thousands given in a Lump at a treaty[.] I have been oblig'd to pay Shirts for what they have already done which I cannot continue to do.

The Numbers of the French have been greatly magnified as your Honour may see by a copy of the inclosd Journal who I sent out to gain Intelligence—I have receivd Letter's from the Governer's of Pensylvania & Maryland Copys of which I also send I am Yr Honrs most Obt & most Hble Servt.

Go: Washington

On the evening of May 27, Washington received a message from the Half-King. As he was coming to join Washington, he had spotted the campsite of some advancing French troops. In his diary, Washington wrote,[21]

.... About eight in the evening I received an express from the Half-King, who informed me, that, as he was coming to join us, he had seen along the road, the tracks of two men, which he had followed, till he was brought thereby to a low obscure place; that he was of opinion the whole party of the French was hidden there.

Washington set out that night in the rain in search of the Half-King and the French encampment.[22]

That very moment I sent out forty men and ordered my ammunition to be put in a place of safety, fearing it to be a stratagem of the French to attack our camp; I left a guard to defend it, and with the rest of my men set out in a heavy rain, and in a night as dark as pitch, along a path scarce broad enough for one man; we were sometimes fifteen or twenty minutes out of the path before we could come to it again, and we would often strike against each other in the darkness:

The following morning, on the twenty-eighth of May, they located the camp of the Half-King and together decided to attack the French forces without waiting for guidance or reinforcements from Washington's commander, Colonel Joshua Fry.[23]

All night long we continued our route, and on the 28th about sun-rise we arrived at the Indian camp, where after having held a council with the Half-King, we concluded to attack them together; so we sent out two men to discover where they were, as also their position and what sort of ground was therabout, after which we prepared to surround them marching one after the other Indian fashion: We had advanced pretty near to them, as we thought, when they discovered us; I ordered my company to fire; my fire was supported by that of Mr. Waggoner and my company and his received the whole fire of the French, during the greater part of the action, which only lasted a quarter of an hour before the enemy were routed.

An intense exchange raged for fifteen minutes, and Washington's forces killed ten of the French, including their commander, Ensign Joseph Coulon de Villers, sieur de Jumonville. In addition, twenty-one of the French troops were captured, including two French officers, Captain Michel Pépin La Force and Ensign Pierre Jacques Drouillon, sieur de Macé.[24]

We killed Mr. De Jumonville, the Commander of the party, as also nine others; we wounded one and made twenty-one prisoners, among whom were M la Force, M. Drouillon and two cadets. The Indians scalped the dead and took away the greater part of their arms, after which we marched on with the prisoners under guard to the Indian camp,...

This was the first battle that Lieutenant Colonel Washington had ever experienced. He emerged unscathed; however, Captain Thomas Waggoner was wounded in the skirmish and one of Washington's troops was killed.

After the battle, Washington and the Half-King returned to the Indian's camp. Washington then told the Half-King that Lieutenant Governor Dinwiddie had requested a meeting in Winchester. The Half-King declined the opportunity to meet with Dinwiddie, stating that he had to defend his people from the French. Washington noted this in his diary.[25]

...where I again held a council with the Half-King, and there informed him that the Governor was desirous to see him, and was expecting him at Winchester; he answered that he could not go just then, as his people were in too imminent danger from the French whom they had attacked; that he must send runners to all the allied nations, in order to invite them to take up the Hatchet.

The following day, Washington sent a dispatch to Lieutenant Governor Dinwiddie informing him of their attack upon the French forces and that the Half-King had declined his invitation to meet in Winchester.[26]

Now Sir, as I have answer'd your Honour's Letter I shall beg leave to acqt you with what has happen'd since I wrote by Mr Gist; I then acquainted you that I had detach'd a party of 75 Men to meet with 50 of the French who we had Intelligence were upon their March towards us to Reconnoitre &ca[.] Abt 9 Oclock the same Night, I receivd an express from the Half King who was Incampd with several of His People abt 6 Miles of, that he had seen the Tract of two French Men xing the Road and believ'd the whole body were lying not far off, as he had an acct of that number passing Mr Gist—I set out with 40 Men before 10, and was from that time till near Sun rise before we reach'd the Indian's Camp, havg Marched in small path, & heavy Rain, and a Night as Dark as it is possible to conceive—we were frequently tumbling one over another, and often so lost that 15 or 20 Minutes search would not find the path again.

When we came to the Half King I council'd with him, and got his assent to go hand in hand and strike the French. accordingly, himself, Monacatoocha, and a few other Indians set out with us, and when we came to the place where the Tracts were, the Half King sent Two Indians to follow their Tract and discover their lodgment which they did abt half a mile from the Road in a very obscure place surrounded with Rocks. I there upon in conjunction with the Half King & Monacatoocha, formd a disposion to attack them on all sides, which we accordingly did and after an Engagement of abt 15 Minutes we killd 10, wounded one and took 21 Prisoner's, amongst those that were killd was Monsieur De Jumonville the Commander, Principl Officers taken is Monsieur Druillong and Monsr Laforc, who your Honour has often heard me speak of as a bold Enterprising Man, and a person of gt subtilty and cunning with these are two Cadets—...

In this Engagement we had only one Man killd, and two or three wounded, among which was Lieutt Waggener slightly—a most miraculous escape, as Our Right Wing was much exposed to their Fire and receivd it all.

The Half King receiv'd your Honour's speech very kind: but desird me to inform you that he could not leave his People at this time, thinking them in great Danger—…

Washington expected the French would react to his attack upon de Jumonville's encampment by sending a retaliatory force from Fort Duquesne. In his letter to Dinwiddie, anticipating the French forces to be much larger than his three hundred, Washington enthusiastically assured the lieutenant governor that they would do battle with the French as long as possible.

As these Runnors went of to the Fort on Sunday last, I shall expect every hour to be attackd and by unequal number's, which I must withstand if there is 5 to 1 or else I fear the Consequence will be we shall loose the Indians if we suffer ourselves to be drove Back, I dispatched an express immediately to Colo. Fry with this Intelligence desiring him to send me Reinforcements with all imaginable dispatch.

Your Honour may depend I will not be surprizd, let them come what hour they will—and this is as much as I can promise—but my best endeavour's shall not be wanting to deserve more, I doubt not but if you hear I am beaten, but you will at the same hear that we have done our duty in fighting as long there was a possibility of hope.

On the twenty-ninth, Washington also sent a note to Colonel Joshua Fry informing his commander of the skirmish with de Jumonville and requesting immediate reinforcements because he was expecting French retaliation. Washington, who attacked de Jumonville without waiting for guidance from his commander, was now hoping that Fry could reinforce him before the French counterattack.[27]

From our Camp at the Gt Meadws [Pa.]
Sir   *29 of Ma⟨y⟩ 1754*

This by an imediate express, I send to infm you that Yesterday I engagd a party of French wherof 11 were kill'd and 20 taken with the loss of only 1 of mine killd and 2 or 3 wounded among which was Lieutt Waggener: by some of their Paper's we can discover that large detachts are expected every day, which we may reasonably suppose are to attack us especially since we have begun.

This is therefore to acquaint you with the necessity there is for a Reinforcet which I hope you will detach imediately as you can be in no manner of danger in your March, for the French must pass our Camp which I flatter myself is not practicable witht my having intelligence thereof especially as there will be Indian's always scouting[.] If there does not come a sufficient Reinforcement we must either quit our gd & retn to you or fight very unequal Number's which I will do before I will give up one Inch of what we have gaind—The great haste I am in to dispatch the bearer prevents me from being particular at this time—I shall conclude Sir with assuring you how sincerely concern'd I am for your indisposition which I hope you'll soon recover from and be able to join us with the Artillery that we may attack the French [in] their Forts I am Sir Yr most Hble Servt

Go: Washington

In a letter to his younger brother John Augustine Washington, dated May 31, George Washington portrayed the essence of his victorious exchange and his ill-founded confidence in a successful defense against the expected retaliation. With a burst of youthful bravado, twenty-two-year-old Washington wrote of his first experience under fire.[28]

[Camp in the Great Meadows, Pa.
Dr John   *31 May 1754]*

Since my last we have arrived at this place, where 3 days agoe we had an engagemt wth the French that is, between a party of theirs & Ours: Most of our men were out upon other detachments, so that I had scarcely 40 men under my Command, and about 10, or a doz. Indians, nevertheless we obtained a most signal Victory. The Battle lasted abt 10, or 15 minutes, sharp firing on both sides, when the French gave ground & run, but to no great purpose; there were 12 killed, among which was Monsr De Jumonville the Commandr, & taken 21 prisoners with whom are Monsieurs La Force, Druillong, together with 2 Cadets. I have sent them to his Honr the Governor at Winchester conducted by Lieut. West & a guard of 20 men. We had but one man killed, 2 or 3 wounded and a great many more within an Inch of being shott; among the wounded on our side was Lieut. Waggoner, but no danger will ensue.

We expect every Hour to be attacked by a superior Force, but shall if they stay one day longer be prepared for them; We have already got Intrenchments & are about a Pallisado'd Fort, which will I hope be finished today. The Mingo's have struck the French & I hope will give a good blow before they have done, I expect 40 odd of them here to night, wch with our Fort and some reinforcements from Colo. Fry, will enable us to exert our Noble Courage with Spirit. I am Yr Affe Bror

Geo. Washington

I fortunately escaped without a wound, tho' the right Wing where I stood was exposed to & received all the Enemy's fire and was the part where the man was killed & the rest wounded. I can with truth assure you, I heard Bulletts whistle and believe me there was something charming in the sound.

On May 30, Washington wrote in his diary that he had the prisoners dispatched to Winchester and began erecting a palisade at the Great Meadows to improve their defenses.[29]

May 30th. Detached Lieutenant West, and Mr Spiltdorph, to take the prisoners to Winchester with a guard of twenty men. Began to erect a fort with small palisades, fearing that when the French should hear the news of that defeat we might be attacked by considerable forces.

The palisade, about fifty-three feet in diameter, included a small fourteen-square-foot cabin for the storage of supplies.[30]

On June 1, Lieutenant Governor Dinwiddie responded to Washington's letter. In this letter, he congratulated him for his victory over the French while warning Washington to not attempt battling a force more numerous than his own. Dinwiddie enthusiastically looked forward to providing additional troops to aid in the effort to drive the French from the forks of the Ohio.[31]

Sir   *Winchester June 1st 1754*

Mr Gist brot Yr Letter & the very agreeable Acct of Yr Killing & taking Monsr Le Force & his whole Party of 35 Men on which Success I heartily congratulate You, as it may give a Testimony to the Inds. that the French are not invincible wn fairly engagd with the English; but hope the good Spirits of Yr Soldiers will not tempt You to make any hazardous Attempts agst a too numerous Enemy. When Colo. Fry's Corps & Capt McKays' Compa. join You, You will be enabled to act with better Vigour. I am in daily Expectatn of seeing or hearing from Colo. Innes, & a Body of Cherokee Inds. which I shall direct to march with all Diligence. I have sent Colo. Cresap to bring away Monsr Le Force & the other Prisoners, which You will deliver him, & be thereby reliev'd from the Anxiety of guarding so may Prisoners with Yr small Number. I have caus'd an Assortmt of Indn Goods to be packt up in order to be sent You immediately; & have engag'd Mr Croghan as an Interpreter to attend the Commander in Chief, assist in delivering the several Presents, & advise You in all matters You may have occasion to consult him about, hoping his faithful demeanour will merit Yr & the Officers kind reception & Entertainmt—I have also sent out of my private Store some rum, which will be sent You with the Goods for this on Monday next—I wait with Impatience the return of Burney to know whether the Half King comes here.

Pray God preserve You in all Yr proceedings & grant Success to our Arms. I remain with great Esteem Sr Yr most humble Servt

On June 3, Washington sent a letter to Dinwiddie informing him that they had completed building the palisade (now named Fort Necessity) within which he could hold off a much larger French force.[32]

We have just finish'd a small palisadod Fort in which with my small Number's I shall not fear the attack of 500 Men.

On June 4, Dinwiddie wrote to Washington informing him of Colonel Fry's accidental death on May 31 when he fell from his horse. Major George Muse was promoted to lieutenant colonel and assumed command of Fry's troops. Dinwiddie informed Washington that he had been promoted to full colonel to command the Virginia regiment. He also informed Washington that Colonel James Innes, commander of the North Carolina regiment, was appointed commander in chief of all the forces.[33]

Sir   Winr June 4th 1754

On the Death of Colo. Fry I have thot it proper to send You the enclos'd Como. To Comd the Virga regimt, & another for Majr Muse to be Lieut. Colo. The eldest Capt. to be Majr & the eldest Lieut. to be Capt. the eldest Ensign to be Lieut. unless You shd have Objectn to them. I think You will want two Ensigns, if so, I recommend Mr Perroney if he has behav'd so as to merit it, the other I leave to You. I have no Como. now here, but send the Names of the Persons to succeed as above & I will send up Commos. to bear equal Date with Yrs so that they may act by Yr Orders 'till that Time. Colo. James Innes, an old experienc'd Officer is daily expected, who is appointed Commander in Chief of all the Forces, which I am very sensible will be very agreeable to You & the other Officers. The Capts. & Officers of the Independt Compas. having their Commos. sign'd by His M[ajest]y immagine they claim a distinguish'd rank & being long trained in Arms expect suitable regards, You will therefore consult & agree with Yr Officers to shew them particular marks of Esteem, which will avoid such Causes of Uneasiness as otherwise might obstruct His Majesty's

Service wherein All are alike engag'd & must answer for any ill Consequences of an unhappy Disagreemt—You cannot believe the Uneasiness & Anxiety I have had for the Tardiness of the Detachmt under Colo. Fry's Commd in not joining You some Time since, as all the Delay in the Provisions, & Ammunition; however I have given strong Instructs. on both these Heads, & hope You will soon be joined with proper Numbers to give the French a total Defeat. Continue in good Spirits, & prosecute Yr usual Conduct & Prudence, which must recommend You to the favo. of His My & Yr Country My Friendship & respect I hope you do not doubt. I therefore remn with great Truth, Sr Your real Friend

Washington received praise for his victory not only from the lieutenant governor but also from the House of Burgesses. Charles Carter, a member of the House of Burgesses, wrote to Washington on June 5, congratulating him and his men on their victory and expressing his hope that "God grant you may be blest" he would soon drive the French out of the Ohio Country. Carter was on the committee that drafted the bill to provide the finances for the expedition to build the fort at the forks of the Ohio. When he learned that Washington's officers were unhappy with their pay, he wrote that he was working on resolving their complaints. In the letter he expressed his compliments to all the officers.[34]

Sr   Fredericksburgh June 5 1754

We had the agreeable news of the victory obtaind by the Partie under your Command I heartily congratulate you and all the Brave gentlen that were of the company. From this happy begining I am lead to hope you will soon make those cruel men know that numbers can't support an unrighteous caus God grant you may be blest with the like success and drive them Out of our Colony I had this affair in the begining much at heart and you are a witness to the share I had in promoting the Bill for defending our Frontiers and you may depend I shall be always ready to serve such brave men to the utmost of my power.

We are told the officers are very uneasy on acct of some late resolves of the Comittee I am not yet satisfied what their complaint is as it comes from a youth in the service I hope much may be imputd to his not being well informd[.] While I was at the Committee I can aver there was the greatest readiness to promote and encourage the officers and men and make the most effectual provision no doubt any just complaint will meet with immediate redress for my part I shall always be a true friend to such deserving men I know the hardships you must suffer and I hope you will be amply rewarded and return crownd with Laurels. I should be glad to know the name of the unfortunate man that died in our Cause please to favour me with an Acct of every Important occurance and the grounds of the Complaint[.] You are so well satisfied of the importance of the trust reposd in you that it would be impertinence to use any Arguments to excite you to a coura-geous discharge of it My compliments to all the officers I am charm with their Bravery[.] I am Sr Yr ,most obligd hume Servt

Ch Carter

PS The above was wrote in the dark but I could not omit an opportunity to congratulate you on this happy occasion.

Washington noted in his diary on June 9 that Lieutenant Colonel Muse and the remaining troops of Colonel Fry's Virginia regiment had arrived at Fort Necessity and that Captain James McKay's independent company from South Carolina had arrived at Wills Creek.[35]

June 9th. The last body of the Virginia regiment, arrived under the command of Colonel Muse, and we learnt that the independent company of Carolina was arrived at Will's Creek.

Captain James McKay arrived with an independent company from South Carolina. Washington was unsure of the interim command struc-ture because Colonel Innes from North Carolina was in charge of all the forces and was not yet in camp. To resolve the confusion, Colonel George Washington wrote to Lieutenant Governor Dinwiddie on June 10 asking for clarification.[36]

Your Honour may depend, I shall myself, and will endeavour to make my Officer's shew Captn McKay all the respect due to his Rank & merit but should have been particularly oblig'd if your Honour had declar'⟨d⟩ whether he was under my Command, or Independant of it. however I shall be studious to avoid all disputes tht may tend to publick prejudice, but as far as I am able will inculcate harmony, and unanimity.

After writing this request for clarification, Captain McKay arrived in camp, and Washington's thoughts about working with the independent company changed significantly because of the lack of British cooperation. He continued writing this letter after McKay's arrival and expressed the confusion caused by the lack of understanding as to who was in command.[37]

Since writing the foregoing, Captn McKay with the Independant Comapny has arriv'd, who I take to be a very good sort of a Gentleman.

For want of proper Instructions from your Honour I am much at a loss to know how to act, or proceed in regard to his company: I made it my particular study to receive him (as it was your Honour's desire) with all the Respect and politeness that was due to his Rank, or that I was capable of shewing: and don't doubt from his appearance and behavr but a strict intimacy will ensue, when matter's are put in a clearer light. but at present I assure your Honour they will rather impede the Service than forward it, for having Commissions from the King they look upon themselves as a distinct Body, and will not incorporate and do duty as our Men—but keep seperate Guards, Incamp seperate &ca. I have not offer'd to controul him in anything, or shewd that I claimd a superior Command, but in giving the Parrole & Countersign which must be the same in an Army consisting of 10 Different Nation's, to distinguish Friends from Foes—He knows the necessity of this, yet does not think he is to receive it from me.

Then who is to give it? am I to Issue these order's to a Company? or is an Independent Captn to prescrive Rules to the Virginia Regiment? this is the Question, but how absurd is obvious.

Captn McKay says that it is not in his power to oblige his Men to work on the Road unless he will engage them a Shilling Sterling a Day which I wd not choose to do and to suffer them to March at their ease whilst our faithful Soldier's are laboriously employd carry's an Air of such distinction that it is not to be wonder'd at, if the poor fellows were to declare the hardship of it[.] He also declares to me that this is not particular to his Company only but that no Soldier's subject to martial law can be obligd to do it for less—I therefore shall continue to compleat the work we have began with my poor fellows—we shall have the whole credit as none other's have assisted.

I hope from what has been said your honour will see the necessity of giving your speedy order's on this head. and I am sensible you will consider the Evil tendancy that will accompany Captn Mckays c[ommandin]g for I am sorry to observe this is what we always hop'd to enjoy—the Rank of Officers which to me Sir is much dearer than the Pay.

Captn McKay brought none of the Cannon very little Ammunition, abt 5 Days allowance of flower, and 60 Beeves. Since I have spun a letter to this enormous size, I must go a little further and beg your Honour's patience to peruse it—I am much grieved to find our Stores so slow advancing[.] God knows when we shall [be] able to do any thing for to deserve better of our Country—I am Honble Sir with the most sincere & unfeigned Regard Yr Honour's most Obt & most Hble Servt

Go: Washington

The Contents of this Letter is a profound Secret.

On June 17, John Carlyle, Washington's brother-in-law and the commissary for the Virginia regiment, wrote Washington congratulating him on his victory. With the arrival at Fort Necessity of Lieutenant Colonel Muse's troops and Captain McKay's South Carolina troops, Carlyle expressed his belief that Washington was now out of danger.[38]

We have no Particular News here only We have had great Rejoyceings on Yr Good Success & are Now out of fear for You As We Are Well Ashured the forces under Muse & Capt. Mackay must have joyn'd you The Latter & his Officers you must Like. I am Dr Sir Yr Very Aff⟨ectionet⟩ &c.

John Carlyle

Sarah Carlyle (daughter of William Fairfax and wife of John Carlyle) wrote to Washington on the same date also congratulating him on his victory and expressing her hope that God would continue to protect him.[39]

Dr Sir   *June 17 1754*

I Received your Letter dated the 15 May, Which gave me both pleasure and pain, the first to heare of your health, the latter to be Informed of the many Risques you run, but am hopeful your good Constitution and a kind protector will bring you out of them all as it has In the last Ingagement preserved you from harm. If I thought my Letters were Agreeabel to you I wou'd continew a Correspondence that I must own Agreeabel to me, but must not Expect it to be Carred on (on my Side) with the Spirret it ought to Inliven you Which wou'd be my desire If I cou'd.

those pleasing reflections on the hours past ought to be banished out of your thoughts, you have now a Noblier prospect that of preserveing your Country from the Insults of an Enimy. and as god has blessed your first Attempt, hope he may Continew his blessings and on your return, Who knows but fortune may have reserved you for Sum unknown She, that may recompence you for all the Tryals past, how⟨ever⟩ you have my Warmest Wishes and may be assurd that I ever am Your Sincear Wellwisher and Your Humbel Servent

Sarah Carlyle

For his expedition to remove the French from the forks of the Ohio, Lieutenant Governor Robert Dinwiddie was unable to get support from Virginia's neighboring colonies. Although threatened by the French, the colonies of Maryland and Pennsylvania failed to authorize funds for troops and supplies. On June 18, 1754, Dinwiddie wrote to Pennsylvania Governor James Hamilton expounding his dissatisfaction over Pennsylvania's lack of support.[40]

> *I am sorry Y'r Assembly is so obstinate and disobedient to the royal Comands, as I had a thorow dependence on You for a Supply of Bread, the want of w'ch puts me to great difficulties. I wish the Bill of £10,000 Supply had passed Y'r Upper House in any Shape, as the Exigency of our Affairs so much wanted it; but You are the best judge of the Clogs in the Bill and the Inconveniency thereof, in reg'd to Your Instructions, w'ch, if possible, You c'd have got pass'd at this Time, with a saving Clause to prevent its being a Precedent for the Future, w'd have been of Infinite Service. I hope you have represented the Affair properly Home, that they may see w't little Dependence there is on Assemblies in this Part of the World, and really I hope the Ministry will take some proper Course to bring all the Colonies into a proper Sense of their Duty.*

On June 20, Dinwiddie wrote to Maryland Governor Horatio Sharpe, expressing his anxiety over the tardiness of the New York and North Carolina forces. He also reemphasized his need for assistance from the colony of Maryland.[41]

> *The two Independent Comp's from N. Y. are gone up to Alex'a in the King's Ship, Capt. Whitwell, Com'd'r. I c'd not review them here, but have order'd Colo. Fairfax to review them and give me a distinct Acc't. I fear they are not so good Compa's as I c'd wish; however, they have my Orders to march directly to join our Camp. The No. Car. Forces are on their March, w'n collected together, they will be few in Comparison with the French. The Gov'r of N. York writes me 30 large Canoes have passed Oswego Fort, full of Men, supposed to reinforce those on the Ohio. It's cruel our neighboring Colonies are so backw'd in granting Supplies, and I find I shall be much straiten'd for Money to furnish*

Provisions, &c. I therefore still have a dependence on some Assistance from your Province, being thorowly convinc'd of your hearty Inclinations; and I hope Your endeavours will be attended with Success.

Bryan Fairfax (the youngest son of William Fairfax) wrote to Washington on June 24. In the letter, he expressed his satisfaction that Major Muse and Captain McKay had arrived at Fort Necessity and would provide sufficient forces to defeat the French in the impending battle. He also let Washington know that the additional forces from New York and North Carolina had arrived in Alexandria and were marching to Fort Necessity.[42]

Dear Sir   Alexandria June 24th 1754

The agreeable and long wished for News of the detachments under the Command of Major Muse and Capt. McKay having joined you in time to prevent the Success of any Attacks from the french was very satisfactory to me; whose mind was continually alarmed with the Apprehensions of your being forced to another battle when unprepared for it.

The Triton arrived here the 22d with the two Companies from New York, tho' not compleat. And a fair Wind yesterday brought up a Schooner with 107 Men, belonging to the No. Carolina Regiment that are on their March.

My Sisters are not yet returned from below, but expected in ten Days. With best Respects to the whole Corps, and wishing you all imaginable Success I remain Yr assured friend and Very humble Servt

Bryan Fairfax

Because correspondence was slow, Carlyle, Dinwiddie, and Fairfax had no idea when they wrote the previously mentioned letters of the difficulties Washington was experiencing. On June 16, Washington decided to advance his forces toward the French at Fort Duquesne and marched the Virginia regiment out of Fort Necessity and headed for Gist's settlement. Gist's camp was located on the path to Redstone Creek, about thirteen miles from the Great Meadow. Upon arriving at Gist's camp, he set up headquarters and directed his men to continue working on the road to the Redstone Creek encampment, which was located on the Monongahela River upstream from Fort Duquesne.

From June 19 to June 21, Washington held a council with the Indian allies. The representatives from the Six Nations of the Iroquois informed Washington that their treaty at Albany precluded them from participating in the war between the French and English. The Indians from the Six Nations of the Iroquois and all of the other tribes decided to not participate in the upcoming skirmish. Washington wrote in his diary:[43]

> *Immediately after the Council was over, notwithstanding all that Mr. Montour could do to dissuade them, the Delawares as also the Half-King, and all the other Indians returned to the Great Meadows;...*
>
> *June 25th. Towards night three men from the Great Meadows came to us, amongst whom was the son of Queen Aliquippa. He brought me a letter from Mr. Croghan informing me what difficulty he had had in finding any Indians willing to come to us; that the Half-King was inclined and was preparing to join us, but had received a blow which was a hindrance to it. I thought it proper to send Captain Montour to Fort Necessity, in order to try if he could persuade the Indians to come to us.*

For ten days his men worked on the sixteen-mile extension of the road from Gist's camp to Redstone Creek, and his troops were exhausted. To make matters worse, the food supply wagons had not arrived, and the rationed men were famished.

On June 28, Washington learned that the French forces at Fort Duquesne had received reinforcements and were advancing with a force of eight hundred men and four hundred Indians. Washington's forces were greatly outnumbered, and there was no support from their Indian allies. Realizing that Gist's camp was not a defensible location, he called a council of officers to discuss their predicament. The council decided to retreat to Fort Necessity.

Since their men were starving and outnumbered, the council of war voted unanimously to return to Fort Necessity. The issues that the officers discussed were detailed in the minutes of the council of war.[44]

At a Council of War held at Mr Gists Ju⟨ne⟩ 28th 1754

After the Junction with our own Detachmt and the Independent Company to Consider what was most prudent & necessary ⟨to⟩ be done in the present Situation of Affairs: It was Unanimously Resolved that it was Absolutly necessary to Return to our Fort at the meadows & Wait there untill Supply'd with a Stock of provisions Sufficient to serve us for some months.

The Reasons for so doing were very Weighty:

Monacattocha a man of Sense and Experience & a gre⟨at⟩ friend to the English Had left the French Fort only two days before & Had Seen the Reinforcemt arrive & heard them declare their Resolution to march and Attack the English with 800 of their own men & 400 Indians.

There was a Reinforcemt hourly expected, we learned from French Deserters.

We knew that two off our men had deserted to them and Acquaintd The Enemy of our Starving Condition and our Numbrs & Situation.

We had wanted meat & Bread for Six days already, and were still uncertain when any would Arrive. We had only about 25 head of Live Cattle the most of them Milch Cows to depend upon for 400 men, and about one quart of Salt to Use with our Meat, or preserve it. The Enemy being thrice our Number & knowing our Cir[c]umstances would not give us a Chance to fight them, but Strive to starve us out by intercepting our Convoys. The Live Cattle were Uncertain ⟨&⟩ the Enemy strove to Block us up. If the Enemy were so Void of knowledge in Military affairs as to Risk a Battle; we must give a Total defeat to thrice our Number, Otherwise be Cut to pieces by so prodigious a Number of their Indians in our Retreat, who are the best people in the World to improve a Victory and at the best lose all our Warlike Stores & Swivles. Compelld by these Reasons it was Unanimously Resolv'd to Decamp directly, and to have our Swivles drawn By the men by Reason of the Scarcity of horses.

Besides the In⟨di⟩ans declar'd that they would have leave us, unless we Returnd to ⟨the⟩ Meadows. The distance Betwixt that & Mr Gist's house, is thirteen miles of hilly Road form'd Naturally for Ambushes. The French could not so Easily Support themselves at the Meadow as at Gists by the reason of distance to Carry the Stores & provisions & their want of horses to do it. They Can come within five miles of Gist's house by water, Thirteen miles further of bad Road was a great Obstruction to them & gave us an Opportunity of Obtaining intelligence, and Securing our Convoys. While we lay at Gist's house, They might pass us unobserv'd by a different Road from Red Stone that Lay about nine miles from us: But at the Meadows, both Roads are United, and the Bearing of the Mountains makes it difficult for an Enemy to Come Near or pass us without Receiving advice of it. From all these Considerations this Resolves Signed by

Washington's Virginia regiment and McKay's South Carolina independent company returned to Fort Necessity on July 1.

They had been informed that the two New York independent companies were at Wills Creek and could be expected to arrive at Fort Necessity shortly. (Later they learned that the New York companies had never left Alexandria.) With the addition of the two New York companies, Washington and McKay believed that they could make a successful stand at Fort Necessity.

But the companies from New York and North Carolina did not arrive at the fort in time to battle the French. Washington's Virginia regiment and McKay's South Carolina independent company provided fewer than three hundred men ready and able to fight.

Two days later, on July 3, seven hundred French and Indians arrived at the Great Meadows and commenced their attack.

The French quickly learned that Washington's forces were within musket range from the tree line. While remaining protected behind the trees, the French were able to pick off Washington's troops located in the trenches. Throughout the day a hard rain fell, and as the trenches around Fort Necessity filled with water, their gunpowder became wet and unusable. Washington's troops were unable to return fire.

Lieutenant Peter Mercier of the South Carolina independent company died after being wounded three times. Of the three hundred men and officers under the command of Washington and McKay, one-third were killed or wounded by the end of the first day's battle.

The French commander, with only twenty casualties (the French reported three killed and seventeen wounded), surprisingly offered a parlay. Washington, with his troops exhausted, starving, badly outnumbered, and their powder too wet to be of use, negotiated terms and surrendered.

The terms of the capitulation allowed Washington to march his forces out of the fort with all the honors of war and with their stores, effects, and baggage.[45]

Articles of Capitulation

July the 3d, 1754, at 8 o'clock at Night.

As our Intentions have never been to trouble the Peace and good Harmony subsisting between the two Princes in Amity, but only to revenge the Assassination committed on one of our Officers, bearer of a Summon, as also on his Escorte, and to hinder any Establishment on the Lands of the Dominions of the King my Master: Upon these Considerations, we are willing to shew Favour to all the English who are in the said Fort, on the following Conditions, viz.

Article I.

We grant Leave to the English Commander, to retire with all his Garrison, and to return peaceably into his own Country; and promise to hinder his receiving any Insult from us French; and to restrain, as much as shall be in our Power, the Indians that are with us.

II.

It shall be permitted him to go out, and carry with him all that belongs to them, except the Artillery, which we reserve.

III.

That we will allow them the Honours of War; that they march out with Drums beating, and one Swivel Gun, being willing thereby to convince them, that we treat them as Friends.

IV.

That as soon as the Articles are signed by both Parties, the English Colours shall be struck.

V.

That To-morrow, at Break of Day, a Detachment of French shall go and make the Garrison file of, and take Possession of the Fort.

VI.

As the English have but few Oxen or Horses left, they are at Liberty to hide their Effects, and to come again, and search for them, when they have a Number of Horses sufficient to carry them off; and that for this End, they may have what Guards they please; on Condition, that they give their Word of Honour, to work no more upon any Buildings in the Place, of any Part on this Side the Mountains.

VII.

And as the English have in their Power, one Officer, two Cadets, and most of the Prisoners made at the Assassination of M. de Jumonville, and promise to send them back, with a safe Guard to Fort du Quesne, situate on the Ohio. For Surety of their performing this Article as well as this Treaty, M. Jacob Vambrane and Robert Stobo, both Captains, shall be delivered to us as Hostages, till the Arrival of our French and Canadians above mentioned. We oblige ourselves on our Side, to give an Escorte to return these two Officers in Safety; and expect to have our French in two Months and a Half at farthest. A Duplicate of this being fixed upon one of the Posts of our Blockade, the Day and Year above mentioned.

James MacKay, Go. Washington
Coulon Villier
pour copie Coulon Villier

William Fairfax had not yet learned of Washington's defeat at Fort Necessity and wrote him on July 5 from Alexandria, telling him that the reinforcements had been delayed and offered advice on methods for extracting the French from Fort Duquesne.[46]

Dear Sir   *Alexandria 5th July 1754*

I came hither at our Governor's Request to view Captn Clarke's Compa. & Captn Rutherford's under the Care & Command of Capt. Ogilve, who I am told have been delayd & retarded many days, By the Muster It appeared they are not compleat. Colo. Innes is at Winchester, waiting for these and two Compas. of his own Men now here, the rest to march from No. Carolina by Land. It will yet require a long Time before They can join You and make You regret the Hours—till then You can do little but Guard, Look out, and now & then bring in a stragling Party of other Embassadors. Thô I sometimes Flatter my Self the brave Dinwiddie & Monacatoocha (whom I desire to take the Name of Washington) will exert their Power & Skill to defeat all the Wiles of the suttle French And as by our Forces not joyning Sooner, the French have gaind the more Time to augment and strengthen their Garrisons, the most effectual & least hazardous Method to regain our Fort and Lands Seems to be, a Prevention of all supply of Provisions which a good Encampment near Them and active Scouts of our brave Indian Warriors might accomplish, And I hope that our Treaty at Albany has engagd the Six Nations & Allies who reside between the Ohio & Canada to intercept all Supplys intended; whereby their present Provisions must Soon be expended. Majr Carlyle dayly expects a £1000 from Mr Allen of Philadelphia, and is to be with the Governor in less than a Fortnight to receive abt £1500, the Governor having applied to the Council who have consented that the Receivr Genl should lend £2000 out of the 2s. per Hhd Fund to the Public Treasurer to answer the Drafts on Him. In short every probable Step has been taken to purchase and send You the necessary Provisions & to assist the March of the Forces that are following. You cannot well guess at the Fatigue Mr Carlyle undergoes to acquit Himself of the various Demands, the different Corps make. It will give Me the greatest Pleasure to know from You that Colo. Innes,

Captns Clarke, Mackay & Olgilvie begin and likely to hold a good Union of Friendship, Councils and joint Operations to fulfil his Majesty's Commands and Expectation from Them—I have no doubt of your friendly Agreement with Them on their own Merit, but may be enlargd for your late Brothers Sake, formerly known to Colo. Innes & Capt. Clarke on the Carthagena Expedition.

Commander in Chief of all the Forces Colonel James Innes was still delayed in Winchester and did not know of the defeat at Fort Necessity. He too wrote on July 5 expressing his anxiety over the New York independent companies' delay. Innes's letter was addressed to James McKay and Washington. Since Innes had not heard of Washington's defeat, he encouraged Washington to be vigilant and erroneously assured him that they would be able to defeat the French.[47]

Gentlmen   Winchester 5 July 1754 Eleven Oclock
*   I have this moment received your Express & am verey glade to find you are Joined. I wish My Regemt, with the New York Companeys were arrived here they are upon ther march, nor cann I laren the reason of there so long Stay att Bell Haven you may depend I will make all the heast in my Power to join you. If you Should be Oblidged to retire you must demolish your Works other ways it is making a Cover for the enemie I have forwarded your Express to the Troops on there march. It is what I daily expected they would by a Strong Detachment inquare about there partey Lost. pray leave no room for A Surprise but be vigilant. & depend We will make them retire in there turne I long to be with you & this would be a fine Oppertunity to prevent there returning to there forte. I wish you good Sucess & am your Most Hue Servtt*

*   James Innes*

The Crown had ordered two companies from New York, but they arrived undermanned, without provisions, and too late to defend Fort Necessity during the July 3, 1754, battle with the French.

Colonel George Washington and Captain James McKay returned to Williamsburg after the capitulation of Fort Necessity. On July 19 they filed a report on the action to Lieutenant Governor Dinwiddie.[48]

Williamsburg 19 July 1754

The third of this Instant July, about 9 o'Clock, we received Intelligence that the French, having been reinforced with 700 Recruits, had left Monongehela, and were in full March with 900 Men to attack us. Upon this, as our Numbers were so unequal, (our whole Force not exceeding 300) we prepared for our Defence in the best Manner we could, by throwing up a small Intrenchment, which we had not Time to perfect, before our Centinel gave Notice, about Eleven o'Clock, of their Approach, by firing his Piece, which he did at the Enemy, and as we learned afterwards killed three of their Men, on which they began to fire upon us, at about 600 Yards Distance, but without any Effect: We immediately called all our Men to their Arms, and drew up in Order before our Trenches; but as we looked upon this distant Fire of the Enemy only as an Artifice to intimidate, or draw our Fire from us, we waited their nearer Approach before we returned their Salute. They then advanced in a very irregular Manner to another Point of Woods, about 60 Yards off, and from thence made a second Discharge; upon which, finding they had no Intention of attacking us in the open Field, we retired into our Trenches, and still reserved our Fire; as we expected from their great Superiority of Numbers, that they would endeavour to force our Trenches; but finding they did not seem to intend this neither, the Colonel gave Orders to fire, which was done with great Alacrity and Undauntedness. We continued this unequal Fight, with an Enemy sheltered behind Trees, ourselves without Shelter, in Trenches full of Water, in a settled Rain, and the Enemy galling us on all Sides incessantly from the Woods, till 8 o'Clock at Night, when the French called to Parley: From the great Improbability that such a vastly superior Force, and possessed of such an Advantage, would offer a Parley first, we suspected a Deceit, and therefore refused to consent that they should come among us; on which they desired us to send an Officer to them, and engaged their Parole for his Safety; we then sent Capt Van Braam, and Mr. Peyronee, to receive their

Proposals, which they did, and about Midnight we agreed that each Side should retire without Molestation, they back to their Fort at Monongehela, and we to Will's Creek: That we should march away with all the Honours of War, and with all our Stores, Effects and Baggage. Accordingly the next Morning, with our Drums beating and our Colours flying, we began our March in good Order, with our Stores, &c. in Convoy; but we were interrupted by the Arrival of a Reinforcement of 100 Indians among the French, who were hardly restrained from attacking us, and did us considerable Damage by pilfering our Baggage. We then proceeded, but soon found it necessary to leave our Baggage and Stores; the great Scarcity of our Provisions obliged us to see the utmost Expedition, and having neither Waggons nor Horses to transport them. The Enemy had deprived us of all our Creatures; by killing, in the Beginning of the Engagement, our Horses, Cattle, and every living Thing they could, even to the very Dogs. The Number of the Killed on our Side was thirty, and seventy wounded; among the former was Lieutenant Mercier, of Captain Maccay's independent Company; a Gentleman of true military Worth, and whose Bravery would not permit him to retire, though dangerously wounded, till a second Shot disabled him, and a third put an End to his Life, as he was carrying to the Surgeon. Our Men behaved with singular Intrepidity, and we determined not to ask for Quarter, but with our Bayonets screw'd, to sell our Lives as dearly as possibly we could. From the Numbers of the Enemy, and our Situation, we could not hope for Victory; and from the Character of those we had to encounter, we expected no Mercy, but on Terms that we positively resolved not to submit to.

The Number killed and wounded of the Enemy is uncertain, but by the Information given by some Dutch in their Service to their Countrymen in ours, we learn that it amounted to above three hundred; and we are induced to believe it must be very considerable, by their being busy all Night in burying their Dead, and yet many remained the next Day; and their Wounded we know was considerable, by one of our Men, who had been made Prisoner by them after signing the Articles, and who, on his Return told us, that he saw great Numbers much wounded and carried off upon Litters.

We were also told by some of their Indians after the Action, that the French had an Officer of distinguishable Rank killed. Some considerable Blow they must have received, to induce them to call first for a Parley, knowing, as they perfectly did, the Circumstances we were in.

In his letter to Colonel James Innes, commander in chief of all the forces, on July 20, Dinwiddie berated Innes for his failure to provide support to Washington and McKay at Fort Necessity.[49]

The Misfortune attending our Expedit'n is entirely owing to the delay of Your Forces, and more particularly the two Ind't Compa's from N.Y.; how they can answer their disobedience to His Majesty's com'ds I know not, and w'n You have review'd them, give me a particular Acc't. As to Y'r regim't I can say little to, as You are talking of disbanding them before they join the other Forces.

On July 24, 1754, Dinwiddie sent an account of the July 3 battle at Fort Necessity to the Lords of Trade. In his account, Dinwiddie blamed the tardiness of the New York and North Carolina companies for their defeat. Pointing out that the neighboring colonies failed to provide timely support in his battle with the French, Dinwiddie requested that the Crown provide support by sending two regiments of His Majesty's troops to engage in his effort to remove the French from the forks of the Ohio.[50]

I beg leave to observe to Y'r L'ds. the Misfortunes attending thro' the Expedit'n. His M'y's orders for two of His Independend't Compa's at N.Y. was trans-mitted me by the E. of H., the latter end of Feb'ry last; I enclos'd the Order to the Gov'r of N.Y. by Express the 1st of Mar. They delay'd com'g here till late in June, and were the 12th of this Mo., only at Winchester, in their way to our Camp. They were unprovided with anything for a March; they had no Tents, Blankets, Knapsacks, Spatterdashes or Kettles, nay only one bl. Of Gun Powder quite spoiled, and the Companies not compleat. The Muster roll and the Capt's Certificate for the deficiency of Men, I have transmitted to the Sec'ry of War, and have given them a proper Supply of every Necessary and directed the supplying them and the other Compa. from So. Car. With Provisions, and hope You will please give Orders how I am to draw for re-imbursement. If these two Compa's had joined our Forces at the Time they sh'd, the French w'd not have attack'd Us or if they had, if these Compa's had behav'd with the Valour and Resolution of the others, in all probability we sh'd have defeated them. The Aid given by No. Car., are in their March, but have not as yet join'd the other Forces; their delay is greatly misfortunate. The other Colonies have not given any Assistance, and I fear do not intend to do anything, unless oblig'd by an Act of Parliam't for a general Poll Tax of half a Crown St'g for conducting this Expedit'n; one Shill'g, by computation, will be two little. I forgot to mention some of the Ind's rem'n with our People, but generally speaking these People side with the Conquerors. The French had pretty many Ind's they bro't from Canada, and high up the river Ohio, who were in the Engagem't and I suspect many of our friendly Ind's on the Ohio, &c., will join them out of fear, and if the French are allow'd a quiet Settlem't on y't river, its more than probable they will ext'd their Incursions into our pres't Settlem'ts; indeed we had several Families settled within a few miles of the Fort they took from Us. I shall comply with the Articles agreed on, by returning the Prisoners, in order to recover our two Capt's who are Hostages for the Performance thereof. Under these Misfortunes I thought proper to order the building of a Fort near Wills's Creek, about seventy Miles from the Place of Action, and to build a large Magazine for Provisions and to keep the People in Pay till I hear from B. and have Orders w't to do hereafter in regard to the Expedition. For the forementioned reasons I fear we shall not be able to dislodge the French from the Fort without Assistance from Britain. This Dom'n has always been in Peace and not accustom'd to War, therefore, their Magazines are quite empty, no Bombs, Coehorns, or Granade Shells, without them we cannot carry on a Siege against a Fort; no Ingineer in the Co't'y, w'ch is much wanted, and in my private Opinion, with't a regim't or two from Home, and proper Supplies of the above Articles, we shall not be able to force them from His M'y's Fort and Lands. And, as the Money granted by our Assembly is now near expended, I have by Proclamat'n called them to meet the 22nd of next Mo., *w'n I hope to prevail with them for a further Supply; but this, if obtain'd, will be of little Service if the other Colonies do not join in a mutual Supply, and then, with't assistance of Forces, &c., from Home, I shall fear want of Success, as I think it will not be proper to march out any Forces, till we can send such a Number as may be able to defeat them.*

Lieutenant Governor Dinwiddie wanted to quickly rebuild the Virginia regiment and send them back into action against the French, but he was unable to get funding from the Assembly.

On September 11, Dinwiddie wrote to Washington explaining to him that because the Assembly failed to provide funds, he was forced to rescind his plans to attack the French. He advised Washington to march to Wills Creek and join the forces of Colonel Innes.[51]

Sir   *Williamsburg Septr 11th 1754*

No doubt You have heard that our Assembly is prorogu'd without granting any Supplies; Under this unexpected Disappointment, I fear we are not Numbers sufficient to attack the Fort taken from Us by the French: Therefore I order You to give a Detachment of Forty or Fifty Men to Capt. Lewis, with them he is to march immediately for Augusta County, in order to protect our Frontiers from the Incursions of small Parties of Indians, & I suppose some French, order him to march immediately & to apply to Colo. Patton the County Lieut. who will direct him where to proceed, that he may be the most usefull—With the remainder of our regiment You are to march to Wills's Creek, to join the other Forces in executing such Orders as I may see proper to direct; Major Carlyle will supply Your Men with Necessaries, not doubting they will agree to have the said Supplies stop't from their Pay; I therefore desire You will immediately march them to the Place above mentioned. You know best whether You can venture to march them from Rock Creek to Wills's—This late Disappointment from the Assembly has entirely defeated the Operations I had proposed; however its probable on their next Meeting they will more seriously consider the great Danger our Country is exposed to & grant proper Supplies—I am sorry my Clerk sent Yr Commission unsigned, it's a very great Omission, if You had sent it down the Date should have been alter'd, I mean a few Day's after Colo. Fry's Death, & I would have signed it & returned it to You....

Let me know the Day You march, & I sincerely wish You Health & Happiness, & I remain Sr Your Friend &ca

Robt Dinwiddie

On October 19, Virginia Lieutenant Governor Robert Dinwiddie and Maryland Lieutenant Governor Horatio Sharpe met with Arthur Dobbs, newly appointed lieutenant governor of the colony of North Carolina, in Williamsburg. Dobbs, having just arrived from Great Britain, announced that His Majesty had provided £20,000 for a campaign to recapture Fort Duquesne and that Sharpe had received the rank of lieutenant colonel by commission of the king and was the commander in chief of all the forces to be sent against the French. Subsequently, Colonel James Innes became the commander of Fort Cumberland located at Wills Creek.[52]

On October 25, Dinwiddie wrote to Sir Thomas Robinson, secretary of state for the Southern Department, proposing to raise ten companies of regular troops, and to eliminate the confusion over the officers' command structure among the different units, he proposed a captain's commission provided by the king for the commanding officers of these companies (similar requests were made on the same date to the Lords of Trade, the Earl of Halifax, Earl Granville, and James Abercromby).[53]

In order to conduct this Expedit'n with a proper Spirit and Forces, I propose raising 10 Companies of 200 Men each. There is an Uneasiness subsist'g between the Officers of His M'y's In't Compa's, and those under my Commissions. The former will not rank with them, and I fear this may be of great Prejudice in case of Action. I w'd, therefore, h'bly propose y't they may be regiment'd, and blank Comiss's sent out to me to fill up as was done on the Expedition to Carthegena, and to the Ind't Compa's comand by Cap'ts and Lieut'ts only; this w'd reconcile all the Officers, and if His M'y sh'd be graciously pleased to give me the Com'd of the Forces raised here, I am perswaded they w'd be greatly pleased, but this I shall submit, as I shall never offer any Thing but w't I conceive absolutely necessary for this important Service.

Washington held the rank of colonel and did not want to be placed in charge of one of these ten companies with the rank of captain. He viewed the potential move as a demotion, and in late October he resigned his commission and returned to civilian life.[54]

Eleven months after receiving instructions from Dinwiddie to drive the French out of the gateway to the Ohio Country, Washington returned to civilian life. During those eleven months he had experienced two fire-fights against the French and had survived without a scratch while nearly one-third of his troops were casualties. Lieutenant Waggoner was injured during the attack upon de Jumonville and Lieutenant Peter Mercier died from three wounds received at Fort Necessity. While many others around him were injured or killed, Washington was unscathed. His survival of these life-threatening experiences reinforced Washington's growing conviction that Providence was protecting him.

On November 4, Colonel William Fitzhugh (commander of the Fort Duquesne campaign in Horatio Sharpe's absence) sent a letter to Washington informing him of Sharpe's offer to retain his rank of colonel if he were to return to the military service.[55]

Dear Sir   *Rousby Hall Novr 4th 1754*

Since I had the Pleasure of Seeing You, I am Convinc'd by the Governour of Maryland that You may Hold Your Commission with Honour & satisfaction. In Regard to Innes he has only a Commission to be Camp Master General which will Confine him to a Separate Duty. I shall have the Honour to Command in the Governours abence, & as I shall Act by his Particular Instructions, You may rest satisfy'd that Every wish be Conducted to your Satisfaction, at least so f⟨ar⟩ as to prevent your being in any Shape oblig'd to Submit to those who have been heretofore under yr Command. The Governr has wrote to Mr Dinwiddie on this

Subject. I inclose you the letter in order to its being Deliver'd in case you return to the Service & If not Please to return it to me.

I am very Confident the Generall has a very Great Regard for you & will in Every Circumstance in his Power make you very Happy. for my Part I shall be Extreamly fond of your Continuing in the Service & wou'd Advise you by no means to Quit. In regard to the Independant Companys they will in no Shape interfere with you, As you will hold your Post, During their Continuance here & when the Regiment is Reduc'd, will have a Separate Duty. Pray Excuse hast as the Messenger Waits & I cou'd by no means miss this Oppertunity. I am Yr Affect. & obedt Sert

Willm Fitzhugh

Washington did not accept Lieutenant Governor Horatio Sharpe's offer. In a letter to Fitzhugh dated November 15, he wrote that he declined because he did not want to serve with an inferior "governor's commission" rank. The Virginia companies that Dinwiddie was proposing would have commissions provided by His Majesty. As noted earlier, the rank of colonel commissioned by Lieutenant Governor Sharpe would be inferior to Dinwiddie's proposed rank of captain commissioned by King George.[56]

To Colo. William Fitzhugh.

Dear Sir,   *Belvoir, November 15th 1754*

I was favoured with your letter, from Rousby-Hall, of the 4th Instant. It demands my best acknowledgments, for the particular marks of Esteem you have expressed therin; and for the kind assurances of his Excellency, Governour Sharp's good wishes towards me. I also thank you, and sincerely, Sir, for your friendly intention of making my situation easy, if I return to the Service; and do not doubt, could I submit to the Terms, that I should be as happy under your command, in the absence of the General, as under any gentleman's whatever: but, I think, the disparity between the present offer of a Company, and my former Rank, too great to expect any real satisfaction of enjoyment in a Corps, where I once did, or thought I had a right to, command; even if his Excellency had power to suspend the orders received in the Secretary of Wars' Letter; which, by the bye, I am very far from thinking he either has or will attempt to do, without fuller Instructions that I believe he has: especially, too, as there has been a representation of this matter by Governor Dinwiddie, and, I believe, the Assembly of this State; we have advices, that it was received before Demmarree obtained his Letter.

All that I presume the General can do, is, to prevent the different Corps from interfering, which will occasion the Duty to be done by Corps, instead of Detachments; a very inconvenient way, as is found by experience.

You make mention in your letter of my continuing in the Service, and retaining my Colo.'s Commission. This idea has filled me with surprise: for if you think me capable of holding a Commission that has neither rank or emolument annexed to it; you must entertain a very contemptible opinion of my weakness, and believe me to be more empty than the Commission itself.

Besides, Sir, if I had time, I could enumerate many good reasons, that forbid all thoughts of my Returning; and which, to you, or any other, would, upon the strictest scrutiny, appear to be well-founded. I must be reduced to a very low Command, and subjected to that of many who have acted as my inferior Officers. In short, every Captain, bearing the King's Commission; every half-pay Officer, or other, appearing with such commission, would rank before me; for these reasons, I choose to submit to the loss of Health, which I have, however, already sustained (not to mention that of Effects) and the fatigue I have undergone in our first Efforts; than subject myself to the same inconveniences, and run the risqué of a second disappointment. I shall have the consolation itself, of knowing, that I have opened the way when the smallness of our numbers exposed us to the attacks of a Superior Enemy; That I have hitherto stood the heat and brunt of the Day, and escaped untouched, in time of extreme danger; and that I have the Thanks of my Country, for the Services I have rendered it.

It shall not sleep in silence, my having received information, that those peremptory Orders from Home, which, you say, could not be dispensed with, for reducing the Regiments into Independant Companies, were generated, hatched, & brought

from Will's-Creek. Ingenuous treatment, & plain dealing, I at least expected—
It is to be hoped the project will answer; it shall meet with my acquiescence
in every thing except personal Services. I herewith enclose Governour Sharp's
Letter, which I beg you will return to him, with my Acknowledgments for the
favour he intended me; assure him, Sir, as you truly may, of my reluctance to quit
the Service, and of the pleasure I should have received in attending his Fortunes:
also, inform him, that it was to obey the call of Honour, and the advice of my
Friends, I declined it, and not to gratify my desire I had to leave the military line.
  My inclinations are strongly bent to arms.

  The length of this, & the small room I have left, tell me how necessary it is
to conclude, which I will do as you always shall find—Truly & sincerely, Your
most hble Servant,

Geo. Washington

Nov. 15th 1754

In his response to Lieutenant Governor Sharpe's offer, Washington
was clear that he did not want to leave the military. He just didn't want to
serve with what he felt would be an inferior rank.

The conflict in rank challenged Washington throughout the year.
His initial year of military service had started with enthusiasm and rapid
promotion to colonel. Then Washington's fortunes changed dramati-
cally. His leadership had been continuously challenged by the British
officers, and his communications with Dinwiddie were disastrously slow.
George Washington, at twenty-two, had experienced the worst of conditions on the battlefield. His command had suffered the full range of
privative living conditions and ended in military defeat and criticism. He
commanded forces that were undermanned, untrained, poorly supplied,
and malnourished. Moreover, his independent actions at Jumonville had
initiated the French and Indian War. The Virginia troops had suffered
extreme casualties during this disastrous campaign, but Washington
was not injured. The year 1754 began with Washington receiving acco-
lades throughout the colonies for his thousand-mile excursion and

confrontation with the French commandant. Nine months later, facing a potential demotion, he resigned from the military. He had survived it all unscathed and had forged a stronger belief in Providence that would shortly be tested yet again.

SOME IMPORTANT SERVICE TO THE COUNTRY

January 1755–August 1755

"As a remarkable instance of this, I may point out to the public that heroic youth Col. Washington, whom I cannot but hope Providence has hitherto preserved in so signal a manner, for some important service to his country."

– August 17, 1755 – Reverend Samuel Davies

W ASHINGTON'S OCTOBER RETIREMENT FROM the military lasted only a few months. In January 1755, Washington learned that the Crown was providing two regiments of British troops to drive the French from the forks of the Ohio and that Major General Edward Braddock had been placed in command of this campaign. Washington, anticipating an opportunity to improve his prospects of a career in the military, negotiated to become an aide-de-camp for General Braddock. To overcome his issue with the ranking of officers, he elected to serve without rank and without pay. This new role enabled him to observe and participate in the campaign's decision-making inner circle ("Braddock's Family"). This decision, however, placed him in another disastrous life-threatening battle where his leadership would again be demonstrated and his belief in a personal Providence would once more be reinforced.

On January 11, 1755, Dinwiddie wrote to Maryland Governor Horatio Sharpe, commander in chief of all forces to be sent against the French, informing him that Sir John St. Clair had arrived with the latest news from Great Britain. Dinwiddie informed Sharpe that St. Clair had been appointed the quartermaster general for the next campaign to take Fort Duquesne and that the two regiments of British troops that Dinwiddie had asked for in his letter of June 24 were about to arrive.[1]

> *Last Night S'r John St. Clair arriv'd here in His M'y's Ship Gilbralter, and with him two L't Colo's for the two Regim'ts to be raised to the No'w'd, and they propose paying their Respects to You soon. S'r Jno. St. Clair is appointed Q'r Mast'r Gen'l of all the Forces; he and I go to Hampton To-morrow Morn'g, to provide an Hospital for the Forces expected from Ireland, w'ch he says may be daily expected to arrive.*

St. Clair also informed Dinwiddie that Major General Edward Braddock would command the two regiments of British troops. This information was included in a letter that Dinwiddie sent on January 14 to William Allen, a Philadelphia merchant.[2]

> *Jan'y 14th, [1755]*
>
> *Dear Sir:*
>
> *Y'r kind Letter by Mr. Donald I duly rec'd, and he sincerely acknowledges the F'dship You was so kind as to shew him. Y'r Observat's on the pres't unhappy Situat'n on our Affairs on the Cont't are very just. His M'y and the Ministry at Home take*

the unjust Invasion of the Fr. on the Ohio sincerely into their Considerat'n, and have ordered out two Regim'ts from Irel'd with large Ordnance Stores, and appointed Gen'l Braddock to com'd, who, with the Forces, are daily expected.

Major General Edward Braddock arrived in Virginia on February 19, 1755. Braddock was the first British general to set foot in North America. Lieutenant Governor Dinwiddie expressed his joy and relief in a letter to James Abercromby on February 24.[3]

I am mighty glad Gen'l Braddock is arrived, w'ch, I hope will give me some Ease, for these 12 mo's past I have been a perfect Slave, and nothing but His M'y's Com'ds, National Service and Good of these Colonies c'd have prevailed on me to undergo such Fatigue, but the Prospect w'n the Troops from Irel'd arrive will raise my Spirits and hope for Success, w'ch I shall esteem an agreeable Issue to all my Troubles; being very much in haste, I am Y'.r affect. h'ble Serv't.

On March 2, Major General Edward Braddock ordered his aide-de-camp, Robert Orme, to invite George Washington to join the campaign to oust the French from the forks of the Ohio while assuring him that any concerns about rank would be resolved.[4]

[Williamsburg, 2 March 1755]
G. Washington

A Copy Of Captn Robt Orme's first Letter to
Sir
  The General having been informd that you exprest some desire to make the Campaigne, but that you declind it upon some disagreeableness that you thought might arise from the Regulation of Command, has orderd me to acquaint you that he will be very glad of your Company in his Family, by which all inconveniences of that kind will be obviated.

I shall think myself very happy to form an acquaintance with a person so universally esteem'd and shall use every oppertunity of assuring you how much I am Sir Your most Obedt Servant &[ca.]

Robt Orme aid de Camp

Williamsburg March 2d 1755

Washington responded to Braddock's invitation in a letter to Robert Orme on March15. In this letter, Washington confessed that his intentions were self-serving: He wanted to acquire knowledge of the military from the able and experienced General Braddock, but he did have concerns over the issue of rank. To resolve the issue he offered to participate in the campaign as a volunteer and suggested a meeting with the general in Alexandria.[5]

[Mount Vernon, 15 March 1755]
Williamsburg

To Robert Orme Esqr. aid de Camp to His Exy General B. In answer to the foregoing—
Sir,

I was not favoured with your polite Letter (of the 2d Inst) til Yesterday; acquainting me with the notice his Excellency Genl Braddock is pleased to honour me with, by kindly inviting me to become one of his Family the ensuing campayn. It is true Sir that I have, ever since I declind my late command, expressd an Inclination to serve the Ensueing Campaigne as a Volunteer; and this inclination is not a little encreasd since it is likely to be conducted by a Gentleman of the Generals Experience.

But, besides this, and the laudable desire I may have to serve (with my best abilitys) my King and Country, I must be ingenuous enough to confess, that I am not a little biassd by selfish, consideratns. To explain, Sir, I wish earnestly, to attain some knowledge on the Military Profession: and, believeing a more favourable oppertunity cannot offer, than to serve under a Gentleman of Generl Braddock's abilities and experience, it does as you may reasonably suppose, not a little contribute to influence my choice.

But Sir, as I have taken the liberty to express my sentimts so freely, I shall beg your Indulgence while I add that the only bar which can check me in the pursuit of this object, is the inconveniences that must necessarily result from, some proceedings wch happen'd a little before the Generals arrival & wch, in some measure had abated the ardour of my desires and determined me to lead a life of retirement into which I was just entering at no small expence; when your favor was presented to me. But, as I shall do myself the honor of waiting upon his Excellency as soon as I hear of his arrival at Alexandria (and woud sooner, was I certain where to find him,) I shall decline saying any thing further on this head till then; begging you will be pleased to assure him that I shall always retain a grateful Sense of the favour with which he is pleasd to honor me; and that I shoud have embraced this oppertunity of writing to him, had I not recently addressed a congratulatory Letter to him on his safe arrival in this Country I flatter myself you will favour me in making a communication of these Sentiments.

You do me a singular favour in proposing an acquaintance, It cannot but be attended with the most flattering prospect of intimacy on my part; as you may already perceive by the familiarity and freedom with which I now enter upon this corrispondence; a freedom, which, even if it is disagreeable you must excuse, as I may lay the blame of it at your door for encourageing me to throw of that restraint which otherwise might have been more obvious in my deportmt on such an occasion. The hope of shortly seeing you will be an ex[c]use for my not adding more than that I shall endeavour to approve myself worthy of your friendship, and that I beg to be esteemd Your most Obedient Servant.

Go: Washington

Mount Vernon March ⟨15th⟩ 1755

General Braddock met with George Washington in Alexandria on March 31, 1755.[6]

Washington wrote to Captain Robert Orme on April 2, 1755, and explained that he needed more time at Mount Vernon to settle affairs and that he would like to join the campaign at Wills Creek at a later date. In the letter, he also requested a provision that he be allowed to return to Mount Vernon upon completion of the campaign. And, if there was an extended delay, he asked to spend that time at Mount Vernon.[7]

[Mount Vernon, 2 April 1755]
Alexandria

To Rorbert Orme Esqr.—
Dear Sir,

The arrival of a good deal of Company (among whom is my Mother, alarmd at the report of my intententions to attend your Fortunes)—prevents me the pleasure of waiting upon you to day as I had intended; I therefore, beg that you'll be kind enough to make my compliments & excuse, to the Generl; who I hope to hear is greatly recoverd from his indisposition; and recruited sufficiently to prosecute his journey to Annopolis.

I find myself much embarrassd with my Affairs; having no person in whom I can confide, to entrust the management of them with. Notwithstanding I am determined to do myself the honour of accompanying you, upon this proviso— that the General will be kind enough to permit my return as soon as the active part of the Campaign is at an end if it is desird Or, if there shoud be a space of inaction long enough, to admit a visit to my home, that I may be endulged in coming to it. I need not add how much I shoud be oblig'd by joining you at Wills Creek instead of doing it at an earlier period and place.—These things Sir, in whatever light they may appear to you at first Sight, will not I hope be thought unreasonable when it is considerd how unprepard I am at present to quit a Family, & an Estate I was just about to settle wch was utmost confusion.

I have inclosd you a Letter from Colo. Fairfax to Governour Shirley, which with his Complts he desird might be given to that Gentleman He also sends his Blessing to you, and desires that by being a good boy you may merit more of them. At present he entertains Sanguine hopes of you—this for your comfort. I herewith send you a small Map of the back Country, which tho' imperfect, &

roughly drawn (for want of proper Instrumts) may, give you a better knowledge
of the parts designated than you have hitherto had an oppertunity of acquiring.

I shall do myself the honour of waiting upon the General as soon as I hear of
His return from Annapolis—My Compliments attends him, Mr Shirley &ca
And I am Sir Yr truely Obedt Servt

Go: Washington

Mount Vernon 2d Apl 1755

General Braddock conceded to Washington's conditions for joining
the campaign. The conditions were that Washington could remain at
Mount Vernon until he was needed, he could return to Mount Vernon if
there were delays in their trek to Fort Duquesne, and Washington could
return to Mount Vernon after the campaign. In a letter dated April 3,
Captain Orme informed Washington that the general had agreed to all
of his terms and conditions.[8]

An Answer to the foregoing   *[3 April 1755]*
Dear Sir

I communicated your desires to the General who expresses the greatest satisfac-
tion in having you of our Party and Orders me to give his Compliments and to
assure you his Wishes are to make it agreeable to yourself and consistant with
your Affairs and therefore desires you will so settle your business at home as to
join him at Wills Creek if more convenient for you and whenever you find it
necessary to return he begs you will look upon yourself as entire Master, and
judge of what is proper to be done.

Pray present my Duty to my Father and assure him if Filial Obedience and
honour for a Parent can secure his Affection I am extreamely safe.

I long with impatience to have you of our Family that I may have frequent
oppertunity's to assure you with how much sincerety I am Dr Sir Yr most obedt
Servant &[ca]

R. Orme

Apl the 3d 1755
Mr Shirley desires his Compliments.

However, General Braddock did not provide Washington with the expected royal commission of colonel; instead, he offered Washington a royal commission of captain with the command of a company. Washington declined his offer. On April 20, in a letter to William Byrd, a member of the Virginia council, Washington explained that he had joined Braddock's campaign as a volunteer and would receive no remuneration.[9]

[Mount Vernon, 20 April 1755]
Westover

To The Honble William Bird Esqr.
Dr Sir

I am sorry it was not in my power to wait upon you at Westover last Christmas—I enjoy'd much satisfaction in the thought of doing it when an unexpected accident put it intirely out of my power to comply either with my promise, of Inclination; both of which prompted me to make this Visit.

I am now prepareing for, and shall in a few days sett off, to serve in the ensueing Campaign; with different views, however, from those I had before; for here, If I can gain any credit, or if I am entitled to the least countenance and esteem, it must be from serving my Country with out fee or rewd for I can truely say I have no expectation of either—To merit its esteem—and the good will of my friends is the sum of my ambition, having no prospect of obtaining a Comn, being well assur'd it is not in Genl Braddocks power to give such an one as I woud accept of; The commd of a Compa. is the highest Comn vested in his gift. He was so obliging as to desire my Company this Campaigne, has honour'd me with particular marks of his Esteem, and has kindly envited me into his Family; a Circumstance which will ease me of expences, that otherwise, must have accrued in furnishing stores Camp equipage &ca; whereas the cost will now be easy, (comparitively speaking) as baggage Horses, Tents, & some other necessarys will constitute the whole of the charge. Yet, to leave a Family just settling, and in the confusion & disorder (mine is in at present) is not a pleasing thing & may be hurtful but be this as it may, it shall be no hindrance to my making this Campaigne. I am Sir with very gt esteem, Your most Obt Servt

Go: Washington

Mount Vernon 20th Apl 1755

John Augustine Washington agreed to manage the plantation so that his brother could leave Mount Vernon.

Before leaving he sent a farewell letter to William Fairfax on April 23. In this letter, he informed Fairfax that General Braddock had held a conference in Alexandria with five governors—Robert Dinwiddie of Virginia, Horatio Sharpe of Maryland, William Shirley of Massachusetts, Robert Morris of Pennsylvania, and James De Lancey of New York—and Commodore Augustus Keppel. In this conference, plans were agreed upon for attacking the French simultaneously on four fronts—Nova Scotia, Crown Point, Fort Niagara, and Fort Duquesne. Washington also wrote that he had begun to doubt the wisdom of Braddock's approach to the Fort Duquesne campaign. In his letter to Fairfax, he wrote that the movement of the heavily loaded train was going to take too long, but few believed his prediction.[10]

[Mount Vernon, 23 April 1755]
prest at Williamsburgh

To The Honble Wm Fairfax Esqr,
Dear Sir,

I cannot think of quitting Fairfax without embracing this last oppertunity of bidding you farewell.

I shall this day set out for Wills Creek, where I expect to meet the Genl, and to stay—I fear too long, as our March must be regulated by the slow movements of the Train, which I am sorry to say, will be tedious—very tedeous indeed—as I have long predicted, tho' few believ'd.

Alexandria has been honourd with 5 Governours in Consultation—A favorable presage I hope, not only of the success of the Expedition, but of the furute greatness of this Town; for surely, such a meeting must have been occasioned by the Commodious, and pleasant situation of the place, which prognosticates population and the encrease of a (now) flourishing Trade.

I have had the Honour to be introduced to the several Governours; and of being well receiv'd by them all; especially Mr Shirley, whose Character and appearance has perfectly charmed me, as I think his every word, and Action discovers in him the Gentn, and Politician. I heartily wish the same unanimity may prevail amongst us, as appeard to exist between him and his Assembly; when they, to expidate the Business, and to forward his journey hither, sat till eleven, and twelve o'clock every Night.

It will be needless as I know your punctuality requires no stimulus to remind you of an Affair abt which I wrote sometime ago—therefore, I shall only beg my compliments to Mr Nicholas and his Lady, an to all Friends who think me worthy of their enquirys. I am Dear Sir Yr most Obedient Servt.

Go: Washington

Mount Vernon 23d of Apl 1755

Washington left Mount Vernon with four horses, but they were unable to withstand the harsh conditions of the march. In a letter to Sarah Cary Fairfax on April 30, he explained that he had to kill one of them and that the other three were no longer fit for the campaign.[11]

[Bullskin Plantation, 30 April 1755]

Belvoir

To Mrs Fairfax—
Dear Madam

In order to engage your corrispondance, I think it is incumbent on me to deserve it; which I shall endeavour to do, by embracing the earliest, and every oppertunity, of writing to you.

It will be needless to dwell on the pleasure that a corrispondence of this kind would afford me, let it suffice to say—a corrispondance with my Friends is the greatest satisfaction I expect to enjoy, in the course of the Campaigne, and that from none shall I derive such satisfaction as from yours—for to you I stand indebted for many Obligations.

If an old Proverb will apply to my case I shall certainly close with success—for no Man could have made a worse beginning than I have done: out of 4 Horses which I brought from home, one I have killd outright, and the other 3 are renderd unfit for use; so that I have been detain here three days already, and how much longer I may continue to be so, time only can discover.

I must beg my Compliments to Miss Fairfax, Miss Dent, and other's that think me worthy of their enquirys. I am Madam Yr most Obedt Servt

Go: Washington

Bullskin Apl the 30th 1755

Washington caught up with Braddock in Frederick, Maryland, on May 1, 1755, and traveled to Winchester, Virginia, the following day. From there, he wrote to William Fairfax about Quartermaster General St. Clair's erroneous advice[12] regarding the existence of a road from Frederick to Wills Creek.[13]

[Winchester, 5 May 1755]
Belvoir

To The Honble Wm Fairfax Esqr.
Dear Sir

I overtook the General at Frederick Town in Maryld from thence we proceeded to this place, where we shall remain till the arrival of the 2d Division of the Train, (which we hear left Alexandria of Tuesday last); after that, we shall continue our March to Wills Creek, from whence it is imagined we shall not stir till the latter end of this Month for want of Waggons, and other conveniences to Transports our Baggage &ca over the Mount⟨n.⟩

You will naturally conclude that to pass through Maryld (when no object requird it) was an uncommon, & extraordinary rout for the Genl. and Colo. Dunbarr's Regiment to this place; The reason, however, was obvious, Those who promoted it had rather that the communication should be opened that way, than through Virginia; but I believe the eyes of the General are now open, & the Imposition detected—consequently the like will not happen again. Please to make my Compts to Colo. G: to whom I shall write by the next oppertunity and excuse haste—I am Sir Yr most Obedt Servt

Go: Washington

Winchester 5th of May 1755

Washington requested a loan from his first employer, Lord Thomas Fairfax, Fifth Lord of Cameron and William Fairfax's cousin, to replace his four horses.[14]

[Winchester, 6 May 1755]
—Greenway Court

To The Right Honble The Lord Fairfax:
My Lord

I have had the misfortune to loose 3 of my Horses since I left home; and not bringing money enough to buy other's, and to answer the contingent expences of the Campaigne, I have made bold to sollicit your Lordships assistance; the granting of which, will infinitely oblige me.

About 40 or 50£ will supply my wants, and for this sum I wou'd gladly pay your Lordship Interest, beside many thanks for the favour, as I am greatly disconcerted at this present, not being able to proceed conveniently without such aid.

The Genl sets out to morrow, and proceeds directly to Wills Creek; which, together with the hurry of Business, that has happened since we came to this place, has been a mean's of depriving me of the pleasure of waiting upon your Lordship, as I intended to have done—please to make my Comp⟨ts⟩ to Colo. Martin. I am Yr Lordships most Obedt & most Humble Servt

Go: Washington

Winchester 6th of May 1755

Colonel Thomas Bryan Martin, Lord Fairfax's nephew, lived with him at his Greenway Court estate.[15]

Braddock's march to Wills Creek was delayed in Winchester for several more days, and once they arrived in Wills Creek, they still had to wait for their supply train of wagons and horses. In his letter to his younger full brother, John Augustine, Washington expressed his frustration with two weeks of delays and the general's adviser's desire to please rather than to move quickly toward their destination.[16]

[*Winchester, 6 May 1755*]
Mount Vernon

To Mr. Jno. Auge Washington
Dear Brother

A very fatigueing Ride; and long round about brought me to the General (the day I parted with you) at Frederick Town; —This is a small Village 15 Miles below the blew Ridge on the Maryland side of Potomac—from thence we proceeded to this place, where we have halted since Saturday last, and shall depart for Wills Creek to morrow.

I find there is no probality of Marching the Army from Wills Creek till the latter end of this Month, or the first of next, you may easily guess then how heavily time will hang upon my hands.

I have met with much complaisance in this Family; especially from the General; who I hope to please withou⟨t⟩ ceremonious attentions or difficulty, for I may add it can not be done with them as he uses, and requires less ceremony than you can easily conceive.

I have orderd the Horse Gist to Bullskin, and my own here, if serviceable; otherwise you must have both carrd down whe⟨n⟩ Countess is sent up: I have conceivd a good Opn of the horse Gist, therefor⟨e⟩ I hope you will not let him want for proper care & good usage, if he shd be s[en]t instead of the Greys; which will be the case if they are able to perform the Journey.

I hope you will have frequent oppertys to particularise the State of my Affairs, wch will admr much satisfn to a Person in my situation—At present I have

nothing to add but my Compts to all friends, particularly to the worthy Family at
Belvoir who I hope are in good health. I am Dr Jack Yr Affe Brother

Go: Washington

Winchester May 6th 1755

Washington's Bullskin plantation was located about fifteen miles from
Winchester, near the present-day city of Charles Town, West Virginia.

On May 14, Washington wrote his half brother Augustine from Fort
Cumberland at Wills Creek about the difficulties delaying the campaign.
Washington also relayed that they had learned the French were sending
reinforcements to Fort Duquesne.[17]

[Fort Cumberland, Md., 14 May 1755]
Westmorland Cty

To Colo. Auge Washington
Dear Brother

I left home the 24th of last Month, and overtook the General at Frederick
Town in Maryland: from whence we proceeded by slow Marches to this place;
where, I fear, we shall remain some-time for want of Horses and Carriages to
convey our Baggage &ca over the Mountains; but more especially for want of
Forage; as it cannot be imagin'd that so many Horses as we require, will be sub-
sisted without a great deal.

We hear nothing particular from the Ohio except that the French are in hourly
expectation of being joind by a large body of Indians; but I fancy they will find
themselves so warmly attackd in other places, that it will not be convenient for
them to spare many.

I am treated with freedom not inconsistent with respect, by the General and his
Family; I have no doubt therefore but I shall spend my time more agreeably than prof-
itably during the Campaigne, as I conceive a little experience will be my chief reward.
Please to give my Love to my Sister &ca. I am Dr Sir Yr most Affecte Brother

Go: Washington

Fort Cumberland 14th of May 1755

On the same date, Washington wrote to his younger brother John Augustine, and expressed his belief that they would have great difficulty transporting their artillery from Wills Creek through the mountains to the forks of the Ohio. He also shared that he felt this appointment would provide him, at twenty-three, with a good opportunity to advance his fortune in the military service.[18]

[Fort Cumberland, Md., 14 May 1755]
Mount Vernon

To Mr Jno. Auge Washington
Dear Brother

As wearing Boots is quite the Mode, and mine are in a declining State; I must beg the favour of you to procure me a pair that is good, and neat, and send them to Major Carlyle, who I hope will contrive them as quick as my necessity requires.

I see no prospect of moving from this place soon; as we have neither Horses nor Waggons enough, and no forage for them to subsist upon except what is expe[c]ted from Philidelphia; therefore, I am well convinced that the trouble and difficulty we must encounter in passing the Mountain for want of proper conveniences, will equal all the other difficulties of the Campaigne; for I conceive the March of such a Train of Artillery in these Roads to be a tremendous undertaking: As to any danger from the Enemy I look upon it as trifling, for I believe the French will be obligd to exert their utmost Force to repel the attacks to the Northward, where Governour Shirley and other's with a body of 8,000 Men will annoy their Settlements and attempt their Forts.

The Genl has appointed me one of his aid de Camp, in which Character I shall serve this Campaigne, agreeably enough, as I am thereby freed from all command but his, and give his Order's to all, which must be implicitly obey'd. I have now a good oppertunity, and shall not neglect it, of forming an acquaintance which may be serviceable hereafter, if I shall find it worth while to push my Fortune in the Military line.

I have wrote to my female corrispondants by this oppertunity, one of which Letters I have inclos'd to you, & beg yr deliverance of it. I shall expect a particular acct of all that has happen'd since my departure. I am Dear Jack Yr most Affecte Brothr

Go: Washington

Fort Cumberland 14th of May 1755

As Braddock's American aide-de-camp, one of Washington's initial assignments was to ride back to Williamsburg and collect additional funds for the campaign. Braddock's instructions were documented as follows:[19]

Camp at Fort Cumberland [Md.] May 15. 1755
Instructions to George Washington Esq.

1. You will repair to Hampton in Virginia with as much expedition as may be; and ⟨immedi⟩ately upon your Arrivel there you will apply ⟨to⟩ John Hunter Esqr. for the Sum of Four tho⟨usand⟩ pounds Sterling, for which you will receive ⟨mutilated⟩ from Mr. Johnston, Deputy paymaster, paya⟨ble⟩ to yourself.

2. You will acquaint Mr Hunter from me that His Majesty's Service under my direction, requires the further Sum of ten thousand pounds Sterling, to be sent to Fort Cumberland at this place, within the Space of two Months at farthest from this day, to be entrusted to the Care of such person as he shall choose for that purpose, who upon his a⟨rrival⟩ at the Fort with it, shall have a proper ⟨mutilated⟩ appointed him for the safe Custody of it.

3. You will also acquaint Mr Hunter that ⟨mutilated⟩ he shall Send with the said Money shall ⟨mutilated⟩ reasonable Allowance for his Trouble; and that ⟨the⟩ Expence of Insurance and all other Charges t⟨hat⟩ may necessarily attend the Sending it shall be allow'd.

4. You will continue at Hampton no longer than two Day's at the farthest, and if you cannot in that time get the whole Sum of four thousand pounds from Mr Hunter, you will return to me as speedily as may be with such part of it as you shall be able to receive.

5. You will take care to bring me a positive Answer from Mr Hunter, whether I may depend upon ten thousand Pounds being sent to Fort Cumberland by the time mention'd in these Instructions.

E. Braddock

Washington rode out of Wills Creek the next day en route to Williamsburg, and from Winchester he forwarded Braddock's request for funds.[20]

[Winchester, 16 May 1755]
Hampton

To Jno. Hunter Esqr.
Sir.

I have Orders from the Genl, and Instructions from Mr Johnston, the Dy Paymaster Genl to receive 4,000£s Sterg at the rate of £4.0.71/4 pr Oz.; which will they say suffice for present contingencies. I have therefore dispatchd this express, with orders to make all imaginable haste to you, who I am told will imediately repair to Wmsburg with the money, and pay it there, according to contract. I must beg your utmost diligence in this affair as I have Order's not to wait, because the whole Army will halt at Wills Creek till I return, at an immense expence.

I have Letter's from the Genl and Paymaster, with Bills and proper Instruction's; all of which I shall deliver when I have the pleasure of meeting you, & this I expect will be (in Williamsburg) on Wednesday next, as I am now upon my way down, and shall delay no time on the journey. I am &ca

G. W.——n

Winchester 16th May 1755

The ride to Williamsburg was very exhausting. There was a drought in the area and feed was scarce. On May 22, seven days into his ride, Washington met the returning express rider. The rider delivered a message from Dinwiddie informing him that John Hunter had gone to New

York to get additional funds and would not return for another two weeks. Washington decided to continue on to Williamsburg, and in a letter to Robert Orme, Washington explained his situation.[21]

[Claiborne's Ferry, 22 May 1755]
Wills Creek

To Robt Orme Esqr. Aid de Camp
Dear Sir

In pursuance of His Excellencys Commands, I proceeded to this place with all convenient dispatch; But, as I apprehd, and Truely, that the getting and posting Horses at proper Stages, in order to expedate my return, woud occasion some delay I dispatchd an express from Winchester to Hampton advising Colo. Hunter of my business, and desiring him to meet me in Williamsburg with the money: This day I met the Express on his return, with a verbal message from Govr Dinwiddie informing me that Colo. Hunter set out to the Northward last Week for money, and woud not be returnd in less than 14 or 15 Days; & that my journey in all probability would be fruitless: however this may be, I shall Continue on till I have other information; but thought it expedient (as I believe the report myself) to give you the earliest notice of it that the Genl may take his measures accordingly.

As I am fatiegued and a good deal disorderd by constant riding (in a drougth that has almost destroyd this part of the Country) I shall proceed more slowly back, unless I am fortunate enough, contrary to expectation, to receive the money, in that case I shall hurry with the utmost dispatch.

If His Excellency finds it necessary that the money shou'd be had, he has nothing more to do than intimate the same to me; when I shall return back from any place that an express can meet me with his Orders. My Compts attds Morris, Shirley and other Friends of our Party in Camp. I am Dr Sir Yrs &ca

G. W———n

Claybourn's Ferry 8 Oclock Thursday Mg

The following day Washington arrived in Williamsburg and met with James Balfour (John Hunter's business partner). Balfour was able to provide the £4,000 that Braddock had requested, and Washington forwarded this information to Robert Orme on May 23.[22]

[Willamsburg, 23 May 1755]

To the Same

Dear Sir

Since writg from Claybourn's Ferry by the express, I arrivd at this place and have met Mr Belfour; who, I believe, will be able with the assistance of the Govr and some other of his Fr[i]ends, to procure the money by the morning; which will enable me to set out at that time and I hope by tuesday to reach Winchester from whence, I shall proceed to the Camp with all possible dispatch.

As Colo. Hunter is gone to the Northward I could get no positive answer concerning the further sum of Ten thousand pounds (which he was desird to send to Wills Creek) but Mr Belfour his partner thinks it may be depended upon. I shall, before I leave Town get his answer in writing, and deliver it on my arrival Interim I am Sir

Williamsburg Friday Noon

For protection from an Indian attack, Braddock ordered that Washington was to be escorted from Winchester to Wills Creek. But when Washington arrived in Winchester on May 27, the escort was not available. Disappointed, he waited two days and finally resorted to arranging for county militia protection. He arrived back at Wills Creek on the thirtieth and described the experience in his memorandum of the trip.[23]

[15–30 May 1755]

The 15th of May I was sent to Colo. Hunter for a Suppely of Money 4,000£ Sterling, and arrivd as far as Winchester on my way thither the day following, from whence I dispatch'd an express to him (fearing he might be out), to provide that sum, and to meet me with it at Williamsburg Proceeded myself thro Fairfax, where I was detaind a Day in getting Horses.

At Claybourns Ferry the 22d I met the express I had sent, as he was returning, who brought a Verbal message from Governour Dinwiddie, informing me that Colo. Hunter was gone to the Northward and that I woud certainly be disappointed in my expectations of money; of this I acquainted Captn Orme by Letter, and proceeded on to Williamsburg where I arrivd the same Day, and met a Mr Belfour the partner of Colo. Hunter with near the sum desird, which was completed the next day; time enough for me to reach Chissels Ordinary on my return. The 27th I arrived at Winchester and expected to have met the troop of Light Horse to Escort me to the Camp, but being disappointed in that I engaged a guard of the Militia with which I set out on the 29th followg and arrived at the Camp the 30th; from Winchester I wrote the following letter to my Brother Jno. Washington.

In his June 7 letter to his patron, William Fairfax, Washington described Braddock's frustration with the colonies' inability to supply provisions. Because there were frequent contract breaches, Braddock blamed the whole population with a fiery temper rather than rationally assigning blame. He ignored the advice of his "Family," and Washington feared that all the colonists were being condemned as dishonest. The colony of Pennsylvania had failed to provide money for the expedition, but their merchants were more than willing to market provisions to the campaign. To expedite the delivery of their necessities, Braddock requested a Pennsylvania road be built to Fort Duquesne. Washington informed Fairfax that Braddock's regiments were finally moving out of Wills Creek and marching toward the forks of the Ohio. He also mentioned that many troops were suffering from the bloody flux (dysentery) and some had died. Washington observed that they had learned the French were sending hundreds of reinforcements to the Ohio, and he was starting to believe that they might be in for a major confrontation.

Washington wondered if war would be declared between France and England and asked for more information from the homeland.[24]

[Fort Cumberland, Md., 7 June 1755]
Belvoir

To the Honble Willm Fairfax Esqr.
Honble Sir

I arrivd with my charge safe in Camp the 30th of last Month, after waiting a Day and piece in Winchester expecting the Cavalry to Escort me up; in which being Disappointed, I was obligd to make use of a small Guard of the Militia of Frederick Cty.

The General, by frequent breaches of Contracts, has lost all Patience; and for want of that temper, & moderation which shoud be used by a Man of Sense upon these occasion's, will, I fear, represent us in a light we little deserve; for instead of blameing the Individuals as he ought, he charges all his Disappointments to publick Supineness; and looks upon the Country, I believe, as void of Honour and Honesty; we have frequent dispu⟨tes⟩ on this head, which are maintaind with warmth on both sides especially on his, who is incapable of Arguing witht; or giving up any point he asserts, let it be ever so incompatable with Reason or commonsense. There is a Line of Communication to be opend from Pensylvania to the French Fort De Quisne, along wch we are to receive, after a little time, all our Convoys of Provisions &ca; and to give all manner of encouragement to a People who ought rather to be chastisd for their insensibility to danger, and disregard of their Sovereigns expectation. They it seems are to be the favored people, because they have furnishd what their absolute Interest alone indueced them to do, that is 150 Waggons, and an Equivalent number of horses.

Majr Chapman with a Detachment of 500 Men & the Quarter Master General, Marchd two or three Days before I arrived here, to open the Road and lay a deposit of Provisions in a small Fort which they are to Erect at the Little meadows.

To morrow Sir Peter Halkett with the first Brigade is to begin their March; and on Monday the General with the 2d will follow.

Our Hospital is fill'd with Sick, and the number's increase daily, with the bloody Flux, which has not yet prov'd Mortal to many. General Innes has accepted of a Commission to be Governour of Fort Cumberland, where he is to reside, and will Shortly receive another to be hang man, or something of that kind & for which he is equally qualified. By a Letter rec'd from Governor Morris of Pennsylvania we have advice that a Party of three hundd Men passd Oswego on their way to Fort Duquisne, and that another, and larger Detachment was expected to pass that place every moment. By the Publick accts from Pensylvania we are assur'd that 900 Men have certainly passd Oswego, to reinfor[c]e the French on Ohio, so that from these accts, we have reason to believe that we shall have more to do than go up the Hills and come down again.

We are impatient to hear what the power's at home are doing; whether Peace or war is like to be the issue of all these Preparations. I am Honble Sir Yr most Obedt Servt

Go: W———n

Camp at Wills Creek 7th of June 1755

When he wrote to John Augustine Washington on June 7, Washington described in more detail the stresses, the awful sickness, and increasing mortality occurring in camp.[25]

[Fort Cumberland, Md., 7 June 1755]
Mount Vernon

To Mr Jno. Auge Washington
Dear Brother

As much as I am hurried at present, I cant think of leaving this place without writing to you; tho I have no time to be particular. I was Escorted by 8 Men of the Militia from Winchester to this Camp; which 8 Men were 2 Days assembling; but I believe they woud not have been more than as many seconds dispersing if I had been attacked. Upon my arrival here, I found that Sir Jno. St Clair with a body of 500 Men had Marchd to prepare the Roads, lay a deposit of Provisions at the little Meadows, and to erect some kind of defensive work there.

Tomorrow Sir Peter Halket with the first Brigade begin their March, and on monday the General and the 2d will follow. We have no certain intelligence from the Ohio: but have advices from Philadelphia that a body of 300 French: passd Oswego on their way to Fort Duquesne, and that a larger Detachment was hourly expected. A Captn of Sir Peter's Regimt with several of the common Soldiers of the different Corps have died since our Incampmt here, and many others are now sick with a kind of Bloody Flux. I wrote to you from Winchester & hope you have receivd it—I shoud be glad of an answer as soon as possible; any Letter's to me, directed to the care of Mr Cox at Winchester, will be certain of a conveyance[.] I am Dr Jack Yr most Affe Brothr

G.W.

Camp at Wills Creek 7th of June 1755

Washington wrote another very lengthy letter to his brother over a period of five days. In this letter, he described General Braddock's progress toward Fort Duquesne.[26]

[Great Crossing of the Youghiogheny, Pa.,
28 June–2 July 1755]
Mount Vernon

To Mr Jno. Auge Washington
Dear Brother

Immediately upon our leavg the C. at Geors. Ck the 14th Inst. (from whe I wrote to yo.) I was siezd wt violt Fevers & Pns in my hd wch con[tinue]d wtout Intermisn till the 23 follg when I was reliev'd by the Genls absolty ordering the Phyns to give me Doctr Jas Powders; (one of the most excelt mede in the W.) for it gave me immee ease, and removed my Fevrs & othr Compts in 4 Days time. My illness was too violent to suffer me to ride, therefore I was indebted to a coverd Waggon for some part of my Transpn; but even in this I cd not conte far for the joltg was so gt that I was left upon the Road with a Guard and necessys, to wait the Arrl of Colo Dunbars Detacht, whh was 2 days M. behind us. The Genl giving me his wd of honr that I shd be brought up before he reachd the French

Fort; this promise, and the Doctrs threats that If I perseverd in my attempts to get on, in the Condn I was, my Life, wd be endangered, determind me to halt for the above Detacht.

Washington explained that it was very dangerous to traverse the road between Wills Creek and the advance guard nearing Fort Duquesne. He let him know that these difficulties meant that his correspondence would be hindered in the near future. General Braddock realized that their progress was slowed by the extensive train of horses and wagons, so he held a council of war to try to decrease its size. Washington set the example by giving his best horse to public service and took half of his normal luggage. But not all the officers were so generous, and the number of wagons was only slightly decreased.[27]

As the Comn betn this & Will's Ck must soon be too dangerous for single persons to pass, it will render the Interce of Lettrs slow & precarious; therefore I shall attempt (and will go through if I have strength,) to give you an acct of our proceedings, of our Situation, & of our prospects at present; which I desire yo. will com[municat]e to Colo. Fairfax: & others, my Corrispts; for I am too weak to write more than this Lettr. In the Lr wch I wrote to you fm Georges Ck I acqd you that unless the numr of Wagns were retrenchd & carryg H[orse]s incrd that we never shd be able to see Duquisne: This in 2 Days afterwards, wch was abt the time they got to the little Meadows with some of their foremost Waggon's and strongest Teams, they themselves were convinced off, for they found that beside the almost imposy of gettg the Wagns along at all; that they had often a Rear of them 3 or 4 Miles in length; & th[a]t the Soldrs Guarding them were so dispersd that if we had been attackd either in Front, Center or Rear the part so attackd, must have been cut of or totally routed before they coud be sustaind by any other Corps.

At the little Meadws there was a 2d Council calld, for there had been one before wherein it was again representd to the Offrs of the difft Corps the urgentcy for Hs. & how laudable a further retrenchment of their Baggage would be that the spare ones might be turned over for Publick Service. In order to encourage this I gave up my best Horse (wch I have nevr hd of since) & took no more baggage than half my Protmanteau wd easily contn. It is said however th[a]t the numbrs reduced by this 2d attempt was only from 210 or 12, to 200 wch had no perceiveable effect.

Their train was still not advancing at the speed anticipated, and Major General Braddock asked Washington for his advice. Washington recommended that the train continue pushing ahead, but encouraged Braddock to deploy an advance detachment of elite troops to capture Fort Duquesne before the French reinforcements arrived.[28]

The Genl before they met in Council askd my prive Opinn concerng the Expn; I urgd it in the warmest terms I was able, to push forward; if we even did it with a small but chosn Band, with such Artillery and light Stores as were absolutely necessary; leavg the heavy Artilly Baggage &ca with the rear division of the Army, to follw by slow and easy Marches, which they might do safely while we were advanced in Front. As one Reason to support this Opinion, I urged that if we cd credt our Intelligence, the French were weak at the Forks at present but hourly expectd reinfts wch to my certain knowledge coud not arrive with Provns or any supplys durg the continuance of the Droughth which we were then experiencing—as the Buffaloe River (River le beauf) down wch was their only commn to Venango, must be as Dry as we now fd the gt xing of the Yaughe; wch may be passd dry shod.

Braddock followed Washington's recommendations and advanced with a select force and minimal baggage. The ailing Washington continued with Colonel Thomas Dunbar, the remaining troops, the supplies, and the women at a less strenuous pace.[29]

This advice prevailed, & it was detd that the Genl, with 1200 Chosen Men and Officers from all the differt Corps, under the following Field Officer's (vizt Sr Petr Halkett who acts as Brigadier, Lt Colo. Gage Lt C: Burton, and Majr

Sparke, with such a certain number of Waggons as the Train wd absolutely require, shoud March as soon as things coud be got in readiness for them; which was compleated, and we on our March by the 19th, leavg Colo. Dunbar & Majr Chapman with the residue of the two Regts, some Indept Companys most of the Women and in short every thing not absolutely necessary behind: carrying our Provision's & other necessarys upon Horses.

The French Indians were able to delay the progress of Braddock's advance detachment by instigating frequent skirmishes and scalping forays.[30]

We set out with less than 30 Carriages (Inclg those that transported the Ammunition for the Howetzers, 12 prs, 6 prs, &ca) & all of them strongly Horsed; which was a prospect that conveyd infinite delight to my mind, tho' I was excessively ill at the time. But this prospect was soon clouded, & my hopes brought very low indeed when I found, that instead of pushing on with vigour, without regarding a little rough Road, they were halting to Level every Mold Hill, & erect Bridges over every brook; by which means we were 4 Days gettg 12 Miles. At this Camp I was left by the Doctrs Advice, and the Genls absolute Orders, as I have already mentioned without which I should not have been prevaild upon to remain behind, as I then imagin'd, and now believe I shall find it no easy matter to join my own Corps again, which is 25 Miles advanced before us; notwithstanding I had the Genls word of Honr pledgd in the most Solemn manner, that I shd be b[rough]t up before he arrived at Fort Duquisne. They have had frequent Alarms and several Men have been Scalp'd, but this is done with no other design than to retard the March; and to harass the Men; who if they are to be turnd out every time a small party attack the Guards at Night; (for I am certain they have not sufficient force to make a serious assault) their ends will be accomplished; by the gaining of time.

Washington ended his letter to John Augustine Washington by saying that he was leaving Dunbar's camp to join the advance guard and General Braddock.[31]

> P.S. *Added afterwards, to the foregoing Letter as follows*
>
> *[Scalping Camp, Pa., 2 July 1755]*
>
> *A Serious inconvenience attended me in my Sickness and that was, looseing the use of my Servant, for poor Jno. Alton was taken abt the same time that I was, & with nearly the same disorder; and was confind as long; so that we did not see each other for several Days. He is also tolerably well recoverd. We are advand almost as far as the gt Meadows; and I shall set out tomorrow morning for my own Corps, with an Excort of 100 Men which is to guard some Provision's up; so that my Fears and doubts on that head are now removd.*
>
> *I had a Letter Yesterday from Orme, who writes me word that they have passd the Yaughyangane for the last time, that they have sent out Parties to scour the Country thereabouts, and have Reason to believe that the French are greatly alarmd at their approach.*
>
> *2d July 1755*

Meanwhile, on July 4, Lieutenant Governor Dinwiddie wrote to Colonel James Innes, governor of Fort Cumberland, without knowing the status of the attack on Fort Duquesne. He expressed his concern over the sickness pervading Fort Cumberland. In this letter he also informed Innes of recent attacks by the French Indians along the Virginia frontier and that he had asked the House of Burgesses for additional funds for defense. Dinwiddie expressed his hope that General Braddock's expedition had taken possession of Fort Duquesne.[32]

> *July 4th, 1755*
>
> Sir:
>
> *I wrote You so lately y't I desire to be refer'd to my former letter. Y'rs of 18th June I received only two Days ago. Y'r Situat'n, with so many Women and sick*

People, is not very agreeable. I shall endeavour very soon to send You forty or fifty Men, as we are inform'd some Parties of Ind's appear'd on our Frontiers and y't of M'yl'd and committed some Murders. I have laid the Intelligence before the Ho. Of Burgesses, and am in hopes they will qualifie me to repell their Designs. I find Mr. Walker charges 100£, p'd You, w'ch I did not know, as You wrote he had no Money. I sent the last £120. Pray advise me how I am to charge y't Sum. I now send You 49 oz. 13 penny w't 6 gr. Gold for the two Bills of 200£ on Colo. Hunter, w'ch I wish safe to Y'r Hands. It comes by Mr. Boyd accord'g to Y'r desire. I hope the Gen'l is in Possess'n of the Fort by y's Time. I am concern'd the Ind's by direct'n of the Fr. Sh'd insult us so near Y'r Fort, and y't You have not Men to chastise them. Pray God protect You and grant us a happy Issue of y's just Expedit'n. I sincerely am,

S'r, Y'r aff. Friend, &c.

P. S.—If any Droves of Cattle for the Army, if possible send an Escort with them. If my L'd Fairfax applies to You for Arms, Ammuniction, &c., I pray [you] supply him.

In a letter to Braddock on the same date, Dinwiddie described in more detail his concerns over the French and Indian attacks on the western settlers, and that he was raising two companies of rangers to march to Fort Cumberland to reinforce Colonel Innes.[33]

July 4th, 1755

Sir:

I wrote You by Mr. Shaw, to w'ch please be refer'd. Since y't I rec'd a Let'r from L'd Fairfax and another from Mr. Martin, copy of w'ch I here enclose You, by w'ch You may observe a No. of Fr. And Ind's got into our Frontiers and have plunder'd and murder'd several Families; Y's is consist't with Y'r Let'r to me. On receipt thereof I order'd the Militia to be in readiness in Case of a Surprize, but am sorry to say they are very ungovernable. I have order'd two Companies of Rangers to be imediately rais'd, each Co'y to be 50 effective Men, to find out the Enemy who lurk in the Woods all Day and do w't Mischief they can in the

Night, but am in hopes by Diligence the above Companies will be liable to reduce them. They are a mixture of Fr. and Ind's, and they comit the most barbarous Murders and destroy every Thing they meet with. This Step I presume was introduced to give a Diversion to Y'r Forces, but I hope before y's You have taken and are in Possess'n of the Fort, and I expect we shall be able to drive the Enemy from our Frontiers. The last Acc't I had, was y't they were near F't Cumberl'd, but I dare say they will not attack y't. I have order'd 50 Men to re-inforce Colo. Innes, and I wrote Gov'r Sharpe to supply the like No. of Men I order'd to be rais'd for y't service, are not yet compleat, but with all possible Diligence I shall send them to him.

As noted in his memorandum on July 8, Washington, although still feeling very weak, arrived in Major General Braddock's encampment where the Monongahela River meets the Youghiogheny River.[34]

[8-9 July 1755]

N.B. The 8th of July I rejoined (in a covered Waggon) the advanced division of the Army under the immediate Comd of the General. On the 9th I attended him on horse back tho. very weak and low—on this day he was attacked and defeated by a party of French & Inds. adjudged not to exceed 300—When all hope of rallying the dismayed troops & recovering the ground, our provisions & Stores were given up I was ordered to Dunbars Camp.

The following day, General Braddock led his troops into a French and Indian ambush. While concealed behind trees in the surrounding hills, they poured down a barrage upon the English troops. The English fought back by standing in formation, making them an easy target for the hidden enemy. By the end of the day's fighting, the British had endured 976 casualties out of a force of 1,469. The French and Indians lost only forty-three out of a force of approximately eight hundred. Once again, George Washington emerged from battle unscathed. During the intense cross fire, Washington had two horses shot from under him and experienced four bullets through his coat.

Washington was at Braddock's side when the general was wounded in the chest.

General Braddock died of his wounds on July 12, 1755, less than five months after his celebrated arrival in America. His last command directed Washington to get reinforcements. Washington, although weakened from his recent illness and exhausted from the day's battle, heroically rode hard all night and into the next day to Gist's camp, which was over fifty miles from the scene of the battle. He later wrote of this night's horrible experience.[35]

> *The shocking Scenes which presented themselves in this Nights march are not to be described, The dead—the dying—the groans—lamentation—and crys along the Road of the wounded for help…were enough to pierce a heart of adamant. The gloom & horror of which was not a little encreased by the impervious darkness occasioned by the close shade of thick woods which in places rendered it impossible for the two guides which attended to know when they were in, or out of the track but by groping on the ground with their hands.*

On July 17, Washington forwarded a letter to Colonel James Innes, governor of Fort Cumberland, ordering preparations for the wounded officers and requesting fresh horses to replace the weak ones toting the officers' litters.[36]

> *[Little Meadows, Md., 17 July 1755]*
> *Fort Cumberland*
>
> To Governour Innis—
> Sir
>   *Captn Orme being confin'd to his Litter & not well able to write, has desir'd me to acknowledge the receipt of your's; He begs the favour of you to have the room that the Genl lodg'd in prepard for Colo. Burton, himself, and Captn Morris;*

who are all wounded; also, that some small place may be had convenient for Cooking; and that, if any fresh Provn and other suitable necessarys for persons in their condition can be had, that you will be kind enough to engage it. He also begs, that, you will order the present wch was sent by Governour Morris to the Genl and his Family, into the care of Mr A. le Roy the Steward, who is sent on for that, and other purposes. The Horses that carry the wounded Gentn in Litters are so much fatiegued that we dread their performance, therefore it is desird, that you will be kind enough to send out 8 or 10 fresh horses for their relief, which will enable us to reach the Fort this Evening. I doubt not but you have had an acct of the poor Genls death by some of the affrighted Waggoners, who ran off without taking leave. I am Sir Yr most Obt Servt

Go; W———n

Little Meadows 15th July 1755

On July 18, Washington wrote letters to his mother, Lieutenant Governor Dinwiddie, and his brother John Augustine Washington describing the battle. To his mother he wrote that nearly all of the troops in the three Virginia companies had been killed but he had luckily escaped unscathed.[37]

[Fort Cumberland, Md., 18 July 1755]
near Fredg

To Mrs Washington
Honour'd Madm
   As I doubt not but you have heard of our defeat, and perhaps have had it represented in a worse light (if possible) than it deserves; I have taken this earliest oppertunity to give you some acct of the Engagement, as it happen'd within 7 miles of the French Fort on Wednesday the 9th inst.
   We Marchd onto that place witht any considerable loss, havg only now and then a stragler pickd up by the French Scoutg Indns. When we came there, we were attackd by a body of French and Indns whose number (I am persuaded) did not exceed 300 Men; our's consisted of abt 1,300 well armd Troops; chiefly

Regular Soldiers, who were struck with such a panick, that they behav'd with more cowardice than it is possible to conceive; The Officers behav'd Gallantly in order to encourage their Men, for which they sufferd greatly; there being near 60 killd and wounded; a large proportion out of the number we had! The Virginia Troops shewd a good deal of Bravery, & were near all killd; for I believe out of 3 Companys that were there, their is scarce 30 Men left alive; Capt. Peyrouny & all his Officer's down to a Corporal was killd; Capt. Polson shard near as hard a Fate, for only one of his was left: In short the dastardly behaviour of thos⟨e⟩ they call regular's, exposd all other's that were inclind to do their duty to almost certain death; and at last, in dispight of all the efforts of the Officer's to the Contrary, they broke, and run as Sheep pursued by dogs; and it was impossible to rally them. The Genl was wounded; of wch he died 3 Days after; Sir Peter Halket was killd in the Field: where died many other brave Officer's; I luckily escapd witht a wound, tho' I had four Bullets through my Coat, and two Horses shot under me; Captns Orme & Morris two of the Aids de Camp, were wounded early in the Engagemt which renderd the duty harder upon me, as I was the only person then left to distribute the Genls Orders, which I was scarcely able to do, as I was not half recoverd from a violent illness that had confin'd me to my Bed, and a Waggon, for above 10 Days; I am still in a weak and Feeble condn which induces me to halt here 2 or 3 Days in hopes of recovg a little Strength, to enable me to proceed homewards; from whence, I fear I shall not be able to stir till towards Sepr, so that I shall not have the pleasure of seeing you till then, unless it be in Fairfax; please to give my love [to] Mr Lewis and my Sister, & Compts to Mr Jackson and all other Fds that enquire after me. I am Hond Madm Yr most Dutiful Son

G. W————n

P.S. You may acqt Priscilla Mullican that her Son Charles is very well, havg only recd a slight wd in his Foot wch will be curd witht detrimt to him in a very small time. We had abt 300 Men killd and as many, ⟨o⟩r more, wounded; and this chiefly done by our own Men.

In his report to Lieutenant Governor Robert Dinwiddie, Washington criticized the performance of the British troops and wrote that the British and Virginia soldiers had experienced devastating casualties. He also was greatly concerned for the safety of the settlers in the back country.[38]

[Fort Cumberland, Md., 18 July 1755]
Williamsburgh

To The Honble Robt Dimwiddie Esqr.
Honble Sir

As I am favourd with an oppertunity, I shoud think myself inexcusable, was I to omit givg you some acct of our late Engagemt with the French on the Monongahela the 9th Inst.

We continued our March from Fort Cumberland to Frazer's (which is within 7 Miles of Duquisne) witht meetg any extraordinary event, havg only a stragler or two picked Up by the French Indians. When we came to this place, we were attackd, (very unexpectedly) by abt 300 French and Indns; Our number's consisted of abt 1300 well armd Men, chiefly regular's, who were immediately struck with such an inconceivable Panick, that nothing but confusion and disobedience of order's prevaild amongst them: The Officer's in genl behavd with incomparable bravery, for which they greatly sufferd, there being near 60 killd and woundd A large Proportion out of the number we had! The Virginian Companies behavd like Men, and died like Soldier's; for I believe out of 3 Companys that were on the ground that Day, scarce 30 were left alive: Captn Peyrouny and all his Officer's down to a Corporal, were killd; Captn Polson shard almost as hard a Fate, for only one of his Escap'd: In short the dastardly behaviour of the Regular Troops exposd all those who were inclin'd to do their duty, to almost certai⟨n⟩ Death; and at length, in despight of every effort to the contrary, broke & run as Sheep before Hounds, leavg the Artillery, Ammunition, Provisions, Baggage & in short every thing a prey to the Enemy; and when we endeavourd to rally them in hopes of regaining the ground and what we had left upon it, it was with as little success as if we had attempted to have stopd the wild Bears of the Mountains or rivulets with our feet, for they wd break by in spite of every effort that could be made to prevent it.

The Genl was wounded in the Shoulder, & the Breast; of wch he died three days after; his two Aids de Camp were both wounded, but are in a fair way of Recovering; Colo. Burton and Sir Jno. St Clair are also wounded, and I hope will get over it; Sir Peter Halket, with many other brave Officers were killd in the Field: It is supposed that we had 300 or more killed; abt that number we brought off wounded; and it is conjectured (I believe with much truth) that two thirds of both receiv'd their shott from our own cowardly Regulars, who gatherd themselves into a body contrary to orders 10 or 12 deep, woud then level, Fire, & shoot down the Men before them.

I Tremble at the consequences that this defeat may have upon our back setlers, who I suppose will all leave their habitation's unless their are proper measures taken for their security.

Colo. Dunbar, who commands at present, intends as soon as his Men are recruited at this place, to continue his March to Philia for Winter Quarter's; consequently there will be no Men left here unless it is the shattered remains of the Virginia Troops; who are totally inadequate to the protection of the Frontiers. As Captn Orme is writg to yr honour I doubt not but he will give you a circumstantial acct of all things, which will make it needless for me to add more than that I am Honble Sir Yr most Obt & most Hble Servt

G. W——n

Fort Cumberland July 18th 1755

To his brother John Augustine Washington he wrote that he believed that Providence had protected him.[39]

[Fort Cumberland, Md., 18 July 1755]
Mount Vernon

To Mr Jno. Ange Washington
Dear Brother
As I have heard since my arrivl at this place, a circumstantial acct of my death and dying Speech, I take this early oppertunity of contradicting the first, and of assuring you that I have not, as yet, composed the latter. But by the all

powerful dispensatns of Providence, I have been protected beyond all human probability & expectation for I had 4 Bullets through my Coat, and two Horses shot under me yet escaped unhurt although death was levelling my companions on every side of me.

We have been most scandalously beaten by a trifling body of men; but fatiegue, and the want of tim⟨e⟩ will prevent me from giving you any of the details untill I have the happiness of seeing you at Mount Vernon; which I now most ardently wish for, since we are drove in thus far. A Weak, and Feeble State of Health, obliges me to halt here for 2 or 3 days, to recover a little strength, that I may thereby be enabled to proceed homewards with more ease; You may expect to see me there on Saturday or Sunday Se'night, which is as soon as I can well be down as I shall take my Bullskin Plantation's in my way. Pray give my Compts to all my Fds. I am Dr Jack Yr most Affecte Brothr

G. W——n

Fort Cumberld 18th July 1755

George Washington returned to Mount Vernon on July 26. On this date, William Fairfax forwarded a note to him expressing how much he and the ladies of Belvoir wanted to see him. He also expressed his belief that Providence had preserved Washington.[40]

Dear Sir   *Belvoir. 26. July 1755*

Your safe Return gives an uncommon Joy to Us and will no Doubt be sympathiz'd by all true lovers of Heroick Virtue. From our first inexpressible affecting Intelligence by Colo. Innes of the total Defeat of our Forces, Genl Braddock and many Officers killd, the whole Artillery taken, We have been in torturing Suspence, Each One for their best belovd. Now You are by a kind Providence preserv'd and returnd to Us, We can say the Castrophy might have been worse. You kindly invite Us over, rightly judging our Curiosity wants to be informd of some particulars yet unacquainted with, And if a Satturday Night's Rest cannot be sufficient to enable you Coming hither to Morrow, the Ladys will try to get Horses to equip our Chair or attempt their Strength on Foot to Salute

You so desirous are They with loving Speed to have an ocular Demonstration of your being the same Identical Gentn that lately departed to defend his Country's Cause.

Mr. Carlyle rec'd a Letter yesterday from G. Fx, at Winchester after his Return from Will's's Creek, expressing his Concern for missing You and accounting that He staid there to meet Lord Fx in Order to consult on the necessary Measures to be taken by the Militia, as Colo. Dunbar Seems to intend Marching, its suppos'd, to Philadelphia or &c. Yrs affecty

W: Fairfax

On July 26, Lieutenant Governor Dinwiddie responded to Washington's letter. In this letter, he expressed his dismay at General Braddock's defeat and his delight that Washington was safe. Dinwiddie wrote that he was surprised to learn that Colonel Dunbar was marching the British forces to Philadelphia for their winter retreat instead of fighting for Fort Duquesne and defending the frontier.[41]

July 26th, 1755.

Dear Washington:

The dismal Defeat of our Forces by such a handful of men gives me very great Concern, as also for the death of the Gen'l and so many brave Officers, entirely owing to the dastardly Spirit of the private Men. Their Panick, I suppose, made them deaft to all Comd's, and in course was the Bane of all our Misfortunes. The train of Artillery being in the Enemy's Possess'n is a monstrious Misfortune. However, I was glad to receive Y'r Let'r, and y't You came safe of with't any Wound, after Y'r gallant Behav'r, on which I congratulate You and thank You for the Acc't You gave me of the Engagem't; but I suppose You c'd not tell the Numb'r of the Enemy y't were kill'd. But pray, S'r, w'th the Numb'r of Men remain'g is there no Possibility of doing someth'g the other Side of the Mount's before the Winter Mo's? I have wrote Colo. Dunbar on y's head, and if the private Men have got over their Panick I think they may do a great deal, as I suppose many of the Fr. Will imediately go up the River Ohio, as they will not expect any attack from y's so soon after the late Defeat. Pray write me Y'r Opinion thereon. I have called the Assembly, and do not doubt of their concurring with me in any Th'g reasonable for the Service. I have order'd three Compa's of Rangers to the Frontiers, but surely You must Mistake. Colo. Dunbar will not march into Winter Qr's in the Middle of Sumer and leave the Frontiers of his Majesty's Colonies open with't proper Fortificat's and expos'd to the Invasions of the Enemy. As he is a better Officer and I have a different opinion of him, I shall wait w'th Impatience an Answer to my Let'r to him by y's Exp's. I thank You for the List of Officers kill'd and Wounded. It gives me much Concern to observe so many brave Men in a manner Murder'd for defect of the private Men's not doing their Duty. I sincerely wish You Health and Happiness & am with great Respect,

S'r, Y'r very h'ble serv't.

Dunbar elected to move the British troops into winter quarters in Philadelphia and marched his troops out of Fort Cumberland on August 1.

With the defeat of Major General Braddock in July and with the retreat of Colonel Dunbar to Philadelphia in August, Dinwiddie requested funding to reestablish the Virginia regiment with an additional 1,200 troops for the defense of the Dominion. The burgesses approved the funding and persuaded Dinwiddie to commission Colonel George Washington to command the regiment.

Philip Ludwell, a member of the governor's council, wrote to Washington from Williamsburg on August 8, and encouraged him to take command of the Virginia forces.[42]

Dear Washington   *Williamsburgh Augt 8 1755*

I most heartily congratulate your safe return from so many Dangers & Fatigues & by this Time I hope you are enough recovered to give us the pleasure of seeing you here which all your Friends are extremely desirous of.

The House has voted 1200 Men but it is very probable they will determine at least for 4000. In Conversation with the Gove about it, I said if this shoud be done, I supposed his Honour woud give the Command of them to Col: Washington for I thought he deserved every thing that his Country cou'd do for him. The Govr made a reply much in yr Favour; tho' I understand there is anor warm Sollicitation for it; & if we coud be so happy as to have you here at this Time, & that it were known you were willing to take such a Command; I believe it woud greatly promote the Success of our Endeavours with the Assembly. Mine, as they have allways been, uniformly continue to procure for such eminent Merit the utmost Encouragement: for, Dear Colo: whilst I am serving so deserving a Man I think with pleasure that I am serving my Country as well as testifying the Sincereity with which I am Sir Your most Obedt Servt

Phi: Ludwell

Burgess Warner Lewis, cousin of George Washington, wrote to him on August 9 and also encouraged him to accept a commission to command the reconstituted Virginia regiment.[43]

Gloster County,

Dear Sir: *Saturday Evening [9 August 1755]*

I am just come from Wmsburgh where your Friends are extreamly impatient to see you, and our Speaker among them, as every one of my acquaintance profess a fondness for your having the command of the men now to be raised, thought proper to send a man to you to acquaint you of it. Shou'd you incline to proceed on this expedition, 'twou'd give a general satisfaction to our Country, and shou'd be glad to see you in Wmsburgh on Wednesday, if your health will permit, as I am of opinion the Assembly will break up the latter end of next week, they have voted forty thousand Pounds to be raised by a Land Tax Pole Tax and 5 per Ct upon all goods imported, and the same out of all Salleries, and to have twelve hundred men imediately raised if possible tho' as yet the number I believe is not fully settled, as a great number of the Members, much incline to raise 4000 Men, in short they all seem to think it absolutely necessary to raise as many men as will be thought sufficient to repel the Enemy, and I believe, were you present that the greatest regard wou'd be shewn any proposals you shou'd think proper with regard to the expedition. I now Sir Most heartily congratulate you upon your safe arrival among us, and most sincerely condole with you, upon your late illness, which by this I hope you have got the better of, to be enabled to protect our Country, and fix immortal honour upon yourself & posterity. I am Dr George yr most affect. Friend & Obedt Hble Servt

Warner Lewis

Washington replied to Warner Lewis on August 14. In this response he described the concerns he had and expressed his reluctance to accept the command.[44]

[Mount Vernon, 14 August 1755]
Gloucester City

To Warner Lewis Esqr.
Dear Sir

After returning you my most sincere, and grateful thanks for your kind condolance on my late indispositions; and for the generous, and give me leave further to say, partial opinion you have entertained of my military ability's; I must express my concern for not having it in my power to meet you, and other Friends, who have signified their desire of seeing me (in Williamsburg). Your Letter only came to hand at nine last Night, and you inform me that the Assembly will break up the latter end of the Week, which allows a time too short to perform a journey of 160 miles especially by a person in my weak and feeble condition for altho' I am happily recover'd from the disorder which brought me to so low an ebb, by a sickness of near 5 Weeks conti[nuanc]e yet, my strength is not returnd to me. Had I got timely notice, I would have attempted the ride by slow and easy journeys, if it had been only for the satisfaction of seeing my Friends, who I flatter myself from what you say, are kind enough to sympathise in my good, and evil Fortunes.

The Chief Reason (next to indisposition) that prevd me from coming down this Assembly was a determination not to offer my Services and that determination proceeded from the following Reason's 1st a belief that I coud not get a command upon such terms as I shoud incline to accept, for I must confess to you I never will quit my Family, injure my Fortune, and (above all) impair my health to run the risque of such Changes and Viscissitudes as I have met with; but shall expect if I am employd again, to have something certain. Again, was I to accept the command, I shoud insist upon somethings which ignorance and inexperience made me overlook before, particularly that of having the Officers in some measure appointed with my advice, and with my concurrance; for I must add, I think a commanding Officer not havg this liberty appear's to me to be a strange thing, when it is considered how much the conduct and bravery of an Officer influences the Men; how much a Commanding Officer is answerable for the behaviour of the inferiour Officer's; and how much his good or ill success in time of action depends upon the conduct of each particular one—especially too in this kind of Fighting, where being dispersd, each and every of them at that time, has greater liberty to misbehave than if they were regularly, and compactly drawn up under the Eyes of their superior Officer's. On the other hand, how little credit is given to a Commander who after a defeat, in relating the cause of it justly lays the blame on some individual whose cowardly behavr betray'd the whole to ruin; how little does the World consider the Circumstances, and how apt are mankind to level their vindictive Censures against the unfortunate Chief, who perhaps merited least of the blame. Does it not appear then that the appointing of Officers is a thing of the utmost consequence; a thing that shoud require the greatest circumspection—Ought it to be left to blind chance? Or what is still worse, to partiality? Shoud it not be left to a Man whose life and what is still dearer, whose honour depends upon their good behaviour.

There are necessary Officer's yet wanting, which no Provison has been made for—A small Military Chest is so absolutely necessary, that it is impossible to do without nor no Man can conduct an affair of this kind that has it not. These things I shoud expect, if the appointment fell upon me.

But besides all these, I had other Reasons whh withd me fr. offering my Services—I believe our Circumstances are brought to that unhappy Dilemma that no Man can gain Honour by conductg our Forces at this time; but will rather loose in his reputation if he attempts it; for I am very confidt the progress of military movements must be slow for want of conveniences to transport our Provisions ammunition and Stores over the Mountains, occasion'd in a great measure by the late ill treatmt of the Waggoner's & Horse driver's, who have recd little compensatn for their Labr and nothg for their lost Horss. & Wagns, wch will be an infallible mean's of preventg all from assistg that are not compelled; so that I am fully sensible, whoever undertakes this command will meet with such insurmountable obstacles that he will be soon viewed in the light of an idle indolent body, have his conduct criticised, and meet perhaps with approbious abuse, when it may be much out of his power to avoid delays as it would be to comd the ragg Seas in a Storm. Viewing these things in the light I do, has no small influence upon me, as I am very apprehensive I shou'd loose what at present constitutes the chief part of my happiness, i. e. the esteem and notice the Country has been pleasd to honour me with.

It is possible you may infer from what I have said that my intention's is to decline at all events, but my meaning is not so: I am determin'd not to offer, because to sollicit the Command, and at the same time to make my proposals, woud be a little incongruous, and carrying with it a face of self sufficiency: But if the command shoud be offerd, the case is then alter'd, as I shd be at liberty to make such objection's as Reason and my small experience had pointed out: I hope you'll make my Compts to all inquiring Fds—I am Dr Warner Yr most Affe Friend and Obt Servt

G. W———n

Mount Vernon Thursday 14th Augt 1755

Dinwiddie, anticipating Washington's acceptance, issued the commission on August 14.[45]

Rob't Dinwiddie, Esq'r, His Majesty's L't G'r, &c., to George Washington, Esq'r:

By Virtue of H. M'y's Royal Com'o. and instruct's appoint'g me L't G'r and Com'd'r-in-Chief in and over y's his Colony and Dom'n of Virg'a, with full

Power and Authority to appoint all Officers, both Civil and Military, within the same, I, repos'g especial Trust in Y'r Loyalty, Courage and good Conduct, do by these Presents appoint You COLONEL of the Virg'a Regim't and Com'd'r-in-Chief of all the Forces now rais'd and to be rais'd for the Defence of y's H. M'y's Colony, and for repell'g the unjust and hostile Invasions of the Fr. and their Ind'n Allies. And You are hereby charg'd with full Power and Authority to act defensively of Offensively, as You shall think for the good and Wellfare of the Service. And I Do hereby strictly charge and require all Officers and Soldiers under Y'r Com'd to be obedient to Y'r Orders and diligent in the Exercise of Y'r several Duties. And I do also strongly enjoin and require You to be Careful in execut'g the great Trust and Confidence y't is repos'd in Y'r Managem't by seeing y't strict Discipline and Order is carefully observ'd in the Army, and y't the Soldiers are duly exercis'd and provided with all convenient Necessaries. Ad You are to regulate Y'r Conduct in every Respect by the Rules and Discipline of War (as herewith given You) and punctually to observe and follow such orders and Direct's from Time to Time as You shall receive from me.

Given under my Hand, &c., Aug'st 14th, 1775. Pay to comence 1st Sep'r.

On August 17, 1755, Reverend Samuel Davies delivered a sermon to Captain Overton's newly formed independent company in Hanover County encouraging the soldiers to develop the "spark" needed to defend the country from the invading French and Indians. In this sermon, "Religion and Patriotism the Constituents of a Good Soldier," Preacher Davies expressed his belief that in the Braddock debacle, Providence had saved Colonel Washington for some future vital service to the country.[46]

As a remarkable instance of this, I may point out to the public that heroic youth Col. Washington, whom I cannot but hope Providence has hitherto preserved in so signal a manner, for some important service to his country.

This was the first public proclamation that Providence was shielding George Washington from harm.[47] Washington, having sufficiently recovered from his illness, decided to accept the command and traveled to Williamsburg as had been requested. He arrived there on August 27.

On September 6, Lieutenant Governor Dinwiddie wrote to the Lords of Trade. In this letter, he expressed his dissatisfaction with Colonel Dunbar's retreat to Philadelphia. He described how he was endeavoring to raise forces for the newly reconstituted Virginia regiment and that he had placed Colonel Washington in command. However, he felt that these forces would be insufficient to protect the frontier settlers from the French and Indian incursions, and requested new orders from the Crown.[48]

Sept'r 6th, 1755.

R't Hon.:

I send Y'r L'd's twenty-two Acts of Assembly y't were pass'd the Sessions ending in June last, as also the Journals of the Council and y't of the Ho. of Burgesses. Money is so extremely scarce in y's Dom'n y't in Order to protect our Frontiers an Act is pass'd for a Lottery to raise £6,000 and to allow the Treasurer's Notes to pass as Money for the Amo. of £20,000, w'ch are to be p'd off next June, and the Subjects have the several Taxes secur'd to them for the s'd Payment, w'ch on our pres't Exigencies I hope will meet with Y'r Approbat'n. The unexpected and fatal Defeat of H. M'y's Forces on the Banks of the Monongahela, under the Com'd of G'l Braddock, the Death of y't brave Gen'l and many other brave officers and Men, rais'd a very great Consternat'n in the People of y's Dom'n. After y's great Loss, w'n all our Artillery also fell into the Hands of the Enemy, the Com'd of the Regular Troops devolved on Colo. Dunbar; he march'd them for F't Cumb'l'd, and on the 2d of Aug. he march'd the Remains of the Army for Philad'a for Winter Q'rs. Y's Step of Colo. Dunbar's increas'd the uneasiness of our People, hav'g left at F't Cumb'l'd some Sick and Wounded and about 250 Provincial Troops to defend our Frontiers, the Consequ'ce thereof was a general Dissatisfaction among our Provincial Troops, y't they deserted daily in great

Numb's (say'g they were left by the Regulars as a Prey for the Enemy), y't now there is not 100 Effective Men at the Fort to protect y't Place and our Frontiers. Colo. Dunbar march'd off with him the three Independ't Compa's H. M'y was graciously pleas'd to send here under my Com'd for the Protect' of y's His Dom'n and to assist us to drive the Enemy from H. M'y's Lands on the Ohio. By w't Power Mr. Dunbar order'd these Compa's to march with him, I know not, but it appears he intended to leave us in as much Distress as was in his Power; he also carried four six Pounders and two Mortars, the last of w'ch was greatly necessary for the defence and protect'n of the Fort. The Road to the Ohio being now open'd and the Fr. know'g the Regulars had march'd 200 Miles from the Fort, w't may not they do if they come over the Allegany Mount's and invade our back Co'try? On y's Conduct of Co. Dunbar's, I imediately rais'd six Comp's of Rangers w'ch I sent to the Frontiers to protect our Settlem'ts to the Westw'd, but they are trifling to oppose an Enemy y't had defeated 1,200 Regulars and pick'd Men. I imediately call'd the Assembly, and by Argum'ts on our pres't distress'd forlorn Condit'n, they voted £40,000, w'ch qualified me to augm't our Forces to 1,000 Men, w'ch I have granted Com'o's to raise 16 Compa's and gave the Com'd to Colo. Geo. Washington, and they are now recruit'g their Men. The Proceedings of y's Assembly, with the Acts, are not yet transcrib'd, but shall soon transmit them to You. Y'r L'd's will please consider our Situat'n; the Regular Forces march'd into Winter Q'rs the middle of Sumer; our neighbour'g Colonies of M'yl'd and Pensylva'a as yet have not granted us any Aid; y't all I possibly can do is to order the Forces rais'd here to be on the Defensive to prevent the Incursions of the Enemy and protect our Frontiers till I receive Orders from Home. I am greatly fatigu'd in rais'g the Men and endeavour'g all in my Power to keep the Spirits of our People with proper Resentm't ag'st the Enemy. They did send in some fly'g parties of Fr. And Ind's who have robb'd and murder'd above 40 Families, but I am in Hopes the Rangers and the Regim'ts now rais'g will in a great Measure prevent these Barbarities for the Future. I shall, under the pres't Situat'n do every Th'g in my Power for H. M'y's Service and the Protect'n of y's his Dom'n. I have the Hono'r to subscribe myself,

R't Hon., Y'r L'ds.' most obd't and f. h'ble serv't.

Although the Braddock campaign was a total disaster, Washington's character, endurance, and leadership were proven on the fields of battle. As a result of this experience, he was now a twenty-three-year-old colonel in sole command of the Virginia regiment. He no longer faced the conflict in rank caused by serving alongside the British regulars. He had survived the Braddock debacle without personal injury, and his belief in Providence's protection was reinforced. Even though debilitated from disease, he faced death and slaughter with calm and courage. And remarkably, his fifty-mile ride through the night to retrieve reinforcements had demonstrated his amazing stamina. Washington had grown tremendously, but his personal development had come at a high cost. His mentor, General Braddock (along with over half of the British forces), had died, many of his countrymen had suffered from disease, Mount Vernon had not been maintained, and the French Indians had become more aggressive along the western frontier.

In July 1753, King George had instructed Dinwiddie "to drive them off by force of arms." But two years later, in 1755, the French still maintained possession of the Ohio Country. Now Washington, in an attempt to execute the king's orders, accepted his new assignment. He had fought two major battles and experienced great personal risk, but the French control had only grown and the British settlers were still being attacked. In his new command, Washington would learn that the settlers could not be protected while the French still occupied Fort Duquesne.

BETWEEN TWO FIRES

August 1755–July 1758

"...and they taking us, for the enemy who had retreated approaching in another direction commenced a heavy fire upon the relieving party which drew fire in return in spite of all the exertions of the Officers one of whom & several privates were killed and many wounded before a stop could be put to it. to accomplish which G. W. never was in more imminent danger. by being between two fires, knocking up with his sword the presented pieces..."

– 1786 George Washington – while writing his biography with

David Humphreys

IT WAS LATE AUGUST 1755 WHEN COLONEL GEORGE Washington accepted the command of the Virginia regiment and commenced a defensive campaign to protect the British settlers along Virginia's western domain. The Virginia Assembly had authorized funds for protecting Virginia's frontier and for conducting an expedition to drive the French from the Ohio Country. Fifteen hundred soldiers were authorized, but Washington was only able to recruit and train a thousand. Because the Virginia frontier extended over three hundred miles, the regiment did not have a sufficient number of soldiers to protect the settlers.

In their authorization, the Assembly included funds for the building of forts along the frontier. Unfortunately, the forts proved to be of little value in battling the mobile and covert French-allied Indian warriors. With only fifty men or fewer stationed in each of the remote forts, only minimal protection for the settlers was provided. The intruders entered the territory freely, attacked the settlers, and disappeared back into the wilderness before soldiers, holed up in the forts, could counterattack.

Dinwiddie sought the participation of the colonies of Maryland and Pennsylvania in the campaign, but the neighboring colonies failed to raise the necessary funds and were unable to participate in the campaign. Without their support, Dinwiddie could not launch a campaign against Fort Duquesne.

In February 1756, John Campbell (Fourth Earl of Loudoun) was named governor of Virginia. Then in March he was named commander in chief of the British forces in Virginia and all of the other colonies as well. On July 1, 1756, eleven months after the Virginia Assembly had authorized funds to launch a campaign against Fort Duquesne, Lieutenant Governor Dinwiddie wrote to Lord Loudoun requesting his support for the campaign.[1]

July 1st, 1756

R T Hon:

   I wrote You by P. Ludwell, Esq're, one of the Council of this Dom., who to deliver You an Address from the Council and myself, as also a State of this Colony, to w'ch I beg to refer Y'r L'd'p. Since writ'g the above one Stalniker' an Inhabit't of Augusta county, &c As I wrote You in my last, we were draught'g the Militia to augm't our Provincial Regim't to 1,500 Men. Unluckily, in the Act of Assembly, those draughted were to pay £10 if they did not go. On w'ch in many Counties they defeated the Law by collect'g the £10. This was contrary to my Opin'n, for I argu'd if they did not go, they sh'd be obliged to send a proper Person in y'r Room, but the Assembly differed from me, and made the Penalty as above, w'ch greatly prevented the rais'g the No. expected; however, I hope w'n collected in a body they will be near 1,200 Men. I must observe to Y'r L'd'p that the two Proprietary Gov'ts of M'yl'd and Pensylvania have been very tardy, in y'r Supplies for the Good of the Expedit'n in gen'l, and seem contented in build'g a few Stockado Forts for protection of y'r Frontiers, w'ch, if cont'd, we shall be forever expos'd to the Invas's, Murders, and Roberies of the Enemy. I have always been of Opin'n and continue in the same, that while we continue on the Defensive, as the Frontiers of the So'ern Colonies are so very extensive, the Enemy will always harrass us in such places w'n we are not provided to receive 'em, and, therefore, I have often propos'd to the neighbour'g Colonies, each to raise a proper quota of Men and Provis's to march to the Ohio and attack F't Du Quesne. If we did not succeed in taking the F't it would be a material Diversion in prevent'g the Fr. And Ind's from proceed'g to Niagara, &c., to join their other Forces, but I have not been able to perswade 'em to go into this Expedit'n, and, indeed, at present, having no Artillery or Ingineers we are in a bad Situation for such Design, but if it s'hd appear eligible to Y'r L'ds'p, the supply'g a small Train of Artillery, with a proper Off'r to to conduct the Expedit'n and some Engineers, w'th Y'r L'd'p's order to the neighbour'g Colonies to raise Y'r Quota of Men, and if tho't proper, a few of the Regul's, w'd put Spirit into the Provincials, and they may be sent by Sea to Alexandria, w'ch is but a'bt 160 miles from F't Cumb'l'd. This I h'bly submit to Y'r superior Knowledge and Judgem't....

On August 4, 1756, Washington wrote to Dinwiddie and expressed his support for Dinwiddie's proposal to Lord Loudoun.[2]

I observe your Honors proposal to Lord Loudon, of carrying on an Expedition against the Ohio. I have always thought it the best and only method to put a stop to the incursions of the Enemy; as they would then be obliged to stay at home, to defend their own possessions.

Six months later, on January 10, 1757, Loudoun had not yet responded to Dinwiddie's request for support from His Majesty. Colonel George Washington took the bold step of writing to Lord Loudoun himself in yet another attempt to get support for the campaign. In his letter he described in extensive detail the obstacles that the Virginia regiment faced in the three-year defensive battle against the Indians and French along their three- hundred-mile frontier. Some of the primary difficulties that he included were inconsistent military law, lack of care for the wounded, shortage of clothing, enlistment and retention problems with the militia, and the severe scarcity of tools and equipment. In his letter, Washington encouraged Lord Loudoun to provide his experience and leadership to resolve the many challenges that they were experiencing.[3]

To John Campbell, Earl of Loudoun

To the Right Honourable The Earl of Loudoun, General, and Commander in Chief of all His Majesty's Forces in North America. and Governor, and Commander in Chief of His Majesty's most Ancient Colony and Dominion of Virginia.

My Lord   Fort Cumberland [Md.] January 10th 1757

The following Sheets contain a Concise, Candid, and Submissive Account of Affairs on this Quarter: particularly of the Grievances which the Virginia Regiment has struggled against for almost three Years. Nothing My Lord, but the most ardent desire of having Your Lordship made thoroughly acquainted with our unhappy Situation; and the pleasing reflections that arise in the hope of seeing an Amendment accomplish'd by that means, coud excuse the boldness of appearing in this manner.

I have my Lord, studied the Nature of this Service with great Care and Attention: have been engaged in it as a principal Actor from the beginning of these Disturbances; and have Noted (as they happened) the most remarkable Occurrences: by which means I am become intimately acquainted with the melancholy Circumstances that retard our Endeavours.

The Funds of Money which have been Granted by this Colony to carry on the War are very considerable: and to reflect to what little purpose these Sums are expended is matter of great concern: and will seem Surprizing to such who are unacquainted with the Causes: and the Confusion in which all our Affairs have hitherto been Conducted; owing to our not pursuing Regular Schemes or Plans of Operation. That I may Convey to Your Lordship the more distinct Idea of the posture of our Affairs, I beg leave to begin with our first Out-setting.

It was not till too late, that we discovered the French were on Ohio: or rather, that we coud be perswaded they came with a design to Invade His Majesty's Dominions—Yea, after I was sent out in November 1753 and brought convincing Testimony even from themselves, it was yet thought a Fiction; and Scheme to promote the Interest of a private Company (by many Gentlemen that had a share in Government.) such lengths did Incredulity and strange Infatuation carry them to.

These unfavourable Surmises caus'd great delays in raiseing the first Men and Money, and gave the active Enemy time to take Possession of the Forks of Ohio (which they now call Duquesne) before we could do it, with Strength sufficient to hold it: which has been the chief Source of all our Past, and Present Misfortunes; for by this Means, the French getting between Us and our Indian Allies, fixed those in their Interest that were wavering and obliged the others to Neutrality, till the unhappy defeat of His late Excellency General Braddock. The Troops, under Colonel Dunbar, going into Quarters so early: and the Inactivity of the neighbouring Colonys, and Incapacity of this, combined to give the French great room to exult, and the Indians little Reason to expect a vigorous offensive War on our Side; which Induced them to join the other that promis'd the greatest Shew of Protection. This is evident, and that all the Ohio Indians did not forsake the English Interest till three Months after the Battle of Monongahela, but waited to see what measures would be concerted to regain our losses and afford them the Protection we had often promis'd.

Virginia it is true, did not lay Idle all this while: on the contrary voted a handsome supply for raiseing Men to carry on the War, or more properly to defend her-

self (as matters now were reduced to this extreamity, for Want of assistance) but even in this, She greatly faild, ariseing I apprehend from the following reasons.

The Men first Levied to repel the Enemy Marched for Ohio the beginning of APRIL—54—without Tents, without Cloaths; In short without any Conveniences to Shelter them (in that remarkably Cold and Wet Season) from the Inclemency of the Weather, and to make the Service tolerably agreeable: in this manner did they continue notwithstanding, till the Battle of the Meadows in July following, never receiving in all that Space one Penny Subsistance, and very often under the greatest Straits and difficultys for want of Provisions.

These things were productive of great murmering and discontent, and renderd the Service so distasteful to the Men, that not being paid immediately upon comeing in, they thought themselves bubbled, and that no reward for their Services ever was intended. This caus'd great Desertion, and the Deserters spreading over the Country recounting their Sufferings and want of Pay (which Rags and Poverty sufficiently testified); fixd in the Populace such horrid Impressions of the hardships they had Encountered, that no Arguments coud remove their prejudices, or Facilitate the Recruiting Service.

This put the Assembly upon enacting a Law to Impress Vagrants; which compleated our Misfortunes: for compelling these abandon'd Miscreants into the Service, who only waited time and opportunity to effect their escape, gave loose to all their vicious Principles, and invented the most unheard of storys to palliate Desertion and gain Compassion; which they not only obtain, but Protection also: so that it was next to impossible to apprehend Deserters while the Civil Officers rather connivd at their Escape, than aided in secureing them.

Thus were Affairs situated when we were orderd in September—55 (as I before observd) to recruit our Forces to Twelve hundred Men. It is easy therefore to conceive the Reason under these Circumstances why the orders were not fulfilled; especially, when the Officers were insufficiently allowd for this Arduous Task: receiving two Pistoles only for each Man (past) and no allowance made for Deserters—also receiving eight pence a day, for maintenance of a Recruit till He joind the Regiment, and oftentimes one Diet woud cost him more—by these means the Officers lost money in proportion as they Recruited Men. however, we continued Recruiting under all these disadvantages till March following.

The Assembly meeting about this time, came to a resolve of augmenting our numbers to Fifteen hundred by Drafting the Militia (who were to continue in the Service till December only) and by a Clause in the Act exempting all who should pay Ten pounds, our numbers were little Increased, one part of the People paying that Sum, and many of the poorer sort absconding.

This was not the only pernicious Clause in the Act, for the Fund ariseing from these Forfeitures were thrown into the Treasury; whereas, had it been deposited in proper hands for Recruiting, the money might have turn'd to very good account: But, a greater Grievance than either of these—was—restraining the Troops from Marching out of the Colony, and ordering them to Build Forts and Garrison them along our Frontiers (of more than three hundred miles extent) how equal they, or any like number is to the Task; and how repugnant a Defensive Scheme is to the true Interest and welfare of the Country, I submit to any Judge to determine, who will consider the following particulars.

First, that evening of Forts at greater Distances than fifteen and eighteen Miles, or a Days March asunder, and Garrisoning them with less than eighty or an hundred Men, is not answering the Intention; because, if they are at greater Distances, it is inconvenient for the Soldiers to Scout between, and gives the Enemy full Scope to make their Incursions without being discovered, till they have Struck the Inhabitants and committed a Ravage: and after they are discovered, the time required in Assembling Troops from Forts more distant, prevents a pursuit being made in time, and allows the Enemy to escape without danger in a Country so Mountainous, and full of Swamps and Hollow-ways covered with Woods. Then—to Garrison them with less than eighty or an hundred Men, the number is too small to afford Detachments but what are very liable to be cut off by the Enemy, whose Numbers in this close Country can scarcely be known 'till they are prov'd; (which we do too often to our cost) as Indian Party's are generally intermix'd with some French, and are so dexterous at Sculking, that their Spies laying about these small Forts for some days make certain discoverys of the

Strength of the Garrison—and observing a Scouting Party go out, may first cut It off, and then attempt the Fort—Instances of this have lately happen'd.

Secondly, Our Frontiers are of such immense extent, that if the Enemy were to make a formidable attack on one side, before our Troops on the other coud March to oppose them, they might overrun great part of the Country; and it is not unlikely if they had a design upon one part, they would make a feint upon the other.

Thirdly, Building a Chain of Forts and removeing Stores and Provisions to each, must necessarily create very great expence, and

Fourthly, and lastly—this expence is never to end; for we may be assured if we don't endeavour to remove the Cause, we are liable to the same Incursions Seven Years hence as now, and more so; because, the French are allowed to possess the Lands in Peace; and will accumulate Indian Interest and grow strong in their Alliances; while we, by our Defensive Schemes and Pusillanimous Behaviour exhaust our Treasury; reduce our Strength and become the Contempt and Derision of these Savage Nations, who are enriching themselves in the meantime with the plunder, and Spoil of our People.

It will evidently appear from the whole tenor of my Conduct, more especially from reiterated Letters, how often I have recommended different Measures to the Govenour and Assembly. and to convince them, by all the Reasoning I was capable of offering, of the Impossibility of Covering so extensive a Frontier from Indian Incursions, without more Force than Virginia coud maintain, I have endeavourd to demonstrate, that it will require fewer Men to remove the Cause, than prevent the Effects while the Cause Subsists.

This nevertheless, as I before observd, was the Scheme concerted, and the Plan under which we acted for Eight Months past, with these disagreeable Reflections; of doing no Singular Service to our Country—Honour to ourselves—or Reputation to the Regiment—however, under all these disadvantages, I must yet presume to say, that the Regiment has not been Inactive: on the Contrary, has perform'd a vast deal of labour and has been very alert in Defending the People; which will appear by observing that notwithstanding we are more contiguous to the French and their Indian Allies, and more expos'd to their frequent Incursions than any of the Neighbouring Colony's, we have not lost half the Inhabitants which they have done; but, considerably more Soldiers in the Defence of the Inhabitants—For in the course of this Campaign: since March I mean, (as we have had but one constant Campaign, and continued Scene of Action since we first entered the Service) our Troops have been engagd in more than Twenty Skirmishes, and we have had near an hundred Men killed and Wounded— From a small Regiment, dispersd over the Country, building of Forts, and acting upon the Defensive, as this is by Order—this, I conceive will not appear inconsiderable to those who are in the least degree acquainted with the Nature of the Service, and Posture of Affairs—However it may to some of our Chimney Corner Politicions that are thirsting for News, & expecting by every express a circumstantial account of the Siege, and reduction of Fort Duquesne—and to hear, in what manner the Garrison was led away Captive by our small Numbers, which they themselves have restrain'd from making the attempt, were our hopes of Success never so rational.

The next thing I beg leave to mention is our Military Laws, and Regulations.

The first Men rais'd, were, if I rightly remember, under no Law; if any, the Militia, (which is the next of Kin to it:) But under this we remaind a short time, and by Instilling Notion's into the Soldiers (who at that time knew no better) that they were Govern'd by the Articles of War, we felt little Inconveniency, and the next Campaign We were join'd with the Regulars, and made Subject to their Laws.

After the Regulars left us, the Assembly, as I before mentioned, Passed an Act, in September following, to raise twelve hundred Men, and in orer (I suppose) to improve upon the Act of Parliament prepard Military Laws of their own; but such, that no Military Discipline coud be preserv'd while they existed.

This being represented in the most pressing, and repeated remonstrances induced the Assembly in October after, to pass a Bill for one Year only; making Mutiny and Desertion Death, but took no Cognizance of many other crimes equally punishable by Act of Parliament; So that no Officer or Soldier accused of Cowardice; holding Correspondence with the Enemy; Quitting a Post, or sleeping upon it and many other Crimes of pernicious Tendency's coud be legally Tryed:

Neither was there any Provision made for Quartering and Billeting of Soldiers; Impressing of Waggons &ca &ca.

But, that which contributed most to render this Law inconvenient and absurd, and at the same time to demonstrate that the Assembly fully intended to prevent any enterprize out of the Colony; was, a Clause forbidding any Courts Martial to sit out of Virginia: by which Means all proceedings held at Fort Cumberland were illegal, and we oblig'd to remove to Virginia for tryal of Offenders; or Act contrary to Law and lay open to Prosecutions (how then were we to behave upon a March—perhaps fifty, Eighty, or an hundred Miles distant?[)] Then again, the Members of General Courts Martial were as in the Act of Parliament obligated not to disclose the Vote or Opinion of any particular Member (unless called upon in certain Cases) and at the sametime, are expressly required to give their proceedings under hand and Seal for the Governors approbation; by which means, the Sentiments of each Individual manifestly appears: for surely no Man will put his hand and Seal to a Sentence that he voted against; and Passed contrary to his Judgement.

These concurring Circumstances to render the Law ineffectual induced me again to recommend an amendment: and I did it with all the Force and Energy I was master of; but no regard hitherto has been paid to my remonstrances, to what cause owing I know not, unless to short sittings and hurry of Business: No other cause upon Earth, can I conceive, why, the Assembly shoud be against Instituting Rules for the Regulation of their Forces, which long experience in Established Army's have fully evinced the necessity of. but to be short. We are under, were, I shoud have said, for at present we are under no Government at all—a Jumble of Laws that have very little meaning in them, unless it is to conspire in making Command Intricate and precarious; and to render it difficult to support Authority and not offend the Civil Powers; who, tenacious of Liberty, and prone to Censure; condemn all Proceedings that are not strictly Lawful, never considering what Cases may arise to make it necessary and excusable.

Another Grievance which this Act Subjects us to, is, the method prescribed to Pay for Deserters—many of our Deserters are apprehended in Maryland— some in Pennsylvania, and for the sake of a reward are brought to the Regiment;

instead thereof, they receive a Certificate that they are entitled to two hundred weight of Tobacco: This Certificate is to be given into a Court of Claims; they refer it to the Assembly, and there it may lay perhaps two or three Years before it is paid: This causes great dissatisfaction; and the ill disposed rather to Aid— than prevent the Escape of Soldiers.

No Regular Provision is establshed for the maimed and Wounded, which is a discourageing Reflection and feelingly Complained of. The Soldiers very justly observe, that Bravery is often rewarded with a broken Leg, Arm, or an Incurable Wound, and when they are disabled and not fit for Service they are discharg'd, and reduced to the necessity of begging from Door to Door, or perishing thrô Indigence—It is true, no Instance of this kind has yet appeard—on the contrary, the Assembly have dealt generously by such unfortunate Soldiers who have met with this Fate—But then this is Curtesy—in no wise Compulsory. and a Man may suffer in the Interim of their Sittings.

After giving this Short and genuine account of our Military Laws; and then observing, that even these Laws are no longer in Force; I conceive there needs few arguments to prove the difficulty of keeping Soldiers under proper Discipline; (who know they are not legally punishable for the most atrocious Crimes): When this happen's to be the case, as it is our's at present, how is it to be wonderd at if Mutiny, Desertion, and all other irregularitys creep into a Camp or Garrison? much less, if we consider that hard Duty, want of Cloaths, and almost every necessary that renders a Soldiers life comfortable and easy are strong Incentives: and to go yet further, when these in themselves intollerable Grievances, are set to view in the most glareing point of Light by a Person lost to all Sense of Honour and Virtue (and building, I am sorry to say, upon a Proclamation inviting the Deserters from the Virginia Regiment, to List in the Royal American Regiment) has made use of every Artifice to represent the Fatigues and hardships of this Service, and the ease and conveniences of the other, to seduce them from their Duty.

Want of Cloathing, may be esteemed among the Principal Grievances which our Soldiers have laboured under.

In the first Twelve Months of their Service they received no cloathing: but in March—54 [1755]—they were presented each with a suit of thin sleazy Cloth without lining, and without Waistcoats except of sorry Flannel. After that, no others were sent for (and two pence stopages drawn from each Mans Pay, Recruits not excepted) till repeated complaints and remonstrances from me, enforced in June last by a representation of many Gentlemen of the Assembly (who had formed an Association and saw the disagreeable Situation of the Soldiers) induced the Committee, to whom these Addresses were presented, to send for Cloathing &ca: These Necessaries were to have been here by the Middle of October, but no news of them yet, which gives the Soldiers some room to suspect finesse. and it is owing to this: Irregular Pay: and the Causes aforementioned that their late disobedience ought to be ascribed; as I can truely and confidently assert, that no Soldiers were ever under better Command than these were before.

It may possibly be asked by Gentlemen not thoroughly acquainted with the Nature of our Service; why the Officers don't see that their Men's Pay is more properly applied? In answer, I must beg leave to observe, that after the Soldiers have appropriated a part for puchaseing fit & reasonable Necessary's; the remainder is barely sufficient to keep them in Shoes: owing to the great consumpt., and exorbitant price of this Article. (I have known a Soldier go upon Command with a new pair of Shoes, which perhaps, have cost him from 7/6 to 10/ and return back without any; so much do they wear in wadeing Creeks, Fording Rivers: climbing Mountains cover'd wt. Rocks &ca.

As great a Grievance as any I have mentioned is yet unnoticed, i.e. the Militia under their present Regulation. A representation of this matter comes better, and more properly from others: Yet, my Zeal for the Service, and my Interest in the Honour and Welfare of the Country obliges me, to speak slightly of somethings, which have filled me with concern.

The difficulties and delays in raising the Militia in time of danger is so preju-dicial, that the Enemy has every opportunity to Plunder, Kill, Scalp, and Escape before they appear: The want of Order, regularity, and Obedience prevent any good effects their assistance and Force might have: For every petty Person must assume Command, direct and advise, otherwise he takes huff. thinks his wisdom and merit affronted, and so Marches off in high Indignation, and great contempt of every Social Law.

The expence of supporting them is, make the best of it, burthensome: but where (Instances are, of) a Captain, Lieutenant, and Ensign; with two or three Sergeants and Six or eight Men going upon Duty at a time, the disproportion of Officers and Men is so remarkable, as to need no proof of the Injustice done the Country.

Their waste of Provisions is very unaccountable, following no method in serving a certain quota to each Man. Speak of an allowance (never so plentiful) and you offer an affront: and they woud sooner suffer, than Condescend to carry Provision on their Backs for conveniency, as other Soldiers do: But heedless and prodigal they regale on the Best, not regarding expence nor the oppression they spread, to Gratify their Humours.

When they come into Service, it is with the utmost difficulty they are prevailed upon, even to take measures for their own Defence: but remain constantly at a Post, using no care or circumspection to guard against Surprizes, and are always exposed to them. In this careless manner was Vass's Fort taken, and Dickenson's found, when the Enemy had got to the Fort Gate, & took the Children from the Walls before they were discovered.

To point out the Causes, that contribute to render the Militia of little use; and to relate all the Grievances which combine to make this Service infinitely hard and disagreeable, woud swell this into a Volume; and require time and a readier Pen than mine. But there are yet a few things which I beg leave to speak of, and the ill judg'd Œconomy that has been exemplified in raising of Men, may be ranked among the first of them.

We are either insensible of danger till it breaks upon our heads, or else, thrô mistaken Notion's of Œconomy evade the expence 'till the blow is Struck, and then run into an extreame of raising Militia: These, after an age is spent in Assembling them: Come up, oppress the Inhabitants; complain of their hardships, and then—return; leaving the Frontiers unguarded as before, although experience convinces Us if reason did not, that the French and Indians watching opportunitys when we are lulled asleep and unprepared to resist them; muster their Force to invade the Country; and by ravaging one part, terrify another, and then retreat as the Militia Assemble: repeating the Stroke as soon as they are dispersed: Sending down small Party's in the Intermedium to discover our Motions, procure Intelligence, and sometimes to divert our Troops. such an Invsion we may expect in March, if Measures to prevent it, are neglected as they have been.

The want of Tools occasions insurmountable difficulty's in carrying on our Works, Offensive or Defensive, and Cartridge Paper is an Article not to be had here.

This My Lord, I beg leave to say is at present my Situation; therefore not to be wondered at, if, under all these concomitant Evils I should be sickened in a Service that promises so little of a Soldiers reward.

I have long since been satisfied of the impossibility of continueing in this Service without loss of Honour: Nay, was fully convinced of it, before I accepted the Command the Second time (seeing the gloom that sat hovering over us) and did, for this Reason, reject the offer till I was ashamed to deny: not careing to expose my Character to Publick Censure: But the Sollicitations of the Country overcame my objections; and another Reason of late has continued me in it, till now; and that is, the Dawn of hope that arose in my Breast when I heard your Lordship was distinguished by His Majesty, with the Important Command of His Armys in America; and Appointed to the Government of His Dominion of Virginia—hence it was I drew my hopes, and fondly pronounced your Lordship our Patron.

Altho̊ I have not the Honour to be known to Your Lordship: Yet, Your Lordship's Name was familiar to my Ear, on account of the Important Services performed to His Majesty in other parts of the World—don't think My Lord I am going to flatter. I have exalted Sentiments of Your Lordships Character, and revere Your Rank; yet, mean not this, (coud I believe it acceptable). my nature is honest, and Free from Guile.

We have my Lord, ever since our Defence at the Meadows, and behaviour under His Excellency General Braddrock been tantalized; nay, bid expect most sanguinely, a better Establishment; and have waited in tedious expectation of seeing this accomplished. The Assembly it is true, have, I believe, done every thing in their Power to bring this about, first, by Sollicitting His Honour the Lieutenant Governor to Address His Majesty: and next, addressing His Majesty themselves in favour of their Regiment, what Success these Addresses have met with I am yet a stranger to.

In regard to myself, I must beg leave to say, Had His Excellency General Braddock survived his unfortunate Defeat, I should have met with preferment equal to my Wishes: I had His Promise to that purpose, and I believe that Gentleman was too sincere and generous to make unmeaning offers, where none were ask'd. General Shirley was not unkind in His Promises—but—He is gone to England.

I don't know My Lord, in what light this plain and disinterested relation of our Circumstances may be received by Your Lordship, but with the utmost candour and Submission it is offer'd. It contains no aggravated Circumstances, nor unjust Reflections.

Virginia is a Country young in War. Untill the breaking out of these Disturbances has Lived in the most profound, and Tranquil Peace; never studying War or Warfare. It is not therefore to be imagined She can fall into proper Measures at once. All that can be expected at Her Hands She cheerfully gives. The Sinews of War. And we only want a Person of your Lordship's Ability and Experience to direct the Application. It is for this Reason, I have presumed to hint these Grievances: That if any thing in them appear worthy of Redress, & Your Lordship will condescend to point out the way; it may be Obtained.

When I look over the Preceeding Pages and find, how far I have exceeded my first Intention, I blush with shame to think of my Freedom. Nothing My Lord, but an Affectionate Zeal to Serve my Country, Steady Attachment to Her Interest, The Honour of Her Arms, and crying Grievances which She is labourg under can plead an Excuse, Untill I am happy enough to have an opportunity of Testifying, with what Profound Respect I have the Honour to be, My Lord, Your Lordship's Most Obedient, and Most Humble Servant,

Go: Washington

On January 28, he wrote a letter to Captain James Cuninghame, Lord Loudoun's aide-de-camp. In this letter, Washington requested that Cuninghame deliver his letter to His Lordship. He also explained to Cuninghame that, five years after the king's orders, they still had not captured Fort Duquesne and driven the French out of the Ohio Country.[4]

Sir   *Fort Loudoun January 28th 1757*

When the inclos'd for His Excellency the Earl of Loudoun was wrote; I (as well as most others) was in hourly Expectation of His Lordships arrival in Virginia. Since then it is reported, and with an Air of great probability, That, Important affairs to the Northward will deprive this Colony of that much desird Honour and Happiness this Season which you may imagine Sir, is cause also for great regret and disappointment to the wellwishers of it.

I wish the inclosd account had more Order, regularity, and Eligance to recommend it. It contains incontestable Facts—plain and perspicuous to All who are in the least degree acquainted with our Affairs; and were thrown together rather as hints that might set His Lordship upon a stricter enquiry than as a full and distinct Account of Our Circumstances—It is in this light I offer it Sir, first to your perusal; after which, if you find any thing contain worth His Lordship's Notice, be pleasd to present it.

That an Offensive Scheme of Action is necessary if it can be Executed, is quite Obvious. Our All in a manner depends upon it. The French grow more and more Formidable by their Alliances, while Our Friendly Indians are deserting our Interest. Our Treasury is exhausting, and Our Country Depopulating—some of the Inhabitants fly intirely of, while others Assemble in small Forts destitute (almost) of the necessary's of Life; to see what Measures will be concerted to relieve their Distresses.

This Sir, I assure you, is at present the Situation of Affairs in Virginia.

I am firmly perswaded that 3,000 Men under good regulation (and surely the 3 Middle Colonies coud easily raize, and support that Number) might Fortifie all the Passes between this and Ohio: Take possession of that River: cut of the Communication between Fort Duquisn and the Lakes, and with a middling

Train of Artillery (with proper Officers & Enjineers) make themselves Masters of that Fortress, which is now become the Terror of these Colonies.

I have presum'd to mention this Sir, from the knowledge I have of the Country, and Enemy; and hope I may, with out vanity say, that there are few Persons who have had better oppertunity's to become acquainted with both, than I have.

I shoud esteem it a particular happiness to be of your Acquaintance—and to have an oppertunity of testifying how much I am Sir Yr Most Obedt Hble Servt

Go: Washington

In response to the requests of Dinwiddie and Washington, Lord Loudoun agreed to meet with them during the conference of governors of the southern colonies in Philadelphia on March 17, 1757. At the conference, Loudoun informed them that he had orders from His Majesty to wage an attack on Quebec and that the campaign would require all the artillery in his possession. Therefore he would not, during the summer of 1757, be able to supply the artillery needed for an advance on Fort Duquesne. Lord Loudoun, as governor of Virginia, failed again to support Lieutenant Governor Dinwiddie's request for military resources to protect the Virginia settlers.

During their meeting, Lord Loudoun announced to the southern governors that he had replaced Lieutenant Governor Horatio Sharpe as the commander of all the forces in the southern provinces with Colonel John Stanwix. With this change in command, Colonel John Stanwix became Colonel George Washington's commanding officer. Thus, Washington's hope of remaining in the colonial command structure was not to be. Instead, once again Washington was under the command of a British officer.[5]

On May 2, Lieutenant Governor Dinwiddie sent a letter to Lord Loudoun and again prodded His Lordship for artillery to wage an attack on Fort Duquesne.[6]

We have lately had near 400 Indians from the Catawbas, Cherokees, Tuscaroras, and some other small Tribes. They are gone to fort Loudoun, and I've order'd 'em out with some of our Men on scalping Parties and to endeavour to observe the Mot'ns of the Enemy, and to obtain Intelligence, it possible, of the No's at Fort Duquesne. If we had an Engineer, with field P's's, with the Provincials from Pennsylvania, Maryland and this Dom'n, we probably might be able to push a stroke on the Ohio; but on the Consultat'ns agreed on at Philad`a I shall strictly adhere to 'em by acting on the Defencive for protect'g our Front's....

On September 17, 1757, Indians attacked the settlements around Stony Creek (about twenty miles southwest of Colonel Washington's headquarters at Fort Loudoun). Approximately thirty settlers were killed.[7] George Washington wrote to Lieutenant Governor Dinwiddie on September 24 and again encouraged an attack on Fort Duquesne to stop the Indian raids. Washington expressed his concern that the offensive needed to be waged by the spring of 1758 or the territory would be lost to the French and Indians.[8]

[Fort Loudoun, 24 September 1757]

To Governor Dinwiddie
Honble Sir
  Enclosed is a copy of a letter which I received from Captn McKenzie.
  Since my last, the different parties I detached in quest of the Enemy (who committed the late depradations in this neighbourhood) are returned; after having prosecuted the most probable measure, and exerted their utmost efforts in vain, in endeavouring to come up with, and prevent the enemys escape: nor is it in any degree surprizing: for, when the vast extent of country; the scattered and distant manner in which the Inhabitants are settled; the nature of the ground, and disposition of the Enemy we have to cope with, are collectively considered: it is next to impossibility that any of our parties should ever see the enemy, except when they possess such advantages as render their victory certain. The inhabitants of this valuable and very fertile valley, are terrified beyond expression. Some have

abandoned their plantations; and many are packing up their most valuable effects, in order to follow them. Another irruption into the heart of this Settlement will, I am afraid, be of fatal consequence to it. I was always perswaded, and almost every day affords new matter for confirming me in the opinion, that the enemy can, with the utmost facility, render abortive every plan which can be concerted upon our present system of Defence; and that the only method of effectually defending such a vast extent of mountains covered with thick woods, as our frontiers, against such an enemy; is by carrying the war into their country. And I think I may, without assuming uncommon penetration, venture to affirm, that, unless an Expedition is carried on against the Ohio next spring; this country will not be another year in our possession.

On October 8, Washington wrote to his commanding officer, Colonel John Stanwix, informing him of the Indian attack of September 17 and of another attack on October 1. As he had advised Dinwiddie in September, Washington expressed his belief that the only way to stop the Indian attacks along the frontier was to go on the offensive and capture Fort Duquesne.[9]

We have had several visitations from the Enemy, and much mischief done, since my last to you: about the 17th ultimo there were upwards of 20 persons killed only 12 miles from this Garrison: and notwithstanding I sent a strong Detachment from hence to pursue them; and ordered the passes of the mountains to be way-laid, by commands from other places; yet we were not able to meet with these Savages.

On friday sennight a body of near, or quite an hundred, fell upon the inhabitants along the great road, between this and Pennsylvania, got 15 more. The mischief would have been much greater, had not an Officer and 20 men of the Regiment, who were then out, fallen in with, and engaged the enemy: finding, however, that his party was over-powered, and like to be surrounded, he retreated to a stockade, not far distant; in which they were besieged for 3 hours: but the firing communicated an alarm from one habitation to another, by which means most of the families were timely apprized of their danger, and happily got safe off. Our party killed one Indian (whose scalp they obtained) and wounded several others.

I exert every means in my power to protect a much distressed country: But it is a task too arduous! To think of defending a frontier as ours is, of more than 350 miles extent, with only 7,00 men, is vain and idle: especially when that frontier lies more contiguous to the enemy than any other.

I am, and have for a long time been, fully convinced, that if we continue to pursue a defensive plan, that the country must be inevitably lost. You will be kind enough, Sir, to excuse the freedom with which I deliver my sentiments; and believe me to be (for I really am) with unfeigned truth and regard, Your most obedt Hble Servant,

G:W.

N.B. These constant alarms, and perpetual movements of the Soldiers of this Garrison, have almost put a total stop to the progress of the public works at this place.

Lieutenant Governor Dinwiddie responded to Washington on October 19, agreeing that an offensive campaign was necessary.[10]

I am Sorry the Enemy Continues their horrid devastations & I wish the Parties you Send out could come up with them to give them a brush, I am Surpriz'd the people shd move Off, Surely the forces with you, those of MaryLand & the regulars under Collo. Stanwix's immediate directions I think Should be Sufficient to protect the frontiers of both Collonies, tho. I am convinc'd the Secret Method the Enemy comes to Attack us, is of great disadvantage, & very difficult to ferret them out of their Lurking places, I always have been of Opinion that unless an Offensive Scheme, is undertaken we Shall always be Expos'd to their villanous Encroachments,...

On October 25, Washington wrote to John Robinson and expressed his frustration with the defensive campaign and suggested that a letter to

Stanwix might help in their effort to make Lord Loudoun aware of their need to wage a campaign against Fort Duquesne.[11]

John Robinson responded to Washington's suggestion on November 3 and informed Washington that Loudoun would not deviate from the campaign for Quebec. He therefore could not provide assistance for a campaign against Fort Duquesne.[12]

> …*I had Occasion to wait on the Govr soon after I received your Letter, when I asked his Honor if he had not received a Letter from You, he told me he had, and asked the same Question of me to which I answered in the Affirmative, and informed him of the Contents, his answer was that he was always of Opinion that an attempt ought to have [been] made last Summer to take Fort Du Quesne, and annoy the Enemy in their Settlements, and that he had pressed Lord Loudon two or three times on the Subject, but his Lordship told him that he had received a Plan of Operations from home and that he would not deviate from it;…*

On November 9, George Washington again succumbed to malaria, left his command, and returned to Mount Vernon to seek treatment. Captain Robert Stewart, now in charge of the regiment, wrote to Colonel Stanwix about Washington's condition.[13]

> *Sir*   *Fort Loudoun November 24th 1757*
>
> *For near Four Months past Colo. Washington has Labour'd under a Bloudy Flux which till of late he did not conceive could be productive of those bad consequences it now too probably will terminate in, at least he would not be prevail'd upon in any Degree to abate the exertion of that steady Zeal for the Interest of the Service he in so emenent a manner has always been remarkable for, however about two weeks ago his Disorder greatly encreas'd and at same time was Seiz'd with Stitches & violent Plueretick Pains under that Complication of Disorders his Strength & viguour diminish'd so fast that in a few days he was hardly able to Walk and was (by the Docr) at length prevail'd upon to leave this place as change of air & quietness (which he could not possibly enjoy here) was the best*

chance that remain'd for his Recovery he is now retir'd to his Seat on Potomack River (about 90 Miles from hence[)] his Physicians give him no room to hope for his speedy Recovery. I heard from him yesterday he expresses much concern for his omission of not giving you previous Notice of the necessity he was under of leaving this place and as he's not in condition to write himself desires me to inform you of the reasons of it which I have now the honr to do & begs leave to subscribe myself Very respectfully Sir &ca

Robert Stewart

The new year brought many significant changes in British leadership and command. William Pitt, secretary of state for the Southern Department, issued a dispatch on December 30, 1757, announcing that Lord Loudoun, who had failed in his northern campaigns, was replaced by Major General James Abercromby. Washington's commander, Colonel Stanwix, was promoted to brigadier general and assigned to Abercromby's northern campaign, leaving Washington anxiously awaiting the assignment of yet another commander.

Also in the new year, the Crown initiated a campaign against Fort Duquesne, and Pitt announced that Adjutant General John Forbes was assigned to lead it. Pitt also ordered Virginia's General Assembly to raise additional forces.[14] Accordingly, the Assembly provided funding to man a corps of fifteen hundred troops for the Second Virginia Regiment with Colonel William Byrd in command.

Lieutenant Governor Dinwiddie, who had been suffering under the strain of his office, requested leave and departed for England on January 12. John Blair, president of the Virginia Council, temporarily replaced Dinwiddie as the colony's lieutenant governor. The king appointed Francis Fauquier as the new Virginia lieutenant governor. He finally arrived in early June, six months after his appointment.

In February, Lord Loudoun, unaware that Pitt had ordered his recall on December 30, 1757 (because the dispatch from England did not arrive in New York until March 4, 1758),[15] initiated plans for a summer 1758 offensive against Fort Duquesne.[16] To bolster this new campaign, he sent his volunteer aide, Colonel William Byrd, to South Carolina to enlist the Cherokee. Byrd successfully recruited over five hundred Cherokee.

On March 4, Washington wrote to Colonel Stanwix to inform his commanding officer that he would be traveling to Williamsburg to seek treatment again for malaria. He notified Stanwix that he would have to resign from the military if he did not improve.[17] On March 5, he set out from Mount Vernon to consult with Dr. John Amson and, under his care, recovered within the month.

On April 10, 1758, Colonel Washington wrote to Colonel Stanwix to congratulate him on his promotion to brigadier general and his assignment to Abercromby's command. In the letter, he also requested that he be recommended to Brigadier General Forbes for the campaign against Fort Duquesne. In addition, Washington encouraged an early campaign for fear the Cherokee would not long remain with them.[18]

To Brigadier-General Stanwix

Dear Sir,   *Ft L[oudoun] April 10th 1758.*

Pe[r]mit me, at the same time I congratulate you (which I most sincerely do) upon the promotion you have met with, and justly merited; to express my Concern at the prospect of parting with you. I can truly say, it is a matter of no small regret to me! and that I shou'd have thought myself happy in serving this campaign under your immediate command. But every thing I hope, is ordered for the best; and it is our duty to submit to the will of our Superior. I must nevertheless beg, that you will add one more kindness to the many I have experienced, and that is, to mention me in favorable terms to General Forbes (if you are acquainted with that Gentleman) not as a person who would depend upon him for further recommendation to military preferment, for I have long conquered all such expectancies (and serve this campaign merely for the purpose of affording my best endeavours to bring matters to a conclusion) but as a person who would gladly be distinguished in some measure from the common run of provincial Officers; as I understand there will be a motley herd of us.

Nothing can contribute more to His Majesty's Interest in this Quarter, than an early campaign, or a speedy junction of the Troops to be employed in this Service. Without this, I fear the Indians with difficulty will be restrained from returning to their nation before we assemble; and in that event, no words can tell how much they will be missed. It is an affair of great importance, and ought to claim the closest attention of the Commanding Officer; for, on the assistance of these people, does the security of our march very much depend.

In mid-April 1758, thirty-two months after the Virginia Assembly authorized funds for an expedition to drive the French out of the Ohio Country, Brigadier General Forbes arrived in Philadelphia and began planning for the expedition to take control of the forks of the Ohio. On April 20, Lieutenant Colonel John St. Clair, deputy quartermaster general for the Forbes campaign, asked Colonel Washington to join the expedition.[19]

Dear Sir   Philadelphia April 20th 1758
I received your agreeable Letter of the 12th by return of the Express I sent to Winchester, it was very acceptable News to General Forbes, Major Halkett and my self to hear you was so well as to be able to make the Campaign with us.—

On April 27, Washington responded to St. Clair's inquiry and agreed to join the campaign.[20]

It gave me real pleasure to hear from you, that my Company this Campaigne was desird by the General, Sir John, and Major Halkett. I shall think my self quite happy, if I should continue to stand well in your good Opinions to the end of the Campaigne; for I have long since given over expecting any other reward for my endeavours in the Service, than what arises from a Consciousness of doing my duty. and from the good liking of my Friends thereupon. I am Sir with very great regard Yr most Obedt & Most Hble Servt

Go: Washington

Major General Abercromby, commander in chief of the British forces in America, informed Forbes that he was to report directly to William Pitt, secretary of state for the Southern Department. Forbes therefore wrote to Pitt on May 1 informing him of his plans to acquire the forces and supplies to capture Fort Duquesne.[21]

Nineteen days later, Forbes informed Pitt that his plans were failing because of the lack of support from the colonies and the defection of the Cherokee Indians.[22]

Philadelphia. May 19th.. 1758.

Sir

I did myself the Honour of writing to you the first of this Month giving you a state of the Military affairs in the Southern Provinces at that time. There has little occurred since only I find that this Province begins to complain that the £100,000 voted for the Service of the Year is mostly expended already, owing to one half of that same being appropriated to clear the Arrears due to their Troops and other demands by which in reality they have only given £50,000 for the Service of this Year.

The striking of their Paper Money has taken up so much time that they had not got £10,000 five days ago. So you see Sir those tardy Proceeding will greatly distress our active operations; however I am still in hopes of getting about 1000 of their Men together (including those that they had on foot) by the 1st of June; But when the rest will be got I can scarce form any Judgement.

The Maryland Assembly has as yet come to no determination, and are in the same situation that I had the honour to acquaint you off, but from some quickening letters that I have lately wrote to that Province I flatter myself they will at least keep the 300 Men now on their pay for this Season and more I scarcely can expect.

The Virginians are going on slowly in compleating their Quota to the 2000 Men that they have agreed to raise, and I shall be well pleased if I get a few more than half their Number by the 1st of June. Colonel Montgomery's Battalion is not yet come from Carolina, altho´ by the last Account I have reason to believe they may be embarking there by this time.

I have therefore marched the three additional Companies of that Battalion, and the 4 Companys of Colo. Stanwix's Battalion into the Back Country, to protect the frontiers until Colo. Montgomery's Battalion arrive, and the new Levies come in.

I am sorry to acquaint you that the Cherokee Indians who have been out upon several scouting party's, and with some Success, begin to weary, and languish after their own homes, complaining that they see no appearance of our Army.

Hitherto I have had the good fortune to amuse them, and keep them from returning, by promises, and presents, but how long I shall be able to continue them with us I cannot say.

But as they are by far the greatest body of Indians that we have ever had to join us, (they being above 700 Men) I thought it my duty to do everything in my power to continue them with us. For which reason I was obliged to purchase the necessarys for equipping of them for Warr, and for presents to them, through this, and all the other Colonies, where such goods and Arms, were to be found. I did imagine that I shou'd have had the Assistance of Sir William Johnston, and of Mr. Atkins in the Manadgement of those Indians, Being informed that those Gentlemen are solely to superintend Indian Affairs, exclusive of any other Person.

But as Sr. William continued at his Settlement 500 Miles North of this, and Mr. Atkins remained at Charlestown 100 Miles to the South, I found myself obliged either to act as I have done or must have seen those Indians return to their own Country disgusted, and probably ready to join the Enemy against us. And even notwithstanding the dilligence I have used in amassing those Goods, there is one Warrior and thirty of his tribe have left us, and another Warriour was actually sett out upon his return, but by sending some Intelligent people after him, have persuaded him and his followers to come back.

So you must easily see, how difficult a task it is, to keep so capricious a sett of people anyways steady.

I have applied to this Province for their Aid and Assistance in furnishing me with Interpreters, Conductors, and such a proportion of presents for the Indians, as they should judge wou'd fall to their Share, considering that So. Carolina and Virginia had both contributed largely, but the Governor has been told by the provinciall Commissioners, that they had no Money, and consequently could allow nothing for that so necessary Service. So that I foresee the whole Expence of the Indians will (in spite of what I can do) fall upon the Crown. I should therefore be extremly Happy to find what I have hitherto done approved of by His majesty with Orders how I am to proceed and conduct myself for the future.

As the Artillery, Arms, Tents &ca. destined for the Service in the Southern Provinces are not yet arrived, nor any Accounts of them, I have been obliged to scrape together some Guns of different Calibres from different places, with all the Ammunition—and three Royal Howbitzers that I have got cast here, in order to form a train, which, with the Assistance of an Officer and nine Men of our own train, that General Abercromby has been so good as to send me, and what I can pick out from among the Provincialls, I hope in some Measure to be able to supply the Disappointment of the Store Ship, and Artillery Men. Having bought and borrowed a good many Firelocks, and provided 300 Tents, which in warm weather must serve them all, as every Man has a Blankett. I have now on the back Frontiers of this Province three Months Provisions for 6000 Men, and I am just entering into a contract for a sufficient number of Waggons and Pack-horses for the transportation of it from one deposite to another, as soon as the troops can be brought up and pushed forward to prepare those stockaded deposites for the reception of he provisions and stores.

I shall lose no time in getting everything in readiness to move forward, as by that Means I may facilitate General Abercromby's operation, by preventing the West Country Indians from going to join the Canadians upon Lake George.

As I have severall people out for Intelligence I hope in a short time to inform you of the Enemy's Strength, and my Generall plan for annoying the Enemy, and shall by the first opportunity, send you a Draught of the Country, with the march I intend to make.

I am Sr. with the greatest respect & regard

Yr. most obt. & most humle. Servt.

Jo: Forbes.

On June 13, St. Clair commanded Washington to march the First and Second Virginia Regiments to Fort Cumberland in Maryland.[23]

[Conococheague, Md., 13 June 1758]

Orders, for Colonel Washington commanding the Troops of the Colony of Virginia.

As you will receive near 700 arms for the 2d Virginia Regiment from Williamsburg, you are to take into your Store at Winchester the Maryland Arms which were deliverd to the 2d Regiment, these Arms are to be deliverd to Govr Sharpe on his Order.

The same proportion of Tools that the 1st Company of Artificers had, to be deliverd to the 2d Company, with an addition of 12 Pick Axe's and 12 Spades or Shovels. The half of the Sand Bags at Winchester to be sent to Connogochieg, and the other half will serve to carry up to Fort Cumberland the Corn that may be got about Winchester and the South Branch.

Five Companies of the first Virginia Regiment to begin their March for Fort Cumberland the 24th of June, with the 2d Company of Artificers of the 2d Regiment. Colo. Byrd with as many Companies as are ready of his Regiment to March the 26th and the rest of that Regiment to follow with Lieutt Colo. Mercer so soon as they can be got ready.

One Company of the 2d Regiment to be station'd at Job Pearsalls on the South Branch & Edwards's till all the Convoys of Provision's have passd and then to Join[.] Whatever Escorts are requird by Mr Commissary Walker are to be furnished to him; he is to lay in Provisions for 1800 Men for Six Weeks at Fort Cumberland from the day of their arrival, and victual them on their March. The officers are only to draw single Ration's of Provisions for themselves as the Genl has no more.

Captn Stewarts Troop of Light Horse are to March up to Fort Cumberland. 30 Barrels of Powder and 100 Boxes of Shott to be carried from Fort Loudoun with 8 Whip Saws to Fort Cumberland. Given under my Hand at Conegocheague this 13th day of June 1758.

John St clair.

Soon thereafter Lieutenant Governor Fauquier arrived in Williamsburg, and Washington wrote him on June 17 congratulating him on his new assignment and requesting additional supplies for the regiments.[24]

[Fort Loudoun, 17 June 1758]

To the Honble Francis Fauquir Govr of Virga
Honble Sir

Although but a poor hand at Complimenting, but permit me, nevertheless to offer your Honr my congratulations on your appointment; and safe arrival to a Government which his Majesty has been graciously pleasd to entrust to your Administration and to assure you, that ⟨I most⟩ sincerely wish your Administration may be attended with pleasure to yourself and ⟨benefit⟩ to the People Governed.

I flatter'd myself with the pleasure of seeing your Honour in Williamsburg, when I was down, but the business that carried me there was of too Urgent a Nature to admit of delay when I had once got it accomplishd. Mr President Blair has, no doubt, informd you of that business—of the State of the Troops here, and situation of other Affairs in this Quarter; I will not, therefore, trouble your Honr with a repetition of them; but Inclose you a Copy of the last Orders which I am preparing to execute with the greatest exactness. Sir John St Clair set out from hence for Connegocheague the 11th Instt, to which place I accompanied him by Summon's from Colo. Bouquet. He proceeded on to Carlyle, and I returnd here; where at present I have the Honr of Command.

I shall transmit your Honour, so soon as I leave this place (I cant well do it before, as alterations are continually happening while the Troops remain here) an exact return of our Stores, agreable to the Presidents Orders. Inclosd is a return of the Strength of the first Regiment—I have directed one to be made out & sent of the 2d Also.

When I was down, the President was pleasd ⟨to forward⟩ 5 blank Commissions to compleat my Regiment with Officers; by mistake I got one less, and must therefore beg the favour of your Honour to send me one now; or, that you woud be pleasd to take the trouble yourself, of appointing Mr Jno. Lawson (who is the oldest Ensign, in my Regiment) to be Lieutenant in Lieutt Colo. Stephen's Company, where there is a Vacancy. This woud have been done before, had not the above mistake happen'd.

I enclose your Honour the Pay Rolls of Captn Rutherfords Company of Rangers, and beg the favour of you to send the money to Mr Thos Rutherford of this place, and he will pay them of in behalf of his Brother, who, being in an ill state of health, got leave to visit Doctr Brown of Maryland, to consult him in the case, and is not yet returnd.

When I was in Williamsburg last, I endeavourd to make Mr President Blair and the Council, sensible of the great want of Cloaths for the first Regiment; and how necessary it is to send to England for a Supply. they declind doing any thing in the case at that time, because the Funds granted by the late act of Assembly were almost exhausted—But I hope it will not escape your Honrs notice if an Assembly shoud be calld. Field equipage of all kinds will also be wanting, and will come better & much cheaper from ⟨there⟩: Colo. Byrd is wanting Cloaths for his Men, if we shoud be late taking the Field; but his redress must be immediate or else useless, as that Regiment by Law will be discharged the first Day of December next—I have the Honr to subscribe myself with gt Respect Yr Hrs most Obedt Hble Servt

Go: Washington

Brigadier General Forbes forwarded a report to Pitt on June 17, 1758, advising that, with the arrival of additional troops and supplies, he was about to set out for the frontier. Forbes noted, however, that the colony of Maryland had failed to provide support and that most of the Cherokee Indians had returned to their homes. He explained to Pitt that he was locating a supply depot every forty miles to facilitate the distribution of provisions along the two-hundred-mile route to Fort Duquesne.[25]

Philadelphia. June 17th.1758.

Sir

Colo. Montgomery's Highland Battalion arrived here the Eight from So. Carolina, and I dispatch'd Capt. Mc Intosh the next day to Admiral Boscawen. The Store Ship with Arms, Tents, Ammunition, & Artillery &ca. arrived here the 11th., which enables me to set out directly for the frontiers, where I have previously assembled all the new Levys of this Province and Virginia. North Carolina I am told has sent 200 Men by sea to Alexandria in Virginia, and have ordered 100 more (which is all they have) to march by the back parts of Virginia in order to join me, at Fort Cumberland, but when they arrive I cannot tell.

The Maryland Assembly broke up without providing any one thing for the present Service, or for the payt. & maintenance of their troops in Fort Cumberland and Fort Frederick, since the eight of October last. By which the Crown becomes bound by the Earl of Loudoun's orders to Mr. Sharpe, for the payment of those Garrisons from October last to the present time, & the necessity of keeping them there, was the preservation of those two Forts from the Enemy. As they are only 300 Men, and have been used to the Woods and the Indian Manner of fighting, I thought it would be a great loss to allow them to disband themselves, upon the province refusing them their by past pay, or continuing them during the Campaign; so have therefore made them an offer to pay them from this time during the rest of the Campaign, and to solicit for their by past pay, either from the Province, or by Virtue of the Earl of Loudoun's promise and orders to Governor Sharpe.

The Cherokee Indians are, (I am afraid) no longer to be kept with us, owing to their natural fickle disposition which is not to be got the better off by fair words nor presents, of both which they have had a great deal, and threats we dare not use, least they change sides, so if the seeing of our Cannon and their Cousins the Highlanders has no Effect upon their stay with us, we shall lose the best part of our Strength as all the Northern Indians mostly our Enemies were kept in awe by the presence of so many Cherokees. As my offensive Operations are clogged with many Difficulties, owing to the great distance & badness of the roads, through an almost impenetrable wood, uninhabited for more than 200 Miles, our back inhabitants being all drove into Carlisle. I am therefore lay'd under the Necessity of having a stockaded Camp, with a Blockhouse & cover for our Provisions, at every forty Miles distance. By which Means, altho' I advance but gradually, yet I shall go more Surely by lessening the Number, and immoderate long train of provision Waggons &c, For I can set out with a fortnight's provisions from my first deposite, in order to make my second, which being finished in a few days, and another fortnight's provision, brought up from the first, to the second, I directly advance to make my third, and so proceed forward, by which I shall have a constant Supply security for my provisions, by moving them forward from Deposite, to Deposite as I advance, and lastly if not thought convenient to settle upon the Ohio, or in that Country, I shall have a sure retreat, leaving a road always practicable to penetrate into those back Countrys, as our Settlements advance towards them, from the side of the Allegany Mountains.

I need not point out to you, Sir, my reasons for these precautions, when you consider that had our last Attempt upon Fort Du Quesne succeeded, we must have retired directly, for want of provisions, and at that time our back Settlements were much nearer advanced to Fort Du Quesne and the Ohio, than they are at present, having properly speaking none to the Westward of Carlisle.

I have used every art and Means to get Intelligence of the strength of the French and Indians (in their Alliance) in those parts, but to little purpose, having various reports, which may indeed be true, as their Savages may be as whimsical as ours, and consequently they may have sometimes numbers and at other times few or none. But by every Account the whole of them in those parts are in a starving Condition, as there has no Provisions been sent to them this Year, either from Canada, nor the Missippi . . . . As the Store Ship was so late of Coming in, I was obliged to purchase a great many Arms in Store, and the new Tents may serve another occasion—I have likewise been obliged to purchase every kind of thing for the Indians who came naked, having had no manner of Assistance from either off the Superintendants of Indian Affairs.

I have now above 400 Men out upon scouting partys, but as they have four or five Hundred Miles in the going and returning, what Intelligence they bring is always of so old a date that there is no trusting to it.

I shall lose no Time in doing every thing in my power for the publick good to the best of my Capacity, and have the honour to be, with the greatest regard and esteem. Sir, Yr. most obedt. & most humble Servt.

Jo: Forbes.

Colonel Henry Bouquet, in command of Forbes's forward detachments, set up camp in Raystown, a small village in Pennsylvania about forty miles northeast of Fort Cumberland. Raystown was in a location that strategically offered the options of traveling to Fort Duquesne via General Braddock's existing route or creating a new road through the Pennsylvania mountains.

To provide for either option, Bouquet wrote to Washington on June 27 and instructed him to build a road from Fort Cumberland, Maryland, to Raystown to provide Forbes's troops access to Braddock's route. In his letter to Washington, Bouquet mentioned that he had written a letter to Colonel Byrd, commander of the Second Virginia Regiment, and instructed him to give protection for Washington's troops while they were building the road.[26]

Sir   *Camp at Reas Town [Pa.], 27th June 1758*

I hope this Letter will find you Safely arrived at Fort CumberLand; as Soon as you are Settled in your Camp, I beg you will begin to cut the Waggon Road to open the Communication between us.

I have ordered Nichols the Pilot to blaze the Road in going, and to Stay wth you.

His Escort may rest one day or two, then come back again.

I have wrote to Col. Byrd to engage the Indians to cover you in your march. I need not recomand you to keep always Strong flanking Parties besides, as you are perfectly acquainted wth the dangers of a Sudden attacq.

We have not discovered yet any trac or appearance of Ennemis, but we expect to be harrassed as Soon as they know our position.

Mr Walker has not engaged I hear to Supply you for more than a fortnight after your arrival, and it will be necessary therefore that we join here as Soon as possible.

You will be pleased to provide for the Safety of the Fort, in leaving a Sufficient Garrison, with Provisions and ammunition. I think the Maryland Troops could be lefft untill we have further orders from the General.

As I allow no other Pay than one Jill of Rum a day here for common Work as Roads & Intrenchments, I beg you will give the Same allowance to your men.

I shall be extremely glad to See you Soon and am wth great Regard Sir Your most obedt & most hble Servant

Henry Bouquet

On July 13, six enemy Indians attacked and killed a Second Regiment soldier and a herdsman and captured another herdsman within a mile of Fort Cumberland. Washington advised Bouquet that he had notified all parties working on the road to Raystown to be on their guard.[27]

Camp at Fort Cumberd abt 9 Thursday Night

Sir   *July 13th 1758*

Abt 4 Oclock this Afternoon—after I had closd my Letter to you—I receivd Information that two Men were killd & a third taken Prisoner on the Road about a Mile from this place. I got the Indians to go, and sent a Command of 50 Men immediately to the spot, where they took the Tract of Six Indians and followd them till near dark when the Indians returnd, as did our Party also.

They discoverd that one of the Men killd was a Soldr of the Second Regiment, and that the other two were herds going to our Grass Guard in the most careless, stragling manner; contrary to repeated, and positive Orders given to prevent small parties stragling from Camp.

The Mischief was done abt 8 this morning—our discovery of it too late to give us a chance to overtake the Enemy—I thought it advisable nevertheless to give you Intelligence that the Enemy are about, and that I expect we shall be pester'd with their Parties all this Moon—haunting our Camps, & watching our Motions.

I have appriz̧d Colo. Mercer, Captn Dagworthy, and all our out parties of this murder, that they may be strictly upon their Guard Marchg—& vigilant in their Camps.

The Inclosd I this Instant receivd from Captn Dagworthy—if it is not in your power to afford him assistance—tis intirely out of mine to do it. I am with great regard Yr Most Obedt Hble Servt

Go: Washington

P.S. Captn Bosomworth &ca are safely arrived here. he & Colo. Byrd join me in their Complimts.

Colonel Bouquet responded to Washington's letter on July 14, thanked him for the notice, and advised him that General Forbes commanded Bouquet to send out scouting parties to harass the enemy more frequently.[28]

Sir   *Camp near Reas Town 14th July 1758*

Having been out to visit the Roads I received this afternoon your two Letters of yesterday.

I am obliged to you for the notice of the Sad Accident happened to your Men. This Warning may prevent more effectually than orders the Carelesnes and disobedience of our People.

The General recommands me to Send frequent Partys to harass the Ennemies at home; I have actually four out, besides the Indians Sent by Col. Byrd: If you Should think proper to Send Some of your brisk young fellows under the Care of a prudent officer, we could keep them busy at home.

As I am entirely unacquainted wth this Country I would look upon it as a favour, if you would let me Know your opinion, upon the Possibility of Sending a Strong Party to the Indian Settlements upon the Ohio; If their houses and familis were in danger, I would think it a great inducemt for them to provide for their immediate defence and leave to the french their own quarrles to fight.

In this July 14 letter, Bouquet also informed Washington that General Forbes wanted Washington's men to reconnoiter and repair Braddock's road to Fort Duquesne because Forbes's strategy was to confuse the enemy by having construction crews on both routes to Fort Duquesne.

The General desires you would Send a Party to reconnoitre Braddocks Road, and begin to clear a few miles, repairing the Bridges &ca.

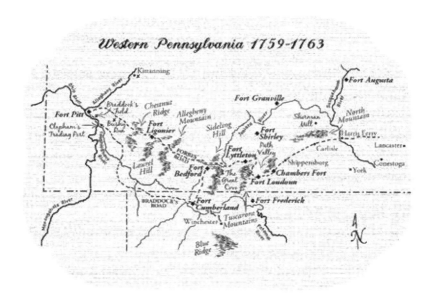

Map of Braddock's Road and Forbes's Road to Fort Duquesne.[29]

Washington was a strong proponent of traveling via Braddock's route to Fort Duquesne while Lieutenant Colonel St. Clair, Forbes's deputy quartermaster general, proposed building a road from Raystown directly across the Allegheny Mountains. St. Clair argued that his option was shorter, crossed fewer rivers, and would provide access to Pennsylvania's frontier. Washington summarized his reasoning in a letter to Francis Halkett, brigade major for the Fort Duquesne expedition. He explained that the construction of a new road over mountains would go slowly and might not be completed before winter weather would end the campaign.[30]

[Fort Cumberland, 2 August 1758]

To Francis Halkett—Brigade Mr
My dear Halkett.

I am just returnd from a Conference held with Colo. Bouquet. I find him fixd—I think I may say fix'd, upon leading you a New way to the Ohio; thro. a Road, every Inch of it to cut, at this advancd Season, when we have scarce time left to tread the beaten Tract; universally confessd to be the best Passage through the Mountains.

If Colo. Bouquet succeeds in this point with the General—all is lost!—All is lost by Heavens!—our Enterprize Ruind; & We stopd at the Laurel Hill for this Winter—not to gather Laurels by the by, desirable in ⟨their effects⟩—The Southern Indians turn against Us—and these Colonies become desolate by such an Acquisition to the Enemy's Strength.

These are the Consequences of a Miscarriage. and a Miscarriage the Consequence of the Attempt—I have drawn my Reason's out at large, and now send them to Colo. Bouquet—He desir'd I woud do so that he might forward them to the General. shou'd this happen you may Judge of their weight.

I am uninfluencd by Prejudice—having no hope or fears but for the General Good—That be assurd of—and my Sincere Sentiments are spoke on this occasion. I am Dear Halkett Most Affectionately Yr Obedt

Go: Washington

When a new route around the Allegheny Mountains was discovered, Forbes decided to follow the advice of St. Clair and advance toward Fort Duquesne by constructing a new road. Colonel Bouquet informed Colonel Washington of the decision on August 3.[31]

Sir   *[Raystown, 3 August 1758]*

I had the pleasure of two Letters from you this morning, and as one of them was upon a most important subject, I read it with great attention, as every thing that has been so seriously considered by you deserves my utmost regard, your arguments are clear, and delivered with that openess and candour that becomes a Gentleman and a Soldier, but give me leave my Dear Sir to answer you in the same stile. At the same time that I was favour'd with your Letter, I received one from the General, with express Orders to begin to open the road from this place across the Allegeny Mountains, and as I shall allwayes oblige the directions of a Superiour Officer with readiness, there was no room left to hesitate, In the present case I shall execute them with the greater pleasure, as Col. Burd who is this Moment arrivd from Edmund Swamp, Whether he had accompanied Sr John St clair, assures me that a very good Waggon road may be made with ease and speed through the Gap that we have lately discovered, and this is the joint opinion of every person who went, they also agree that there are great numbers of fine springs the whole way, and good food for Horses so far as they have yet gone, Sir John went forward this morning, and sent me back word by a person coming from Major Armstrong, that as far as he had gone he found the road good, and every other thing answering our expectations I cannot therefore entertain the least doubt that we shall all now go on hand in hand and that the same zeal for the service that has hitherto been so distinguishing a part of your character will carry you by Reas Town over the Alligeny Mountains to Fort du Quesne

On September 4, Bouquet wrote to Washington, who was still at Fort Cumberland, advising him to move along the Braddock route to continue the attempt to deceive the enemy. At Salt Lick (near modern-day Melcroft, PA), he was to join forces with St. Clair's troops building the new road. Meanwhile, on September 7, Major James Grant, commander of the Highlanders, convinced Colonel Bouquet that he could reconnoiter Fort Duquesne and cause some injury to the French. Colonel Bouquet described his conversation with Major Grant at Loyalhanna Camp in a letter to General Amherst.[32]

> *The day on which I arrived at the camp, which was the 7th, it was reported to me that we were surrounded by parties of Indians, several soldiers having been scalped, or made prisoners.*
>
> *Being obliged to have our cattle and our horses in the woods, our people could not guard or search for them, without being continually liable to fall into the hands of the enemy.*
>
> *Lieutenant Col. Dagworthy and our Indians not having yet arrived, I ordered two companies each of a hundred men to occupy the path ways and try to cut off the enemies in their ambush and release our prisoners. These detachments being ready to march, Major Grant drew me aside and said that he was surprised that I took this method, after so many proofs that these little parties never did anything, and served to lose our men and discourage our people; but if I would give him five hundred men, he would go to the fort, reconnoitre the roads and forces of the enemy, which according to all our reports does not exceed six hundred French and Indians, that this was confirmed by a party which had entered the town, and that whatever detachments they could make, they could not send out more than they have, and that by erecting an ambuscade he could take prisoners....*

On September 12, Major Grant departed Loyalhanna with 900 chosen men, including 150 Virginians, 100 Marylanders, and 100 Pennsylvanians. Two days later while reconnoitering Fort Duquesne, the enemy launched an offensive resulting in major losses for the Virginia detachment: Six of the eight officers and sixty-two soldiers, a devastating forty-eight percent, were killed in action. In his September 25 report to Lieutenant Governor Faquier, Washington provided his critique of Grant's reconnoitering efforts.[33]

[Raystown, 25 September 1758]

To The Honorable Govr Fauquier.

Honble Srt.

   I think it incumbent upon me to give you the following account, altho' it is with very great concern I am furnished with the occasion.

   The 12th instant Major Grant, of the Highland-Battalion, with a chosen Detachment of 8,00 men, marched from our advanced Post, at Loyal-Hannon, for Fort du Quesne, what to do there (unless to meet the fate he did) I can not certainly inform you: however, to get intelligence and annoy the Enemy, was the ostensible plan. On the 13th in the night, they arrived near that place—formed upon the Hill in two columns, and sent a Party to the Fort to make discoveries, which they accomplished accordingly, and burned a Log-house not far from the walls without interruption: Stimulated by this success the Maj. kept his post and disposition until day, then detached Major Lewis, and part of his command 2 miles back to their Baggage-guard, and sent an Engineer with a covering party in full view of the fort, to take a plan of the works—at the same time causing the Revilé to beat in several different places.

   The enemy hereupon sallied out, and an obstinate Engagement began—for the particulars of which I beg leave to refer your Honr to the enclosed letters and return of the Regt. Major Lewis it is said met his fate in bravely advancing to sustain Maj. Grant. Our Officers and men have acquired very great applause for their gallant Behaviour during the action—I had the honor to be publickly complimented yesterday by the Genl on the occasion—The Havock that was made of them is a demonstrable proof of their obstinate defence; having 6 officers killed, and a 7th wounded, out of 8. Major Lewis, who chearfully went upon this Enterprize (when he found there was no dissuading Colonel Bouquet from the attempt) frequently there and afterwards upon the march, desired his friends to remember, that he had opposed the undertaking to the utmost. He is a great loss to the Regiment and is universally lamented. Captn Bullett's behaviour is matter of great admiration: and Capt Walter Stewart, the other surviving officer, distinguished himself greatly while he was able to act—he was left in the Field, but made his escape afterwards.

What may be the consequence of this affair, I will not take upon me to decide; but this I may venture to declare, that our affairs in general appear with a greater gloom than ever; and I see no probability of opening the Road this Campaign: How then can we expect a favourable issue to the Expedition? I have used my best endeavours to supply my men with the necessaries they want: 70 Blankets I got from the General, upon the promise to return them again: I therefore hope your Honor will direct that number to be sent to Winchester for his use. I must also beg the favour of having blank-commissions sent to me—it will take near a dozen for the promotions and vacancies: I must fill up the vacancies with the volunteers I have, and some of the best Sergeants. I marched to this camp the 21st instant, by order of the General.

Having little else of moment to relate; I beg leave to assure your Honour that I am your most obedient, & most humble Servant,

G:W.

Camp, at Rays-town, the 25th Septemb. 1758.

After defeating Major Grant's reconnaissance effort, a large body of French and Indian troops were sent out to attack Bouquet's troops. On October 13, a battle raged for several hours until the French and Indians were driven off. Colonel Forbes learned of the attack and ordered Washington's First Virginia Regiment to march from Raystown to Stony Creek to reinforce Colonel Bouquet.[34]

Instead, upon arriving at Stony Creek, Washington's regiment was ordered to escort the artillery from Stony Creek to Loyalhanna per the orderly book for October 16.[35]

[16 October 1758]

Camp at Stony Creek Octr 16. 1758 Monday
G.O.
Parole Winchester
  The Artillery is to March to Morrow under the Escort of Colo. Washingtons Detachmt & w[ha]t Remains of the 1st B. Pensilvanians, these Troops as well

as the road Cutters are to take provis. for the 20th Inclusive they are to draw bread the Meat as Soon as the Bullocks arrive, the light Horse & the Detachmt that Came from Loyal Hann[o]n with the Men of the Second Battallion of pensilvs. are to draw provisions for the 18th Inclusive & to March to morrow with Colo. Bouquet.

On November 6, still some forty miles from Fort Duquesne, General Forbes initiated discussions among his senior officers regarding the strategic options of pursuing the campaign to Fort Duquesne or delaying it until next season. Washington documented his opinions in a letter to Colonel Bouquet on the same day.[36]

Dear Sir   [Loyalhanna, 6 November 1758]
You will be surprisd (till I give you a reason for it) at receiving a Letter from a Person in the same Camp with you, and who has free access at all times to your Tent. but when I tell you that we were interrupted while conversing on a very important matter, and that I did not certainly know whether I might have another oppertunity of renewing the Conservation till you had some how or other settled the point with the General, I flatter myself you will excuse the freedom I now beg leave to use with you.

I don't doubt Sir but you have thoroughly considerd the practicability of the Scheme you this Night mentiond to me—and the good or evil consequences to be derivd therefrom, according to its success—it might therefore seem unseasonable to offer the following crude thoughts, did I not believe you are desirous of hearing opinion's—at least—on this occasion.

How far then do you believe our Stock of Provisions—to say nothing of other Matters—will allow you to execute this Plan? will it last till we coud reduce Fort Duquesne and March back to the Inhabitant—or receive a Supply else where? if it woud do this, the Measure may be right; but if it will not what is the consequence? Is it not neglecting the strengthening of this place—consuming the Provisions that shoud support a Garrison here, and ab[and]oning our Artillery either to the Enemy or a general destruction—It appears to me in that light.

Now suppose the Enemy gives us a meeting in the Field and we put them to the Rout what do we gain by it? perhaps triple their loss of Men in the first place, thô our numbers may be greatly superior (and If I may be allow'd to judge from what I have seen of late, we shall not heighten much that good opinion they seem to have of our skill in woods fighting)—therefore to risk an Engagement when so much depends upon it, without having the accomplishment of the main point in view, appears in my Eye, to be a little Imprudent. coud we suppose the Enemy woud immediately evacuate their Fort in case of a defeat in the woods—or as I before observd coud we be certain of Provisions in the other event—I think not a moments time is left for hesitation—but one or tother of these we ought to be assurd of. you I am sensible stand very little in need of any of these suggestion's—which are thrown together in haste, as I waited till this moment almost, expecting to see you—You will at least pardon this liberty & believe me to be Your Most Obedt Hble Servt

Go: Washington

Monday
9 Oclock p.m.

On November 11, General Forbes called a council of war with his commanding officers to discuss their campaign strategy. The challenge of battling the French into submission appeared daunting in light of the shortage of supplies and the deteriorating travel conditions. The attending officers recommended abandoning the pursuit of their objective for the season and Brigadier General John Forbes concurred.

But the following evening, the enemy attacked Lieutenant Colonel George Mercer's Virginia corps. Washington, upon hearing the intense fire, requested that he lead an additional detachment to reinforce Lieutenant Colonel Mercer. At twilight, with the light failing, Washington's troops approached the scene of the battle. The two Virginia detachments mistakenly fired upon each other with devastating consequences. To stop the action, Washington placed his well-being in the hands of Providence and stepped in the line of fire. Using his sword, he struck up the weapons of his troops while commanding them to cease firing. Washington later described this encounter in 1786 while preparing his biography with David Humphreys, and expressed his feeling that this skirmish was his most life-threatening military encounter.[37]

"During the time the Army lay at Loyal haning, a circumstance occurred wch involved the life of G. W. in as much Jeopardy as it had ever been before or since the enemy sent out a large detachment to reconnoitre our Camp, and to ascertain our strength; in consequence of Intelligence that they were within 2 Miles of the Camp. a party commanded by Lt Colo. Mercer of the Virga line (a gallant & good Officer) was sent to dislodge them between whom a severe conflict & hot firing ensued which lasting some time & appearing to approach the Camp it was conceived that our party was yielding the ground upon which G. W. with permission of the Genl called (for dispatch) for Volunteers and immediately marched at their head to sustain, as was conjectured the retireing troops. led on by the firing till he came within less than a half a Mile, & it ceasing, he detached Scouts to investigate the cause & to communicate his approach to his friend Colo. Mercer advancing slowly in the meantime—But it being near dusk and the intelligence not having been fully dissiminated among Colo. Mercers Corps, and they taking us, for the enemy who had retreated approaching in another direction commenced a heavy fire upon the releiving party which drew fire in return in spite of all the exertions of the Officers one of whom & several privates were killed and many wounded before a stop could be put to it. to accomplish which G. W. never was in more imminent danger. by being between two fires, knocking up with his sword the presented pieces"

Washington also described this tragic event in a conversation with William Finley. In 1818, Finley published his recollection of the conversation.[38]

"Since I am in the way of writing about Washington, I will add one serious scene through which he passed, which is little known, and with which he concluded this

conversation. He asked me how near I lived to Layalhana old Fort, and if I knew a run from the Laurel Hill that fell into the creek near it. I told him the distance of my residence, and that I knew the run. He told me that at a considerable distance up that run his life was in as great hazard as ever it had been in war. That he had been ordered to march some troops to reinforce a bullock-guard on their way to the camp—that he marched his party in single file with trailed arms, and sent a runner to inform the British officer in what manner he would meet him. The runner arrived and delivered his message, but he did not know how it was that the British officer paid no attention to it, and the parties met in the dark and fired on each other till they killed thirty of their own men; nor could they be stopped till he had to go in between the fires and threw up the muzzles of their guns with his sword"

Two officers and thirty-eight men were lost in the fiasco and many were wounded. Washington miraculously survived the encounter unscathed. His confidence in the protection of Providence became a firm conviction.

During the battle, three prisoners were captured, and Colonel Forbes learned that the French at Fort Duquesne were suffering, weakened because of the lack of supplies. With this new information, he reversed his November 12 decision and ordered his men to form and march on the fort. The order book for November 14 provided the details.[39]

[14 November 1758]

Camp at Loyal Hannon Novr 14th 1758
Parole Barbadoes
Field Officer for to morrow Majr Jameson.
Whereas the Circumstances of the times require that a Disposition be immediately made of the Troops under Brigadeer Genl Forbes Commandr[,] the Army is to be divided into three Bodys and to be Commanded by Colo. Bouquet Montgomrie and Washington who is to Act as Brigadiers receiving all reports & givining orders &c. regarding their respective division⟨s⟩ or Brigades the right

Wing to be Commanded by Colo. Washington to Consist of the 1st Virginia regimt[,] two Companies of Artificers, N. Caroleneans, Marylandrs and Lower County's.

The Senter to be Commanded by Colo. Montgomrie and to Consist of the Highlanders and 2d Virginia Regiment.

The left wing to be Commanded by Colo. Bouquet Consisting of the three Battallions of Pensilvanians and Royall Americans.

The reserve to be Commanded by [ ] to Consist of 200 highlanders 200 of the 2d V. Regimt & 200 of the Pensilvanians.

The Meantime the Virginians to be under the Command of Brigadier Washington.

The Highlanders under the Command of Brigadier Montgomrie, and the Pensilvas. Under the Command of Colo. Bouquet.

The first Division to March to morrow Morning and to draw 8 Days provisions and meat for 4 Days driving Cattle with them to Compleat them with the rest.

The 2d Division to march with the field Train of Artillery at one oClock with the same Qty of Provisions and the third Division to be Comple[te]d to morrow with the same Number of Days as the former.

On November 17, Forbes sent a report of the encounter between the Virginia detachments to General James Abercromby.[40]

"Two hundred of the ennemy came to attack our live Cattle and horses on the 12th—I sent 500 men to give them chace with as many more to Surround them, there were some killed on both sides, but unfortunately our partys fired upon each other in the dark by which we lost two officers and 38 private kill'd or missing. Wee made three prisoners from whom wee have had the only Intelligence of the Enemys strength, and which if true gives me great hopes"

On November 24, Forbes's men were within ten miles of their goal and were in good spirits and anxious to strike. At dawn, the Third Light

Horse was sent to reconnoiter the French fort. In the evening, as they approached Fort Duquesne, they found that the French had evacuated the fort, set it afire, and burned it to the ground. General Forbes's army finally took possession of the forks of the Ohio on November 25.

It was November 25, 1758, when His Majesty's commands were finally enforced. Five years and twenty-five days after Major George Washington embarked on a diplomatic mission to require the French to vacate their forts, the Ohio Country was finally open for the British colonists to pursue their relentless westward migration. On November 26, Forbes wrote to General James Abercromby about their successful campaign.[41]

"I have the pleasure of acquainting you with signall success of His Majesties Arms over all His Enemies on the Ohio, by having obliged them to burn, and abandon their Fort Duquesne, which they effectuated upon the 24th Inst; and of which I took possession with my light troops the same Evening, and with my little Army the next day—"

In this third and final drive to gain control of the forks of the Ohio, Washington had again placed himself in harm's way. With absolute belief in Providence, he had risked his life to stop a raging friendly fire-fight. Since the French no longer were battling for control of the Ohio Country, Washington retired from the military and returned to civilian life. On January 6, 1759, George Washington—at the age of twenty-six—married Martha Custis and settled into the peace and quiet of plantation living.

COMMANDER IN CHIEF
January 1759–September 1776

"I shall rely therefore, confidently, on that Providence which has heretofore preservd, & been bountiful to me, not doubting but that I shall return safe to you in the fall—"

– June 18, 1775 – George Washington

FTER CAPTURING FORT DUQUESNE FROM THE French in late 1758, Washington returned to Mount Vernon anticipating the felicity and serenity of plantation living. But because of the mismanagement of his accounts by his British brokers and unfair British taxes, the operation of Mount Vernon became increasingly challenging for Washington. After sixteen years of intensifying mercantile frustrations, Washington finally agreed in 1775 to join the growing movement to oust the British. He rejoined the military and would soon put Providence to the test yet again.

It was early in 1759 when Washington began his transition from life in the military to that of a civilian. Prior to returning to Mount Vernon and taking up the life of a plantation owner, he had married Martha

Custis and taken his seat in the House of Burgesses. The House of Burgesses honored his return with the following resolution.[1]

Resolution of the House of Burgesses

[Williamsburg, 26 February 1759]

Resolved, Nemine contradicente,

  That the Thanks of this House be given to George Washington, Esq; a Member of this House, late Colonel of the first Virginia Regiment, for his faithful Services to his Majesty, and this Colony, and for his brave and steady Behaviour, from the first Encroachments and Hostilities of the French and their Indians, to his Resignation, after the happy Reduction of Fort Du Quesne: And accordingly Mr Speaker, from the Chair, returned him (he standing in his Place) the Thanks of the House.

In early April, George Washington began preparations to bring his bride, Martha, home to Mount Vernon. On April 5, he wrote to John Alton, his body servant, and instructed him on how to arrange the beds.[2]

Jno.   *[Thursday Morning 5 April 1759]*

  I have sent Miles on to day, to let you know that I expect to be up to Morrow, & to get the Key from Colo. Fairfax's which I desire you will take care of—You must have the House very well cleand, & were you to make Fires in the Rooms below it, wd Air them—You must get two of the best Bedsteads put up—one in the Hall Room, and the other in the little dining Room that use to be, & have Beds made on them against we come—you must also get out the Chairs and Tables, & have them very well rubd & Cleand—the Stair case ought also to be polishd in order to make it look well.

  Enquire abt in the Neighbourhood, & get some Egg's and Chickens, and prepare in the best manner you can for our coming: you need not however take out any more of the Furniture than the Beds Tables & Chairs in Order that they may be well rubd & cleand. I am Yr Fd &ca

G. Washington

Then, on May 1, Washington wrote his broker in Great Britain, Robert Cary & Co., and advised them of his marriage and his assumption of the affairs of Martha's estate.[3]

Gentn   *Williamsburg May 1. 1759.*

The Inclosd is the Ministers Certificate of my Marriage with Mrs Martha Custis—properly as I am told—Authenticated, you will therefore for the future please to address all your Letters which relate to the Affairs of the late Danl Parke Custis Esqr. to me. as by Marriage I am entitled to a third part of that Estate, and Invested likewise with the care of the other two thirds by a Decree of our Genl Court which I obtaind in order to Strengthen the Power I before had in consequence of my Wifes Administration.

I have many Letters of yours in my possession unanswerd, but at present this serves only to advise you of the above Change and at the sametime to acquaint you that I shall continue to make you the same Consignments of Tobo as usual, and will indeavour to encrease it in proportion as I find myself and the Estate benefitted thereby.

The Scarcity of the last Years Crop; and the high prices of Tobo consequent thereupon woud in any other Case, have inducd me to sell the Estates Crop (which indeed is only 16 Hhds) in the Country but for a present, & I hope small advantage only I did not care to break the Chain of Corrispondance that has so long Subsisted, and therefore have, according to your desire, given Captn Talman an offer of the whole.

On the other side is an Invoice of some Goods which I beg of you to send me by the first Ship bound either to Potomack or Rappahannock, as I am immediate want of them, Let them be Insurd, and in case of accidents reshipd witht Delay. Direct for me at Mount Vernon Potomack River Virginia; the former is the name of my Seat the other the River on which 'tis Situated. I am Gentn Yr Most Obedt Hble Servt

GO: Washington

Washington's arrangement with his broker, Robert Cary & Co., enabled him to sell his tobacco in Great Britain. With the proceeds from tobacco sales, Cary would then purchase the goods that Washington ordered. Because Cary was responsible for both sales and purchases, Washington was dependent upon his brokers and frequently expressed his dissatisfaction. In his letter to Cary on September 28, 1760, Washington explained his concerns.[4]

Gentn   Mount Vernon 28th Septr 1760

Your Letter of the 31st May Via Bristol came to hand a few days ago; and I take the oppertunity by Captn Johnston of Inclosing you my Second Bill of Lading, which is all that Captn Talman gave; as my Steward informd me. You will find by that there was only 50 Hhds Tobacco Shipd pr the Cary, four by mistake being left out (as I wrote you in a Letter of the 28th of April last) which went afterwards in the Russia Merchant with 12 Others consignd to yourselves—I hope they are safe arrivd.

By this conveyance & under the same cover of this Letter, you will receive Invoices of such Goods as are wanting, which please to send as there directed by Captn Johnston in the Spring—and let me beseech you Gentn to give the necessary directions for purchasing of them upon the best Terms—It is needless for me to particularise the sorts, quality, or taste I woud choose to have them in unless it is observd; and you may believe me when I tell you that instead of getting things good and fashionable in their several kind we often have Articles sent Us that coud only have been usd by our Forefathers in the days of yore — 'Tis a custom, I have some Reason to believe, with many Shop keepers, and Tradesmen in London when they know Goods are bespoke for Exportation to palm sometimes old, and sometimes very slight and indifferent Goods upon Us taking care at the sametime to advance 10, 15 or perhaps 20 prCt upon them—My Packages pr the Polly Captn Hooper are not yet come to hand, & the Lord only, knows when they will, without more trouble than they are worth—As to the Busts a future day will determine my choice of them if any are wrote for—Mrs Washington sends home a Green Sack to get cleand, or fresh dyed of the same colour—made

up into a handsome Sack again woud be her choice, but if the Cloth wont afford
that, then to be thrown into a genteel Night Gown. The Pyramid you sent me last
year got hurt, and the broken pieces I return by this oppertunity to get New ones
made by them—please to order that they be securely Packd.

I now address Copies of my last by Mr Fairfax, in the Ship Wilson Captn
Coolage; and take occasion again to assure you, that the Crops of Tobacco this
year will be shorter than you seem to expect—A Very wet Summer was the Cause
of a good deal of Tobaccos drawing in the low Grounds, and of its firing on the
high Lands—My Steward on York River writes me that their Expectations in
those parts are greatly fallen, mine here is not a little shortned—however, if the
Frosts dont take what little I have remaining, I purpose to Ship you 40 or 50
Hhds of my own Crop from this River, but how much I shall be able to send
you from York River I really cant say till I go down there, which will happen in a
very few days, and from thence I will write you again. I shall endeavour however to
contribute something towards the dispatch of your Ship. The Bill which I thought
I shoud have occasion to draw in favour of Mr Clifton passd my hands the 20th
Ulto for £30 Sterling. I have neither seen—nor heard—any thing concerning the
Salt from Liverpool yet. I am Gentn Yr Most Obedt Hble Servt

Go: Washington

P.S. Since writing the foregoing Letter, I recollect the expediency of having the Bill
of Lading mention'd to be Inclosd in the first part recorded before I part with it for
fear of Accidents—this will consequently prevent its going by Johnston: but the first
outward bound Ship from York or James River after I (get) down shall carry it.

In May 1762, Washington learned of the sales price for the tobacco
that he had shipped to Great Britain some six months earlier. He wrote
of his aggravation and dissatisfaction to his broker and asked why his
tobacco had not received the highest available price.[5]

Gentlemen, Mount Vernon 28th May 1762
Your unacknowledged favours of the 26th June 10th Augt 16 & 19th Septr
and the 19th of Octr following now lye before—in that one of Augt 10th I

perceive you bring the shortness of some of the Bundles of the Tobo Shipped in the Bland to acct for the lowness of the Price—That some of the Tobo was small I shall not undertake to dispute, but at the sametime I must observe that it was clean & neatly handled which I apprehended woud have rendered the other objection of very little weight—As to stemming my Tobo in the manner you recommend I woud readily do it if the returns woud be equivalent to the trouble, & loss of the Stem, and of this I shall be a tolerable judge as I am at no small pains this year to try the quality with the advantages & disadvantages of differ-ent kinds of Tobos and shall at the sametime find out the difference between a hhd of Leaf & a hhd of Stemmd Tobo by comparing then the loss of the one with the extra price of the other I shall be able to determine which is the best to pursue & follow that method which promises the most certain advantages.

Some of the Tobo which I put on board the Unity Captn Cuzzens got damaged in carrying to the Warehouses for Inspection & had a part cut of which will no doubt deface it a little but as this happened while I was at Williamsburg I am able to give you no exact Information concerning it—In this parcel of Tobo there are three kinds which please to give me yr opinions upon—No. 1 to 6 Inclusive are of one kind—from 9 to 14 are of another—& 15 to 16 are of a third sort—the rest are of the same kinds of these three but made on other Plantations.

As I have ever laid it down as an established Maxim to believe that every per-son is, (most certainly ought to be) the best judges of What relates to their own Interest & Concerns I very rarely undertake to propose Schemes to others which may be attended with uncertainty & miscarriage—this will at once acct for my being among the last who shoud advise your sending a Vessell into Potomack for the accomodation of your Friends there. That I have often thought of it as a desireable thing for the Shippers, I will readily confess and have as often concluded that so soon as you found an established consignment formed here you woud do it of course—and sooner we ought not to expect it—Since you have proposed the matter yourself to me—I certainly must approve of it, and as you are so obliging to write that you shall direct the Matter to be under my notice I hope you will be perswaded to believe that I shall readily contribute my best advice and assistance towards his dispatch—The Tobacco's of most of your friends upon Potomack (or that Ships from thence) lyes within 15 Miles above & below this place, and as good, or best harbour (Piscataway) is within sight of my Door—It has this great advantage besides good Anchorage & laying safe from the Winds that it is out of the way of the Worm which is very hurtful to Shipping a little lower down & lyes in a very plentiful part of the Country—I thought it incumbant upon me to mention these things after which do as you please. If I had receivd any Intimation of your sending a Vessell into this River I shoud not have engaged any part of my Tobo to Cuzzens, & while I remain in expectation of her arrival will not seek a freight else where for the residue of what I intend your house from this River which probably may amount to about 30 hhds more.

My Letter of the 25th of Jany will inform you how the Interest of the Bank stock is to be applied—as that fund was appropriated towards the payment of Miss Custis's Fortune I am informed that the Stock ought to be transferred to her. you will please therefore to have it done accordingly and whatever charges may arise in so doing place to her own Acct. I hope Messrs Hill & Co. will send the wine into this River for I had rather have it in Madeira than York.

Thus far had I wrote & was going to conclude when your favour of the 18th Jany was presented to me—I am sorry to hear the Accts given of the Tobo Shipped in Boyes but as you don't particularize the proprietor's names who suffered most I am in hopes my 70 hhds have pretty well escaped the ge[ne]r[a]l complaint—If it has not I confess it to be an Art beyond my skill, to succeed in making good Tobo as I have used my utmost endeavours for that purpose this two or 3 years past—& am once again urged to express my surprize at finding that I do not partake of the best prices that are going—I saw an Acct rendered by Mr Athaws of some Tobo which he sold for Mr Fairfax at 12½d. the Tobo went from this River & I can aver was not better that 12 hhds of my Mountn Crop which you receivd in the Sarah & Bland last Summr—In fact Mr Fairfax's Plantation's & mine upon Shannondoah lye in the same neighbourhood—The Tobo brought to the same Inspection—and to be short, is in all respects exactly alike—none of mine however sold for more that 11d. or 3½ which you please while his went of a little before at the price of 12½ aforesaid—this is a difference *really too great & I see it with concern—however Gentlemen I hope to find it otherwise for the time to come. I am Yr Most Obedt Hble Servt.*

Go: Washington

Washington, although frustrated with the difficulties of trading with Great Britain, became even more alarmed with the passage of the Stamp Act of 1765. The British Parliament passed the act to force the colonies to service the debt created by the French and Indian War. This measure would increase his costs substantially, and in September, Washington wrote to Francis Dandridge, Martha's uncle in London, expressing his dissatisfaction.[6]

Sir,   *Mount Vernon 20 Septr 1765.*

If you will permit me after six years silence—the time I have been married to your Niece—to pay my respects to you in this Epistolary way I shall think myself happy in beginning a corrispondance which cannot but be attended with pleasure on my side.

I shoud hardly have taken the liberty Sir, of Introducing myself to your acquaintance in this manner, and at this time, least you shoud think my motives for doing of it arose from sordid views had not a Letter which I receivd some-time this Summer from Robt Cary Esqr. & Co. given me Reasons to believe that such an advance on my side woud not be altogether desagreeable on yours[.] before this I rather apprehended that some disgust at the News of your Nieces Marriage with me—and why I coud not tell—might have been the cause of your silence upon that event, and discontinuing a corrispondance which before then you had kept up with her—but if I coud only flatter myself, that you woud in any wise be entertaind with the few occurrances that it might be in my power to relate from hence I shoud endeavour to attone for my past remissness, in this respect, by future punctuality.

At present few things are under notice of my observation that can afford you any amusement in the recital—The Stamp Act Imposed on the Colonies by the Parliament of Great Britain engrosses the conversation of the Speculative part of the Colonists, who look upon this unconstitutional method of Taxation as a direful attack upon their Liberties, & loudly exclaim against the Violation— what may be the result of this—& some other (I think I may add) ill judgd Measures, I will not undertake to determine; but this I may venture to affirm, that the advantage accrueing to the Mother Country will fall greatly short of the expectations of the Ministry; for certain it is, our whole Substance does already in a manner flow to Great Britain and that whatsoever contributes to lessen our Importation's must be hurtful to their Manufacturers—And the Eyes of our People—already beginning to open—will perceive, that many Luxuries which we lavish our substance to Great Britain for, can well be dispensd with whilst the necessaries of Life are (mostly) to be had within ourselves—This consequently will introduce frugality, and be a necessary stimulation to Industry—If Great Britain therefore Loads her Manufacturers with heavy Taxes, will it not facili- tate these measures? they will not compel us I think to give our Money for their exports, whether we will or no, & certain I am none of their Traders will part from them without a valuable consideration—where then is the Utility of these Restrictions?

As to the Stamp Act, taken in a single view, one, & the first bad consequences attending it I take to be this—Our Courts of Judicature must inevitably be shut up; for it is impossible (or next to kin to it) under our present Circumstances that the Act of Parliamt can be complyd with were we ever so willing to enforce the execution; for not to say, which alone woud be sufficient, that we have not money to pay the Stamps, there are many other Cogent Reasons to prevent it; and if a stop be put to our Judicial proceedings I fancy the Merchants of G. Britain trad- ing to the Colonies will not be among the last to wish for a Repeal of it.

I live upon Potomack River in Fairfax County, about ten Miles below Alexandria & many Miles distant from any of my Wifes Relations; who all reside upon York river, & who we seldom see more than once a year—not always that—My wife who is very well & Master and Miss Custis (children of her former Marriage) all join in making a tender of their Duty & best respects to yourself & their Aunt—My Compliments to yr Lady I beg may also be made acceptable & that you will do me the justice to believe that I am Dr Sir Yr Most Obedt Hble Servt

Go: Washington

On May 5, 1768, Washington wrote to Robert Cary & Co. informing them that he was again shipping some tobacco to them. With this shipment, he wrote that he expected to receive the highest price available and threatened to cancel their business arrangement if they failed.[7]

Gentn   Williamsburg 5th May 1768

I have just time before I leave this place to acknowledge the receipt of your Letters of the 22d of Decr by Eston and 1st of Feby by Captn Outram. By the Latter I shall send you all my own Tobo consisting of Fifteen Hhds and about Twenty-five of Mastr Custis's—on both which parcels please to Insure Ten pounds pr Hhd. As the scarcity of Tobo, and high prices thereof in the Country are facts too well known to be doubted of, it consequently becomes unnecessary for me to add that unless the Sales with you are high, we shall be a considerable looser by adhering to our usual custom of assisting your Ships here, this we hope you will endeavour to avoid, and make the advantages reciprocal; at least that we do not suffer by our Attachment to your House.

Herewith you will receive a Bill of Exchange drawn by James Kirk on Messrs Crosbies & Trafford for One hundred and Seven pounds ten shillings Sterlg— as also two other Bills of Mr J. Wales's drawing on Messrs Farrel & Jones of Bristol amounting together to One hundd and twenty pounds Sterg—which Sums when receivd please to give my Acct credit for—At present I shall only add that I am Gentn Yr Most Obedt Hble Servt

Go: Washington

On July 10, 1773, Washington placed an order with Robert Cary & Co. for articles needed upon the death of his stepdaughter for the second mourning. He requested delivery on the first ship to the Potomac River and he complained once more about the quality of the merchandise that he was receiving. This is Washington's last known order to Robert Cary & Co. and there is no record that the goods were delivered.[8]

Gentn   *Mount Vernon [10 July 1773]*

Inclosed you have an Invoice of such Goods as I want for my own use, which please to send by the first Ship to this River as many of the Articles will be wanted by the time they can arrive; among which the Second Mourning for Miss Custis, who we had the misfortune to loose on the 19th Ulto will be necessary—Your Acct against this young Lady may remain as stated in your Books till further advise, in the meanwhile please to send me an exact transcript thereof. As I shall have occasion soon, I expect, to send for many Articles preparatory to Mr Custis's Housekeeping, when he returns from College, no Goods are sent for on his Acct by this oppertunity, but a small Invoice of Sundries for Mr Lund Washington is forwarded that they may be dispatchd with mine. The Shoes by Captn Grig are safe arrivd; so are the Goods by Peterson, saving a Bale of Cotton (of mine) which Mr Hill writes me is damaged, but as he is not particular in the Acct I do not know to what degree, or whether worth speaking of; I have wrote to him however on this head, & expect his answer, when I shall be better able to inform you—He complains a good deal of the enormous size of the Grindstones; adding that, some of them (if they had been of the proper quality) were full large enough for Millstones.

I have directed him to put all my Tobo on Board of Peterson, as also Mr Custis's except a few Hhds for Mr Hanbury; but as he has not yet furnished me with the respective quantities, it is not, at this time, in my power to order Insurance. As soon as it is I will advise you thereof, and shall hope notwithstanding the Stagnation, and indeed Consternation which the trading World seems to have been thrown into of late that you will endeavour to render us agreeable Accts of Sale for these Tobacco's, for if a steady adherence to one House carrys any merit along with it none I am Sure has a better claim to your particular Attention than my Ward and self hath.

As I shall probably have occasion to write to you again in a few days for Insurance &ca I shall add no more at present than that I am Gentn Yr Very Hble Servt

Go: Washington

After a decade of Parliament's failed attempts at taxation, the protestations of the colonies erupted in direct action. On December 16, 1773, the colonists destroyed the taxed tea by throwing it into Boston Harbor. To support the residents of Boston, the colonies began appointing delegates to meet in Philadelphia to discuss what actions to take. The following June, Thomas Johnson, a delegate from Maryland, wrote to George Washington, informing him of the Maryland resolutions and their plans to convene with the other colonies in Philadelphia.[9]

Sir   *Annapolis [Md.] 28 June 1774*

I take the Freedom to inclose you the Resolutions of our general Committee for the Province on the Bills respecting the Massachusetts Governmt and the Act for blocking up the Harbour of Boston—If our general Scheme of Conduct should be adopted by the Congress I think even so strict an Association will be kept by the people of Maryland with good Faith I have sanguine Hopes that your Colony will readily join in effectual Measures—I am sorry to hear that your abrupt Dissolution has thrown you into Difficulties about Officers Fees we have unhappily been for some Time much embarrassed about the Fees of Office here and as you may remember have had some Controversial Pieces on the Subject I preserved a paper which contains the last no Answer having been yet given to it and inclose it you as indeed I would all on the Subject if I had them not from any Opinion the Matter may not be as well handled in Virginia as with us but from an Apprehension that any Thing on the Subject which may tend to an Investigation of the Truth will at this Time be agreeable to you. I have stong Expectations from pensylvania but have heard Nothing material from New York. I am sir Your most obedt Servant

Ths Johnson Junr

In early August, Virginia held a convention and elected George Washington as one of their delegates to meet with the other colonies in Philadelphia.

On August 24, before traveling to Philadelphia, Washington wrote to Bryan Fairfax, the youngest son of his patron, William Fairfax, expressing his belief that Parliament had passed an illegal tax on the colonies. He informed Fairfax that he had agreed to be a Virginia delegate and meet in Philadelphia with the representatives of the other colonies to determine how to support the opposition in Boston.[10]

Dear Sir   *Mount Vernon Augt 24th 1774*

Your Letter of the 5th Instt came to this place, forwarded by Mr Ramsay, a few days after my return from Williamsburg; and I delayed acknowledging of it sooner, in hopes that I should find time, before I began my other journey to Philadelphia, to answer it fully, if not satisfactorily, but as much of my time has been engrossd since I came home by Company; by your Brother's Sale & the business consequent thereupon; In writing Letters to England; and now in attending to my own domestick affairs previous to my departure as above; I find it impossible to bestow so much time and attention to the Subject matter of your Letter as I could wish to do, & therefore must rely upon your good nature & candour in excuse for not attempting it. In truth, perswaded as I am that you have read all the Political Pieces which compose a large share of the Gazettes, at this time, I should think it, but for your request, a piece of inexcusable arrogance in me, to make the least essay towards a change in your Political Opinion's; for I am sure I have no new lights to throw upon the Subject, or any arguments to offer in support of my own doctrine than what you have seen; and could only in general add, that an Innate Spirit of freedom first told me, that the Measures which Administration hath for sometime been, and now are, most violently pursuing, are repugnant to every principle of natural justice; whilst much abler heads than my own, hath fully convinced me that it is not only repugnant to natural Right, but Subservsive of the Laws & Constitution of Great Britain itself; in the Establishment of which some of the best Blood in the Kingdom hath been Spilt;

Satisfied then that the Acts of a British Parliament are no longer Govern'd by the Principles of justice—that it is trampling upon the Valuable Rights of American's, confirm'd to them by Charter, & the Constitution they themselves boast of; & convinc'd beyond the smallest doubt, that these Measures are the result of deliberation; & attempted to be carried into Execution by the hand of Power is it a time to trifle, or risk our Cause upon Petitions which with difficulty obtain access, and afterwards are thrown by with the utmost contempt—or should we, because heretofore unsuspicious of design and then unwilling to enter into disputes with the Mother Country go on to bear more, and forbear to innumerate our just causes of Complaint—For my own part, I shall not undertake to say where the Line between Great Britain and the Colonies should be drawn, but I am clearly of opinion that one ought to be drawn; & our Rights clearly ascertaind. I could wish, I own, that the dispute had been left to Posterity to determine, but the Crises is arriv'd when we must assert our Rights, or Submit to every Imposition that can be heap'd upon us; till custom and use, will make us as tame, & abject Slaves, as the Blacks we Rule over with such arbitrary Sway.

I intended to have wrote no more than an apology for not writing, but find I am Insensibly running into a length I did not expect, & therefore shall conclude with remarking, that if you disavow the Right of Parliament to Tax us (unrepresented as we are) we only differ in respect to the mode of opposition; and this difference principally arises from your belief that they (the Parliament I mean) want a Decent oppertunity to Repeal the Acts; whilst I am as fully convinc'd, as I am of my existance, that there has been a regular Systematick Plan form'd, to enforce them; and that nothing but Unanimity in the Colonies (a stroke they did not expect) and firmness can prevent it; It seems, from the best advices from Boston, that Genl Gage is exceedingly disconcerted at the quiet ⟨& steady⟩ Conduct of the People of the Massachusets Bay, and at the Measures pursuing by the other Governments; as I dare say he expected to have forc'd those oppressd People into compliance, or irritated them to acts of violence before this, for a more colourable pretence of Ruling that, and the other Colonies with a high hand. But I am done.

I shall set off on Wednesday next for Philadelphia whither if you have any
Commands I shall be glad to oblige you in them. being Dr Sir, with real regard
Yr Most Obedt Servt

Go: Washington

P.S. Pray what do you think of the Canada Bill?

All of the colonies, except Georgia, convened on September 5, 1774, and voted to call the assembly the First Continental Congress.[11]

Wasington used the term "Canada Plan" in referring to the Quebec Act that was passed by Parliament in June 1774.[12]

Robert McKenzie[13] wrote to George Washington on September 13, 1774, expressing his view of events as a British soldier stationed in Boston. McKenzie believed that the British military had the responsibility to control the rebellious residents.[14]

Dear Sir   *Boston Camp [Mass.] Septr 13th 1774*

I am happy to take the Advantage of my Friend Mr Atchison's Return to
Virginia to pay my Respects where they are so much due as to yourself, espe-
cially as he expects to find you at Philadelphia engaged in the present impor-
tant Affairs in America. No Class of People wish more cordially for a happy
Accommodation than those of my Profession, and among them there is not one
who is under stronger Obligations to do so than myself.

Mr Atchison can sufficiently inform you of the State of this unhappy Province,
of their tyrannical Oppression over one another, of their fixed Aim at total
Independance, of the Weakness and Temper of the main Springs that set the
whole in Motion, and how necessary it is that abler Heads and better Hearts shd
draw a Line for their Guidance: Even when this is done 'tis much to be feared
they will follow it no further than where it coincides with their present Sentiments.

Amidst all these Jarrings we have until lately lived as in a Camp of Pleasure,
but the rebellious and numerous Meetings of Men in Arms, their scandalous
and ungenerous Attacks upon the best Characters in the Province, obliging them
to save their Lives by Flight, and their repeated but feeble Threats to dispossess

the Troops have furnished sufficient Reasons to Genl Gage to put the Town in a formidable State of Defence, about which we are now fully employed, and which will be shortly accomplished to their great Mortification.

I shall endeavour to quit this disagreeable Scene when the Regiments retire into Quarters, and hope that going or returning from James's River to pay my Respects in Person.

Col. Robt Stuart Dr John Stuart, and Col. Mercer were among the last Persons I parted with in London last April—I mention them as your Acquaintances— 'Tho' they all had a long Detail of Grievances, neither their Health or Spirits seem to have suffered at that Time. I have the Honour to be Dear Sir, your very respectful and most obedient Servant

Robert Mackenzie
Lieutt 43d Foot

On April 19, 1775, the first engagement between the British and Continental forces erupted in the Battles of Lexington and Concord, igniting the American Revolutionary War. While attending the Second Continental Congress in Philadelphia, Washington wrote to George William Fairfax describing how the conflict began and justifying America's right to freedom.[15]

Dear Sir,   *Phildelphia May 31st 1775.*

Since my last (dated about the first of April) I have received from Mr Craven Peyton the Sum of £193.6.10 (as you may see by the inclosed Account) with which, and the Balance of the former Money, I now remit you the following Bills; to wit, one drawn by Mr Thomas Contee on Mr Mollison, for £40 Sterling, and another drawn by Lyonel Bradstreet on Mr William Tippell of London for the like Sum (indorsed by Mr Contee; the strongest assurances being given me, that they are both good) Mr Contee is Mr Mollison's principal Factor, or Agent, in Maryland, and is besides a Man of property himself; but notwithstanding this, the times are so ticklish, that there is no such thing as answering for the payment of Bills. You must therefore, either take the chance of receiving bad ones, or suffer your Money to lay dead.

I have also, since coming to this place, purchased a Bill from Messieurs Willing and Morris of £161.5.10 Sterling, which will, I believe, for I have not a state of our Account with me, about Balance it. With the Copy of Mr Peyton's Account, you will receive a List of the Rents which he collected since last settlement; and these, as I have not been favoured with a Line from you, since your Letter of June, is all I recollect at present worth communicating relative to your business.

Before this Letter can reach you, you must, undoubtedly, have received an Account of the engagement in the Massachusetts Bay between the Ministerial Troops (for we do not, nor cannot yet prevail upon ourselves to call them the King's Troops) and the Provincials of that Government; But as you may not have heard how that affair began, I inclose you the several Affidavits that were taken after the action.

General Gage acknowledges, that the detachment under Lieutenant Colonel Smith was sent out to destroy private property; or, in other Words, to destroy a Magazine which self preservation obliged the Inhabitants to establish. And he also confesses, in effect at least, that his Men made a very precipitate retreat from Concord, notwithstanding the reinforcement under Lord Piercy; the last of which may serve to convince Lord Sandwich (and others of the same sentiment) that the Americans will fight for their Liberties and property, however pusilanimous, in his Lordship's Eye, they may appear in other respects.

From the best accounts I have been able to collect of that affair; indeed from every one, I believe the fact, stripped of all colouring, to be plainly this, that if the retreat had not been as precipitate as it was (and God knows it could not well have been more so) the Ministerial Troops must have surrendered, or been totally cut off: For they had not arrived in Charlestown (under cover of their Ships) half an hour, before a powerful body of Men from Marblehead and Salem were at their heels, and must, if they had happened to have been up one hour sooner, inevitably intercepted their retreat to Charlestown. Unhappy it is though to reflect, that a Brother's Sword has been sheathed in a Brother's breast, and that, the once happy and peaceful plains of America are either to be drenched with Blood, or Inhabited by Slaves. Sad alternative! But can a virtuous Man hesitate in his choice? I am, with sincere Regard and Affectionate compliments to Mrs Fairfax, Dear Sir, Your Most obt servant,

G. Washington

In the summer of 1775, George Washington returned to the military service, this time not in support of the British colonial empire but in opposition to their tyranny. During the next twelve years, Washington, on numerous occasions, placed himself in harm's way as he bravely led the colonies toward independence.

By June 17, 1775, the Continental Congress appointed George Washington commander in chief of the American forces. Before he left Philadelphia to lead the ragtag Continental army against the powerful British military machine, he wrote to Martha Washington. He expressed his concern for how it would inconvenience her and suggested that she move to Alexandria while he was away from Mount Vernon. In his letter, he affirmed his reliance upon the protection of Providence and assured his Patcy that he would safely return. He also let her know that his personal lawyer had drafted a will to clarify the distribution of his property.[16]

My Dearest,   *Philadelphia June 18th 1775.*

I am now set down to write to you on a subject which fills me with inexpressable concern—and this concern is greatly aggravated and Increased when I reflect on the uneasiness I know it will give you— It has been determined in Congress, that the whole Army raised for the defence on the American Cause shall be put under my care, and that it is necessary for me to proceed immediately to Boston to take upon me the Command of it. You may believe me my dear Patcy, when I assure you, in the most solemn manner, that, so far from seeking this appointment I have used every endeavour in my power to avoid it, not only from my unwillingness to part with you and the Family, but from a consciousness of its being a trust too great for my Capacity and that I should enjoy more real happiness and felicity in one month with you, at home, than I have the most distant prospect of reaping abroad, if my stay was to be Seven times Seven years. But, as it has been a kind of destiny that has thrown me upon this Service, I shall hope that my undertaking of it, is design'd to answer some good purpose—You might, and I suppose did perceive, from the Tenor of my letters, that I was apprehensive I could not avoid this appointment, as I did not even pretend ⟨t⟩o intimate when I should return—that was the case—it was utterly out of my power to refuse this appointment without exposing my Character to such censures as would have reflected dishonour upon myself, and given pain to my friends—this I am sure could not, and ought not to be pleasing to you, & must have lessend me considerably in my own esteem. I shall rely therefore, confidently, on that Providence which has heretofore preserv'd, & been bountiful to me, not doubting but that I shall return safe to you in the fall—I shall feel no pain from the Toil, or the danger of the Campaign—My unhappiness will flow, from the uneasiness I know you will feel at being left alone—I therefore beg of you to summon your whole fortitude & Resolution, and pass your time as agreeably as possible—nothing will give me so much sincere satisfaction as to hear this, and to hear it from your own Pen.

If it should be your desire to remove into Alexandria (as you once mentioned upon an occasion of this sort) I am quite pleased that you should put it in practice, & Lund Washington may be directed, by you, to build a Kitchen and other Houses there proper for your reception—if on the other hand you should rather Incline to spend good part of your time among your Friends below, I wish you to do so—In short, my earnest, & ardent desire is, that you would pursue any Plan that is most likely to produce content, and a tolerable degree of Tranquility as it must add greatly to my uneasy feelings to hear that you are dissatisfied, and complaining at what I really could not avoid.

As Life is always uncertain, and common prudence dictates to every Man the necessity of settling his temporal Concerns whilst it is in his power—and whilst the Mind is calm and undisturbed, I have, since I came to this place (for I had not time to do it before I left home) got Colo. Pendleton to Draft a Will for me by the directions which I gave him, which Will I now Inclose—The Provision made for you, in cas⟨e⟩ of my death, will, I hope, be agreeable; I have Included the Money for which I sold my own Land (to Doctr Mercer) in the Sum given you, as also all other Debts. What I owe myself is very trifling—Cary's Debt excepted, and that would not have been much if the Bank stock had been applied without such difficulties as he made in the Transference.

I shall add nothing more at present as I have several Letters to write, but to desire you will remember me to Milly & all Friends, and to assure you that I am with most unfeigned regard, My dear Patcy Yr Affecte

Go: Washington

P.S. Since writing the above I have receivd your Letter of the 15th and have got two suits of what I was told wa⟨s⟩ the prettiest Muslin. I wish it may please you—it cost 50/. a suit that is 20/. a yard.

On June 23, Washington wrote again to Martha, informing her that he was leaving Philadelphia and traveling to Boston to lead the American forces against the British. In this letter, he once more stated his belief that he would be protected by Providence and he would soon return to her.[17]

My dearest,   *Phila. June 23d 1775.*

As I am within a few Minutes of leaving this City, I could not think of departing from it without dropping you a line; especially as I do not know whether it may be in my power to write again till I get to the Camp at Boston—I go fully trusting in that Providence, which has been more bountiful to me than I deserve, & in full confidence of a happy meeting with you sometime in the Fall—I have not time to add more, as I am surrounded with Company to take leave of me—I retain an unalterable affection for you, which neither time or distance can change, my best love to Jack & Nelly, & regard for the rest of the Family concludes me with the utmost truth & sincerety Yr entire

Go: Washington

Commander in Chief General George Washington arrived at the Continental army's Boston encampment on July 2 and was surprised by the many diverse commands and their lack of discipline. He wrote to Samuel Washington on July 20 and expressed his concerns. In this letter to his brother, Washington pointed out that the casualty count from the June 17 Battle of Bunker Hill was far higher for the British army than for the Continental army, and with a few more similar successes, the British would soon concede.[18]

Camp at Cambridge about ⟨5⟩ Miles from Boston

Dear Brother,   *July 20. 1775.*

Agreeable to your request I am now set down to write to you, although in the first place I have scarce time to indulge an Inclination of the kind, and in the next place do not know how or whether it may ever get to your hands.

I came to this place the 2d Instant & found a numerous army of Provincials under very little command, discipline, or order—I found our Enemy who had drove our People from Bunkers Hill strongly Intrenching, and from Accts had reason to expect before this, another attack from them; but, as we have been incessantly (Sundays not excepted) employed in throwing up Works of defence I rather begin to believe now, that they think it rather a dangerous experiment; and that we shall remain sometim⟨e⟩ watching the Motions of each other, at the distance of little more than a mile & in full vie⟨w⟩—from the best Accts we have been able t⟨o⟩ get, the number of the Enemy amounts to between 10 and 12,000 Men; part of which are in Boston, & part on Bunkers Hill just by—our numbers including Sick, absent &ca are between 16 & 18,000; but then, having great extent of Lines & many places to defend, & not knowing where the attack may be made (as they have the entire command of the Water & can draw their whole force to any one point in an hour or twos time without any person but the Commanding Officer who directs it having the least previous notice of it) our situatio⟨n⟩ is a little unfavourable. but not so bad that I think we can give them a pretty warm reception if they think proper to make any advances towards us—their situation is such as to secure them from any attack of ours.

By what we can learn, they are sadly distressd for want of fresh Provisions—Beef (the Milch Cows in Boston) sells from One shilling to 18d. Sterg pr lb.—Mutton higher, & these only to be had for the Sick. the number of thos⟨e⟩ killed & wounded in the engagement on Bunker⟨s⟩ Hill could not fall short of 1100, ours did not exceed 450—a few more such Victories woul⟨d⟩ put an end to their army and the present contest.

The Village I am in, is situated in the midst of a very delightful Country, and is a very beautiful place itself, th⟨ou⟩gh small—a thousand pities that such a Country should become the theatre of War—A Month from this day will bring on some Capitol change I expect; for if the Enemy are not able to penetrate into the Country, they may as well, one would think, give up the point & return home; for if they stay at Boston & a⟨t⟩ Bu⟨n⟩kers Hill (which is another Peninsula lef⟨t⟩ unto it, & seperated by a small Ferry over to Charles Town which is part of the Nec⟨k⟩ I say if they stay at those places f ⟨or⟩ ever, the end for which they were se⟨nt⟩ cannot be accomplished; & to compel them to remain there, is the principal object we have in view indeed the onl⟨y.⟩

We have seen nothing of the Rifle men yet, nor have we heard any thing certain of them. I have only time to add my love to my Sister & the Family & to assure you that I am with unfeigned regard & truth Dr Sir Yr Affecte Brother and frien⟨d⟩

Go: Washington

P.S. In the late Ingagemt of the 17th Ulto the Enemy by the best Accts we can get had 1043 Men killed & W⟨o⟩und⟨e⟩d Wh⟨ere⟩ of 92 Were Officers—our loss amounted to 13⟨9⟩ killed 278 Wounded & 36 Missing—pray rememb⟨er⟩ me kindly to Mr Warner Washington ⟨and Family⟩ when you see them.

Washington spent the summer organizing his forces, reinforcing his position, and monitoring the movements of the British in Boston. After the defeat at Bunker Hill, the British replaced Commander in Chief Gage with General William Howe. When November arrived, Washington expressed concern about maintaining his army through the winter and called a council of war to discuss strategy. The council met in Cambridge on November 2, 1775, and decided to attack the British immediately rather than wait until the spring of 1776, when they anticipated that the British forces would be reinforced.[19]

> *As the Situation of American Affairs with respect to Great Britain, may be such, as to render it indispensably necessary, to attempt to Destroy the Ministerial Troops in the Town of Boston, before they can be reinforced in the Spring; even if it should be by Bombarding, & Firing the Town, is it advisable to Erect any kind of Works upon Dorchester point, before Frost setts in; & what Kind?*

The council decided to transport the cannons from Fort Ticonderoga, on Lake George in New York, to Boston. Washington wrote to Nathaniel Woodhull, president of the New York Provincial Congress, on November 16, advising him that Colonel Henry Knox would be passing through New York on his way to Fort Ticonderoga to acquire military stores. He asked Woodhull to assist Knox in every way for the benefit of the country.[20]

> *Sir*   *Cambr⟨idge 16th Novr 1775⟩*
> *it was determined at t⟨he Conference⟩ held here in the Last Month, th⟨at Such Military⟩ Stores as Coud be spared from N⟨ew york Crown point⟩ Ticonderoga &a shoud be Sent he⟨re for the use of⟩ the Continental Army—as it wa⟨s not clear to me,⟩ whether I was to send for, or that they ⟨were to be sent⟩ to me, I desired Mr Reed on his way to ⟨Philada⟩ to enquire into this Matter—as I have ⟨not heard⟩ from him on this Subject, And the Seaso⟨n advanceing⟩ fast, I have thought it necessary to se⟨nd Hen.⟩ Knox Esqr. who will deliver you this— after ⟨he⟩ forwards what he Can get at your place, ⟨he will⟩ proceed to General Schuyler on this very imp⟨ortant⟩ business. I request the favour of you Si⟨r⟩ and the Gentlemen of your Congress to give ⟨Mr⟩ Knox all the Assistance in your power, ⟨by So⟩ doing you will render infinite Service to y⟨our Country⟩ and vastly Oblige Sir Your most Ob. ⟨H: St⟩*
>
>   *Go: Washi⟨ngton⟩*

Colonel Knox arrived at Fort George at the southern end of Lake George, and based on scouting intelligence, he reported to Washington that it would take ten days to move the cannons across the lake to Fort George.[21]

Fort George [N.Y.]

May it please Your Excellency   *Decr 5. 1775.*

I arriv'd here Yesterday & made preparation to go over the lake this morning but General Schuyler reaching here before day prevents my going over for an hour or two. He has given me a list of Stores on the other side from which I am enabled to send an Inventory of those which I intend to forward to Camp—The Garriso⟨n⟩ at Ticonderoga is so weak, The conveyance from the fort to the landing is so difficult the passage accross the lake so precarious that I am afraid it will be ten days at least before I can get them on this side—when they are here—the conveyance from hence will depend entirely on the sleding—if that is good they shall immedia[tel]y move forward—without sleding the roads are so much gullied that it will be impossible to move a Step.

General Schuyler will do every thing possible to forward this buisiness. I have the honor to be with the greatest Respect Your Excellencys most Obedient Humble Servan⟨t⟩

Henry Knox

P.S. General Schuyler assures me that although the Navigation thro' Lake George should be stopt Yet if there is any sleding they shall move on another way.

Warm weather and the lack of snowfall made sledding almost impossible. By January 5, the convoy of cannons had only traveled as far as Albany. Knox explained the situation in the following letter to Washington.[22]

Sir   *Albany Jany 5 1776*

I did myself the honor to address your Excellncy from Fort George on the 17 Ult.—I then was in hopes that we should have been able to have had the

Cannon at Cambridge by this time the want of Snow detain'd us some days &
now a cruel thaw, hinders from Crossing Hudsons River which we are oblig'd to
do four times from Lake George to this Town—the first severe night will make
the Ice on the river sufficiently strong 'till that happens the Cannon & mortars
must remain where they are most of them at the different crossing places & some
few here—these inevitable delays pain Me exceedingly as my mind is fully sensible
of the importance of the greatest expedition in this Case—In eight of nine days
after the first severe frost they will be at Springfield from which place we can get
them easily transported Altho there should be no snow—but to that the roads are
So excessively bad Snow will be necessary—We got over 4 more dble fortified 12
pounders after my last to your excellency—I send a duplicate of the List for fear
of miscarriage of the other List, General Schuyler has been exceedingly assidious
In this matter, as to myself my utmost endevers have been & still shall be use[d]
to forward them with the utmost dispatch. I have the honor to be with the greatest
Respect Your Excellencys Most Obdt Hble Servt

H. Knox

After further delays, Knox finally arrived with the cannons on
January 18. Washington called a council of generals on February 16.
They decided to locate the cannons on Dorchester Heights overlooking
British-held Boston and bombard the enemy into submission. On the
weekend of March 3, the Continental forces shelled Boston. In retali-
ation, the British planned to storm Dorchester Heights and drive the
Continental army out of this strategic location. However, a ferocious
late winter nor'easter arose at the time of the crossing and forced the
British to abandon that plan. In a letter to Lieutenant Colonel Joseph
Reed, Washington concluded that the high winds that had prevented the
British from crossing the channel were an act of Providence.[23]

Dear Sir,   *Cambridge 26th Feby [–9 March] 1776*
    A Line or two from you by Colo. Bull, which came to hand last Evening, is
the only Letter I have receivd from you since the 21st of Jany—this added to

my getting none from any other Corrispondant to the Southward, leads me to apprehend some miscarriage. I am to observe thô that the Saturday's Post is not yet arrived—by that I may, possibly, get Letters.

We have, under as many difficulties perhaps (on Acct of hard frozen ground) as ever working Parties Ingaged, compleated our Work on Litchmores point—we have got some heavy pieces of Ordinance placed there—two Platforms fixed for Mortars, and every thing, but the thing, ready for any offensive operation— Strong Guards are now Mounted there, and at Cobble Hill.

About ten days ago the severe freezing Weather formed some pretty strong Ice from Dorchester to Boston Neck, and from Roxbury to the Common—this I thought (knowing the Ice could not last) a favourable oppertunity to make an Assault upon the Troops in Town—I proposed it in Council; but behold! though we had been waiting all the year for this favourable Event, the enterprize was thought too dangerous! perhaps it was—perhaps the irksomeness of my Situation led me to undertake more than could be warranted by prudence—I did not think so, and am sure, yet, that the Enterprize, if it had been undertaken with resolution must have succeeded; without it, any would fail; but it is now at an end, and I am preparing to take Post on Dorchester to try if the Enemy will be so kind as to come out to us. Ten Regiments of Militia you must know had come in to strengthen my hands for Offensive Measures—but what I have hear said respective the determinations in Council & possessing of Dorchester Point is spoken under the rose.

March 3d 1776. The foregoing was intended for another Conveyance, but being hurried with some other matters, & not able to compleat it, it was delayed; since which your favours of the 28th Jany and first & 8th of Feby are come to hand. for the agreeable Accts contain in one of them, of your progress in the Manufacture of Powder, & prospect of getting Arms, I am obliged to you; as there is some consolation in knowing that these useful Articles will supply the Wants of some part of the Continental Troops, although I feel too sensibly, the Mortification of havg them with-held from me—Congress not even thinking it necessary to take the least notice of my application for these things.

I hope in a few Nights to be in readiness to take Post on Dorchester as we are using every means in our power to provide materials for this purpose, the Ground being so hard froze yet, that we cannot Intrench, & therefore are obliged to depend entirely upon Chandaliers, Fascines, & screw'd Hay for our Redoubts. It is expected that this Work will bring on an Action between the King's Troops and ours....

March 7th. The Rumpus, which every body expected to see between the Ministerialists in Boston and our Troops has detain'd the bearer till this time. On Monday Night, I took possession of the Heights of Dorchester with two thousand Men under the Command of General Thomas—previous to this, and in order to divert the Enemy's attention from the real object & to harrass we began on Saturday Night a Canonade and Bombardment which with Intervals was continued through the Night. the same on Sunday—and on Monday a Continued Roar from Seven Oclock till day light was kept up between the Enemy and us. In this time we had an Officer and one private killed & 4 or 5 Wounded—and through the Ignorance I suppose of Our Artillery men burst 5 Mortars (two 13 Inch & 3 ten Inch) the Congress one of them. What damage the Enemy has sustain'd is not known as there has not been a creature out of Boston since. The Canonade &ca except in the destruction of the Mortars answer'd our expectation fully; for though we had upwards of 300 teams in motion at the same Instant carrying on our Fascines & other Materials to the Neck & the Moon Shining in its full lustre we were not discover'd till day light on Tuesday Morning.

So soon as we were discover'd every thing seem'd to be preparing for an Attack, but the tide failing before they were ready about One thousand only were able to Imbark in Six transports in the Afternoon and these falling down towards the Castle were drove on Shore by a violent storm which arose in the Afternoon of that day & continued threw the Night. Since that they have been seen returning to Boston—and whether from an apprenshion that our Works are now too formidable to make any Impression on, or from what other causes I know not, but their hostile appearances have subsided & they are removing their Ammuniti⟨on⟩ out of their Magazine whether with a view to move Bag & Baggage or not I cannot undertake to say—but if we had Powder (and our Mortars replaced, which I am about to do by new cast ones as soon as possible) I would, so soon as we were sufficiently strengthened on the Heights, to take possession of the point just opposite to Boston Neck give them a dose they would not well like.

We had prepared Boats, a Detachment of 4000 men &ca &ca for pushing in to the West part of Boston if they had made any formidable attack upon Dorchester. I will not lament or repine at any Act of Providence because I am in a great measure a convert to Mr Popes opinion that whatever is, is right, but I think every thing had the appearance of a successful Issue if we had come to an Ingagement on that day. It was the 5th of March which I recalled to their remembrance as a day never to be forgotten—an Ingagement was fully expected—& I never saw spirits higher, or more ardour prevailing.

General Howe made no further attempt to attack Washington's forces. Shortly thereafter, the defeated British decided to abandon Boston. On March 19, Washington advised Brigadier General Lord Sterling, the commander of the Continental army in New York City, that Howe had sailed out of Boston Harbor. Although he did not know Howe's plans, Washington advised Sterling to expect the British to attack New York City.[24]

My Lord   *Cambridge March 19. 1776*
I am now to acknowledge the receipt of your favour of the 11th Instant & to give you my congratulations upon your late appointment by the Honourable Congress.

If the intelligence is true and to be depended on, which was brought by the Gentn to New York, I think with you, that we shall have an Opportunity of securing & putting the Continent in a tolerable posture of defence, and that the operations of the Summers Campaign will be not so terrible, as we were taught to expect, from the accounts and denunciations which the Ministry have held forth to the publick.

I have the pleasure to inform you, that on the morning of the 17 Instant General Howe with his Army abandon'd the Town of Boston without destroying It, an event of much importance and which must be heard with great satisfaction, and that we are now in full possession—Their embarkation & retreat were hurried and precipitate and they have left behind 'em stores of one thing and another to a pretty considerable amount, among which are several peices of Heavy Cannon & one or two Mortars which are spiked—The Town is in a much better situation and less Injured, than I expected from the reports I had received, tho to be sure It is much damaged, and many Houses despoiled of their valuable furniture.

The Fleet is still in King and Nantasket Roads and where they Intend to make a descent next, is altogether unknown, but supposing New York to be an Object of much importance & to be in their view, I must recommend your most strenuous and active exertions in preparing to prevent any designs or Attempts they may have against It—I have detached the Riflemen & Five Batallions from hence to your Assistance, which will be followed by others as circumstances will allow—These with what forces you have & can Assemble If there shou'd be an occasion, I trust will be sufficient to hinder the Enemy from possessing the City or making a Lodgement 'till the main body of this Army can arrive. I am My Lord with great esteem Your Most Obedt & Humble servt

Go: Washington

General Howe and his seven thousand troops lingered just offshore for ten days before sailing to Halifax, Nova Scotia. When the British fleet finally sailed away, Washington, in anticipation of Howe's next objective, issued orders for the Continental army to march from Boston to New York City. Washington then sent a letter to Nicholas Cooke, Lord Stirling, Brigadier General William Thompson, and Jonathan Trumbull Sr. informing them of his move to New York City.[25]

Sir   Head Quarters Cambridge 27th March 1776
I take this earliest opportunity to acquaint you that the Men of War and Transports with the Ministerial troops sailed this afternoon from Nantasket

Harbour. There is only a Man of War and two or three other armed Vessels now remaining there.

In consequence of this movement I have ordered a Brigade to march to morrow morning for New York, and shall follow with the remainder of the Army as soon as I can receive certain information of the Fleet being clear of the Coast, and that we are in no further danger of their returning to attack us at a disadvantage. I shall leave a few Regiments at Boston to protect the Continental Stores, and to assist in fortifying the Town and Harbour agreeable to the directions that may be given by the General Assembly of this Colony. I have the honor to be most respectfully Sir Your obedient humble Servant

G. Washington

On April 2, John Hancock wrote to Washington and informed him that the Continental Congress ordered a gold medal be struck to memorialize his success in Boston and the approbation of the country.[26]

Sir,   *Philadelphia April 2d 1776.*

It gives me the most sensible Pleasure to convey to you, by Order of Congress, the only Tribute, which a free People will ever consent to Pay; the Tribute of Thanks and Gratitude to their Friends and Benefactors.

The disinterested and patriotic Principles which led you to the Field, have also led you to Glory: and it affords no little Consolation to your Countrymen to reflect, that, as a peculiar Greatness of Mind induced you to decline any Compensation for serving them, except the Pleasure of promoting their Happiness, they may, without your Permission, bestow upon you the largest Share of their Affections and Esteem.

Those Pages in the Annals of America, will record your Title to a conspicuous Place in the Temple of Fame, which shall inform Posterity, that under your Directions, an undisciplined Band of Husbandmen, in the Course of a few Months, became Soldiers; and that the Desolation meditated against the Country, by a brave Army of Veterans, commanded by the most experienced Generals, but employed by bad Men in the worst of Causes, was, by the Fortitude

of your Troops, and the Address of their Officers, next to the kind Interposition
of Providence, confined for near a Year, within such narrow Limits, as scarcely to
admit more Room than was necessary for the Encampments and Fortifications,
they lately abandoned.

Accept therefore, Sir, the Thanks of the United Colonies, unanimously declared
by their Delegates, to be due to you, and the brave Officers and Troops under your
Command: and be pleased to communicate to them, this distinguished Mark of
the Approbation of their Country.

The Congress have ordered a Golden Medal, adapted to the Occasion, to be
struck, and when finished, to be presented to you. I have the Honour to be, with
every Sentiment of Esteem, Sir, your most obedt and very hble Servt.

John Hancock Presidt

Washington arrived in New York City on April 13, 1776. Upon arriving, he issued general orders thanking the officers who had established the defenses of the city. Along with his compliments, Washington set the standards for troop deportment.[27]

Head Quarters, New-York, April 14th 1776

Parole, New-York.   *Countersign Prosperity.*

The General compliments the Officers who have successively commanded at this
Post, and returns his Thanks to them, and to all the Officers, and Soldiers, under
their Command, for the many Works of Defence, which have been so expedi-
tiously erected, and doubts not but the same Spirit of Zeal for the service, will
continue to animate their future conduct.

Exact Returns of all the Regiments and Corps, to be made up and sent to the
Adjutant General as soon as possible—The Commanding Officers at the out-
posts, are also to send a Report of the Numbers under their command, where,
and how disposed of—Exact Returns also, of all the Ordinance, and military
Stores, Provisions, Stores in the Department of the Quarter Master General

&c., to be forthwith deliver'd to the Commander in Chief, signed by the proper Officer of the Head of each department.

All persons infected with the Small-Pox are to be immediately removed to a secure place to be provided by the Qr Mr General, who will consult the Magistrates of the City thereupon. A proper Guard, to be composed of men, who have had that Disorder, to be fixed at this Hospital, to prevent any intercourse but such as the manager shall licence.

Pay-Abstracts are to be made out for each Regiment, and Corps in this department, to the 1st of April exclusive; (each Month seperate) and lodged with Major Harrison Aid-de-Camp to the General, that provision may be made for payment.

As the General is unacquainted at present, with the various Orders for the good Government of the Troops here, or the reasons which induced the giving of them; He directs, that those, and all General Orders be duly attended to, and obeyed until countermanded by himself.

As the General flatters himself, that he shall hear no Complaints from the Citizens, of abuse, or ill-treatment, in any respect whatsoever; but that every Officer, and Soldier, of every Rank and Denomination, will pride themselves (as Men contending in the glorious Cause of Liberty ought to do) in an orderly, decent and regular deportment.

One Captain, four Subalterns, four Serjeants, four Corporals, two Drums, and one hundred Privates, to parade this Afternoon at four O'Clock, to go as Guard to Governor's Island.

Two Field Officers, four Captains, eight Subalterns, sixteen Serjeants, four Drums & Fifes and four hundred men from Heath's and Lord Stirling's Brigades, to parade at Six O'Clock to morrow Morning, with three days provisions, to go as a working party to Governor's Island—Genl Putman will order Boats to be ready at the Ferry to transport them.

For the future the Commissary General is not to issue any Rum to working parties, unless the Return is signed by the Officer commanding the whole party.

Washington then ordered the expansion of the defenses of New York City. Colonel Henry Knox followed Washington's strategy and then reported that he had placed 121 cannons in and around the city.[28]

New York June 10 1776

Your Excellency will please to observe by the above summary that there are now mounted and fit for action in this City and the neighbouring posts one hundred and twenty one heavy and light Cannon. To each Cannon it will be necessary to have ten men including the mortar and contingent Services. this would make twelve hundred an[d] ten men. we have in the regiment six hundred officers included, of these about forty are on Command at distant posts, and about as many more perhaps sick or unfit for service, this would reduce the numbers to five hundred and twenty, of these about fifty are officers—if your Excellency should think it proper that all the artillery should be mann'd at the same time we shall want six hundred more men. It is usual in the British Service to draught men from the Battalions as additional artillery men for such time as the Commander in cheif shall think necessary. as most of the Battalions now in the service are considerably defficient in arms a draught might be made without any prejudice to the strength of the regiments—and that part of the army which will be of no use in action put upon a Service of the utmost importance. the men who may be draughted to be muster'd and paid by their respective Colonels. as the Corps of artillery is always more on detachments than any other Corps an additional number of officers will be necessary—The above is Most respectfully submitted by Yr Excellencys Most Obedt Hble Ser.

H. Knox

On June 30, 1776, the British sailed into New York Harbor. Washington wrote to John Hancock to inform him that 110 British ships had been observed before it became too dark to continue counting.[29]

Sir   *New York June 30. 1776*

I had the pleasure of receiving your favor of the 29th early this morning with which you have been pleased to honor me, together with the Resolves for a further augmentation [of] our Army.

The Battallion of Germans which Congress have ordered to be raised, will be a Corps of much service, and I am hopefull that such persons will be appointed Officers as will complete their Inlistments with all possible expedition.

I shall communicate to Col. Stevenson and One of his Field Officers what you have requested and direct them to repair immediately to Philadelphia.

It is an unlucky circumstance that the Term of Inlistment of these three Companies and of the Rifle Battallion should expire at this time, when a hot Campaign is in all probability about to commence.

Canada It is certain would have been an Important acquisition, and well worth the Expences incurred in the pursuit of It. But as we could not reduce It to our possession, the retreat of our Army with so little loss under such a variety of distresses, must be esteemed a most fortunate event. It is true the Accounts we have received, do not fully authorize us to say, that we have sustained no loss, but they hold forth a probable ground for such conclusion. I am anxious to hear It confirmed.

I have the honor of transmitting you an Extract of a Letter received last night from Genl Ward. If the Scheme the privateers had in view, and the measures he had planned have been carried into execution, the Highland Corps will be tolerably well disposed off, but I fear the fortunate event had not taken place.

In General Wards Letter was Inclosed one from Lt. Colo. Campbell, who was made prisoner with the Highland Troops. I have transmitted you a Copy. This will give you a full and exact Account of the number of prisoners, that were on board the four Transports, and will prove beyond a possibility of doubt, that the evacuation of Boston by the British Troops was a matter neither known or expected when he received his orders. Indeed so many facts had concurred before to settle the matter, that no additional proofs were necessary.

When I had the honor of addressing you Yesterday, I had only been informed of the arrival of Forty five of the fleet in the morning, since that I have received *authentic Intelligence from sundry persons, among them from Genl Greene, that One hundred & Ten Sail came in before night that were counted, and that more were seen about dusk in the Offing. I have no doubt but the whole that sailed from Halifax are now at the Hook.*

Just as I was about to conclude my Letter, I received one from a Gentleman upon the Subject of calling the Five Regiments from Boston to the defence of Canada, or New York, and to have Militia raised in their lieu. I have sent you a Copy and shall only Observe that I know the Author well, his handwriting is quite familiar to me—he is a Member of the General Court, very sensible, of great Influence and a warm and zealous friend to the cause of America. the expedient proposed by him is submitted to Congress. I have the honor to be with Sentiments of the highest esteem Sir Your Most Obed. Servt

Go: Washington

Washington also wrote to his brother John Augustine Washington and described their preparations for defending the colony against Howe's invasion.[30]

Dear Brother   *New York July 22d 1776.*

Whether you wrote to me or I to you last, I cannot undertake to say; but as it is sometime since a Letter has past, and as I expect every hour to be engaged in two busy a Scene to allow time for writing private Letters, I will take an oppertunity by this days post to address you a few Lines, giving a brief acct of the Situation of Affairs in this Quarter.

To begin then—we have a powerful Fleet within full view of us—distant about 8 Miles—We have General Howes present Army, consisting by good report of abt Eight or Nine thousand Men upon Staten Island, covered by their Ships—We have Lord Howe just arrived (that is about 10 days ago)—and we have Ships now popping In which we suppose, but don't know, to be part of the Fleet with the expected Reinforcement—When this arrives, if the Report of Deserters, Prisoners, and Torries are to be depended upon the Enemy's numbers will amount at least to 25,000 Men. ours to about 15,000—more indeed are expected, but there is no certainty of their arrival as Harvest and a thousand other excuses are urged for the Reasons of delay. what kind of opposition we shall be able to make time only can shew—I can only say that the Men appear to be in good Spirits, and if they will stand by me the place shall not be carried without some loss, notwithstanding we are not yet in such a posture of defence as I cd wish.

Two Ships, to wit, the Phoenix of 44 Guns, and Rose of 20, Run by our Batteries on the 12th; exhibiting a proof of what I had long most religeously believed, and that is, that a Vessel with a brisk Wind and strong Tide, cannot (unless by a chance Shott) be stopp'd by a Battery without you could place some obstruction in the Water to impede her Motion within reach of your Guns. We do not know that these Ships received any Capitol Injury—in their Rigging they were somewhat damaged, & several Shot went through their Hulls; but few if any Lives were lost. they now, with three Tenders which accompanied them lye up the North or Hudsons River abt 40 Miles above this place and have totally cut off all Communication (by Water) between this City and Albany; & this Army and that of ours upon the Lakes—they may have had other motives inducing them to run up the River, such as supplying the Tories with Arms &ca &ca but such a vigilant watch has hitherto been kept upon them that I fancy they have succeeded but indifferently in those respects notwithstanding this Country abounds in disaffected Persons of the most diabolical dispositions & Intentions, as you my have perceived by the several publications in the Gazette relative to their designs of destroying this Army by treachery and Bribery, which was provadentially discover'd.

It is the general Report of Deserter[s] and Prisoners, and a prevailing opinion here, that no attempt will be made by Genl How till his reinforcement arrives, which as I said before is hourly expected—Our Situation at present, both with respect to Men, & other matters is such, as not to make it advisable to attempt any thing against them, surrounded as they are by Water & covered with Ships, least a miscarriage should be productive of unhappy and fatal consequences. It is provoking nevertheless to have them so nea⟨r with⟩out being able in their weakest

⟨*part to give*⟩ *them any disturbance.* ⟨*The ships*⟩ *that past us are also saf*⟨*ely moored*⟩ *in a broad part of the River, out* ⟨*of reach*⟩ *of shott from either shore.*

Mrs Washington is now at Philadelphia & has thoughts of returning to Virginia as there is little or no prospect of her being with me any part of this Summer. I beg of you to present my Love to my Sister and the Children—and Compliments to any enquiring friends & do me the justice to believe that I am Dr Sir Yr most Affecte Brother

Go: Washington

Washington wrote to John Hancock on August 13 advising him that the British were about to launch their offensive. In the letter, he informed Hancock that he was shipping his important papers to Congress in Philadelphia to protect them from the imminent invasion.[31]

Sir   *New York Augt 13th 1776*

As there is reason to believe that but little Time will elapse before the Enemy make their Attack, I have thought It advisable to remove All the papers in my hands respecting the Affairs of the States from this place. I hope the Event will shew the precaution was unnecessary, but yet prudence required that It should be done, Lest by any Accident they might fall into their hands.

They are all contained in a large Box nailed up & committed to the care of Lt. Colo. Reed, Brother of the Adjt Genl to be delivered to Congress, In whose Custody I would beg leave to deposit them, untill our Affairs shall be so circumstanced as to admit of their return. The Enemy since my Letter of Yesterday have received a further augmentation of Thirty Six Ships to their Fleet, making the whole that have arived since Yesterday morning Ninety Six. I have the Honor to be with great respect Sir yr most Obed. Servt

Go: Washington

P.S. I would Observe that I have sent off the Box privately that It might raise no disagreable Ideas, & have enjoined Colo. Reed to Secrecy.

G.W.

To advise Congress on the actions of the British fleet, Washington increased the frequency of his letters to John Hancock. On August 15, he informed Hancock that it was apparent that the British intended to land on Long Island.[32]

> *Sir*   *New York Augt 15th 1776*
>
> *   As the situation of the Two Armies must engage the attention of Congress and lead them to expect, that, each returning day will produce some Important Events, This is meant to Inform them that Nothing of Moment has yet cast up. In the Evening of Yesterday there were great movements among their Boats and from the Number that appeared to be passing and repassing about the Narrows, we were Induced to beleive they Intended to land a part of their force upon Long Island, but having no report from Genl Greene, I presume they have not done It. I have the Honor to be with my duties to Congress yr & their most Obedt Servt*
>
> *   Go: Washington*

Washington joined the forces on Long Island as the confrontation with the British was about to commence. Lieutenant Colonel Robert Hanson Harrison reported to John Hancock that with the general busy commanding his troops, Harrison would be reporting to Congress on behalf of Washington. Harrison wrote to Hancock informing him that the British had attacked on several fronts and that both General Sullivan and Lord Stirling had been captured.[33]

> *Sir*   *New York Augt 27. 1776 Eight OClock. P.M.*
>
> * I this minute returned from our Lines on Long Island where I left his Excellency the General. From him I have It in command to Inform Congress that Yesterday he went there & continued till Evening when from the Enemy's having landed a considerable part of their Forces and many of their Movements, there was reason to apprehend they would make in a little time a Genl Attack. As they would have a Wood to pass through before they could approach the Lines, It was thought expedient to place a number of Men there on the different Roads*

leading from whence they were stationed in order to harrass and annoy them in their March—This being done, early this Morning a Smart engagement ensued between the Enemy and our Detachments, which being unequal to the force they had to contend with, have sustained a pretty considerable loss—At least many of our Men are missing, among those that have not returned are Genls Sullivan and Lord Stirling—The Enemy's loss is not known certainly, but we are told by such of our Troops that were in the Engagement and that have come in, that they had many killed and wounded—Our party brought off a Lieutt, Sergt, and Corporal with 20 privates prisoners. While These Detachments were engaged, a Column of the Enemy descended from the Woods and marched towards the Center of our Lines with a design to make an Impression, but were repulsed— This Evening they appeared very numerous about the Skirts of the Woods where they have pitched Several Tents, and his Excellency Inclines to think they mean to attack and force us from our Lines by way of regular approaches rather than in any other manner.

Today Five Ships of the Line came up towards the Town where they seemed desirous of getting, as they turned a long time against an unfavourable Wind, and on my return this Evening I found a Deserter from the 23d Regmt, who Informed me that they design as soon as the Wind will permit 'em to come up, to give us a Severe Cannonade and to Silence our Batteries, If possible. I have the Honor to be in great Haste Sir Your Most Obedt

Rob. H. Harrison.

On August 28 and 29, it rained heavily and prevented further aggression by the British. On the night of August 29, Washington withdrew his troops from Long Island and returned to Manhattan. That night, with the British only a few hundred yards away, Washington, under a cloud of heavy weather, transported all of the Continental troops across the East River to Manhattan without being detected.

General Thomas Mifflin was stationed in the rear guard while the Continental troops retreated across the East River. Late that night, he mistakenly was informed that Washington wanted him to proceed to the

East River and withdraw. General Washington observed Mifflin's movements and commanded him to return to his position of guarding their withdrawal. By returning to the rear guard position, Mifflin's party risked being discovered and captured as daylight approached. But the heavy weather enabled Mifflin's troops to safely escape too.[34]

Mifflin's party promptly faced about and reoccupied their stations until dawn, when Providence again "interposed in favor of the retreating army." To have attempted to withdraw in clear daylight would have been a hazardous experiment for these regiments, but just before dawn a heavy fog began to settle over Long Island, and the covering party was safe. … When the final order, therefore, came about sunrise for Mifflin's men to retire to the ferry, they were enabled to do so under cover of the fog without exciting any suspicion of their movements in the enemy's camp. "We kept up fires, with outposts stationed," says Lieutenant-Colonel Chambers, "until all the rest were over. We left the lines after it was fair day and then came off." As our soldiers withdrew they distinctly heard the sound of pickaxe and shovel at the British works. Before seven o'clock the entire force had crossed to New York, and among the last to leave was the commander-in-chief. "General Washington," adds Chambers, "saw the last over himself."

General Washington informed John Hancock of their losses and retreat in a letter on August 31.[35]

Sir   New York Augt 31st 1776

Inclination as well as duty would have Induced me to give Congress the earliest Information of my removal and that of the Troops from Long Island & Its dependencies to this City the night before last, But the extreme fatigue whic⟨h⟩ myself and Family have undergone as much from the Weather since the Engagement on the 27th rendered me & them entirely unfit to take pen in hand—Since Monday scarce any of us have been out of the Lines till our passage across the East River was effected Yesterday morning & for Forty Eight

Hours preceding that I had hardly been of[f] my Horse and never closed my Eyes so that I was quite unfit to write or dictate till this Morning.

Our Retreat was made without any Loss of Men or Ammunition and in better order than I expected from Troops in the situation ours were—We brought off all our Cannon & Stores, except a few heavy peices, which in the condition the earth was by a long continued rain, we found upon Trial impracticable—The Wheels of the Carriages sinking up to the Hobs, rendered it impossible for our whole force to drag them—We left but little provisions on the Island except some Cattle which had been driven within our Lines and which after many attempts to force across the Water we found Impossible to effect, circumstanced as we were—I have Inclosed a Copy of the Council of War held previous to the Retreat, to which I beg leave to refer Congress for the Reasons or many of them, that led to the adoption of that measure. Yesterday Evening and Last night a party of our Men were employed in bringing Our Stores, Cannon, Tents &ca from Governors Island, which they nearly compleated—Some of the Heavy Cannon remain there still, but I expect will be got away to day.

In the Engagement on the 27th Generals Sullivan & Stirling were made pris-oners; The former has been permitted on his parole to return for a little time—From My Lord Stirling I had a Letter by Genl Sullivan a Copy of which I have the Honor to transmit—That contains his Information of the Engagement with his Brigade—It is not so full and certain as I could wish; he was hurried most probably as his Letter was unfinished—Nor have I been yet able to obtain an exact account of Our Loss, we suppose It from 700 to a Thousand, killed & taken—Genl Sullivan says Lord Howe is extremely desirous of seeing some on the Members of Congress for which purpose he was allowed to come out & to communicate to them what was passed between him & his Lordship—I have consented to his going to Philadelphia, as I do not mean or conceive It right to withold or prevent him from giving such information as he possesses in this Instance.

I am much hurried & Engaged in Arranging and making new Dispositions of our Forces, The Movements of the Enemy requiring them to be immediately had, and therefore have only time to add that I am with my best regards to Congress Their & Your Most Obedt He Servt

Go: Washington

Both the battles of Boston and Long Island were determined by wildly unseasonable weather. Washington believed these abnormal conditions were attributable to the protection of Providence. In Boston, the British assault on Dorchester Heights had been turned back by a violent storm. On Long Island, Washington's successful retreat had been enabled by a heavy fog. These two experiences validated his claim to Martha when he first left home fourteen months earlier: Acts of Providence would protect him in the fight against the Crown's superior forces.

Following the loss of Long Island, Washington retrenched in Manhattan and planned the defense against Britain's drive to control the Hudson River. The British planned to unite their forces with Burgoyne from the north and Howe from the south to bifurcate the colonies.

YOU ALONE CAN DEFEND US

October 1776–January 1777

"...your patience and fortitude can have no bounds after sustaining so severe a trial as you have lately had. God grant you may not meet with such another, Permit me to say (without flattery) that it is plain Providence designed you as the favorite Instrument in working the Salvation of America, it is you alone that can defend us against our foreign and, still more dangerous, domestic Enemies,..."

– January 16, 1777 – Bartholomew Dandridge

AFTER LOSING THE FIGHT AGAINST GENERAL HOWE on Long Island, Washington crossed the East River and established camp in Manhattan. General Howe marched his army north of the city in pursuit of the British plan to capture the Hudson. General Howe was to capture the southern portion of the Hudson and General Burgoyne was to capture the northern portion of the Hudson. Washington, who had been outmaneuvered by Howe on Long Island, moved quickly and blocked Howe's movements by stationing his troops in the highlands of White Plains. In an intense firefight on October 28, 1776, Howe failed to dislodge the American forces from the hills around White Plains and was forced to forfeit his plans to capture the Hudson. Howe's next move would be to send his troops across New Jersey and attempt to capture Philadelphia. And once more, Providence would influence the destiny of the young country and its forty-four-year-old commander in chief.

Washington's victory at White Plains forced General Howe to abandon the Hudson campaign, which left General Burgoyne isolated and vulnerable at Albany. Washington, in the following report to John Hancock, presiding president of Congress, outlined his plans to defend against Howe's next movements.[1]

Sir   *White plains Novr the 6th 1776*

I have the honor to inform you, that on yesterday morning the Enemy made a sudden and unexpected movement from the Several posts they had taken in our Front. they broke up their whole Encampments the preceding night, and have advanced towards King's bridge and the North river. the design of this manuvre, is a matter of much conjecture and speculation, and cannot be accounted for with any degree of certainty. the Grounds we had taken possession of, were strong and advantageous and such, as they could not have gained without much loss of blood in case an attempt had been made. I had taken every possible precaution to prevent their outflanking us, which may have led to the present measure. they may still have in view their original plan; and by a sudden wheel try to accomplish it. detachments are constantly out to observe their motions, and to harrass them as much as possible.

In consequence of this movement, I called a Council of Genl Officers to day to consult of such measures as should be adopted in case they pursued their retreat to New York. the result of which, is herewith transmitted. In respect to myself, I cannot indulge an Idea, that General Howe, supposing he is going to New York, means to close the Campaign and to sit down without attempting something more. I think it highly probable and almost certain, that he will make a descent with a part of his Troops into Jersey, and as soon as I am satisfied that the present manuvre is real and not a feint, I shall use every means in my power to forward a part of our force to counteract his designs. nor shall I be disappointed, if he sends a Detachment to the Southward for the purpose of making a Winter Campaign. from the information I have received, there is now a number of Transports at Red Hook with about three thousand Troops on board. their destination as given out, is, to Rhode Island, but this seems altogether improbable for various reasons, among others, the Season is much against it. in the Southern States they will find it milder and much more favourable for their purposes. I shall take the liberty of mentioning, that it may not be improper to suggest the probability of such a measure to the Assemblies and Conventions in those States, that they may be on their guard, and of the propriety of their establishing and laying up magazines of provisions & other necessaries in suitable places. this is a matter of exceeding importance, and what cannot be too much attended to.

From the approaching dissolution of the Army, and the departure of the New Levies which is on the eve of taking place, and the little prospect of levying a New One in time, I have wrote to the Eastern States by the unanimous advice of the General Officers, to forward Supplies of Militia in the room of those, that are now here, and who it is feared, will not be prevailed on to stay any longer than the time they are engaged for. The propriety of this application, I trust will appear, when it is known, that not a Single Officer is yet commissioned to recruit, and when it is considered how essential it is to keep up some shew of force and shadow of an Army.

I expect the Enemy will bend their force against Fort Washington and invest It immediately. from some advices it is an Object that will attract their earliest attention.

I am happy to inform you that in the Engagement on Monday Sennight, I have reason to beleive our Loss was by no means so considerable as was conjectured at first. By some deserters & prisoners we are told that of the Enemy was tolerably great. some accounts make it about Four Hundred in killed & wounded—All agree that among the former there was a Colo. Carr of the 35th Regiment.

The force that will be sent to Jersey after I am satisfied of Mr How's retreat, in addition to those now there, according to my present opinion, will make it necessary for me to go with them, to put things in a proper channel, and such a way of defence, as shall seem most probable—to check the progress of the Enemy in case they should attempt a descent there or a move towards Philadelphia. I have the Honor to be with great respect Sir Yr Most Obedt Sert

Go: Washington

After the Continental troops stopped Howe's northward movement, Howe then initiated plans to march across New Jersey and capture Philadelphia. In response, Washington moved his troops into New Jersey across from Manhattan to block Howe's campaign. On November 10, he instructed Major General Charles Lee to remain at White Plains until Washington could be confident of General Howe's movements.[2]

Sir   *[White Plains, 10 November 1776]*

The late movement of the Enemy, and the probability of their having designs upon the Jerseys (confirmd by Sundry accts from Deserters & Prisoners) rendering it necessary to throw a body of Troops over the North River, I shall immediately follow, & the Command of the Army which remains (after Genl Heaths Division Moves to Pecks kiln's) devolving upon you, I have to request[:]

That you will be particularly attentive that all the Intrenching & other Tools (except those in immediate use) be got together, and delivered to the Quarter master Genl or Majr Reed, who heretofore has been Intrusted with the care of them.

That you will direct the Commanding officer of Artillery to exert himself in having the Army well supplied with Musket Cartridges—for this purpose a convenient place, at a distance, should be fixed on, that the business may go on uninterupted.

That no Troops who have been furnished with arms, accoutrements, or Camp Utensils, be suffered to depart the Camp before they have delivered them either to the Commissary of Stores, or the Quarter Master Genl (or his assistant) as the case may be; taking receipts therefor in Exoneration of those which they have passed. In a particular manner let the Tents be taken care of, and committed to the Quarter masters care.

A Little time now, must manifest the Enemys designs, and point out to you, measures proper to be pursued by that part of the Army under your Command[.] I shall give no direction therefore on this head, having the most entire confidence in your Judgment, and Military exertions—One thing however I will suggest— namely, that as the appearance of Imbarking Troops for the Jerseys may be intended as a feint to Weaken us, & render the strong Post we now hold more vulnerable; or, if they find that Troops are Assembled with more expedition, and in greater numbers than they expected on the Jersey shore to oppose them—I say, as it is possible that from one or the other of these motives they may yet pay the Army under your Command a visit, It will be unnecessary, I am perswaded, to recommend to you the propriety of Putting this Post if you stay at it, into a proper posture of defence; and guarding against Surprizes—But I would recommend it to your Consideration, whether under the Suggestion above, your retiring to Croton Bridge, & some strong Post still more Easterly (covering the other Passes thro^ the Highlands) may not be more advisable than to run the hazard of an attack with unequal Numbers. At any rate, I think all your Baggage and Stores except such as are necessary for immediate use ought to be to the Northward of Croton River.

In case of your Removal from hence, I submit to the consideration of your self & the General Officers with you, the Propriety of destroying the Hay to prevent the Enemy from reaping the Benefit of it.

You will consider the Post at Crotons (or Pines) Bridge as under your immediate care; as also that lately occupied by Genl Parsons, and the other at Wrights Mill—the first I am taught to believe is of consequence—the other two can be of little use while the Enemy hover about the North River, and upon our right Flank.

General Wooster from the State of Connecticut and by Order of the Governor, with several Regiments of Militia are now, I presume, in or about Stamford. they were to receive Orders from me. of course they are to do it from you. There are also some other Regiments of Connecticut Militia who came out with Genel

Saltonstall, and were annex'd to Genl Parsons's Brigade, & others, which you must dispose of as occasion & Circumstances shall require—but as by the late return many of those Regiments are reduced to little more than a large Company, I recommend the discharge of all supernumerary Officers, and the others annexed to some Brigade.

As the Season will soon oblige the Enemy to betake themselves to Winter Quarters, and will not permit our Troops to remain much longer In Tents, it may be well to consider in time where Magazines of Provision's & Forage should be laid In for the army on the East side of Hudsons River. Peaks kiln of the Neighbourhood, would, I should think, be a very advantageous Post for as many as can be supported there—Croton Bridge may possibly be another good deposit—& somewhere more Easterly for the rest, as the Commissary, Quarter Master, &ca may assist in pointing out.

It may not be amiss to remind you, for it must (as it ought) to have some Influence upon your deliberations & measures, that the Massachusets Militia stand released from their contract the 17th of this Instt; & that the Connecticut Militia are not engaged for any fixed Period; & by what I can learn begin to grow very impatient to return, few indeed of whom being left.

Washington concluded this letter with instructions for Lee to quickly move his forces from White Plains to New Jersey if General Howe crossed the Hudson River and confronted Washington's forces.

If the Enemy should remove the whole, or the greatest part of their Force to the West side of Hudsons River, I have no doubt of your following with all possible dispatch, leaving the Militia, & Invalids to cover the Frontiers of Connecticut &ca in case of Need. Given at Head Quarters near the White Plains this 10th day of Novr 1776.

Go: Washington

You are hereby authorized & Impower'd to appoint General Courts Martial for Tryals in all Cases whatsoever—to approve, or disapprove of the Judgment and to order Execution.

Go: Washington

In a letter to his brother John Augustine, he wrote that although his army was disorganized and undermanned, they were able to outmaneuver the British forces and prevent them from moving northward. Washington had very little time to write; therefore, he wrote whenever he had the opportunity. This letter was started on November 6 while he was in White Plains and was completed in Hackensack, New Jersey, on the nineteenth.[3]

Dear Brother,   *White plains Novr 6[–19]th 1776.*
   I have had the pleasure to receive your Letter of the 6th Ulto. We have, I think, by one Manouvre and another, and with a parcel of—but it is best to say nothing more about them —Mixed, & ungovernable Troops, spun the Campaign out to this time without coming to any decisive Action, or without letting Genl How obtain any advantage which, in my opinion, can contribute much to the completion of the business he is come upon, or to the Honour and glory of the British Arms, and those of their Auxilaries—Our numbers from the Beginning have been disjointed and confused, and much less than were apprehended. had we ever hazarded a general Action with them therefore, unless it had been in our Works at New York, or Harlem heights, we undoubtedly should have risked a good cause upon a very unfavourable Issue.
   Whilst we lay at the upper end of York Island (or the heights of Harlem) How suddenly Landed from the best Accts we cd get, about 16,000 Men above us, on a place called Frogs point on the East River, or Sound, this obliged Us, as his design was evidently to surround us, & cut of our Communication with the Country, thereby stopping all Supplies of Provisions (of which we were very

scant) to remove our Camp and out Flank him, which we have done, & by degrees got Strongly posted on advantageous Grounds at this place.

It is not in my power to furnish you with so extensive a Draft as you require, as I have none but printed Maps of the Country you want to see deleniated, & have no person about me that has time enough to Copy one, but a rough sketch of the Country in wch we have been Manouvreing, & which I had taken off to carry in my pocket, I enclose you, as it will afford some Idea of the parts adjacent to New York.

Before moving his army into New Jersey, General Howe returned to Manhattan and attacked Fort Washington, the crucial fortifications controlling the Hudson.[4] On November 16, after a heated battle, the British overran the fort and captured more than two thousand colonial troops. This was the largest single loss of American troops in the Revolutionary War.

In Hackensack, New Jersey, on the nineteenth, Washington continued his letter to his brother, writing about the fall of Fort Washington and his worries over the declining fortunes of the Continental army.

Novr 19th at Hackensac: I began this Letter at the White plains as you will see by the first part of it; but by the time I had got thus far the Enemy advanced a Second time (for they had done it once before, & after engaging some Troops which I had posted on a Hill, & driving them from it with the loss of abt 300 killed & wounded to them, & little more than half the number to us) as if they meant a gene[ra]l Attack but finding us ready to receive them, & upon such ground as they could not approach without loss, they filed of & retreated towards New York.

As it was conceived that this Manouvre was done with a design to attack Fort Washington (near Harlem heights) or to throw a body of Troops into the Jerseys, or what might be still worse, aim a stroke at Philadelphia, I hastend over on this side with abt 5000 Men by a round about March (wch we were obliged to take on Acct of the shipping opposing the passage at all the lower Ferries) of near 65 Miles, but did not get hear time enough to take Measures to save Fort Washington tho I got here myself a day or two before it surrendered, which happened on the 16th Instt after making a defence of about 4 or 5 hours only.

We have no particular Acct of the loss on either side, or of the Circumstances attending this matter, the whole Garrison after being drove from the out lines & retiring within the Fort surrendered themselves Prisoners of War, and giving me no Acct of the terms. By a Letter wch I have just receivd from Genl Greene at Fort Lee (wch is opposite to Fort Washington) I am informd that "one of the Train of Artillery came across the River last Night on a Raft—by his Acct the Enemy have suffered greatly on the North side of Fort Washington—Colo. Rawlings's Regiment (late Hugh Stephenson's) was posted there, and behaved with great Spirit—Colo. Magaw could not get the Men to Man the Lines, otherwise he would not have given up the Fort.

This is a most unfortunate affair and has given me great Mortification as we have lost not only two thousand Men that were there, but a good deal of Artillery, & some of the best Arms we had. And what adds to my Mortification is, that this Post after last Ships went by it, was held contrary to my Wishes & opinion; as I conceived it to be a dangerous one: but being determind on by a full Council of General Officers, & receiving a resolution of Congress strongly expressive of their desires, that the Channel of the River (which we had been labouring to stop a long while at this place) might be obstructed, if possible; & knowing that this could not be done unless there were Batteries to protect the Obstruction I did not care to give an absolute Order for withdrawing the Garrison till I could get round & see the Situation of things & then it became too late as the Fort was Invested. I had given it, upon the passing of the last Ships, as my opinion to Genl Greene under whose care it was, that it would be best to evacuate the place—but—as the order was discretionary, & his opinion differed from mine, it unhappyly was delayd too long, to my grief, as I think Genl Howe considering his Army & ours, would have had but a poor tale to have told without it & would have found it difficult, unless some Southern Expedition may prove successful, to have reconciled the People of England to the Conquest of a few pitiful Islands, none *of wch were defensable considering the great number of their ships & the power they have by Sea to Surround & render them unapproachable.*

Your Letter to the 30th of Octr was delivered to me a few days ago by Colo. Woodford— It is a matter of great grief and surprize to me, to find the different States so slow, and inattentive to that essential business of levying their quota's of Men—In ten days from this date, there will not be above 2000 Men, if that, on this Side Hudson's River (of the fixed & establish'd Regiments) to oppose Howes whole Army, and very little more on the other to secure the Eastern Colonies and the Important Passes leading through the Highlands to Albany & the Country about the Lakes. In short it is impossible for me in the compass of a Letter to give you any Idea of our Situation—of my difficulties—& the constant perplexities & mortifications I constantly meet with, derived from the unhappy policy of short enlistments, & delaying them too long. Last fall or Winter, before the Army which was then to be raised, was set about, I represented in clear & explicit terms the evils wch would arise from short Inlistments—the expence that must attend the raising of an Army every year—the futility of such an Army when raised; and, in a word, if I had spoke with a prophetick spirit, could not have foretold the evils with more accuracy than I did—all the year since I have been pressing them to delay no time in engaging Men upon such terms as would Insure success, telling them that the longer it was delayed the more difficult it would grow; but the measure was not set about till it was too late to be effected, & then in such a manner as to bid adieu to every hope of getting an Army from which any Services are to be expected. the different States without regard to the merits or qualifications of an Officer, quarrelling about the appointments; & nominating such as are not fit to be Shoe Blacks from the local attachments of this or that Member of Assembly.

I am wearied almost to death with the retrog[r]ade Motions of things, and Solemnly protest that a pecuniary rewd of 20,000 £s a year would not induce me to undergo what I do; and after all perhaps, to loose my Character as it is impossible, under such a variety of distressing Circumstances to conduct Matters agreeable to public expectation or even of those who employ me—as they will not make proper allowances for the difficulties their own errors have occasioned.

I am glad to find by your last Letter that your family are tolerably well recoverd from the Indispositions they labourd under. God grant you all health & happiness—nothing in this world would contribute so much to mine as to be once more fixed among you in the peaceable enjoymt of my own vine, & fig Tree. Adieu my dear Sir—remember me Affectionat(e)ly to my Sister & the Family, & giv(e) my Compliments to those who enqui(re) after Yr Sincerely Affectionate Brother

Go: Washington

On November 20, only four days after capturing Fort Washington, the British crossed the Hudson and attacked Fort Lee in New Jersey. With only three thousand men remaining, General Washington elected to withdraw without a fight rather than risk his men again. On November 21, Washington described their dire conditions in a letter to John Hancock.[5]

21st. The unhappy affair of the 16th has been succeeded by further misfortunes. Yesterday morning a large body of the Enemy landed between Dobb's Ferry and Fort Lee. their object was evidently to inclose the whole of our Troops & Stores that lay between the North & Heckensec Rivers, which form a very narrow neck of Land. for this purpose they formed and marched as soon as they had ascended the High Grounds towards the Fort. Upon the first information of their having landed & of their movements, our Men were ordered to meet them, but finding their numbers greatly superior & that they were extending themselves to seize on the Passes over the River, It was thought prudent to withdraw our Men, which was effected and their retreat secured. We lost the whole of the Cannon that was at the Fort, except Two twelve Pounders, and a great deal of baggage—between Two & three hundred Tents—about a Thousand Barrells of Flour & other Stores in the Qr Master's department. this loss was inevitable. As many of the Stores had been removed, as circumstances & time would admit of. the Ammunition had been happily got away. Our present situation between Heckensec & Posaic Rivers being exactly similar to our late one, and our force here by no means adequate to an opposition that will promise the smallest prob-

ability of Success, we are taking measures to retire over the Waters of the latter, when the best disposition will be formed that circumstances will admit of.

Also on November 21, Washington sent a letter to Lee explaining that the British had moved across the Hudson River and urged him to immediately move his men to New Jersey and reinforce Washington's dwindling army.[6]

Dear General   Hackinsack [N.J.] November 21. 1776.

It must be painful to you as well as to us to have no News to send you but of a melancholy Nature. Yesterday Morning the Enemy landed a large Body of Troops below Dobb's Ferry & advanced very rapidly to the Fort called by your Name. I immediately went over & as the Fort was not tenable on this side & we in a narrow Neck of Land the passes out of wch the Enemy were attempting to seize directed the Troops consisting of Bealls, Heards[,] the Remainder of Ewing's Brigades & some other Parts of broken Regiments to move over to the West Side of Hackinsack River. A Considerable Quantity of Stores & some Artillery have fallen into their Hands—We have no Account of their Movements this Morning. But as this Country is almost a dead Flat, we have not an intrenching Tool, & not above 3000 Men, & they much broken & dispirited not only with our ill Success but the Loss of their Tents & Baggage; I have resolved to avoid any Attack tho by so doing I must leave a very fine Country open to their Ravages, or a plentiful Store House, from which they will draw voluntary Supplies.

Your Favour of the 19th is just come to Hand—I approve of your Step with Respect to the Rhode Island Officers, as I am unacquainted with their Merits, I was obliged to leave the Determination of this Matter much to Gen. Greene hoping I confess that he would make an Arrangement acceptable to his Countrymen—however I am well satisfied with what you have done & must leave it upon that Footing.

With Respect to your Situation I am very much at a Loss what now to determine, there is such a Change of Circumstances since the Date of your Letter as seems to call for a Change of Measures. Your Post undoubtedly will answer some important Purposes, but whether so many or so great as your Removal is well worthy of Consideration—You observe it prevents a fine fertile Country affording them Supplies—but now they have one much more so & more contiguous—They have already traversed a Part of that Country leaving little behind them: is it probable they will return—if not the Distance must be too great in Winter Time to render it effectually serviceable—Upon the whole therefore I am of Opinion & the Gentlemen about me concur in it that the publick Interest requires your coming over to this Side with the Continental Troops—leaving Fellows & Wadsworths Brigades to take Care of the Stores during their Short Stay at the Expiration of which I suppose they will set out home.

My Reasons for this Measure & which I think must have Weight with you are—that the Enemy are evidently changing the Seat of War to this Side of the North River—that this Country therefore will expect the Continental Army to give what Support they can & failing in this will cease to depend upon or support a Force from which no Protection is given to them. It is therefore of the utmost Importance that at least an Appearance of Force should be made to keep this Province in the Connection with the others—if that should not continue it is much to be feared that its Influence on Pennsylvania would be very considerable & more & more endanger our publick interests—Unless therefore some new Event should occur, or some more cogent Reason present itself I would have you move over by the easiest & best Passage. I am sensible your Numbers will not be large & that perhaps it may not be agreeable to the Troops—as to the first, Report will exaggerate them & present an Appearance of an Army which will at least have an Effect to encourage the desponding here, & as to the other—you will doubtless represent to them that in Duty & Gratitude their Service is due wherever the Enemy make the greatest Impression, or seem to intend so to do.

The Stores at North Castle[,] Croton Bridge & Kings Ferry are to be removed to Pecks Kiln so as to be under Genl Heaths Eye—this we hope there will be Time & Means to do.

Col. Puttnam who has been surveying the Country thinks the Bridge at Croton River a very important Place & that Troops would be necessary there—you will

please to regard it accordingly by leaving or ordering one Regiment there. I am Sir
with great regard Yr Most Obedt Servt

G.W.

Without Lee's reinforcements, Washington no longer had sufficient manpower to stand against the British. As General Howe's forces
aggressively pursued Washington, he rapidly retreated across New Jersey.
In dire need of support, Washington wrote to Lee again expressing the
necessity that his forces move quickly to New Jersey.[7]

Dear Sir   New Ark Novr the 27th 1776
I last night received the favor of your Letter of the 25th. My former Letters
were so full and explicit as to the necessity of your marching as early as pos-
sible, that it is unnecessary to add more on that Head. I confess I expected you
would have been sooner in motion. The force here when joined by yours, will not
be adequate to any great opposition, at present it is weak, and it has been more
owing to the badness of the weather that the Enemys progress has been checked,
than any resistance we could make. They are now pushing this way—part of
'em have passed the Posaic. Their Plan is not entirely unfolded, but I shall not
be surprized if Philadelphia should turn out the Object of their movement.
The distress of the Troops for want of Cloaths, I feel much, but what can I do?
Having formed an enterprize against Roger's &c. I wish you may have succeeded.
I am Dr Sir with great esteem Yr Most Obedt St.

On December 1, after moving his headquarters to Brunswick, New
Jersey, Washington reported to John Hancock that the British were
advancing with their overwhelming numbers. He informed Hancock
that he would have to concede New Jersey, retreat across the Delaware
River, and regroup in Pennsylvania.[8]

Sir   Decr 1st 1776 ½ after 7. P.M.
In a little time after I wrote you this Evening, the Enemy appeared in several
parties on the Heights opposite Brunswic and were advancing in a large body

towards the crossing place. We had a smart cannonade whilst we were parading our Men but without any or but little loss on either side. It being impossible to oppose them with our present force with the least prospect of success, we shall retreat to the West side of Delaware & have advanced about Eight miles, where it is hoped we shall meet a reinforcement sufficient to check their Progress. I have sent Colo. Humpton forward to collect the necessary boats for our transportation and conceive it proper, that the Militia from Pensylvania should be ordered towards Trentton, that they may be ready to Join us and act as occasion may require. I am Sir Yr Most Obedt Servt

Go. Washington

P.S. I wish my Letters of Yesterday may arrive safe, being informed that the return Express who had 'em was idling his time & shewing 'em on the Road.

To facilitate crossing the Delaware, Washington wrote to Colonel Richard Humpton and instructed him to secure boats at Trenton, New Jersey, to transport the army to Pennsylvania.[9]

Sir   Brunswick [N.J.] Decemr 1. 1776.

You are to proceed to The Two ferry's near Trentown and to see all the boats there put in the best Order with a sufficiency of Oars and poles and at the same time to Collect all the Additional Boats you [can] from both above and below and have them brought to those ferry's and Secured for the purpose of Carrying over the Troops & Baggage in most expeditious Manner: & for this purpose you will get every Assistance in the power of the Quarter Master General & any person in his Department. you will particularly attend to the Durham Boats which are very proper for the purpose. The Baggage & Stores of the Army should be got over the River as soon as possible and placed at some Convenient place a little back from it. I am Sir Yr Most Obt Servt

Go: Washington

On December 8 (only eighteen days after Howe initiated his attack on the Continental forces in New Jersey), Washington informed Hancock that all his troops were now in Pennsylvania. He also wrote that he still did not know the status of General Lee's army.[10]

Sir   *Mr Berkley's Sommerseat Decr 8th 1776*

   Colo. Reed would inform you of the Intelligence which I first met with on the Road from Trenton to Princeton Yesterday. Before I got to the latter, I received a Second express informing me, that as the Enemy were advancing by different Routs and attempting by One to get in the rear of our Troops which were there & whose numbers were small and the place by no means defensible, they had judged it prudent to retreat to Trenton—The retreat was accordingly made, and since to this side of the River.

   This information I thought it my duty to communicate as soon as possible, as there is not a moments time to be lost in assembling such force as can be collected and as the object of the Enemy cannot now be doubted in the smallest degree. Indeed I shall be out in the conjecture (for it is only conjecture), if the late imbarkation at New York, is not for Delaware river, to cooperate with the Army under the immediate command of Genl Howe, who I am informed from good authority is with the British Troops and his whole force upon this Route.

   I have no certain intelligence of Genl Lee, although I have sent frequent Expresses to him and lately a Colo. Humpton to bring me some accurate Accounts of his situation. I last night dispatched another Gentn to him—Major Hoops, desiring he would hasten his march to the Delaware in which I would provide Boats near a place called Alexandria for the transportation of his Troops. I can not account for the slowness of his March.

   In the disordered & moving state of the Army I cannot get returns, but from the best accounts we had between Three thousand & 3500 Men before the Philadelphia Militia and German Batallion arrived, they amount to about Two thousand. I have the Honor to be with great respect Sir Yr Most Obedt Servt

                                                    Go: Washington

Ever since Howe's return to America in August 1776, the Americans had been in full retreat. They were exhausted and demoralized after five months of fighting losing battles. Driven out of New Jersey and enduring winter blizzards without shelter, poorly clothed, and famished, they anxiously waited for January 1, the expiration date of their enlistments.

The British were encamped only a few miles from Philadelphia, and the decimated Continental army was unable to prevent their attack on America's capital. On December 12, 1776, the Continental Congress, recognizing their tenuous state, passed a resolution to relocate to Baltimore, Maryland, and relinquished civilian control of military operations to Commander in Chief General George Washington.[11]

> *Resolved, That this Congress be, for the present, adjourned to the town of Baltimore, in the state of Maryland, to meet on the 20th instant, unless a sufficient number to make a Congress shall be there sooner assembled; and that, until the Congress shall otherwise order, General Washington be possessed of full power to order and direct all things relative to the department, and to the operations of war. That the several matters to this day referred, be postponed to the day to which Congress is adjourned.*

Fifteen days later, on December 27, 1776, the Continental Congress, now seated in the city of Baltimore, passed another resolution that specifically identified the powers delegated to General Washington and limited the term of his newly specified powers to six months.[12]

> *Resolve, That General Washington shall be, and he is hereby, vested with full, ample, and complete powers to raise and collect together, in the most speedy and effectual manner, from any or all of these United States, 16 battalions of infantry, in addition to those already voted by Congress; to appoint officers for the said batallions; to raise, officer, and equip three thousand light horse; three regiments of artillery, and a corps of engineers, and to establish their pay; to apply to any of the states for such aid of the militia as he shall judge necessary; to form such magazines of provisions, and in such places, as he shall think proper; to displace and appoint all officers under the rank of brigadier general, and to fill up all vacancies in every other department in the American armies; to take, wherever*

he may be, whatever he may want for use of the army, if the inhabitants will not sell it, allowing a reasonable price for the same; to arrest and confine persons who refuse to take the continental currency, or are otherwise disaffected to the American cause; and return to the states of which they are citizens, their name, and the nature of their offenses, together with the witnesses to prove them:

That the foregoing powers be vested in General Washington, for and during the term of six months from the date hereof, unless sooner determined by Congress.

The Continental Congress entrusted Washington with the power he needed to effectively command the Continental army. This decision was a turning point in the war against Great Britain. Washington utilized his newly assigned authority to rebuild his devastated army. He assigned commands to better-qualified officers, increased the number of regiments, appropriated supplies from the civilian population, and unilaterally extended the tours of duty for new enlistees.

The concentration of all military power in the hands of the commanding general could have caused the downfall of the fledgling American democracy and facilitated a dictatorship. But Washington, true to his character, believed that the power of the military should never be permanently held by one individual, and he returned control to the Continental Congress once he defeated the British.

On December 13, Major General Lee was captured by the British. Two days later Washington received notice of Lee's capture from Major General John Sullivan.[13]

My dear General   *Germantown [N.J.] Decemr 13. 1776*
It gives me the most pungent pain to inform your Excellency of the sad Stroke America must feel in the loss of General Lee, who was this morning taken by the Enemy near Veal Town. He ordered me yesterday morning to march for this place early, which I did—and by some fatality he was induced to go to Barnell's Town, nearer the Enemy by three Miles than we were. Some Tories doubtless gave information, and this morning 70 of the Light Horse surrounded the

House, and after a gallant resistance by him and his Domesticks, he was made a prisoner.

I have taken every step to regain him, but almost despair of it. I received your Excellency's Letters to him of the 10th & 11th instant, and shall endeavour to join the Army as soon as possible. A french Gentleman whose name is wrote on the Cover that incloses this, (Capt. De Vernejoul,) behaved with great bravery in defending the General, & had his advice been taken, the General would have escaped.

Dear General I most heartily sympathize with you and my Country in this affecting Loss, and am Your most Obedient Servant

Jno. Sullivan

Washington's army was exhausted, and he was concerned about whether the Continental forces could withstand the British attack. He wrote to Lund Washington, who was managing his plantation, on December 17 and advised him to prepare for the removal of his papers from Mount Vernon.[14]

I wish to Heaven it was in my power to give you a more favourable Acct of our situation than it is—our numbers, quite inadequate to the task of opposing that part of the Army under the Command of Genl Howe, being reduced by Sickness, Desertion, & Political Deaths (on & before the first Instt, & having no assistance from the Militia) were obliged to retire before the Enemy, who were perfectly well informed of our Situation till we came to this place, where I have no Idea of being able to make a stand,...

Matters to my view, but this I say in confidence to you, as a friend, wears so unfavourable an aspect (not that I apprehend half so much danger from Howes Army, as from the disaffection of the three States of New York, Jersey & Pensylvania) that I would look forward to unfavorable Events, & prepare Accordingly in such a manner however as to give no alarm or suspicion to any one; as one step towards it, have my Papers in such a Situation as to remove at a

short notice in case an Enemy's Fleet should come up the Rive—When they are
removd let them go immediately to my Brothers in Berkeley.

On December 18, Washington wrote to his brother Samuel and
expressed his anxiety over their situation. He detailed the many concerns that he had, which included the defection of the residents of
New Jersey, New York, and Pennsylvania and subsequent support for
General Howe's imminent attack on Philadelphia. Washington confided
to Samuel that although their situation was dire, they would ultimately
succeed because their cause was righteous.[15]

Camp near the Falls at Trenton
Dear Brother,   *Decr 18th 1776.*
  In the number of Letters which necessity compels me to write, the recollection of
any particular one is destroyed, but I think my last to you was from Hackinsack
about the 20th of Novr.
  Since that period, and a little before our affairs took an adverse turn but not
more than was to be expected from the unfortunate measures which had been
adopted for the establishment of our Army.
  The Retreat of the Enemys Army from the White Plains led me to think
that they would turn their thoughts to the Jerseys, if no further, and induced
me to cross the North River with some of the Troops in order if possible to
oppose them—I expected to have met at least 5000 Men of the Flying Camp
and Militia; instead of wch I found less than one half and no disposition in
the Inhabitants to afford the least aid—This being perfectly well understood by
the Enemy they threw over a large body of Troops which pushed us from place
to place till we were obliged to cross the Delaware (into Pensylvania) with less
than 3,000 Men fit for duty owing to the Dissolution of our Force by short
Inlistments—the Enemys Numbers by the best Accts exceeding Ten, and by
others 12,000 Men.
  Before I removed to the Southside of this River I had all the Boats and other
vessels brot over or destroyed from Philadelphia upwards for 70 Miles, and by

guarding the different Fords have, as yet, baffled all their attempts to cross but from some late movements of theirs I am left in doubt whether they are Inclining to Winter Quarters or making a feint to throw us off our Guard.

Since I came on this side I have been reinforced by about 2000 of the City Militia, and understand that some of the Country Militia (from the back Counties) are on their way—but we are at present in a very disaffected part of the Provence, and between you and me I think our Affairs are in a very bad way—not so much from the Apprehension of Genl Howes Army as from the defection of New York, New Jersey, and Pensylvania—In short the conduct of the Jersey, has been most Infamous—Instead of turning out to defend their Country and affording aid to our Army they are making their Submissions as fast as they can—If they had given us any Support we might have made a stand at Hackensack, and after that at Brunswick, but the few Militia that were in Arms disbanded themselves or slunk off in such a manner upon the approach of danger as to leave us quite unsupported, & to make the best shift we could without them.

I have no doubt but that General Howe will still make an attempt upon Philadelphia this Winter—I see nothing to oppose him in a fortnight from this time, as the term of all the Troops except those of Virginia, (reduced almost to nothing) and Smallwoods Regiment from Maryland (in the same condition) will expire in that time. In a word my dear Sir, if every nerve is not straind to recruit the New Army with all possible Expedition I think the game is pretty near up—owing in great Measure to the insidious Arts of the Enemy and disaffection of the Colonies beforementioned, but principally to the accursed policy of Short Inlistments and depending too much on Militia, the Evil consequences of which were foretold 15 Months ago with a spirit almost prophetick.

Before this reaches you, you will no doubt have heard of the Captivity of Genl Lee—this is an additional Misfortune, and the more vexatious as it was the effect of folly & Imprudence (without a view to answer any good) that he was taken—going three Miles out of his own Camp (for the sake of a little better lodging) & within 20 of the Enemy a rascally Tory gave information in the

Night and a party of light Horse in the Morning seiz'd and carried him off with every mark of triumph and Indignity.

You, at a distance, can f⟨orm⟩ no Idea of the perplexity of my Situa⟨tion. No⟩ Man I be⟨li⟩eve ever had a greater c⟨hoice of⟩ difficulties & less the means of extri⟨cating⟩ himself than I have—However und⟨er a⟩ full perswation of the justice of our Ca⟨use⟩ I cannot but think the prospect will bri⟨ghten⟩ allthough for wise purposes it is, at pres⟨ent⟩ hid under a cloud.

My love & sincere regards attend My Sister & the Family. My Compliments also to our friends at Fairfield &ca and with every Sentiment of friendship as well as love I am Dr Sir Yr Affecte Brothr

Go: Washington

In his letter to John Hancock on December 20, Washington acknowledged the congressional resolution and expressed his concern over this assignment of power to one individual. He restated his intention to use this newly delegated power to bring about peace with the British and paraphrased a prophecy in the Book of Isaiah of a future where there would be peace among all humankind.[16]

> *It may be said, that this is an application for powers, that are too dangerous to be intrusted. I can only add, that desperate diseases, require desperate remedies, and with truth declare, that I have no lust after power but wish with as much fervency as any man upon this wide extended Continent for an Opportunity of turning the Sword into a ploughshare; But my feelings as an Officer and a man, have been such, as to force me to say, that no person ever had a greater choice of difficulties to contend with than I have.*

To monitor Howe's preparations for the impending attack on Philadelphia, Washington sent Colonel Joseph Reed back across the Delaware to observe their movements. On December 22, Reed reported that his scouts had found few British in the southern portion of New Jersey and that Colonel Samuel Griffin, with a militia of six hundred, had advanced with very little resistance to Mount Holly, NJ, located only twenty miles from Trenton. Reed encouraged Washington to return to New Jersey and attack Trenton as a diversionary tactic. He believed that the triumph of such a bold action would raise the spirits of the troops and the country. Reed also pointed out that the Continental army enlistments would expire shortly and a successful raid would bolster spirits throughout the country and enable Washington to rebuild his army.[17]

Dear Sir   *Briston [Pa.] Decem. 22. 1776*

    Pomroy whom I sent by your Order to go to Amboy & so through the Jersey & round by Princeton to you returned to Burlington yesterday—he went to South Amboy but was not able to get over—upon which he came up to Brunswick pass'd on to Princeton—& was prevented going to Pennington—upon which he returned to Burlington by Way of Cranberry.

    His Intelligence is that he saw no Troops, Baggage Waggons or Artillery going to New York except about 8 Waggons which he understood had the Baggage of some of the light Horse who had been relieved & were going into Quarters—At Cranberry he saw 16 Waggons going down to South Amboy for the Baggage of about 500 Men who were to quarter about Cranberry—inlisted Tories commanded by one Lawrence—at Brunswick he saw 4 peices of Cannon—the Number of Men he could not learn but they did not exceed 600 or 800—Princeton he says was called Head Quarters and there he saw a very considerable Body of Troops coming out of the College, Meeting House & other Places where they quartered. He understood they were settled in their Winter Quarters & had given over farther Operations till the Spring.

    In Burlington County he found them scattered thro all the Farmers Houses, 8, 10, 12 & 15 in a House & rambling over the whole Country.

    Col. Griffin has advanced up the Jerseys with 600 Men as far as Mount Holly within 7 Miles of Their Head Quarters at the Black Horse—he has wrote over here for 2 peices of Artilly & 2 or 300 Volunteers as he expected an Attack very soon. The Spirits of the Militia here are very high—they are all supporting him—Col. Cadwallader & the Gentlemen here all agree that they should be indulged—we can either give him a strong Reinforcement—or make a separate Attack—the latter bids fairest for producing the greatest & best Effects—it is therefore determined to make all possible Preparation to day & no Event happening to change our Measures the main Body here will cross the River tomorrow Morning & attack their Post between this & the Black Horse, proceeding from thence either to the Black Horse or the Square where about 200 Men are posted as Things shall turn out with Griffin. If they should not attack Griffin as he expects it is probable both our Parties may advance to the Black Horse if Success attends the intermediate Attempt. If they should collect their Force & march against Griffin our Attack will have the best Effects in preventing their sending Troops on that Errand, or breaking up their Quarters & coming in upon their Rear which we must endeavour to do in order to save Griffin.

We are all of Opinion my dear General that something must be attempted to revive our expiring Credit give our Cause some Degree of Reputation & prevent a total Depreciation of the Continental Money which is coming on very fast— that even a Failure cannot be more fatal than to remain in our present Situation in short some Enterprize must be undertaken in our present Circumstances or we must give up the Cause—In a little Time the Continental Army is dissolved the Militia must be taken before their Spirits & Patience are exhausted & the scattered divided State of the Enemy affords us a fair Oppy of trying what our Men will do when called to an offensive Attack—Will it not be possible my dear Genl for your Troops or such Part of them as can act with Advantage to make a Diversion or something more at or about Trenton—the greater the Alarm the more likely Success will attend the Attacks—If we could possess ourselves again of New Jersey or any considerable Part of it the Effects would be greater than if we had never left it—Allow me to hope that you will consult your own good Judgment & Spirit, & not let the Goodness of your Heart subject you to the Influence of Opinions from Men in every Respect your Inferiours. Something must be attempted before the 60 Days expires which the Commissioners have allowed—for however many affect to despise it—it is very evident that a very serious Attention is paid to it—& I am confident that unless some more favourable Appearance attends our Arms & Cause before that Time a very great Number of the Militia Officers here will follow the Example of those of Jersey, & take Benefit from it.

I will not disguise my own Sentiments that our Cause is desperate & hopeless if we do not take the Oppy of the Collection of Troops at present to strike some Stroke. Our Affairs are hasting fast to Ruin if we do not retrieve them by some happy Event. Delay with us is now equal to a total Defeat.

Be not deceived my dear General with small flatterg Appearances, we must not suffer our selves to be lulld into Security & Inacti[o]n because the Enemy does not cross the River—It is but a Reprieve the Execution is the more certain for I am very clear that they can & will cross the River in Spite of any Opposition we can give them.

Pardon the Freedom I have used, the Love of my Country, a Wife & 4 Children in the Enemys Hands, the Respect & Attachment I have to you—the Ruin & Poverty that must attend me & thousands of others will plead my Excuse for so much Freedom. I am with the greatest Respect & Regard D. Sir Your Obed. & Affect. Hbble Servt

J. Reed

On December 24, Brigadier General Philemon Dickinson wrote to Washington informing him that he had sent a scout to reconnoiter Trenton and report his findings to Washington on the morning of the twenty-fifth, Christmas Day. As Dickinson wrote the letter, he received additional intelligence and was able to inform Washington that there were about two thousand Hessians[18] in Trenton.[19]

Sir   Yardly's Farm [Bucks County, Pa.] 24 Decr 1776
I have this moment dispatch'd a proper Person over the river, to make the followg enquires, (& to return tomorrow morng, at which time a Horse will be provided for him, to wait upon your Excellency, with such Information as he may obtain) Viz: what Guards are posted upon the different roads leading into Trenton, the number on the Mill-bridge, where the Cannon lay & what number; to ascertain the number of the Enemy in Trenton, & whether any reinforcements have lately

arrived, or any Troops march'd out, & such other Intelligence as he can possibly procure.

By a Person just returned from Jersey, I am informed that a certain Benj: Combes whom your Excellency lately released, went immediately to Amboy, has since returned, & now acts as Commissary to Genl Howe at Penny town, where he is giving out a large quantity of Continental Pork, to the Poor & protected Inhabitants of that State; The Person who gives this Information, made application for some Pork, but was refused, because he had not taken Protection. I am allso informed that the number of the Enemy now in Trenton, amounts to 2,000 men, all Hessians, except a few British Troops. I have order'd a Capt. & 25 men to Genl Stevens's Quarters, agreable to Genl Green's request, there to wait your Excellency's Orders—the Bearers Capt. Mott with a few others, now waits upon my Lord Sterling to give him some Information about certain roads, agreable to his Lordships requests—Capt. Mott is a man that may be relied upon in every respect. I am extremely sorry for the occasion of my Absence at present, have been detained till near 1 OClock to compleat the above orders, hope to meet with my Mother in Philada & to return immediately. I have the honor to be, Your Excellencys, Most Ob. Servt

Philemon Dickinson

With the latest intelligence and Reed's advice, the commander in chief called upon his men to join in battle one more time and issued general orders to attack Trenton on December 25, 1776.[20]

[Bucks County, Pa., 25 December 1776]

Each Brigade to be furnish'd with two good Guides.

General Stevenss Brigade to form the advanced party & to have with them a detachment of the Artillery without Cannon provided with Spikes and Hamners to Spike up the enemies Cannon in case of necessity or to bring them off if it can be effected. the party to be provided with drag ropes for the purpose of dragging off the Cannon. General Stevens is to attack and force the enemies Guards and seize such posts as may prevent them from forming in the streets and in case

they are annoy'd from the houses to set them on fire. The Brigades of Mercer &
Lord Stirling under the Command of Major General Greene to support General
Stevens, this is the second division or left wing of the Army and to march by the
way of the Pennington Road.

St Clairs Glovers & Sargents Brigades under Major General Sullivan to
march by the river road, this is the first division of the Army and to form
the right wing. Lord Stirlings Brigade to form the reserve of the left wing and
General St Clairs Brigade the reserve of the right wing. These reserves to form
a second line in Conjunction or a second Line to each division as circumstances
may require—Each Brigadier to make the Colonels acquainted with the posts
of their respective Regiments in the Brigade and the Major Generals will inform
them of the posts of their Brigades in the Line.

Four peices of artillery to march at the head of each Column, three peices at
the head of the second Brigade of each Division and two peices with each of the
Reserves. The troops to be assembled one Miles back of McKonkeys ferry and
as soon as it begins to grow dark the troops to be March'd to McKonkeys ferry
and embark onboard the boats in following order under the direction of Colonel
Knox.

General Stevens Brigade with the detachment of Artillery men to embark
first General Mercers next; Lord Stirlings next, Genl Fermoys next who will
march in the rear of the Second Division and file off from the Penington to the
Princeton Road in such direction that he can with the greatest ease & safety
secure the passes between Princeton & Trenton. the Guides will be the best judges
of this. he is to take two peices of artille[r]y with him.

St. Clair Glover & Sargents Brigades to embark in order. Immediately upon
their debarkation the whole to form & march in Subdivisions from the Right.

The Commanding Officers of Regiments to observe that the Divisions be
equal & that proper officers be appointed to each—a profound silence to be
enjoyn'd & no man to quit his Ranks on the pain of Death—each Brigadier
to appoint flanking parties—the reserve Brigades to appoint the rear Guards of
the Columns—The heads of the Columns to be appointed to arrive at Trenton
at five oClock.

Capt. Washington & Capt. Flahaven with a party of 40 men each to march before the Divisions & post themselves on the road about three miles from Trenton & make prisoners of all going in or coming out of Town.

General Stevens will appoint a Guard to form a chain of centries round the landing place at a sufficient distance from the river to permit the troops to form This Guard not to suffer any person to go in or come out—but to detain all persons who attempts either this Guard to join their Brigade when the troops are all over.

On the evening of December 25, 1776, General Washington and his troops began crossing the Delaware River during a raging blizzard, and there were frequent setbacks during the night. Once across the river, they had to wait in subfreezing weather until all of the men and equipment arrived on the New Jersey side of the Delaware. They had planned to have everything across by midnight, but it was 3:00 a.m. on the twenty-sixth before they were ready to march on Trenton. They expected to be in position to attack at dawn, but the intense storm made it difficult to traverse the rugged roads. By the time they had marched the nine miles and formed ranks, it was 8:00 a.m. Although the battle began later than they had planned, they were still able to launch a surprise attack. Washington again ignored all personal risk and led his troops into an intense barrage of enemy fire.

After a ferocious battle, the British surrendered with losses of more than nine hundred due to death, injury, or captivity. There were two American officers wounded in the attack while they were securing two Hessian cannons. Captain William Washington (a cousin of George Washington's) was shot in each hand, and Lieutenant James Monroe (future president of the United States) was shot in his shoulder. Providentially, Washington was uninjured.

Although victorious, Washington was disappointed that several hundred Hessians managed to escape. Washington had planned for the militia to cross downstream and prevent the Hessians from escaping, but these plans were not executed because of the icy conditions on the Delaware where the militia were to cross.

The strategy was for Brigadier General James Ewing and six hundred militia to cross the Delaware River at Trenton Ferry to prevent the Hessians from retreating across Assunpink Creek Bridge. But General Ewing elected not to cross because of the hazardous, ice-filled Delaware. Also, Colonel John Cadwalader was to cross farther downstream and attack the Hessians in towns south of Trenton. Cadwalader was able to move his troops across the Delaware, but was not able to transport the artillery. He therefore abandoned the effort, and he and his troops returned to Pennsylvania.

Captain Thomas Rodney described Cadwalader's abortive effort to cross the Delaware River in his diary on December 25.[21]

About dark I received orders to march immediately to Neshaminy ferry and await orders.

We march off immediately without the knowledge of the families where we were staying and met Col. Matlack at the ferry, he being the advance party of the brigade from Bristol. We soon received orders to march to Dunkers ferry on the Delaware, and after we arrived there the whole brigade came up, and also Col. Hitchcock Brigade of New England Regulars.

Our light Infantry Battalion [the Dover company and four companies of Philadelphia militia under Capt. George Henry] were embarked in boats to cover the landing of the Brigade.

When we reached the Jersey shore we were obliged to land on the ice, 150 yards from the shore; the River was also very full of floating ice, and the wind was blowing very hard, and the night was very dark and cold, and we had great difficulty in crossing but the night was very favorable to the enterprise. We advanced about two hundred yards from the shore and formed in four columns of double files.

About 600 of the light troops got over, but the boats with the artillery were carried away in the ice and could not be got over.

After waiting about 3 hours we were informed that Gens. Cadwalader and Hitchcock had given up the expedition, and that the troops that were over were ordered back. This greatly irritated the troops that had crossed the River and they proposed making the attack without both the Generals and the artillery but it was urged, that if Gen. Washington should be unsuccessful and we also, the cause would be lost, but if our force remained intact it would still keep up the spirit of America; therefor this course was abandoned.

We had to wait about three hours more to cover the retreat, by which time the wind blew very hard and there was much rain and sleet, and there was so much floating ice in the River that we had the greatest difficulty to get over again, and some of our men did not get over that night. As soon as I reached the Pennsylvania shore I received orders to march to our quarters, where I arrived a little before daylight very wet and cold.

Washington's army regrouped, and in a driving rain and sleet storm, they marched back to the Delaware and safely crossed back into Pennsylvania, returning at daybreak.

On December 27, Tench Tilghman, Washington's secretary, wrote to his father, James Tilghman, Esq., and noted that General Washington had not only planned and executed the attack on Trenton, but that he had also personally led his troops into battle.[22]

Head Quarters Newtown 27th Decemr 1776

Hond Sir:

I have the pleasure to inform you that I am safe and well after a most successful Enterprise against three Regiments of Hessians consisting of about 1500 Men lying in Trenton, which was planned and executed under his Excellency's immediate command. Our party amounted to 2400 Men, we crossed the River at McKonkeys Ferry 9 Miles above Trenton the Night was excessively severe, both cold and snowey, which the Men bore without the least murmur. We were so much delayed in crossing the River, that we did not reach Trenton till eight OClock, when the division which the General headed in person, attacked the Enemy's out post. The other Division which marched the lower Road attacked the advanced post at Phil Dickinson's, within a few minutes after we began ours. Both parties pushed on with so much rapidity, that the Enemy had scarce time to form, our people advanced up to the Mouths of their Field pieces, shot down their Horses, and brought off the Cannon. About 600 run off upon Bordenton Road the moment the Attack began, the remainder finding themselves surrounded laid down their Arms. We have taken 30 officers and 886 privates among the former Colo Rahls the Commandant who is wounded. The General left him and the other wounded Officers upon their parole, under their own Surgeons, and gave all the privates their Baggage. Our loss is only Capt Washington and his Lieutenant slightly wounded and two privates killed and two wounded. If the Ice had not prevented Genl Ewing from crossing at Trenton Ferry, and Colo Cadwalader from doing the same at Bristol, we should have followed the Blow and drove every post below Trenton. The Hessians have laid all waste since the British Troops went away, the Inhabitants had all left the Town and their Houses were stripped and torn to pieces. The Inhabitants about the Country told us, that the British protections would not pass among the Hessians. I am informed that many people have of choice kept their Effects in Philada, supposing if Genl Howe got possession that they would be safe, so they may be, if he only carries British Troops with him, but you may depend it is not in his power, neither does he pretend to restrain the Foreigners. I have just snatched time to scrawl these few lines Colo Baylor, who is going to Congress —

I am your most dutiful and affect— Son

Tench Tilghman.

Major George Johnston provided a detailed description of the battle action and Washington's bold and courageous leadership in a letter to Colonel Leven Powell.[23]

" the two forlorn Hopes, (the right wing composed of N. Englanders, the left of Virginians,) pressed on, attacked their advanced Guards and drove them to their main Body. Our noble countryman, the Gen'l, at the head of the Virginia

Brigades, exposed to the utmost danger, bid us follow. We cheerfully did so in a long trot, till he ordered us to form, that the cannon might play. Still, the forlorn hopes pursued to the very middle of the Town, where the whole Body of the Enemy, drawn up in a solid column, kept up a heavy fire with Cannon and Muskets, till our Cannon dispersed and threw them in confusion. The fight continued obstinately about ½ an hour…. The fight became a chase. Our Brigade being on the left wing and nearest the course the Enemy took, were ordered to pursue them with all expedition. We stepped off with alacrity, in full cry, and fortunately got into the thickest of them, while they were fording a small creek. L'd Stirling's brigade soon came to our assistance"

On December 27, Washington reported to John Hancock that the events of the twenty-sixth had proven successful.[24]

Sir   Head Quarters Newtown [Pa.] 27th Decemr 1776
I have the pleasure of congratulating you upon the Success of an Enterprize, which I had formed against a Detachment of the Enemy lying in Trenton, and which was executed yesterday Morning.
The Evening of the 25th I ordered the Troops intended for this Service to parade back of McKonkey's Ferry, that they might begin to pass as soon as it grew dark, imagining we should be able to throw them all over, with the necessary Artillery, by 12 OClock, and that we might easily arrive at Trenton by five in the Morning, the distance being about nine Miles. But the quantity of Ice, made that Night, impeded the passage of Boats so much, that it was three OClock before the Artillery could all be got over, and near four, before the Troops took up their line of march.
This made me despair of surprizing the Town, as I well knew we could not reach it before the day was fairly broke, but as I was certain there was no making a Retreat without being discovered, and harassed on repassing the River, I determined to push on at all Events. I formed by Detachment into two divisions one to march by the lower on River road, the other, by the upper or Pennington Road. As the Divisions had nearly the same distance to march, I ordered each

of them, immediately upon forcing the out Guards, to push directly into the Town, that they might charge the Enemy before they had time to form. The upper division arrived at the Enemys advanced post, exactly at eight OClock. and in three Minutes after, I found from the fire on the lower Road that, that Division had also got up. The Out Guards made but small Opposition, tho', for their Numbers, they behaved very well, keeping up a constant retreating fire from behind Houses.

We presently saw their main Body formed, but from their Motions, they seem'd undetermined how to act.

Being hard pressed by our Troops, who had already got possession of part of their Artillery, they attempted to file off by a road on their right leading to Princeton, but perceiving their Intention, I threw a Body of Troops in their Way which immediately checked them. Finding from our disposition, that they were surrounded, and that they must inevitably be cut to pieces if they made any further Resistance, they agreed to lay down their Arms. The Number, that submitted in this manner, was 23 Officers and 886 Men. Colo. Rall the commanding Officer and seven others were found wounded in the Town. I dont exactly know how many they had killed, but I fancy not above twenty or thirty, as they never made any regular Stand. Our Loss is very trifling indeed, only two Officers and one or two privates wounded.

I find, that the Detachment of the Enemy consisted of the three Hessian Regiments of Lanspatch, Kniphausen and Rohl amounting to about 1500 Men, and a Troop of British Light Horse; but immediately, upon the beginning of the Attack, all those, who were not killed or taken, pushed directly down the Road towards Bordentown. These would likewise have fallen into our hands, could my plan have been compleatly carried into Execution. Genl Ewing was to have crossed before day at Trenton Ferry, and taken possession of the Bridge leading out of Town, but the Quantity of Ice was so great, that tho' he did every thing in his power to effect it, he could not get over. This difficulty also hindered Genl Cadwallader from crossing, with the Pennsylvania Militia, from Bristol, he got part of his Foot over, but finding it impossible to embark his Artillery, he was obliged to desist. I am fully confident, that could the Troops, under Generals

Ewing and Cadwallader, have passed the River, I should have been able, with their Assistance, to have driven the Enemy from all their posts below Trenton. But the Numbers I had with me, being inferior to theirs below me, and a strong Battalion of Light Infantry being at Princetown above me, I thought it most prudent to return the same Evening, with the prisoners and the Artillery we had taken. We found no Stores of any Consequence in the Town.

In justice to the Officers and Men, I must add, that their Behaviour upon this Occasion, reflects the highest honor upon them. The difficulty of passing the River in a very severe Night, and their March thro' a violent Storm of Snow and Hail, did not in the least abate their Ardour. But when they came to the Charge, each seemed to vie with the other in pressing forward, and were I to give a preference to any particular Corps, I should do great injustice to the others.

Colo. Baylor, my first Aid de Camp, will have the honor of delivering this to you, and from him you may be made acquainted with many other particulars; his spirited Behaviour upon every Occasion, requires me to recommend him to your particular Notice. I have the Honor to be with great Respect Sir Your most obt Servt

Go: Washington

Inclosed you have a particular List of the Prisoners, Artillery and other Stores.

With the Continental army's complete dominance of the British forces in Trenton, there was a dramatic change in the fortunes of war. The call to arms was suddenly and enthusiastically supported, and the militias of New Jersey and Pennsylvania found their ranks swelling.

The British, who believed that they were going to end the war by capturing Philadelphia, were now faced with an invigorated and aggressive enemy. Hessian Captain Ewald summed up the change in the war in his diary.[25]

"Thus had the Times Changed!" wrote Hessian Captain Ewald. "The Americans had constantly run before us. Four weeks ago we expected to end the war with the capture of Philadelphia, and now we had to render Washington

the honor of thinking about our defense. Due to this affair at Trenton, such a
fright came over the army that if Washington had used this opportunity we would
have flown to our ships and let him have all of America. Since we had thus far
underestimated our enemy, from this unhappy day onward we saw everything
through the magnifying glass."

The Hessians, having been routed by the Continental troops,
retreated across New Jersey to South Amboy. Washington, now with a
rapidly expanding army and with the Hessians in full retreat, decided to
return to Trenton. On December 28, he wrote to Major General William
Heath, who was located in Peekskill, New York, that he was planning
on another attack and instructed Heath to march from New York into
northern New Jersey and execute a diversionary attack on Howe's army.[26]

Dear Sir   Head Quarters Newtown [Pa.] 28th Decemr 1776
Since I had the pleasure of informing you Yesterday of our Success at Trenton,
I have received Advice that Count Donnop with the remainder of the Enemy's
Army, immediately upon the News, decamped, and was on his Retreat towards
South Amboy. On hearing this Genl Ewing and Colo. Cadwallader passed the
River with the Troops under their command, and Genl Mifflin will follow this
day with a considerable Body of Militia from Pennsylvania, from whence large
Reinforcements are coming in. I purpose to go over myself with the whole of
the Continental Troops as soon as they are refreshed and recovered of their late
Fatigue. These added together will make our Force very respectable.
I have wrote to Genl McDougall and Genl Maxwell who are at Morris Town,
and have desired them to collect as large a Body of Militia as they possibly can,
and whether the Enemy advance or retreat harass them on Flank and Rear. If
they cannot be brought to that, to keep them embodied, till they are joined by our
regular Troops. Things being in this Situation, I think a fair Opportunity is
offered of driving the Enemy intirely from, or at least to the Extremity of the
province of Jersey. I would therefore have you advance as rapidly as the Season
will admit with the Eastern Militia by the way of Hackensack, and proceed

downwards till you hear from me. I dont think there is the least danger of the Enemy's making any move towards the Highlands at this Season of the Year. That they cannot do it by Water is most certain. I am dear Sir Yr most obt Servt

Go: Washington

On December 29, Washington informed John Hancock that his troops were again embarking on a difficult crossing of the Delaware and that Colonel John Cadwalader and Brigadier General Thomas Mifflin were also moving into New Jersey with their force of around 3,400 men. The combined forces totaled about six thousand men.[27]

Sir   *Newtown [Pa.] Decr 29th 1776*

I am just setting out, to attempt a second passage over the Delaware with the Troops that were with me on the morning of the 26th. I am determined to effect it, if possible but know that it will be attended with much fatigue & difficulty on account of the Ice, which will neither allow us to cross on Foot, or give us an easy passage with Boats. Genl Cadwalader crossed from Bristol on the 27th and by his Letter of Yesterday was at Borden Town with about Eighteen Hundred Men. In addition to these, Genl Mifflin sent over Five hundred from Philadelphia on Friday, Three hundred yesterday Evening from Burlington and will follow to day with 7 or 800 more. I have taken every precaution in my power for subsisting of the Troops, & shall without loss of time and as soon as circumstances will admit of, pursue the Enemy in their retreat—try to beat up more of their Quarters and in a word, in every instance, adopt such measures as the exigency of our affairs requires & our situation will justifye. had it not been for the unhappy failure of Genls Ewin and Cadwalader in their attempts to pass on the night of the 25, and if the several concerted attacks could have been made, I have no doubt but that our views would have succeeded to our warmest expectations. What was done, occasioned the Enemy to leave their Several Posts on the Delaware with great precipitation. The peculiar distresses to which the Troops who were with me, were reduced by the severities of Cold, rain, Snow & Storm—the charge of the Prisoners they had taken, and another reason that might be mentioned and the little prospect of receiving succours on account of the Season & situation of the River, would not authorize a further pursuit at that time. Since transmitting the List of Prisoners a few more have been discoverd & taken in Trentown, among 'em a Lieutt Colo. & a Deputy Adjutt Genl, The whole amounting to about a Thousand.

I have been honoured with your Letter of the 23d and Its several Inclosures, to which I shall pay due attention. A Flag goes in this Morning with a letter to Genl Howe & Another to Genl Lee. For the latter, Rob. Morris Esqr. has transmitted a Bill of Exchange drawn by Two British Officers for 116:9:3 on Major Small for money furnished them in South Carolina, which I trust will be paid. This supply is exclusive of the Sum you have resolved to be sent him and which Mr Morris will procure in time. I have the Honor to be with great respect Sir Yr Most Obedt servt

Go: Washington

P.S. I am under great apprehensions about obtaining proper supplies of Provisions for our Troops. I fear it will be extremely difficult if not impraticable, As the Enemy from every account, has taken & collected every thing they could find.

On December 30, Washington arrived in Trenton, set up his headquarters, and began encouraging his troops to extend their enlistments. After some prodding and a promise of a ten-dollar[28] bonus, they agreed to extend their enlistments for six more weeks. An unknown soldier wrote about the experience many years later.[29]

"While we were at Trenton, on the last of December, 1776, the time for which I and most of my regiment had enlisted expired. At this trying time General Washington, having now but a little handful of men and many of them new recruits in which he could place but little confidence, ordered our regiment to be paraded, and personally addressed us, urging that we should stay a month longer. He alluded to our recent victory at Trenton; told us that our services were greatly needed, and that we could now do more for our country than we ever could at any further period; and in the most affectionate manner entreated us to stay. The

drums beat for volunteers, but not a man turned out. The soldiers worn down with fatigue and privations, had their hearts fixed on home and the comforts of the domestic circle, and it was hard to forego the anticipated pleasures of the society of our dearest friends.

"The General wheeled his horse about, rode in front of the regiment, and addressing us again said, "'My brave fellows, you have done all I asked you to do, and more than could be reasonably expected; but your country is at stake, your wives, your houses, and all that you hold dear. You have worn yourselves out with fatigue and hardships, but we know not how to spare you. If you will consent to stay only one month longer, you will render that service to the cause of liberty, and to your country, which you probably never can do under any other circumstances. The present is emphatically the crisis, which is to decide our destiny.' The drums beat the second time. The soldiers felt the force of the appeal. One said to another, 'I will remain if you will.' Others remarked, 'We cannot go home under such circumstances.' A few stepped forth, and their example was immediately followed by nearly all who were fit for duty in the regiment, amounting to about two hundred volunteers. An officer enquired of the General if these men should be enrolled. He replied,— 'No! Men who will volunteer in such a case as this, need no enrolment to keep them to their duty'"

Washington then wrote to the commanding officer at Morristown on December 31, advising him of his success in extending the term of enlistment with the troops at Trenton and encouraged the commander to do the same with his troops. Washington also instructed the commanding officer to pursue a diversionary attack on the British forces.[30]

Sir   Head Quarters Trenton 30th Decemr 1776
   I have the pleasure to acquaint you that the Continental Regiments from the Eastern Governments have to a Man agreed to stay Six Weeks beyond their Term of Inlistment which was to have expired the last day of this Month. For this extraordinary Mark of their Attachment to their Country, I have agreed to give them a Bounty of Ten dollars per Man, besides their pay running on.

I hope this noble Example will be followed by the four Regiments under your command, promise them the same Reward and endeavour to work upon them by every Means in your power. let them know the Militia are pouring in from all Quarters and only want Veteran Troops to lead them on. Since our Success at this place on the 26th the Enemy have evacuated all the Country below, they went off in the greatest hurry and Confusion. I beg you will collect all the Men you possibly can about Chatham, and after gaining the proper Intelligence endeavour to strike a stroke upon Elizabeth Town or that Neighbourhood, at any Rate be ready to co operate with me. Let me hear what success you have with your Troops as soon as possible. I am Sir.

When he learned that Lieutenant General Charles Cornwallis was preparing to attack Trenton, Washington held a council of war on January 1, 1777. The council decided to increase their forces in Trenton, and Washington ordered Cadwalader at Crosswicks (about eight miles southeast of Trenton) and Mifflin at Bordentown (about seven miles southeast of Trenton) to march overnight and be in Trenton by five o'clock in the morning.[31]

Dear Sir   Trenton 9 Oclock P.M. Janry 1st 177[7].
Some pieces of Intelligence renders it necessary for you to March your Troops immediately to this place—I expect your Brigade will be here by five O'clock in the Morning without fail. at any rate do not exceed 6. I am very sincerely Yr Most Obedt Sert

Go: Washington

The following morning Cornwallis formed his British forces of over six thousand men in Princeton and commenced to march on Washington's army in Trenton. Washington needed time to organize the newly arriving forces and establish a defensive perimeter. To accomplish this, Colonel Edward Hand's Pennsylvania riflemen were positioned to ambush and impede the advance of the British. The riflemen were successful, and the British arrived at Trenton too late in the day to form for battle. Cornwallis elected to wait for daylight the following morning to attack the Continentals.

But during the night, as Cornwallis's troops prepared for a morning attack, Washington and his army stealthily slipped out of their encampment in Trenton and moved overnight to attack Princeton in the morning. On the morning of January 3, Cornwallis was awakened by the far-off sounds of the Continental army's attack on Princeton.

When the Continental troops arrived at Stony Bridge, about a mile and a half from Princeton, Washington divided his forces to attack Princeton from both the south and the east. General Mercer's brigade (about two hundred men) was ordered to advance directly into Princeton. Two British regiments were preparing to march out of Princeton to reinforce Cornwallis at Trenton when they spotted Mercer's brigade approaching. They set themselves to ambush the Continentals. Mercer's brigade suffered greatly, and although they were quickly reinforced, the Continentals were overpowered and retreated under the incessant fire of the British regiments.

When Washington heard the sounds of battle, he raced to join Mercer's retreating troops. He placed himself between the lines of fire and took command of the Continental forces. After reforming his retreating Continentals, he successfully repulsed the British and captured Princeton. As a result of Washington's successes at both Trenton and Princeton, General Howe removed all British forces from these towns and canceled his plans to attack Philadelphia by marching through New Jersey.

Delaware Militia Captain Thomas Rodney's diary provides a poignant description of the late night escape from Trenton and the subsequent early morning skirmish at Princeton.[32]

At two o'clock this morning the ground having been frozen firm by a keen N. West wind secret orders were issued to each department and the whole army was at once put in motion, but no one knew what the Gen. meant to do. Some thought that we were going to attack the enemy in the rear; some that we were going to Princeton; the latter proved to be right. We went by a bye road on the right hand which made it about 16 miles; During this nocturnal march I, with the Dover Company and the Red Feather Company of Philadelphia Light Infantry led the van of the army and Capt. Henry with the other three companies of Philadelphia light Infantry brought the rear.

The Van moved on all night in the most cool and determined order but on the march great confusion happened in the rear. There was a cry that they were surrounded by the Hessians and several corps of Militia broke and fled towards Bordentown but the rest of the column remained firm and pursued their march without disorder, but those who were frightened and fled did not recover from their panic until they reached Burlington.

When we had proceeded to within a mile and a half of Princeton and the van had crossed Stony Brook, Gen. Washington ordered our Infantry to file off to one side of the road and halt. Gen. Sullivan was ordered to wheel to the right and flank the town on that side, and two Brigades were ordered to wheel to the Left, to make a circuit and surround the town on that side and as they went to break down the Bridge and post a party at the mill on the main road, to oppose the enemy's main army if they should pursue us from Trenton.

The third Division was composed of Gen. Mercers brigade of Continental troops, about 300 men, and Cadwaladers brigade of Philadelphia militia to which brigade the whole of our light Infantry Regiment was again annexed.

Mercers brigade marched in front and another corp of infantry brought up the rear.

My company flanked the whole brigade on the right in an Indian file so that my men were very much extended and distant from each other; I marched in front and was followed by sargeant McKnatt and next to him was Nehemiah Tilton [afterwards Lieut.-Col. Tilton].

Mercers brigade which was headed by Col. Haslet of Delaware on foot and Gen. Mercer on horseback was to march straight on to Princeton without Turning to the right or left.

It so happened that two Regiments of British troops that were on their march to Trenton to reinforce their army there, received intelligence of the movements of the American army (for the sun rose as we passed over Stony brook) and about a mile from Princeton they turned off from the main road and posted themselves behind a long string of buildings and an orchard, on the straight road to Princeton.

The first two Divisions of our army therefore passed wide to the right and left and leaving them undiscovered went on to Princeton.

Gen. Mercers Brigade owing to some delay in arranging Cadwaladers men had advanced several hundred yards ahead and never discovered the enemy until he was turning the buildings they were posted behind, and then they were not more than fifty yards off.

He immediately formed his men, with great courage, and poured a heavy fire in upon the enemy, but they being greatly superior in number returned the fire and charged bayonets, and their onset was so fierce that Gen. Mercer fell mortally wounded and many of his officers were killed, and the brigade being effectually broken, began a disorderly flight.

Col. Haslet retired some small distance behind the buildings and endeavored to rally them, but receiving a bullet through his head, dropt dead on the spot and the whole brigade fled in confusion. At this instant Gen. Cadwalader's Philadelphia Brigade came up and the enemy checked by their appearance took post behind a fence and a ditch in front to the buildings before mentioned, and so extended themselves that every man could load and fire incessantly; the fence stood on low ground between two hills; on the hill behind the British line they had eight pieces of artillery which played incessantly with round and grape shot on our brigade, and the fire was extremely hot. Yet Gen. Cadwalader led up the head of the column with the greatest bravery to within 50 yards of the enemy, but this was rashly done, for he was obliged to recoil; and leaving one piece of his artillery, he fell back about 40 yards and endeavored to form the brigade, and some companies did form and gave a few vollies but the fire of the enemy was so hot, that, at the sight of the regular troops running to the rear, the militia gave way and whole *brigade broke and most of them retired to a woods about 150 yards in the rear; but two pieces of artillery stood their ground and were served with great skill and bravery.*

At this time a field officer was sent to order me to take post on the left of the artillery until the brigade should form again, and, with the Philadelphia Infantry keep up a fire from some stacks and buildings, and to assist the artillery in preventing the enemy from advancing.

We now crossed the enemies fire from right to left and took position behind some stacks just on the left of the artillery; and about 30 of the Philadelphia Infantry were under cover of a house on our left and a little in the rear.

About 15 of my men came to this post, but I could not keep them all there, for the enemies fire was dreadful and three balls, for they were very thick, had grazed me; one passed within my elbow nicking my great coat and carried away the breech of Sargeant McKnatts gun, he being close behind me, another carried away the inside edge of one of my shoesoles, another had niched my hat and indeed they seemed as thick as hail.

From these stacks and buildings we, with the two pieces of artillery kept up a continuous fire on the enemy, and in all probability it was this circumstance that prevented the enemy from advancing, for they could not tell the number we had posted behind these covers and were afraid to attempt passing them; but if they had known how few they were they might easily have advanced while the two brigades were in confusion and routed the whole body for it was a long time before they could be reorganized again, and indeed many, that were panic struck, ran quite off.

Gen. Washington having rallied both Gen. Mercers and Gen. Cadwaladers brigade they moved forward and when they came to where the artillery stood began a very heavy platoon fire on the march. Thus the enemy bore but a few minutes and then threw down their arms and ran.

We then pushed forward towards the town spreading over the fields and through the woods to enclose the enemy and take prisoners.

The fields were covered with baggage which the Gen. ordered to be taken care of.

Our whole force met at the Court House and took there about 200 prisoners and about 200 others pushed off and were pursued by advance parties who took about 50 more.

In this engagement we lost about 20 killed, the enemy about 100 men killed and lost the field.

William S. Stryker, in his classic 1898 book, *The Battles of Trenton and Princeton*, described how his fellow officers viewed Washington's courageous efforts to reverse the flow of the battle.[33]

The sight of the great chieftain placing himself in such peril between the two armies at the turning point of the conflict lent new courage to the weary troops, and they promptly came up to the work. This voluntary exposure seemed dreadful to Washington's gallant aide, Lieutenant-Colonel John Fitzgerald, who, expecting every moment to see a bullet pierce the heart of his commander, endeavored to avoid the appalling sight. A moment later the shout which greeted Washington's brave act, the heavy firing and the eager advance of the men startled the worried aide-de-camp, and he looked up but to see the general coming forth uninjured from the smoke of battle and to hear himself calmly addressed in an order, "Bring up the troops, Colonel Fitzgerald; the day is our own!"

An officer on the Continental line, writing from Morristown a few days after this gallant but hazardous exploit, used these words, "Our army love the general very much, but they have one thing against him, which is the little care he takes of himself in any action."

In his report to John Hancock on January 5, Washington described the events leading up to the confrontation with Cornwallis, their late night march on Princeton, and the Continental army's successful surprise attack upon the British.[34]

Sir   Pluckamin [N.J.] January 5th 1777

I have the honor to inform you, that since the date of my last from Trenton, I have removed with the Army under my command to this place. The difficulty of crossing the Delaware on account of the ice made our passage over it tedious, and gave the Enemy an opportunity of drawing in their cantonments and assembling their whole Force at Princeton. Their large Picquets advanced towards Trenton, their great preparations & some intelligence I had received, added to their knowledge, that the first of January brought on a dissolution of the best part of our Army, gave me the strongest reasons to conclude, that an attack upon us was meditating.

Our situation was most critical and our force small. to remove immediately was again destroying every dawn of hope which had begun to revive in the breasts of the Jersey Militia, and to bring those Troops which had first crossed the Delaware, and were laying at Croswix's under Genl Cadwalader & those under Genl Mifflin at Bordenton (amounting in whole to about 3600) to Trenton, was to bring them to an exposed place; One or the other however was unavoidable, the latter was preferred & they were ordered to join us at Trenton, which they did by a Night march on the 1st Instt.

On the 2nd according to my expectation the Enemy began to advance upon us, and after some skirmishing the Head of their Column reached Trenton about 4 OClock, whilst their rear was as far back as Maidenhead. They attempted to pass Sanpink Creek, which runs through Trenton at different places, but finding the Fords guarded, halted & kindled their Fires—We were drawn up on the other side of the Creek. In this situation we remained till dark, cannonading the Enemy & receiving the fire of their Field peices which did us but little damage.

Having by this time discovered that the Enemy were greatly superior in number and that their design was to surround us, I ordered all our Baggage to be removed silently to Burlington soon after dark, and at twelve OClock after renewing our fires & leaving Guards at the Bridge in Trenton and other passes on the same stream above, marched by a roundabout Road to Princeton, where I knew they could not have much force left and might have Stores. One thing I was certain of, that it would avoid the appearance of a retreat, (which was of course or to run the hazard of the whole Army being cut off) whilst we might by a fortunate stroke withdraw Genl Howe from Trenton and give some reputation to our Arms. happily we succeeded. We found Princeton about Sunrise with only three

Regiments and three Troops of light Horse in it, two of which were on their march to Trenton—These three Regiments, especially the Two first, made a gallant resistance and in killed wounded and Prisoners must have lost 500 Men, upwards of One hundred of them were left dead in the Feild, and with what I have with me & what were taken in the pursuit & carried across the Delaware, there are near 300 prisoners 14 of which are Officers—all British.

This piece of good fortune is counterballanced by the loss of the brave and worthy Genl Mercer, Cols. Hazlet and Potter, Captn Neal of the Artillery, Captn Fleming who commanded the first Virginia Regiment and four or five other valuable Officers who with about twenty five or thirty privates were slain in the feild—Our whole loss cannot be ascertained, as many who were in pursuit of the Enemy, who were chaced three of four Miles, are not yet come in.

The rear of the Enemy's Army laying at Maidenhead (not more than five or Six miles from Princeton) was up with us before our pursuit was over, but as I had the precaution to destroy the Bridge over Stoney Brooke (about half a mile from the Feild of action) they were so long retarded there as to give us time to move off in good order for this place. We took Two Brass Feild peices but for want of Horses could not bring them away. We also took some Blankets—Shoes—and a few other trifling Articles—burnt the Hay & destroyed such other things as the shortness of the time would admit of.

My Original plan when I set out from Trenton was to have pushed on to Brunswic, but the harrassed State of our own Troops (many of them having had no rest for two nights & a day) and the danger of loosing the advantage we had gained by aiming at too much induced me by the advice of my Officers to relinquish the attempt, but in my Judgement Six or Eight hundred fresh Troops upon a forced march would have destroyed all their Stores and Magazines—taken as we have since learnt their Military Chest containing 70,000£, and put an end to the War. The Enemy from the best intelligence I have been able to get were so much alarmed at the apprehension of this, that they marched immediately to Brunswick without halting except at the Bridges, (for I also took up those on Millstone on the different routs to Brunswick) and got there before a day.

From the best information I have received, Genl Howe has left no men either at Trenton or Princeton. The truth of this I am endeavouring to ascertain that I may regulate my movements accordingly—The Militia are taking spirit and I am told, are coming in fast from this State, but I fear those from Philadelphia will scarcely submit to the hardships of a winter Campaign much longer, especially as they very unluckily sent their Blankets with their Baggage to Burlington—I must do them justice however to add, that they have undergone more fatigue and hardship than I expected Militia (especially Citizens) would have done at this inclement Season. I am just moving to Morris town where I shall endeavour to put them under the best cover I can. hitherto we have been without any and many of our poor Soldiers quite bear foot & ill clad in other respects. I have the Honor to be with great respect Sir Yr Most Obedt

Go: Washington

The American army endured the loss of six officers and twenty-five to thirty privates in the battle at Princeton. The officers died in the following manner: Brigadier General Hugh Mercer received seven bayonet wounds and died eleven days after the battle; Colonel John Haslett received a shot to the head while fighting alongside General Mercer; Lieutenant Bartholomew Yeates of the First Virginia Infantry Regiment died from a shot in the breast and head along with thirteen bayonet wounds; Ensign Anthony Morris Jr. with the First Battalion Philadelphia Associators died from shots to the chin, the knee, and the right temple. The following officers also died, but their cause of death was not recorded: Captain Daniel Neil, assigned to General Knox's artillery brigade; Captain John Fleming, commanding the First Regiment Virginia Infantry; and Captain William Shippin with the Pennsylvania militia.[35]

Cornwallis's advance forces arrived in Princeton as Washington's trailing forces were leaving. Cornwallis decided to not pursue Washington. He was concerned about protecting the extensive supplies that were stored in Brunswick and elected to defend them instead. Washington too broke off from the confrontation and continued northward to Morristown where he settled in for the winter and began rebuilding his army for the summer's campaign. On January 7, Washington wrote to John Hancock from Morristown apprising him of the latest intelligence on the British and the need to encamp the exhausted American forces.[36]

Sir   *Morristown January the 7th 1777*

I am happy to inform you, that the account of Genl Mercer's death, transmitted in my last, was premature, though it was mentioned as certain by many who saw him after he was wounded; By intelligence from princeton yesterday evening, he was alive, and seemed as if he would do well; Unhappily he is a prisoner. had it not been for the information I had of his death, I would have tried to have brought him away, tho I believe it could not have been effected.

The Enemy have totally evacuated Trent & Prince towns & are now at Brunswick & the several posts on the communication between that & Hudson's river, but chiefly at Brunswick. Their numbers and movements are variously reported, but all agree, their force to be great. There have been Two or three little skirmishes between their parties & some detachments of Militia, in which the latter have been successfull and made a few prisoners, the most considerable was on Sunday morning near Springfeild, when Eight or Ten Waldeckers were killed and wounded, and the remainder of the party, Thirty nine or Forty, made prisoners with Two Officers, by a force not superior in number & without receiving the least damage.

The Severity of the Season has made our Troops, especially the Militia, extremely impatient, and has reduced the number very considerably. Every day more or less leave us. Their complaints and the great fatigues they had undergone, induced me to come to this place, as the best calculated of any in this quarter, to accomodate and refresh them. The situation is by no means favourable to our views, and as soon as the purposes are answered for which we came, I think to remove, though I confess, I do not know how we shall procure covering for our Men elsewhere. I have the Honor to be with much esteem Sir Yr Most Obedt Servt

Go: Washington

George Washington was not the only one who believed that he was under the protection of Providence. In his letter to Washington on January 16, 1777, Bartholomew Dandridge, Washington's brother-in-law, reflected on the strife that Washington and his army had endured and made the observation that Providence's design was for Washington to save America.[37]

Dear Sir   *Wmsburg [Va.] January 16. 1777.*

It is probably a very unseasonable time to interrupt that attention you must be constantly paying to the momentous concerns you are engaged in, but I could not omit so good an Opportunity as offers by Mr Walker to let you know that I am alive and in good health, and that all our Relations at present enjoy the same blessing, as far as I know or have heard, for it is seldom I have the pleasure of seeing them, being desirous of making up in some measure by diligence what I want in other respects, towards the discharge of the trust reposed in me by my Country, I have not had the least Opportunity of seeing my Sister, tho' there is hardly any thing I am more desirous of; The rest you will read or not as you have leisure—I cannot help mentioning (tho' it is impossible to express) the anxiety I have suffered from the critical situation you have been in for sometime past, but I have the pleasure of hoping, from various Reports, that matters have now taken a more favorable turn with you, and that you have so far improved your glorious Victory at Trenton as to have stoped the Ravages of our cruel Enemies, and greatly lessened the fatigue and danger to which you have been exposed, we have no authentic Accounts of your transactions since, but such as we have seem to deserve credit.

It is certainly astonishing and will hardly be credited hereafter that the most deserving, the most favorite General of the 13 united American States, should be left by them, with only about 2500 Men, to support the most important Cause that mankind ever engaged in agst the whole Power of British Tyranny, my Indignation against the Authors of such measures admits of no bounds, they are concealed at present, but that Providence that has hitherto protected you, will, I hope, in due time unveil their dark Designs (or timid Counsels) and subject them to be despised and punished as they deserve—it is however some consolation to me, to reflect that measures which disgraced America in General afforded an Opportunity of adding honour to you, your patience and fortitude can have no bounds after sustaining so severe a trial as you have lately had. God grant you may not meet with such another, Permit me to say (without flattery) that it is plain Providence designed you as the favorite Instrument in working the Salvation of America, it is you alone that can defend us against our foreign and, still more dangerous, domestic Enemies, I wish these Considerations would caution you against exposing your Person too much, in all other Things I rely on you most stedfastly, but I am sure you can have no Idea of your real value to us—If you were not at the head of our Affairs we should have ten Tories in Virginia where we have one, a personal attachment to you, weighs more with some than any attachment to the glorious cause in which you are engaged, and I am sorry to say that I am afraid there others who would sacrifice the most sacred Friendship to their pernicious Principles, or their Fears—if a fair Opportunity offered.

The State of Jersey seems to have been in the same situation with respect to America in General as Norfolk was to Virginia—both left to combat a Power singly, that united we seemed unable or unwilling to resist; the Conduct of our Generals upon these Occasions appear indeed in a very different light, and I hope will be attended with different consequences.

I sincerely congratulate you and the publick upon the necessary Accession of Power you have received from the Congress, as it appears the only means of rendering your endeavors successful, you may depend on what the executive Power here can contribute to your Assistance and nothing can have greater force in Virginia than a request from you—I have the pleasure to inform you that the business of recruiting goes on well, and that we have a fair prospect of raising our new Regiments in good time.

Several of the young Gent. who have lately come here from your Army are taken with the Small Pox in different Places which I am afraid will be attended with bad consequences.

If there is no impropriety in the Commission we have given Mr John Walker, I hope for the future to have, thro his means, a more frequent, and more perfect account of you and your situation than we have been hitherto able to get. May all that is great & good attend you is the sincere Prayer of Dear Sir Your affectionate & obedt Ser.

B. Dandridge

In a letter to his stepson, John Parke Custis, on January 22, 1777, Washington described how challenging his military command had become, and that, remarkably, Providence had saved them again.[38]

Dear Sir,   *Morris Town Jany 22d 1777*

Your letter of the 7th came to my hands a few days ago, and brot with it the pleasing reflection of your still holding me in remembrance.

The misfortune of short Inlistments, and an unhappy dependance upon Militia, have shewn their baneful Influence at every period, and almost upon every occasion, throughout the whole course of the War. at no time, nor upon no occasion were they ever more exemplified than since Christmas; for if we could but have got in the Militia in time, or prevaild upon those Troops whose times expired (as they generally did) on the first of this Instt to have continued (not more than a thousand or 1200 agreeing to stay) we might, I am perswaded, have cleard the Jerseys entirely of the Enemy. Instead of this, all our movements have been made with inferior numbers, & with a mix'd, motley crew; who were here today, gone tomorrow, without assigning a reason, or even apprising you of it. In a word, I believe I may with truth add, that I do not think that any Officer since the Creation ever had such a variety of difficulties & perplexities to encounter as I have—How we shall be able to rub along till the New Army is raised I know not. Providence has heretofore saved us in a remarkable manner, and on this we must principally rely. Every person, in every State, should exert himself to facilitate the raising and Marching the New Regiments to the Army with all possible expedition.

I have never seen (but heard of) the Resolve you mention, nor do I get a Paper of Purdies once a Month—those who want faith to believe the Acct of the shocking wastes committed by Howes Army—of their Ravaging—Plundering—&

abuse of Women, may be convinced to their Sorrow perhaps, if a check cannot be put to their progress.

It is painful to me to hear of such illiberal reflections upon the Eastern Troops as you say prevails in Virginia—I always have, and always shall say, that I do not believe that any of the States produce better men, or Persons capable of making better Soldiers; but it is to be acknowledged that they are (generally speaking) most ⟨wretchedly officered—⟩ to this, and this only, ⟨their demerits⟩ is to be attributed. the Policy of those States has been, to level men as much as possible to one standard. the distinction therefore ⟨between officers⟩ & Soldiers, is lost—⟨determination mutilated⟩ is destroyed—and that hunger, & thirst after glory which spurs on the ⟨mutilated⟩ to distinguish Acts, has ⟨mutilated⟩ Officers; which, for the most part, ⟨mutilated⟩ are men of low Character, Friends persons, & such as have had Influence (perhaps undue Influence) to raise Men—entering the Service probably, ⟨mutilated⟩ of pay which they gain by, for Gentlemen cannot live upon it.

This is the true secret, and we have found, that wherever a Regiment is well Officered, the Men have behaved well—when otherwise, ill—the ⟨misconduct⟩ or cowardly behaviour always originating with the Officers, who have set the example. Equal Injustice is done them, in depriving them of Merit in other respects; for no People fly to Arms readier than they do, or come better equip'd, or with more regularity into the Field than they.

With respect to your enqu⟨iries about the payment⟩s made Mr Matzai ⟨I cannot⟩ answer them with precision, b⟨ut I am ex⟩ceedingly mistaken if I have not made him two, for both you and myself. indeed I am as sure of it as I can be of any thing from the badness of my Memory—I think I made him one payment myself, and the Treasurer, or Hill made him the other. The Book however in which I keep your Accts will shew it (the parchment covered Quarto one) as you will, I suppose, find your self charged by me, with the payments made Matzai.

In my Letter to Lund Washington I have given the late occurrances—& to avoid repetition I refer you to him. My love to Nelly—& Compliments to Mr Calvts Family & all other enquiring friends leaves me nothing else to add than that I am Yr Affecte

Go: Washington

The battles of Trenton and Princeton proved to be the turning point in the American Revolutionary War. Before these victories, Washington's army was close to total annihilation and the British were about to capture Philadelphia. But these victories initiated an enthusiastic fervor to enlist, and the ranks of the American army quickly swelled.

The sudden turn of events surprised General Howe, and he went into winter quarters in New York City. While encamped in New York City he strategized a new approach to capture Philadelphia.

Eighteen months into the campaign against the British, Washington remained unscathed. Throughout these trying months, his belief in the protection of Providence did not waver. This unswerving conviction had been further reinforced at the battles of Trenton and Princeton. His pre-war assurances to Martha Washington were proving to be prophetic.

PROVIDENCE WHICH HAS NEVER FAILED US

August 1777–July 1778

"A Retreat however was the fact, be the causes as they may; and the disorder arising from it would have proved fatal to the Army had not that bountiful Providence which has never failed us in the hour of distress, enabled me to form a Regiment or two (of those that were retreating) in the face of the Enemy, and under their fire, by which means a stand was made..."

– July 4, 1778 – George Washington

IN AUGUST 1777, BRITISH GENERAL WILLIAM HOWE launched his second campaign to capture Philadelphia. Rather than marching across New Jersey, this time he sailed up the Chesapeake Bay and landed at Head of Elk, Maryland. The British began disembarking on August 25.

On the following day, Washington was reconnoitering the movements of the British army when a storm arose. He and his accompanying officers took shelter in a farmhouse located perilously close to the British forces. The officers encouraged him to ride on to a less dangerous location, but he was confident of his safety and elected to stay. In his *Memoirs*, Major General Lafayette noted that Washington understood the danger.[1]

> *The army stationed itself on the heights of Wilmington, and the enemy disembarked on the Elk River, at the head of Chesapeake Bay. The same day that the enemy landed, General Washington imprudently exposed himself to danger. After a long reconnaissance, he was overtaken by a storm, on a very dark night. He took shelter in a farmhouse, very close to the enemy, and, because of his unwillingness to change his mind, he remained there with General Greene and M. de Lafayette. But when he departed at dawn, he admitted that a single traitor could have betrayed him....*

Later Washington defended his risky behavior in a letter to Landon Carter, a wealthy Virginia planter. He explained that when duty required, he would put himself in harm's way. And he knew that he was under the protection of his staff while reconnoitering at Head of Elk.[2]

> *Dear Sir   Philadelphia County [Pa.] Octr 27th 1777*
>
> *Accept my sincere thanks for your sollicitude on my Acct—and for the good advice contained in your little paper of the 27th Ulto—at the sametime that I assure you, that It is not my wish to avoid any danger which duty requires me to encounter I can as confidently add, that it is not my intention to run unnecessary risques. In the Instance given by you, I was acting precisely in the line of my duty, but not in the dangerous situation you have been led to believe. I was reconnoitring, but I had a strong party of Horse with me. I was, as (I afterwards found) in a disaffected House at the head of Elk, but I was equally guarded agt friend and Foe. the information of danger then, came not from me.*

Upon completing his reconnaissance, Washington wrote to John Hancock on August 27, 1777, to convey his findings.[3]

Sir.   *Wilmington [Del.] August 27th 1777.*

I this morning returned from the Head of Elk, which I left last night. In respect to the Enemy, I have nothing new to communicate. they remain where they debarked first. I could not find out from inquiry what number is landed—nor form an estimate of It, from the distant view I had of their Encampment, But few Tents were to be seen from Iron Hill and Greys Hill, which are the only eminences about Elk. I am happy to inform you, that all the Public stores are removed from thence, except about seven thousand Bushels of Corn. This I urged the Commissary there to get off as soon as possible, and hope it will be effected in the course of the few days if the Enemy should not prevent, which their situation gives them but too easy an opportunity of doing; The scarcity of Teams in proportion to the demand will render the removal rather tedious though I have directed the Quarter Master to send some from hence to expedite the measure. A part of the Delaware Militia are stationed there, and about nine hundred more from Pensylvania are now on the March that way—I also intended to move part of the Army that way to day, but am under the necessity of defering it, till their Arms are put in order and they are furnished with ammunition, both having been greatly injured by the heavy rains that fell yesterday and last Night. I have the honor to be Sir your most Obet Servt

Go: Washington

To stop the British advance on Philadelphia, General Washington selected Brandywine Creek, Pennsylvania (located between Head of Elk and Philadelphia), to make a stand. The British attacked Washington's forces on September 11, 1777, and Washington yet again faced his destiny. When the fighting began, Washington rode out for a closer view of the enemy's deployment. A British rifleman, Captain Patrick Ferguson,[4] saw the general and took aim, but elected not to pull the trigger. Ferguson wrote about his experience in a letter dated January 31, 1778, to an unknown recipient.[5]

Whilst Knyphausen was forming the Line within amile of the Rebells Camp to wait for G Howes attack, their Rifle men were picking off our men very fast by random shots from a wood some hundred yards in front as it is easy to do execution upon such large objects I had only 20 men with me (a few having been disabled by the Enemy the rest from fatigue) who however proved sufficient for my lads first dislodged them from the skirts of the wood then drove them from a breast work within it after which our purpose being answered we lay down at the further skirt of the wood not unnessarily to provock an attack being so few without support. We had not lyn long when a Rebell Officer remarkable y a huzzar Dress passed towards our army within 100 yards of my right flank, not perceiving us—he was followed by another in Dark Green or blue mounted on a very good bay horse with a remarkable large high cocked hat. I ordered three good shots to steal near them and fire at them but the idea disgusted me and I recalled them. The Huzzar in returning made a circuit but the other passed within 100 yards of us upon which I advanced from the wood towards him, upon my calling he stopd but after looking at me proceeded. I again drew his attentionm, and made signs to him to stop levelling my piece at him, but he slowly continued his way. As I was within that distance at which in the quickest firing I have seldom missed a sheet of paper and could have lodged a half a dozen balls in or about him before he was out of my reach I had only to determine but it was not pleasant to fire at the back of an unoffending individual who was acquitting himself very cooly of hi duty so I let him alone. The day after I had just been telling this story to some wounded officers who lay in the same room with me when one of our surgeons who had been dressing the wounded Rebell Officers came in and told us that they had been informing him that Genl Washington was all morning with the Light Troops generally in their front and only attended by a French Officer in a huzzar Dress he himself mounted and dressed as above described, the oddness of their dress had puzzled me and made me take notice of it—I am not sorry that I did not know all the time who it was.

further this deponent saith not, as his bones were broke a few minutes after— I am yr most

p. F.

Philadelphia
Jan: 31: 1778

On the front lines, the Continental army experienced only minimal action from the British because General Howe had marched his main force several miles upstream and outflanked Washington's army. The Continental troops were caught by surprise and retreated from the battlefield before they were encircled. Howe then advanced on Philadelphia and eleven days later, on September 26, entered the city.

To dislodge the British from Philadelphia, on October 4, Washington attacked the British at Germantown, Pennsylvania, where a major contingent of the British army was encamped. As Washington advanced with the central column, the British broke and retreated. But one British detachment, led by Colonel Musgrave, took refuge in a stone house (Chew's House) and made a stand against the Continentals. General Henry Knox convinced Washington to halt there to bombard Musgrave's regiment into submission while the flanks continued their push on the retreating British. But the flanks, hearing the action by the central column, reversed their direction and returned to Chew's House to support Washington's troops. This delay cost the Americans dearly in casualties, gave the British army an opportunity to regroup, and enabled them to reverse the flow of the battle. In an unsuccessful attempt to turn his retreating troops and attack the British, Washington courageously exposed himself to the hottest fire of the enemy. Major General John Sullivan rode to Washington's side and encouraged him to move away from the enemy's intense action. In a letter to Meshech Weare, chairman of the New Hampshire Committee of Safety, on October 25, 1777, Sullivan described his efforts to ensure his commander's safety.[6]

my Division with a Regiment of North Carolinians Commanded by Col°
Armstrong & assisted by part of Conways Brigade having Driven the Enemy
a mile & a half below Chews House & finding themselves unsupported by
any other Troops Their Cartridges all Expended the force of the Enemy on the
Right Collecting to the Left, to oppose them being alarmed by the firing at Chews
House So far in their Rear & by the Cry of a Light Horse man on the Right

that the Enemy had got round us & at the Same time Discovering Some Troops flying on our Right retired with as much precipitation as they had before advanced against Every effort of their officers to Rally them—when the Retreat took place they had been Engaged near three Hours which with the march of the Preceeding night rendered them almost unfit for fighting or retreating—we however made a Safe retreat Though not a Regular one—our Loss in this Action amount to Less than 700 mortly wounded. The Enemys by Accounts from their own officers to 2500—I can only Say it must have been considerable—we Lost some valuable officers among which were the brave General Nash & my Two Aid De Camps Majors Sherburne & White whose singular Bravery must Ever do Honor to their memorys—our army Rendevousd at Paulens Mills & Seem very Desirous of another Action. The misfortunes of this Day were principally owing to a Thick Fog which being rendered still more So by the Smoke of the Cannon & musketry prevented our Troops from Discovering the motions of the Enemy or Acting in Concert with Each other—I cannot help observing That with great Concern I saw our brave Commander Exposing himself to the hottest fire of the Enemy in such a manner that regard to my Country obliged me to ride to him & beg him to retire—he to gratify me & Some others withdrew a Small Distance but his anxiety for the fate of the Day Soon brought him up again where he remained till our Troops had retreated.

In his memoirs, Major Benjamin Tallmadge described the Battle of Germantown and George Washington's efforts to muster the American forces.[7]

Having marched from our camp on the evening of the 3rd of October, '77, by 3 o'clock the next morning we found ourselves close in upon the scene of action. Just before the dawn of day, the troops were put in motion, and in a few moments the firing commenced. The out-posts and advanced guards of the enemy were driven in with great precipitation, and by 9 o'clock we found ourselves almost in the heart of Germantown. A very heavy fog prevented our corps from discovering one another, so as to distinguish, in some cases, friend from foe. Hitherto the progress of our troops had been entirely successful, and it seemed as if the victory must be ours. Some of the regiments on the flanks had reached the centre of the village, and had then more prisoners than troops of their own; and in this situation, finding themselves separated from their own brigades, were captured by the enemy.

At this critical moment, Col. Musgrave, of the British army, threw his regiment into a large stone house directly in front of our division in the centre, from which he poured a heavy and galling fire upon our troops. All attempts to dislodge them were ineffectual, and although they would have been harmless in a few minutes if we had passed them by, yet through the importunity of Gen. Knox (which I distinctly heard), Gen. Washington permitted him to bring his field artillery to bear upon it, but without effect. During this transaction time elapsed, the situation of our troops was uncomfortable, their ardor abated, and the enemy obtained time to rally. In less than thirty minutes, our troops began to retire, and from the ardor of pursuit, were in full retreat. This not being general through the line, of necessity left the flanks of some divisions and brigades uncovered and exposed to the assaults of an exasperated foe. From this moment the prospects of victory were changed, and notwithstanding all our attempts to rally the retiring troops, it seemed impossible to effect it, even by the presence of the Commander-in-Chief. I threw my squadron of horse across the road, by order of Gen. Washington, repeatedly, to prevent the retreat of the infantry; but it was ineffectual. In addition to this, after our attack had commenced, Lord Cornwallis had commenced his march from Philadelphia with the grenadiers and light troops, and had reached Germantown. This relieved the enemy greatly; but they pursued us very cautiously. After our army had passed Chestnut Hill, the enemy halted, as did also our troops. Thus in an unexpected moment, when everything seemed to look favorable to the cause, victory turned into defeat, and the fugitive enemy was the cautiously pursuing foe.

Although Washington waged two major battles against the British in the fall of 1777, the British successfully gained control of Philadelphia. On December 19, Washington ended the campaign and moved his forces into winter quarters at Valley Forge, Pennsylvania, twenty miles west of Philadelphia. Valley Forge provided a defensible position for the Revolutionary Army and enabled them to monitor the movement of the British troops.

However, the 1777–1778 winter cantonment at Valley Forge proved to be calamitous for Washington's soldiers. The devaluation of Continental money and the superior monetary strength of the British pound meant that the Continental army's commissary general was unable to purchase the provisions needed for the eleven thousand men wintering in Valley Forge. Without sufficient shelter, food, clothing, and medical care the soldiers suffered widespread starvation, disease, frostbite, and infection.

The conditions at Valley Forge became so severe that Washington was unable to rouse his army to confront the British. Thus, for the first time, the Americans mutinied and deserted en masse. On December 23, 1777, Washington wrote to Henry Laurens, who had recently replaced John Hancock as president of the Continental Congress, and reiterated their dire circumstances and expressed his anxiety over the lack of congressional support.[8]

Sir   *Valley Forge Decemb. 23d 1777.*

Full as I was in my representation of matters in the Commissary's department yesterday, fresh and more powerful reasons oblige me to add, that I am now convinced beyond a doubt, that unless some great and capital change suddenly takes place in that line this Army must inevitably be reduced to one or other of these three things. Starve—dissolve—or disperse, in order to obtain subsistence in the best manner they can. rest assured, Sir, this is not an exaggerated picture, and that I have abundant reason to support what I say.

Yesterday afternoon receiving information that the Enemy, in force, had left the City, and were advancing towards Derby, with apparent design to forage and draw subsistence from that part of the Country, I ordered the Troops to be in readiness, that I might give every Opposition in my power; when behold! to my great mortification, I was not only informed, but convinced, that the Men were unable to stir on account of provision, and that a dangerous mutiny, begun the night before and which with difficulty was suppressed by the spirited exertions of some Officers, was still much to be apprehended for want of this Article.

This brought forth the only Commissary in the purchasing line in this Camp, and with him this melancholy and alarming truth, That he had not a single hoof of any kind to slaughter, and not more that 25 Barrells of Flour! From hence form an opinion of our situation, when I add, that he could not tell when to expect any.

All I could do under these circumstances was, to send out a few light parties to watch and harrass the Enemy, whilst other parties were instantly detached different ways to collect, if possible, as much provision as would satisfy the present pressing wants of the Soldiery—But will this answer? No Sir: three of four days bad weather would prove our destruction. What then is to become of the Army this Winter? and if we are as often without Provisions now, as with them, what is to become of us in the Spring, when our force will be collected, with the aid perhaps of Militia, to take advantage of an early campaign before the Enemy can be reinforced? These are considerations of great magnitude—meriting the closest attention, and will, when my own reputation is so intimately connected and to be affected by the event, justify my saying that the present Commissaries are by no means equal to the execution of the Office, or that the disaffection of the people is past beleif. The misfortune however does in my opinion proceed from both causes, and though I have been tender heretofore of giving any opinion or lodging complaints, as the change in that department took place contrary to my Judgement, and the consequences thereof were predicted; yet finding that the inactivity of the Army, whether for want of provisions, Cloaths, or other essentials is charged to my account, not only by the common vulgar, but those in power, it is time to speak plain in exculpation of myself. With truth then I can declare, that no Man in my opinion ever had his measures more impeded that I have, by every department. Since the month of July we have had no assistance from the Quarter Master General, and to want of assistance from this department, the Commissary General charges great part of his deficiency—to this I am to add, that notwithstanding it is a standing order and often repeated, that the Troops shall always have two days provisions by them, that they might be ready at any sudden call, yet no opportunity has scarely ever offered of taking advantage of the Enemy, that has not been either totally obstructed, or greatly impeded on this account: and this the great & crying evil is not all. Soap—Vinegar and other articles allowed by Congress we see none of, nor have we seen them, I believe, since the battle of Brandywine. The first indeed we have now little occasion for, few men having more than one shirt—many only the moiety of one, and some none at all. In addition to which, as a proof of the little benefit received from a Cloathier General, and at the same time, as a farther proof of the inability of an Army under the circumstances of this, to perform the common duties of Soldiers, besides a number of Men confined to Hospitals for want of Shoes, & others in Farmers Houses on the same account, we have by a Field return this day made, no less than 2898 Men now in Camp unfit for duty, because they are barefoot and otherwise naked; and by the same return it appears, that our strength in continental Troops, including the Eastern Brigades which have joined since the surrender of Genl Burgoyne, exclusive of the Maryland Troops sent to Wilmington, amount to no more than 8200—in Camp fit for duty. Notwithstanding which, and that since the 4th Instant our numbers fit for duty from the hardships and exposures they have undergone, particularly on account of Blankets (numbers having been obliged and still are, to set up all night by fires, instead of taking comfortable rest in a natural and common way) have decreased near 2000 Men, we find Gentlemen without knowing whether the Army was really going into Winter Quarters or not (for I am sure no Resolution of mine would warrant the Remonstrance) reprobating the measure as much, as if they thought the Soldiery were made of Stocks or Stones, and equally insensible of Frost and Snow; and moreover, as if they conceived it easily practicable for an inferior Army, under the disadvantages I have described ours to be, which is by no means exaggerated, to confine a Superior one, in all respects well appointed and provided for a Winters Campaign, within the City of Philadelphia, and to cover from depredation and waste the States of pensylvania, Jersey, &ca. But what makes this matter still more extraordinary in my eye is, that these very Gentlemen, who were well apprized of the nakedness of the Troops from occular demonstration, who thought their own Soldiers worse clad than others and advised me near a month ago, to postpone the execution of a plan I was about to adopt in consequence of a Resolve of Congress for seizing Cloaths, under strong assurances, that an ample supply would be collected in ten days agreable to a decree of the State (not one article of which, by the bye, is yet come to hand) should think a Winters Campaign, and the covering these States from the invasion of an Enemy so easy and practicable a business. I can assure those Gentlemen, that it is a much easier and less distressing thing, to draw Remonstrances in a comfortable room by a good fire side, than to occupy a cold, bleak hill, and sleep under frost & snow without Cloaths or Blankets: However, although they seem to have little feeling for the naked and distressed Soldier, I feel superabundantly for them, and from my soul pity those miseries, which it is neither in my power to releive or prevent. It is for these reasons therefore, I have dwelt upon the subject, and it adds not a little to my other difficulties and distress, to find that much more is expected of me, than is possible to be performed; and, that upon the ground of safety and policy, I am obliged to conceal the true state of the Army from public view, and thereby expose myself to detraction & calumny.

The Honble Committee of Congress went from Camp fully possessed of my Sentiments respecting the Establishment of this Army—the necessity of Auditors of Accounts—Appointment of Officers—New Arrangements &c. I have no need therefore to be prolix on these Subjects, but shall refer to them, after adding a word or two to shew, First, the necessity of some better provision for binding the Officers by the tye of Interest to the service (as no day, nor scarcely an hour passes without an Offer of a resigned Commission) Otherwise, I much doubt the practicability of holding the Army together much longer. In this, I shall probably be thought more sincere, when I freely declare, that I do not myself expect to derive the smallest benefit from any establishment that Congress may adopt, Otherwise than as a Member of the Community at large in the good which I am persuaded will result from the measure, by mak-ing better Officers and better Troops; And Secondly, to point out the necessity of making the appointments, arrangements, &ca without loss of time. We have not more than three months to prepare a great deal of business in—if we let these slip or waste, we shall be labouring under the same difficulties all next

Campaign, as we have done this, to rectify mistakes, and bring things to order for Military arrangements and movements, in consequence like the Mechanism of a Clock, will be imperfect, and disordered, by the want of a part. In a very sensible degree, have I experienced this in the course of the last Summer— Several Brigades having no Brigadiers appointed to them till late & some not at all. by which means it follows, that an additional weight is thrown upon the Shoulders of the Commander in Cheif to withdraw his attention from the great line of his duty. The Gentlemen of the Committee, when they were at Camp, talked of an expedient for adjusting these matters, which I highly approved and wish to see adopted; namely that two or three Members of the Board of War—or a Committee of Congress should repair immediately to Camp where the best aid can be had, and with the Commanding Officer, or a Committee of his appointment prepare and digest the most perfect plan, that can be divised for correcting all abuses—making New arrangements—considering what is to be done with the weak & debilitated Regiments (If the States to which they belong will not draft men to fill them, for as to enlisting Soldiers it seems to me to be totally out of the question) together with many other things that would occur in the course of such a conference: and after digesting matters in the best manner they can, to submit the whole to the ultimate determination of Congress. If this measure is approved of, I would earnestly advise the immediate execution of it. And that the Commissary General of purchases, whom I rarely see, may be directed to form Magazines without a moments delay in the Neighbourhood of this Camp in order to secure provision for us in case of bad weather. The Quarter Master General ought also to be busy in his department—In short, there is as much to be done in preparing for a Campaign, as in the active part of it. In fine every thing depends upon the preparation that is made in the Several departments in the course of this Winter and the success or misfortunes of next Campaign will more than probably originate with our activity or Supineness this Winter. I have the Honor to be Sir Your Most Obedt Servant

Go: Washington

In early February 1778, Washington wrote to William Buchanan, the commissary general responsible for provisioning the Continental army, and described how grim circumstances had become.[9]

Sir,   *Head Quarters Valley Forge 7th Feby 1778*

The occasional deficiencies in the Article of provisions, which we have often severely felt, seem now on the point of resolving themselves into this fatal crises—total want and a dissolution of the Army. Mr. Blaine informs me, in the most decisive terms, that he has not the least prospect of answering the demands of the army, within his district, more than a month longer, at the extremity. the expectations, he has from other quarters, appear to be altogether vague and precarious; and from any thing, I can see, we have every reason to apprehend the most ruinous consequences.

The spirit of desertion among the soldery never before rose to such a threatening height, as at the present time—The murmurs on account of Provisions are become universal, and what may ensue, if a better prospect does not speedily open, I dread to conjecture. I pretend not to assign the causes of the distress, we experience, in this particular, nor do I wish, to throw out the least imputation of blame, upon any person. I only mean to represent our affairs as they are, that necessity may be proprerely felt, of exerting the utmost care and activity, to prevent the mischiefs; which I cannot forbear anticipating, with inexpressible concern. I am Sir Your most obedt servant

Go: Washington

P.S. I shall be glad to have from you a just state of what we have to expect, at the expiration of this month and in the course of the ensuing spring.

With no solution in sight, Washington, even though he no longer commanded with the full powers that had been authorized by Congress in December 1776, took matters into his own hands, and on February 12 commanded Major General Nathanael Greene to scavenge the countryside for livestock, forage, and food.[10]

Sir,   *[Valley Forge, 12 February 1778]*

The good People of the State of Pennsylvania living in the vicinity of Philadelphia & near the Delaware River having sufferd much by the Enemy carrying off their property without allowing them any Compensation, thereby distressing the Inhabitants—supplying their own Army & enabling them to protract the cruel & unjust war that they are now waging against these States— And whereas by recent intelligence I have reason to expect that they intend making another grand Forage into this Country, it is of the utmost Consequence that the Horses Cattle Sheep and Provender within Fifteen or Twenty miles west of the River Delaware between the Schuylkil and the Brandywine be immediately removed, to prevent the Enemy from receiving any benefit therefrom, as well as to supply the present Emergencies of the American Army.

I do therefore Authorise impower & Command you forthwith to take Carry off & secure all such Horses as are suitable for Cavalry or for Draft and all Cattle & Sheep fit for Slaughter together with every kind of Forage that may be found in possession of any of the Inhabitants within the Aforesaid Limits Causing Certificates to be given to each person for the number value & quantity of the horses Cattle Sheep & Provender so taken.

Informing them that notice will be given to the holders of such Certificates by the Commissaries & Quarter master General when & where they may Apply for Payment that they may not be disappointed in calling for their money.

All Officers civil and military, Commissaries, Quarter masters &ca, are hereby Orderd to obey and assist you in this necessary business.

All the Provinder on the Islands between Philadelphia and Chester which may be difficult of Access or too hazardous to attempt carrying off, you will immediately Cause to be destroyed, giving Direction, to the Officer or Officers to whom this Duty is assign'd, to take an account of the Quantity together with the Owners Names, as far as the nature of the Service will admit. Given under my hand at head Quarters this 12th day of Feby 1778.

Go: Washington

By the end of February, General Greene's forays began to resolve the supply crisis at Valley Forge. In the general orders issued on March 1, General Washington acknowledged the improved conditions and expressed his admiration for how well his troops had withstood the deprivations of the winter camp.[11]

Head-Quarters V. Forge Sunday March 1st 1778.

Parole Arnold—   *C. Signs Ashford—Almbury.*

The Commander in Chief again takes occasion to return his warmest thanks to the virtuous officers and soldiery of this Army for that persevering fidelity and Zeal which they have uniformly manifested in all their conduct; Their fortitude not only under the common hardships incident to a military life, but also under the additional sufferings to which the peculiar situation of these States have exposed them, clearly proves them worthy the enviable privilege of contending for the rights of human nature, the Freedom & Independence of their Country; The recent Instance of uncomplaining Patience during the scarcity of provisions in Camp is a fresh proof that they possess in an eminent degree the spirit of soldiers and the magninimity of Patriots—The few refractory individuals who disgrace themselves by murmurs it is to be hoped have repented such unmanly behaviour, and resolved to emulate the noble example of their associates upon every trial which the customary casualties of war may hereafter throw in their way— Occasional distress for want of provisions and other necessaries is a spectacle that frequently occurs in every army and perhaps there never was one which has been in general so plentifully supplied in respect to the former as ours; Surely we who are free Citizens in arms engaged in a struggle for every thing valuable in society and partaking in the glorious task of laying the foundation of an Empire, should scorn effeminately to shrink under those accidents & rigors of War which mercenary hirelings fighting in the cause of lawless ambition, rapine & devastation, encounter with cheerfulness and alacrity, we should not be merely equal, we should be superior to them in every qualification that dignifies the man or the soldier in proportion as the motive from which we act and the final hopes of our Toils, are superior to theirs. Thank Heaven! our Country abounds with provision & with prudent management we need not apprehend want for any length of time. Defects in the Commissaries department, Contingencies of weather and other temporary impediments have subjected and may again subject us to a deficiency for a few days, but soldiers! American soldiers! will despise the meaness of repining at such trifling strokes of Adversity, trifling indeed when compared to the transcendent Prize which will undoubtedly crown their Patience and Perseverence, Glory and Freedom, Peace and Plenty to themselves and the Community; The Admiration of the World, the Love of their Country and the Gratitude of Posterity! Your General unceasingly employs his thoughts on the means of relieving your distresses, supplying your wants and bringing your labours to a speedy and prosperous issue—Our Parent Country he hopes will second his endeavors by the most vigorous exertions and he is convinced the faithful officers and soldiers associated with him in the great work of rescuing our Country from Bondage and Misery will continue in the display of that patriotic zeal which is capable of smoothing every difficulty & vanquishing every Obstacle.

Within the remarkably short period of time between April 18 and April 23, five significant events occurred that gave the Americans the upper hand in both political and military affairs.

First, the Continental Congress directed Washington to convene his generals and plan the summer campaign. The open discussions that occurred in the council enabled Washington to establish a set of alternatives that were plans based upon potential British actions. Henry Laurens wrote to Washington to inform him of the congressional resolution.[12]

Sir   York Town [Pa.] 18th April 1778

I beg leave to refer Your Excellency to my Letter of yesterday by McClosky.

This will cover Copy of a Petition by several Officers Civil & Military of New Jersey to His Excellency the Governor of that State. Also Copy of a Representation by the Legislative Council & General Assembly of the same State to Congress; together with an Act of Congress of the 17th Inst. Resolved upon the Report of a Committee to whose consideration the Papers above-mentioned had been referred. I have the honour to be With the highest Esteem & Respect Sir Your Excellency's Most Obedient & most humble servant.

Henry Laurens, President of Congress.

P.S. Your Excellency will also find an Act of Congress of this day for forming a plan for the general operations of the Campaign.

The act of Congress that authorized Washington to convene the council was written as follows:[13]

> *"Resolved, That general Washington be authorized and directed forthwith to convene a council to consist of the major generals in the State of Pennsylvania and the general officer commanding the corps of engineers, and with the advice of the said council to form such a plan for the general operations of the campaign, as he shall deem consistent with the general welfare of these States:*
>
> *"That major generals Gates & Mifflin, members of the board of war, have leave to attend the said council"*

Major General William Heath informed Washington of the second and third significant events in a letter on April 21, 1778.[14] Heath's letter announced that first, the French had become American allies and second, surprisingly, the British were planning to offer a resolution to the war!

Dear General   Head Quarters Boston April 21st 1778
Mr Deane Brother to the Hon. Silas Deane Esqr. being on his way to Congress Charged with Dispatches of the most Happy & Interesting nature to the United States of america and being anxious to proceed Immediately I have not Time to write Save to Congratulate your Excellency on the Court of France having acknowledged the Independence of these United States and having entered into Two Treaties with our Agents One of amity and Commerce the other of Defence guaranteing our Independence & Territory Great Britain is in

the greatest Consternation Lord North has Changed his Tone Commissioners are to Come out to treat with us, The Safest way is Sword in Hand, all Europe appear to be preparing for war Imagining that your Excellency will Immediately have the particulars from Congress I will not add but that I have the Honor to be with great respect your Excellency most obt Sert.

Fourth, on April 21, Generals Washington and Howe came to an agreement on the prisoner exchange, and Major General Charles Lee was returned to the American forces. Washington wrote to Lee the following day to congratulate him on his release and asked him to report to headquarters as soon as he was able.[15]

Dear Sir,   *Valley-forge Aprl 22d 1778*

Mr Boudinot, at Comy Lorings request, met at German town yesterday; from whence he is just returned, after having agreed on a final exchange of yourself and other Officers with that Gentleman.

That delay may not produce danger, I shall send in a flag tomorrow for your parole—when obtained, I shall most cordially, and sincerely, congratulate you on your restoration to your Country, and to the Army—I could not however refrain, till this happy event should take place, rejoicing with you on the probability of it, and to express my wish of seeing you in Camp, as soon as you possibly can make it convenient to yourself, after you are perfectly at liberty to take an active part with us; of which I shall not delay giving you the earliest notice.

I have received your favour of the 13th Instt from York—the contents shall be the subject of conversation when I have the pleasure of seeing you, in a condition to mount your hobby horse, which I hope will not, on tryal, be found quite so limping a jade as the one you set out to york on. I am sincerely & affectionately Dr Sir yr obt sert

Go: Washington

The fifth momentous event was the change in British command. Washington wrote Henry Laurens on April 23 to inform him that

General William Howe had been recalled and replaced by General Henry Clinton.[16]

> *P.S. It is confidently reported and I have little doubt of the truth of it, that Sir Wm Howe is recalled, & that Genl Clinton is to succeed him in command. I have also the pleasure to transmit a List of sundry Officers exchanged on the 21st Inst.*

Thus, in the remarkably short span of six days, these five events provided Commander Washington with the crucial change in conditions for the Americans to turn the tide of the war. Following that week of decisive activity, Edmund Pendleton, Washington's personal lawyer, prophesied that destiny was preserving him to rescue the country.[17]

> *Dear Sir*   *Caroline Virga April 27th 1778.*
>
> *It gave me infinite pleasure to hear by my Worthy Friend Woodford that you was in fine health, a circumstance the more pleasing, as it could scarcely have been expected, after such uncommon & unremitted toil For near three years. I am not Superstitious, nor disposed to offend you by what I know you abhor, yet it is firmly my creed that Heaven has raised & will preserve you For the Sake of the Milions whom you are now engaged in rescuing From Slavery—May the divine Favor be unlimited, and after directing you to that great end, & making you many-many years a Spectator as well as partaker of the happiness you shall have procured Us, compleat your own in immortality. I am sorry yr Countreymen have not appear'd lately so well disposed to come to your Assistance, as Formerly—The Spirit of Avarice seems to have pervaded every breast almost, and expel'd all the manly sentiments, so that paper money is as eagerly sought after as if it contain'd in itself the essence of meat, drink and cloathing or even of all the virtues, tho' the graspers at the same time effect to decry it, as of no more value than Oak leaves; I think however the Martial Spirit is some what recovering & am not without hopes that the Militia will with tolerable alacrity obey your call for them, if you find it necessary. I will not trouble you with news,*

Genl Woodford, will better retail any little we may have—but what do you think of the Commissioners From London to treat with Congress, acknowledging independence? I suppose it another Verse of the old Syren's Song which has preluded each Campaign, composed at first to take you off yr guard, but that hope abandon'd, is continued to make the people of England & timid Americans believe that the want of Peace is the fault of Congress. I thank you For yr kind remembrance of me by my friend, & beg leave to assure you I have the Honr to be wth the Warmest zeal Yr Exclys devoted friend & Obt Servt

Edmd Pendleton

On May 5, 1778, General Washington, complying with the resolution passed by the Continental Congress on April 18, convened the council of war. The generals discussed three options that Washington had presented to them. The first two options were to wage an offensive battle against the enemy in either Philadelphia or New York. The third choice was defensive: to await the movements of General Clinton's troops. The unanimous decision of the generals was the third option, and the conclusions drawn from the council of war were documented and signed on May 9.[18]

Camp at Valley Forge May 9th 1778

Having maturely considered the state of facts and representations submitted to us in Council, by His Excellency the Commander in Chief, with a request, that "each member, after a full and candid discussion of the matter in council would furnish him with his sentiments on some general plan, which considering all circumstances, ought to be adopted for the operations of the ensuing campaign."

We beg leave to offer it as our opinion, after a free and unreserved discussion of the subject, that the line of conduct most consistent with sound policy, and best calculated to promote the interest and safety of the United States—is to remain on the defensive and wait events; without attempting any offensive operation of consequence, unless the future circumstances of the enemy, should afford a fairer opportunity, than at present exists, for striking some successful blow; in the mean time employing our utmost exertions, to put the army in the most respectable state, possible, both with respect to numbers, appointments and discipline; and to establish and fill our magazines, with arms, military stores, provisions and necessaries of every kind; so as to be upon a proper footing more effectually to counteract, any measures of offence, which may be hereafter adopted, by the enemy, or to undertake, at a more convenient season, any offensive entreprise, that may be found necessary against them....

By remaining on the defensive we put nothing to the hazard. Our army will increase in number and improve in discipline. Our Arsenals and magazines will be more respectable and more adequate to the exigencies of the service. A large emission of public money will be saved, which will have a negative efficacy, in raising its value. We have the chance of events, resulting from the important treaties lately concluded between France and America, which may oblige the enemy, to withdraw their force, without any further trouble to us. If this does not happen, and they make a vigorous effort the ensuing campaign, which seems to be a necessary alternative, we shall be in a much better situation to give them opposition. We can then rely on the aid and cooperation of the Militia, who having been left in a state of repose to cultivate their lands, and persue their other private avocations and domestic concerns will more cheerfully come to our assistance.

Thus circumstanced, we shall have a much fairer prospect of disappointing the future attempts of the enemy, and terminating the campaign, to our own honor and advantage. Unanimously agreed to in Council.

Horatio Gates
Nathanael Greene
Stirling,
Thomas Mifflin
the Marquis de lafayette
The Baron deKalb
John Armstrong
de Steuben
H. Knox
the Chevalier duportail

Major General Charles Lee did not attend because he had not yet recovered from his imprisonment and illness. When his health returned, General Lee traveled to the Valley Forge encampment and on May 22 added his signature to the general plan.

On May 16, General Washington anticipated General Clinton's evacuation of Philadelphia and ordered Major General Nathanael Greene, the quartermaster general, to store provisions along the road leading to the Hudson River.[19]

Dr Sir   *Head Quarters [Valley Forge] 16th May 1778*
From many concurrent circumstances it appears that the enemy are preparing to evacuate Philadelphia, whether their design is to withdraw altogether from the Continent or to concenter their forces at new york cannot be ascertained—in case the latter shd be the case it will be proper to have provision of forage made on the road to the No. River for such body of Troops as may be ordered to march from hence in consequence.

If you could employ an intelligent confidential person to go into new york and inform you of what passes there, it would be of infinite use in the present conjecture as any similar preparations on the part of the enemy in that place would evince their intention of generally abandoning the Territories of the United States. I am with great regard &c.

The following day, Washington also advised Brigadier General Henry Knox to prepare the artillery to move against the British. Knox responded to Washington on the same day, expressing his concerns for their shortage of teams of horses and weapons.[20]

sir   *Park Artillery [Valley Forge] 17th May 1778*
I received your Excellency's Letter of this morning respecting the probable evacuation of Philadelphia by the enemy. The peices of Artillery with the ammunition belonging to them now in Camp will be completed with horses and Geers so as to be mov'd in a day or two. I must depend on the Quarter Master General

for Horses and some Waggons to move the Spare Ammunition, and he will be very soon able to supply the demand.

Colonel Flower Commissary Genl Military Stores will supply the small Arms provided he has them, he is now in Lebanon.

I gave positive Orders to Mr Cheever Commissary Stores at Springfield in February to send on to Lebanon with the utmost expedition 3500 new Arms. It was impossible he says then to send them as there was no money and teams could not be procur'd without. I was at Springfield on the 25th March and then again give him positive written instructions to procure teams by any means in his power and send on 2000 Arms—The whole number in the Magazines in Massachusetts being about 5000, the remaining 3000 being necessary to arm the recruits in that State and Connecticut.

At Albany there were 2460 Muskets fit for Service. On the 30th March I wrote from Fish-Kill to Major Stevens at Albany and in the Strongest terms order'd him to send on to Lebanon or Head Quarters with the greatest expedition 2000 Arms with Bayonets complete. I expected both of those parcels on by the 1st May and believe nothing has detain'd them but want of teams occasion'd by the derangement of the Quarter Master Generals department. I shall send off two Conductors immediately one towards albany and the other towards Springfield to meet and expedite them on to this Army

Under the present appearance of thi⟨ngs⟩ I submit it your Excellency whether it would not be proper to dispatch new orders respecting the Artillery lately order'd on to this Camp from the east Side Hudsons River. I am with the utmost Respect Your Excellencys most Obedient Humble Servant

H. Knox

Then in the general orders on May 18, Washington commanded "The whole Army are desired to prepare in the best manner possible for an immediate and sudden Movement."[21]

In anticipation of the campaign, Washington assigned Major General Charles Lee to command Major General Nathanael Greene's division until the actual engagement. He announced his decision in general orders dated May 23, 1778.[22]

> Head-Quarters V. Forge saturday May 23 1778. Parole Bunker hill— C. Signs Brandewine. Bennington—
>
> 'Till some further Arrangement of the Army is made—Major General Lee is to take charge of the division lately commanded by Major General Greene, and in Case of Action or any general Move of the Army the three eldest Major Generals present fit for duty are to command the two Wings and second line according to their seniority.
>
> The Commanding Officers of Regiments & Corps will immediately apply for orders on the Commissary of Military Stores for all the Arms & Accoutrements wanting to compleat their men.
>
> The Quarter Masters of Brigades will also make out returns and apply for orders for ammunition to complete each man to forty rounds and two flints.
>
> All Officers are called upon to see that their Mens Arms and Accoutrements are put in the best order possible—They will likewise take particular Care that their men have wooden drivers fixed in their pieces at the hours of Exercise to prevent an unnecessary waste of Flints—They are not to be absent from Camp on any pretence but be in actual readiness to march at a moments warning.

On May 30, Washington wrote to his friend Landon Carter, commenting that he believed the British were going to abandon Philadelphia and march across New Jersey to New York City.[23] In this letter he reiterated that his primary thanks were to Providence for his safety and guidance during the dangerous times he had experienced.[24]

> My dear Sir,   Valley-forge May 30th 1778
>
> Your favors of the 10th of March (ended the 20th;) and 7th Instt, came safe to hand after a good deal of delay. I thank you much for your kind and affectionate remembrance & mention of me; & for that sollicitude for my welfare which breathes through the whole of your Letters—were I not warm in

my acknowledgments for your distinguished regards, I should feel that sense of ingratitude which I hope will never constitute a part of my character, not find a place in my bosom. My friends therefore may believe me sincere in my professions of attachment to them, whilst Providence has a just claim to my humble, and grateful thanks for its protection & direction of me, through the many difficult & intricate scenes which this contest hath produced; & for its constant interposition in our behalf when the clouds were heaviest, & seemed ready to burst upon us. To paint the distresses, & perilous situation of this army in the course of last Winter for want of Cloaths, Provisions, and almost every other necessary, essential to the well being (I may say existance) of an Army, would require more time, and an abler pen than mine; nor, since our prospects have so miraculously brightned, shall I attempt it, or even bear it in remembrance, further that as a memento of what is due to the great author of all the care & good that has been extended in relieving us in difficulties and distress....

The Enemy seem to be upon the point of evacuating Phila. & I am perswaded are going to New York—whether as a place of rendezvous of their whole force, for a general imbarkation, or to operate upon the North River—or to act from circumstances in not quite so clear—My own opinion is, that they must either give up the Continent, or their Islands; which they will do, I cannot say—which they ought to do, is clear; and yet, I think they will endeavour to retain New York, if they can, by any means, spare Troops enough to Garrison it. Reinforcements will, undoubtedly be sent to Canada, Nova scotia &ca; & I presume must go from their Army in America, as I trust full employment will be found for their Subscription, and other Troops in England & Ireland. Equally uncertain is it, whether the Enemy will move from Phila. by Land, or Water; I am inclined to think the former, and lament that the number of our Sick (under inoculation &ca)—the Situation of our Stores, & other matters, will not allow me to make a large detachment from this Army till the Enemy have actually crossed the Delaware and begun their March for South Amboy. then it will be too late; so that we must give up the idea of harrassing them much in their March through the Jerseys, or attempt it at the hazard of this Camp, & the Stores which are covered by the Army that lays in it if we should divide our force or remove it wholly which by the by circumstanced as the Quarter master's department is, is impracticable.

While waiting for General Clinton's Philadelphia forces to make their move, Washington wrote his brother John Augustine Washington and expressed his anxiety over the delays. He also informed his brother that though his troops had experienced a devastating winter encampment, Washington was heartened by their high morale in anticipation of the upcoming campaign.[25]

Dear Brother,   Camp near Valley forge June 10th 1778

I do not recollect the date of my last to you, but although it is not long ago, I cannot let so good an oppertunity, as Captn Turberville affords, slip me. Your favors of the 10th of April from Bushfield, and 8th of May from Berkeley, are both before me, and have come to hand, I believe, since my last to you.

We have been kept in anxious expectation of the Enemy's evacuating Phila. for upwards of fourteen days; and I was at a loss, as they had Imbarked all their Baggage, Stores, &ca on Board Transports, and had passed all those Transports (a few only excepted) below the Cheveaux de Frieze, to acct for their delay; when behold on Friday last the additional Commissioners, to wit, Lord Carlisle, Govr Johnson, & Mr Willm Eden arrived at the City—whether this, heretofore, has been the cause of the delay I shall not undertake to say, but, more than probably, it will detain them for some days to come—they give out, as I understand, that we may make our own terms provided we will but return to our dependance on Great Britain; but, if this is their expectation, & they have no other powers than the Acts (which we have seen) give them, their will be no great trouble in manageing a negotiation; nor will their be much time spent in the business I apprehend. They talk, as usual, of a great reinforcement; but whether the situation of affairs between them and France will admit of this, is not quite so clear—my wishes lead me, together with other circumstances, to believe that they will find sufficient employment for their reinforcements at least, in other Quarters—time however will discover, & reveal things more fully for us.

Out of your first and Secd draught by which we ought to have had upwards of 3500 Men for the Regiments from that State, we have received only 1242 in all. I need only mention this fact in proof of what other States do—of our prospects also—and, as a criterion by which you may form some estimate of our real numbers when you hear them, as I doubt not you often do, spoke of in magnified terms. From report, however, I should do injustice to the States of Maryland & New Jersey, were I not to add, that they are likely to get their Regiments nearly compleated.

The extreme fatigue & hardship which the Soldiers underwent in the course of the Winter, added to the want of Cloaths, &, I may add, Provisions, have rendered them very sickly, especially in the Brigade you have mentioned (of No. Carolina)—many deaths have happened in consequence—& yet the Army is in exceeding good Spirits.

You have, doubtless, seen a publication of the Treaty with France—the Message of the King of France by his Ambassader to the Court of London, with the Kings Speech to, and addresses of, Parliament upon the occasion—If one was to judge of the Temper of these Courts from these documents, War I should think must have commenced long before this, & yet the Commissioners (but we must allow them to lye greatly) say it had not taken place the 28th of April, & that the differences between the two Courts was likely to be accomodated—but I believe not a word of it—& as you ask my opinion of Lord North's Speech & Bills, I shall candidly declare to you, that they appear to me, to be a compound of Fear, art, & villainy, & these ingredients so equally mixed, that I scarcely know which predominates.

I am sorry to hear of Billy Washingtons ill health, but hope he is recovered—Mrs Washington left this the day before yesterday for Mt Vernon. My love to my Sister & the Family is most sincerely offered, and I am with the truest regard and affection Yrs Most sincerely

Go: Washington

Three weeks after receiving his command, Major General Charles Lee questioned Washington's May 23 general orders regarding the reassignment of battalions at the time of action and also disagreed with Washington's premise that the British were about to depart Philadelphia and march across New Jersey to New York City.[26]

Dr General   Camp [Valley Forge] June the 15th 1778

As your time must necessarily be taken up by more and a greater variety of busyness than perhaps ever was impos'd on the Shoulders of any one Mortal, the most clear simple and agreeable method of communicating my sentiments on any matters of importance must certainly be by throwing em on paper. You will have more leisure to weigh and consider the stregnth or weakness of my arguments—and I flatter myself that what I now, or, I hope, shall at any time, offer will not be imputed to presumption impertinence or a spirit of criticism, but to my zeal for the publick service You will pardon me then when I express freely my thoughts freely—on the present arrangement with respect to the command of the General Officers, which I cannot help thinking not only extremely defective but that it may be productive of the worst consequences—We are, it seems, to have the superintendance of one division in the present situation of affairs, (that is, as long as We remain tranquil and undisturb'd,) but the instant our tranquility is disturb'd and a movement is to be made, We are to quit this division and abruptly to take the command of another—by these means, We are put out of all possibility of becoming acquainted with the names faces and characters of the Officers who are to execute the orders We give, and the Soldiers who are to look up to us in the hour of tryal must be strangers to our voices and persons—They cannot consequently have that confidence in us which is so necessary and which habit and acquaintance usually inspire—indeed it appears to me not only repugnant to the rules of war, but of common prudence to introduce, for the first time, a General to his Officers and Soldiers, in the moment of attack—I must intreat your pardon, therefore in urging the expediency of affixing without, loss of time, the respective Generals to the line wings or divisions which They are to command in real action, so that the Commanders and Commanded may not fall into the mistakes blunders and distractions which otherwise from their being Strangers to each other must inevitably ensue.

Yesterday and the day before I had some conservation with Mr Budenot—He is from many circumstances fully persuaded that it is not the Enemy's intention to pass through the Jerseys to N. York—I have myself from the beginning been inclin'd to the same opinion—and on the supposition that this is not their design We ought to consider with ourselves what They most probably will do—my opinion is, that (if They are in a capacity to act offensively,) They will either immediately from Philadelphia, or by a feint in descending the River as far as New Castle, and then turning to the right march directly and rapidly towards Lancaster, by which means They will draw us out of our present position, and oblige us to fight on terms perhaps very disadvantageous—or that They will leave Lancaster and this Army wide on the right, endeavour to take Post on the lower parts of the Susquehanna, and by securing a communication with their Ships sent around into the Bay for this purpose, be furnished with the means of encouraging and feeding the Indian War broke out on the Western Frontier—this last plan I mention as a possibility but as less probable that the former.

If They are not in a capacity to act offensively, but are still determind to keep footing on the Continent, there are strong reasons to think that They will not shut themselves up in Towns, but take possession of some tract of Country which will afford em elbow room and sustenance, and which is so situated as to be the most effectually protected by their command of the Waters—and I have particular reasons to think that They have cast their eyes for this purpose on the lower Counties of Delawar and some of the Maryland Counties on the Eastern Shore—that They had thoughts of adopting this measure some time ago I learnt from Mr Wellin when They entertaind an idea of offering or assenting to, if propos'd, a cessation of hostilities—as to any apprehensions from the unwholesomeness of the climate They laugh at it—if They are resolv'd on this plan it certainly will be very difficult to prevent'em or remove em afterwards as their Shipping will give em such mighty advantages. whether They do or do not adopt any one of these plans there can no inconvenience arise from considering the subject, nor from devising means of defeating their purposes on the supposition that They will—in short I think it woud be proper to put these queries to ourselves, shoud They march directly towards Lancaster and the Susquehanna

or indirectly from N. Castle what are We to do? shoud They (tho it is less prob-
able), leave this Army and even Lancaster wide on the right or endeavour to
establish themselves on the lower parts of the Susquehanna, what are We to do?
and should They act only on the defensive and attempt to secure to themselves
some such tract of Country as I have mentiond what measures are We to pur-
sue? these are matters, I really, think worthy of consideration—We have many
and, I believe, able Field Engineers in the Camp or at York; why cannot They
be employ'd in some essentials, in surveying well the Country on both sides the
Susquehanna—determining on the most proper Fords for our Army if on any
occasion They shou'd be obligd to ford it, in examining well all the best positions
which may be taken betwixt the head of Elk and the Delawar, as also betwixt
Philadelphia Wilmington and Lancaster—what use may be made of Conestoga
Creek if We are obligd to cover Lancaster—and (to extend their task further)
how Baltimore may be put in a more defensible state—and what posts and defiles
there are in one line of direction from Baltimore to York—and in another line
from that part of the lower Susquehanna, where it is most probable the Enemy
woud chuse for their landing place, to York—but I am swelling out my paper to
a most insufferable bulk—and intreat Dr General that You will excuse not only
it's length but whatever You find ill-time'd or impertinent in the contents as I am,
most sincerely and devotedly Yours

Charles Lee

On the same day, June 15, Washington provided a tactful reply thanking General Lee for his opinion and counsel, especially since his com-
ments were not being overly critical. Then Washington explained that
Congress controlled the assignment of officers and he had not received
a response to his proposal. Therefore he made temporary moves to
prepare for the upcoming battle and assigned Lee to march with one
division until an engagement began, and then he would assign Lee to a
different division. Washington assured Lee that he had considered Lee's
suggestions but felt it best to proceed as planned.[27]

Dear Sir,   *Head Quarters [Valley Forge] June 15th 1778*

I have received your Letter of this date, and thank you, as I shall do any Officer over whom I have the honor to be placed for his opinion and advice, in matters of importance; especially when they proceed from the fountain of candor, & not from a captious spirit, or an itch for criticism.

No man can be more sensible of the defects of our present arrangement than I am—No man more sensible of the advantage of having the Commander, & commanded of every Corps well known to each other—and the Army properly organized than myself—Heaven & my own Letters to Congress can witness, on the one hand, how ardently I have laboured to effect these points during the past Winter & Spring—The Army on the other, bear witness to the effect. Suspended between the old & new establishment, I could govern myself by neither, with propriety; & the hourly expectation of a Comee for the purposes of reducing some Regiments, & changing the establishment of all rendered a mere temporary alteration (which from its uncertainty & shortness could effect no valuable end) unnecessary—that I had a power to shift regiments, & alter Brigades (every day if I chose to do it) I never entertain a doubt of, but the efficacy of the measure I have very much questioned; as frequent changes, without apparent causes, are rather ascribed to caprice & whim, than to stability & judgment.

The mode of shifting the Major Generals from the commd of a division in the present tranquil state of affairs to a more important one in action & other capitol movements of the whole army is not less disagreeable to my Ideas, than repugnant to yours, but is the result of necessity; for having recommended to Congress the appointment of Lieutt Generals for the discharge of the latter duties, & they having neither approved, or disapproved the measure, I am hung in suspence, and being unwilling on the one hand to give up the benefits resulting from the Command of Lieutt Generals in the cases abovementd; or to deprive the Divisions of their Major Genls for ordinary duty, on the other, I have been led to adopt a kind of medium course which, tho not perfect in itself, is, in my judgment the best that circumstances will admit of, till Congress shall have decided upon the proposition before them—your remark upon the disadvantages of an Officers being suddenly removed from the command of a divn to a Wing, tho not without foundation as I have before acknowledged does not apply so forceably in the present case as you seem to think it does—There is no Majr Genl in this Army that is not pretty well known, and who may if he chooses it soon become acquainted with such Officers as may be serviceable to him—Their Commands being anounced in genl ords & the Army prepared for their receptn a Major Genl may go with the same ease, to the comd of a Wing consisting of five Brigades, as to a division composed of two, & will be received with as little confusion, as the Brigades remain perfect, & no changes have happened in them.

Mr Boudenots conjecture of the enemys intention, altho it does not coincide with mine, is nevertheless worthy of attention; and the evils of the measure have been guarded against as far as it has been in my power, by removing the Stores, Provisions &ca as fast as possible from the Head of Elk, the Susquehanna &ca—and by exploring, the Country, Surveying the Roads, & marking the defiles, & Strong grounds, an Engineer & three Surveyors haveing been employed in this work near a Month though their report is not yet come in. Boats are also prepared on the Susquehanna for the Transportation of our Troops in case we should find it necessary to move that way. But nevertheless, it gives me real pleasure to find you have turned your thoughts that way and are revolving the questions contained in your Lettr—& here let me again assure you that I shall be always happy in a free communication of your Sentiments upon any important subject relative to the Service, & only beg that they may come directly to myself—the custom which many Officers have of speaking freely of things & reprobating measures which upon investigation may be found to be unavoidable is never productive of good, & often very mischievous consequences. I am &ca

G. W.

On June 17, Washington called a council of war and informed his generals that the British were in the process of evacuating Philadelphia and summarized the intelligence on the strength of the British and the American forces. He offered them six proposed strategies based upon the movements of the British and requested that they provide a written response to his proposed stratagem of attacking if there was an opportunity.[28]

[Valley Forge, 17 June 1778]

At a Council of War held at Head Quarters Valley Forge the 17th day of June 1778

Present

His Excellency The Commander in chief

Major Generals	*Brigadier Generals*
Lee	*Smallwood*
Greene	*Knox*
Arnold	*Poor*
Sterling	*Patterson*
Fayette	*Wayne*
Steuben	*Woodford*
	Mughlenberg
	Huntington
	Portail

The Commander in Chief informs the council, that from a variety of concurring intelligence, there is the strongest reason to believe the enemy design speedily to evacuate Philadelphia;...

He observes to them also, that on a junction of the enemy's force in and near Philadelphia, and that which they already have at New York and its dependencies, their number will amount to between 14 & 15000—That, on our part, when this army shall be united to the one on the North River, we shall have near 14000 Continental troops, fit for service.

Having stated these facts, for the information of the council, The commander in Chief requests, after a personal discussion of the subject, that each member will favour him with his opinion, in writing, on the conduct, which it will be adviseable for this army to observe on the present occasion, and under present appearances, in determining which, though he would not wish to confine the attention of the Council solely to these objects—He recommends the following questions to their mature consideration.

Whether any enterprise ought to be undertaken against the enemy in Philadelphia, in their present circumstances?

Whether this army should remain in the position it now holds, 'till the final evacuation of the city or move immediately towards the Delaware?

Whether any detachment of it shall be sent to reinforce the Brigade in the Jerseys, or advanced towards the enemy to act as occasion shall require and endeavour to take advantage of their retreat?

If the army remain on its present ground 'till the enemy quit the city, and if they march, through the Jerseys towards Amboy, will it be practicable, from the obstructions they may probably receive, from the troops already there, in conjunction with the Militia, to arrive, in time, with this army, to give them any material interruption? Will it be prudent to attempt it, or not rather more eligible to proceed to North River, in the most direct and convenient manner, to secure the important communication between the Eastern and Southern states?

In case such measures should be adopted, as will enable this army to overtake the enemy in their march, will it be prudent, with the aid, which may reasonably be expected from the Jersey Militia, to make an attack upon them, and ought it to be a partial or a general one?

In case of an immediate removal of this army, what precautions will be proper for the security of the sick belonging to it, and of the stores in this state?

Each of the generals provided Washington with their answers to his questions within a day. Major General Charles Lee's written response again challenged Washington's premise. Once more he questioned whether they should attack the British, whether the British were evacuating Philadelphia, and whether the British would march across New Jersey to New York City.[29]

[18 June 1778]

1st As the Enemy are suppos'd already to have transported their stores &cc. over the River—and as Philadelphia is peculiarly circumstancd to secure their rear from any considerable annoyance—an attack upon 'em coud answer no important end altho ever so successfull, but perhaps might furnish a pretext for setting fire to that noble City—I shoud therefore think any attack upon 'em highly imprudent.

2'd If any position can be taken nearer the Delaware from whence if occasion requires, this Army may gain one or two days time to transport itself into the Jerseys, and at the same time, if it appears that the Enemy does not intend to march through the Jerseys may equally cover this Country the stores Sick &cc.—it would be prudent to move but on a mere supposition that it is the Enemys intention to march through that State, it would be unjustifyable to leave this Country uncover'd by moving from the present Position.

3'd As it is far from being certain that it is the Enemy's intention to march thro' the Jerseys—detaching a part of this Army wou'd be imprudent, but I see no obje⟨ction⟩ to one division moving one days march towards the Delaware if so great reliance can be placd in those who give intelligence from Philadelphia, that there will be no danger of this detachd division not falling back in time to rejoin this Army if the Enemy repass in force the Delaware.

4th and 5th on this question it is difficult to give an opinion—the possibility or impossibility of being in time to give any material interruption to the Enemy in their march to Amboy—depends on the obstructions thrown in their way by the Militia to which We are Strangers—but to risk an action in our present circumstances wou'd be to the last degree criminal—and marching directly to the North River when We are not ascertaind of their designs woud be extremely imprudent.

6th If this Army Moves, the sick and stores ought undoubtedly to be sent to convenient places up the Country.

Charles Lee

On that same day, June 18, Elias Boudinot,[30] who had traveled to Philadelphia to check on the prisoners, wrote to General Washington to inform him that the British had evacuated Philadelphia and had marched southeast toward Haddonfield, New Jersey.[31]

German Town [Pa.]
June 18 1778 8 oClock P.M.

Dr Sir

 I am this Moment returned from the Point opposite to Gloucester—As soon as the City was a little reconnoitered, and prudent precautions taken, I went down with two or three chosen Persons to the Point from whence the Enemy had just gone over—We plainly discovered their rear & indeed the direction of the whole Party from the Dust—Two Deserters came over to us while we were there, one swam the River the other came in a Canoe—From the whole, I think your Excellency may depend on the following facts—That the main Body passed over at Coopers ferry—The flying Army as it is called passed to Gloucester to serve as a Covering Party—This last Body halted about two or three Hours at Gloucester, buried their Scows dressed two Days Provision and marched towards Haddonfield about three or four oClock, where it is said they are to join the Main Body this Evening—One thing only puzzeled me, it was clearly discernible that the last of the main Body, who were in sight when we entered the City, marched down from Coopers ferry along the River, to Gloucester—The only way I can Account for this, is to suppose them part of the flying Army—I asked the Deserter how it came that this flanks division marched to the right of the main Body instead of the left—He answered me that it was reported the Genl wayne with his Division had crossed from Wilmington—we have sent off two or three proper Persons in their rear.

 a light Horseman comes in with your Excellency⟨'s⟩ Letter of this date, but the Contents are as fully answered by the above, as I am now capable of; every possible measure shall be taken by me to endeavour to watch the Enemy's movements.

 Notwithstanding every endeavour used to the Contrary, they have embarked all our Prisoners except a very few—They persist in taking the Officers with them, but say they will disembark the Privates in the River when their Prisoners arrive—I have given for Answer, that under so notorious a Violation of a solemn Agreemt for the purpose, I could not say whether your Excellency would

suffer another of their Prisoners to be sent in at any rate. I am Your Excellency's
Most Obedt & Most Hble Servt

Elias Boudinot

Following the plan agreed upon by the generals in their May 9 council of war, Washington moved his troops out of Valley Forge and began tracking the British forces as they retreated across New Jersey toward New York City. In the general orders issued on June 19, Washington instructed the troops to march at 4:00 a.m.[32]

Head-Quarters Doctor Shennons [Pa.]
Friday June 19th [17]78

Parole   *C. Signs*

The Commanding Officers of Corps are to pay the greatest attention to keeping their men within their Encampment and prevent stragling, that they may be in constant readiness for moving at the shortest notice—They are likewise to forbid under the severest Penalties, marauding and the Destruction of the Inclosures, Fruit-Trees or other Property of the Inhabitants. The General will beat tomorrow morning at 3 óClock, the troop in half an hour afterwards and the whole line is to march precisely at four.

If through mistake any part of the baggage should not have marched in the order of the Brigades, the Waggon-Master General is to have the matter rectified so that the whole may move tomorrow in proper order.

If any of the Troops have marched without the proper quantity of cooked Provisions they are to cook enough this afternoon to serve them tomorrow and the next day provided their rations are of salt meat. The old and new Guards will parade in the road opposite Mr Shennon's precisely at half past three óClock in the morning.

In future the Camp-Kettles are always to be carried by the Messes—each soldier of the Mess taking it in his turn, and no man is on any Account to presume to put the Camp Kettle belonging to the Mess in a Waggon—No soldier is to put his Musquet in a Waggon unless on Account of his Inability to carry it, in which Case he is to obtain leave from a Field-Officer of the day, Commanding Officer of the Regiment or from the Officer of the Baggage guard who shall make themselves judges of the circumstances.

The Officers of the day are authoriz'd to punish on the spot such as transgress the foregoing Orders.

The indulgence of suffering Women to ride in Waggons having degenerated into a great abuse, and complaint having been made by the Officers of the day that the Plea of leave from Officers is constantly urged when the Waggon Masters order such Women down.

It is expressly ordered that no Officer grant such leave for the future but the Commanding Officers of a Brigade or the Field Officers of the day who are to grant it only on account of Inability to march, and in writing.

The General is far from supposing that any Officer will act in opposition to a positive order, but he is determined in Case a Violation should happen that it shall not pass unnoticed.

The Officers of the day are to report the names of those who are guilty of a breach thereof.

Washington's army closed in on General Clinton's army as they approached Monmouth, New Jersey, and on June 24, Washington called a council of war to determine whether to attack the British army or to continue annoying them with skirmishes. The generals counseled that 1,500 troops should advance upon the British rear guard to observe their reaction.[33]

[Hopewell, N.J., 24 June 1778]
At a Council of War held at Hopewell Township, New Jersey, June 24th 1778
Present
The Commander in Chief

Major Genls	*Brigadier Generals*
Lee	*Knox*
Greene	*Poor*

Stirling	*Wayne*
Fayette	*Woodford*
Steuben	*Patterson*
	Scott
	Portail.

His Excellency informs the Council, that by the latest advices, he has received, the Enemy are in two columns, one on the Allen Town and the other on the Border Town road, The front of the latter near the Drawbridge, at which the Two roads unite in the main Cranbury road; Their force from the best estimate he can form is between 9 & 10,000 rank & file.

That the strength of the Army on this Ground, by a field return made two days since consisted of 10,684 rank & file; besides which, there is an advanced Brigade under General Maxwell, of about 1200. That in addition to this force, from the amount given by Genl Dickinson there appear to be about 1200 Militia, collected in the Neighbourhood of the Enemy, who in conjunction with General Maxwell are hovering on their flanks & rear and obstructing their march.

He further informs the Council, that measures have been taken to procure an aid of Pensylvania militia; which have not as yet produced any material effect. Genl Cadwalader with fifty or Sixty Volunteers and a Detachment of Continental Troops, amounting to about 300 were to cross the Delaware yesterday morning and fall in with the Enemy's rear—General Lacy had crossed with 40 men.

He observes to the Council that it is now the seventh day since the Enemy evacuated Philadelphia during which time, they have marched less than 40 miles; That the obstructions thrown in their way, by breaking down Bridges, felling Trees &c. were insufficient to produce so great delay, as is the opinion of Genl Dickinson himself, who has principally directed them; and that the opposition, they have otherwise received, has not been very considerable.

Under these circumstances and considering the present situation of our national affairs, and the probable prospects of the Enemy, the General requests the sentiments of the Council on the following questions.

Will it be adviseable for us, of choice, to hazard a general action?

If it is, should we do it, by immediately making a general attack upon the Enemy, by attempting a partial one, or by taking such a position, if it can be done, as may oblige them to attack us?

If it is not, what measures can be taken, with safety to this Army, to annoy the Enemy in their March, should it be their intent⟨ion⟩ to proceed through the Jerseys?

In fine, what precise line of conduct will it be best for us to pursue?

Answer to the first question—It will not be adviseable. to the second—This is involvedand answered in the first. to the third—A detachment of fifteen hundred men to be immediately sent to act as occasion may serve, on the enemy's left flank and rear, in conjunction with the other Continental troops and militia, which are already hanging about them; and the main body to preserve a relative position, so as to be able to act as circumstances may require. To the fourth—This is partly answered in the foregoing and may be referred to farther consideration.

H. Knox
Charles Lee
Stirling,
Nath. Greene
The Marquis de lafayette
Steuben M.G.
Poor
Jno. Patterson
Wm Woodford
Chs Scott
Duportail

After the council of war, Major General Lafayette wrote to Washington to comment that the generals' advice was evenly divided: Six of them wanted to use the 1,500 troops just to observe the movements of the British, and the other six really wanted to advance in order to draw the British into a general action. Lafayette noted that General Lee preferred to observe the British movements while he personally favored an attack.[34]

dear general   [Hopewell, N.J., 24 June 1778]

   I have Sign'd the paper because I have been told I schould Sign it, and because almost all the others who were of the same opinion as I am have also sign'd—for, Sir, I will easely schow you that there were Six gentlemen for more than fifteen hundred and only six for fifteen hundred. they are as follows.

general lee	baron de Stueben	Some of the Second
lord Stirling	general portaïl	column were for
general woodfort	general waïne	2500, but would
general Scot	general patterson	like much better
general knox	general greene	2000 than 1500, as
general poor	general Lafayette	they have a notion
		of attaking, and the
		others only a notion
		of scouting

   Now, my dear general, I beg leave to tell some few words about my opinion—it is that morgan be directed towards the Rear of the Right flank, and in a word the militia be directed to act about as it has been told and as I will not Repeat, for indeed I did not like theyr motions to be So minutely dictated by the council.

   but for what Regard the detachement from this army I am Clearly of the opinion, that a choosen corps of two thousand five hundred or at least two thousand Selected men ought to have been Sent or are to be Compleated towards the ennemy's left flank or rear—not to Scout as Some Say, but to attak any part of the english army or of theyr baggage as will furnish a proper opportunity—Some Certainly may be depend upon for Many Reasons too long to mention and very obvious or any body who knows how an army marches.

   I would want the column of the main army to be at a proper distance along the left flank of the ennemy—I wish'd however our army would be rather towards the rear, that it would never run risk to be turn'd by the Right, which may be easely avoided—if by chance the Corps would put such confusion among the *ennemy, that a general attak might be advantageous, then I would not think that with ten thousand men it is not proper to attak ten thousand english—but let us only speack of what is likely to happen.*

I do'nt doubt but a detachment of 2000 or 2500 Selected men will find an occasion of attaking Some part of the ennemy with advantage—of even beating those tremendous grenadiers if they fight with them—in a word I would lay my fortune, all what I possess in the world that if Such a detachement is Sent in proper time, some good effect, and no harm schall arise of it.

the other five gentlemen are of my opinion but principally general portaïl and baron de stueben have begg'd me if the matter was yet spoken off to explain you an english how sorry, how distressed they we[re] to See that we were going to loose an occasion which may be reputed as one of the finest ever offered.

in a word I think the measure consistent with prudence, military principles, with the honor of the american army and every one in it, and I am very far from entertaining the Same opinion of this we are going to take—I have perceiv'd my dear general, that you were rather inclin'd to follow the same way I so ardently wish for, and I would a council of war would never have been call'd.

Such a council is a school of logic, it may come an occasion of disputes for these gentlemen May come personal, it will never be a mean of doing what is consistent with the good of the Service, the advantage of the occasion, and indeed the authority of the commander in chief.

but I forget that I write to the general, and I was ready to speack freely to my friend—I will finish in begging leave to add a word of protestation to my signature if you think that signature of mine may engage to believe that I did approuve of the project.

The Marquis de lafayette

On the following day, June 25, General Washington, in apparent agreement with Lafayette's observations, gave him instructions to attack the British if—and when—possible.[35]

Sir   *[Kingston, N.J., 25 June 1778]*

You are immediately to proceed with the detachment commanded by Genl Poor and form a junction as expeditiously as possible with that under the commanded of Genl Scott. You are to use the most effectual means for gaining the enemys left flank and rear, and giving them every degree of annoyance—all continental parties that are already on the lines will be under your command and you will take such measures in concert with Genl Dickinson as will cause the enemy most impediment & loss in their march—for these purposes you will attack them as occasion may require by detachment, and if a proper opening shd be given by operating against them with the whole force of your command.

You will naturally take such precautions as will secure you against surprise— and maintain your communication with this army. Given at Kingston this 25th June 1778.

When Major General Lee learned that Lafayette was to attack the British if the opportunity arose, he wrote to Washington and asked that he lead the assault. He felt that his seniority in command qualified him to lead the attack force rather than Major General Lafayette.[36]

Dr General   *Camp at Kingston [N.J.] June the 25th [1778]*

When I first assented to the Marquis of Fayette's taking the command of the present detachment, I confess I viewd it in a very different light than I do at present I considerd it as a more proper busyness of a Young Volunteering General than of the Second in command in the Army—but I find that it is considerd in a different manner; They say that a Corps consisting of six thousand Men, the greater part chosen, is undoubtedly the most honourable command next to the Commander in Chief, that my ceding it woud of course have an odd appearance I must intreat therefore, (after making a thousand apologies for the trouble my rash assent has occasion'd to you) that if this detachment does march that I may have the command of it—so far personally, but to speak as an Officer—I do not think that this detachment ought to march at all, untill at least the head of the Enemy's right column has pass'd Cranbury—then if it is necessary to march the whole Army, I cannot see any impropriety in the Marquis's commanding this detachment or a greater as advance Guard of the Army—but if this detachment with Maxwells Corps Scotts, Morgans and Jacksons are to be considerd as a separate chosen active Corps and put under the Marquis's Command until the Enemy leave the Jerseys—both Myself and Lord Steuben will be disgrac'd. I am, Dr General Yours

C. Lee

On the eve of battle, General Washington wrote to Lee to address his request and inform him of a compromise.[37]

Dear Sir   Cranbury [N.J.] June 26 1778

   Your uneasiness, on account of the command of yesterday's detachment, fills me with concern, as it is not in my power, fully, to remove it without wounding the feelings of the Marquiss de la Fayette—I have thought of an expedient, which though not quite equal to either of your views, may in some measure answer both; and that is to make another detachment from this Army for the purpose of aiding and supporting the several detachments now under the command of the Marquiss & giving you the command of the whole, under certain restrictions; which, circumstances, arising from your own conduct yesterday, render almost unavoidable. The expedient which I would propose is, for you to march towards the Marquiss with Scot's & Varnum's Brigades. Give him notice that you are advancing to support him—that you are to have the command of the whole advanced body; but as he may have formed some enterprize with the advice of the Officers commanding the several Corps under his command, which will not admit of delay or alteration, you will desire him to proceed as if no change had happened, and you will give him every assistance and countenance in your power. This, as I observed before, is not quite the thing; but may possibly answer, in some degree, the views of both. That it may do so, and the public service receive benefit from the measure, is the sincere wish of Dr Sir Yr Most Obedt & Affect. Servant

Go: Washington

On the morning of the twenty-eighth, Washington sent a short note to President Laurens to advise him that Lee's detachment was to attack the rear guard of the British at Monmouth Court House. Meanwhile, Washington would lead the main body of the army and march rapidly toward Monmouth to join in the battle.[38]

English town 6 miles from Monmouth [N.J.]

Sir   June 28: [1778] ½ after 11 a.m.

I was duly honored with your favor of the 20th instant, with the report to which it referred, and trust my situation will apol[og]ize for my not answering it before.

I am now here with the main body of the Army and pressing hard to come up with the Enemy. They encamped yesterday at Monmouth Court House, having almost the whole of their front, particularly their left wing, secured by a Marsh and thick wood & their rear by a difficult defile, from whence they moved very early this morning. Our advance, from the rainy weather and the intense heat, when it was fair (though these may have been equally disadvantageous to them) has been greatly delayed. Several of our men have fallen sick from these causes, and a few unfortunately have fainted and died in a little time after. We have a select and strong detachment more forward under the general command of Major Genl Lee, with orders to attack their rear if possible. Whether the Detachment will be able to come up with it is a matter of question, especially before they get into strong grounds. Besides this, Morgan with his Corps and some bodies of Militia are on their flanks. I cannot determine yet, at what place they intend to embark. Some think they will push for Sandy Hook—whilst others suppose they mean to go to Shoal Harbour. The latter opinion seems to be founded in the greater probability, as, from intelligence, Several Vessels and Craft are lying off that place. We have made a few prisoners, and they have lost a good many men by desertion. I cannot ascertain their number, as they came into our advanced parties & pushed immediately into the Country; I think five or Six Hundred is the least number that have come in, in the whole. They are chiefly foreigners. I have the Honor to be with great respect Sir Yr Most Obedt servt

G. Washington

Lee's strategy was to encircle the rear column of the British, but as his force of five thousand were forming, General Cornwallis's returned to Monmouth with an additional six thousand troops and forced Lee to abort his plans for encirclement.

General Washington arrived and observed Lee leading a chaotic retreat. Washington confronted Lee and, after a heated discussion, replaced General Lee and took command of the battle. Joseph Plumb Martin, a soldier in the Continental army, described Washington's actions in his *A Narrative of a Revolutionary Soldier.* He wrote that he saw Washington confront General Lee, relieve him of his command, and then saw Washington ride to the front of the action, exposing himself to fierce enemy fire.[39]

> *We had to fall back again as soon as we could, into the woods; by the time we had got under the shade of the trees, and had taken breath, of which we had been almost deprived, we received orders to retreat, as all the left wing of the army (that part being under the command of Gen. Lee) were retreating. Grating as this order was to our feelings, we were obliged to comply. We had not retreated far before we came to a defile, a muddy sloughy brook; while the Artillery were passing this place, we sat down by the road side;—in a few minutes the Commander-in-chief and suit crossed the road just where we were sitting. I heard him ask our officers "by whose order the troops were retreating," and being answered, "by Gen. Lee's;" he said something, but as he was moving forward all the time this was passing, he was too far off for me to hear it distinctly; those that were nearer to him, said that his words were— "d—n him;" whether he did thus express himself or not I do not know, it was certainly very unlike him, but he seemed at the instant to be in a great passion, his looks if not his words seemed to indicate as much. After passing us, he rode on to the plain field and took an observation of the advancing enemy; he remained there sometime upon his old English charger, while the shot from the British Artillery were rending up the earth all around him. After he had taken a view of the enemy, he returned and ordered the two*

Connecticut Brigades to make a stand at a fence, in order to keep the enemy in check while the Artillery and other troops crossed the before-mentioned defile....

Washington, now in command of the American army, refocused his army, motivated them to hold their lines against the hard-charging British, and then successfully drove the British into a retreat. As night settled, General Clinton withdrew his troops from the battle. That evening, Washington and his exhausted troops slept on the Monmouth battlefield. By the following morning, the British had marched a distance of thirteen miles from the battle grounds, and Washington found it inexpedient to pursue the engagement further. Two days later, on July 1, the British began their embarkation at Sandy Hook, New Jersey.

General George Washington had faced the enemy's fire and survived without a scratch. He attributed his survival to the protection of Providence as he had always done when he placed himself in harm's way. On July 4, Washington wrote his brother John and confided that Providence had saved him again from the intense fire of the rapidly converging British.[40]

Dear Brother,   *Brunswick in New Jersey July 4th 1778*

Your Letter of the 20th Ulto came to my hands last Night—before this will have reached you, the Acct of the Battle of Monmouth propably will get to Virginia; which, from an unfortunate, and bad beginning, turned out a glorious and happy day.

The Enemy evacuated Philadelphia on the 18th Instt—at ten oclock that day I got intelligence of it, and by two oclock, or soon after, had Six Brigades on their March for the Jerseys, & followed with the whole Army next Morning—On the 21st we compleated our passage over the Delaware at Coryells ferry (abt 33 Miles above Philadelphia) distance from Valley forge near 40 Miles—From this Ferry we moved down towards the Enemy, and on the 27th got within Six Miles of them.

General Lee having the command of the Van of the Army, consisting of fully 5000 chosen Men, was ordered to begin the Attack next Morning so soon as the enemy began their March, to be supported by me—But, strange to tell! when he came up with the enemy, a retreat commenced; whether by his order, or from other causes, is now the subject of enquiry, & consequently improper to be discanted on, as he is in arrest and a Court Martial sitting for tryal of him. A Retreat however was the fact, be the causes as they may; and the disorder arising from it would have proved fatal to the Army had not that bountiful Providence which has never failed us in the hour of distress, enabled me to form a Regiment or two (of those that were retreating) in the face of the Enemy, and under their fire, by which means a stand was made long enough (the place through which the enemy were pursuing being narrow) to form the Troops that were advancing, upon an advantageous piece of Ground in the rear. hence our affairs took a favourable turn, & from being pursued, we drove the Enemy back, over ground they had followed us, recovered the field of Battle, & possessed ourselves of their dead. but, as they retreated behind a Morass very difficult to pass, & had both Flanks secured with thick Woods, it was found impracticable with Men fainting with fatigue, heat, and want of water, to do any thing more that Night. In the Morning we expected to renew the Action, when behold the enemy had stole off as Silent as the Grave in the Night after having sent away their wounded. Getting a Nights March of us, and having but ten Miles to a strong pass, it was judged inexpedient to follow them any further, but move towards the North River least they should have any design upon our posts there.

We buried 245 of their dead on the field of Action—they buried several themselves—and many have been since found in the Woods, where, during the action they had drawn them to, and hid them—We have taken five Officers and upwards of One hundred Prisoners, but the amount of their wounded we have not learnt with any certainty; according to the common proposition of four or five to one, their should be at least a thousand or 1200—Without exaggerating, there trip through the Jerseys in killed, Wounded, Prisoners, & deserters, has cost them at least 2000 Men & of their best Troops—We had 60 Men killed—132 wounded & abt 130 Missing, some of whom I suppose may yet come in. Among our Slain Officers is Majr Dickenson, & Captn Fauntleroy, two very valuable ones.

I observe what you say concerning voluntary enlistments, or rather your Scheme for raising 2000 Volunteers; & candidly own to you I have no opinion of it— these measures only tend to burthen the public with a number of Officers without adding one jot to your strength, but greatly to confusion, and disorder—If the several States would but fall upon some vigorous measures to fill up their respective Regiments nothing more need be asked of them, but while these are neglected, or in other words ineffectually & feebly attended to, & these succeedaniums tried, you never can have an Army to depend upon.

The Enemy's whole force Marched through the Jerseys (that were able) except the Regiment of Anspach, which, it is said, they were affraid to trust, & therefore sent them round to New York by Water, along with the Commissioners; I do not learn that they have received much of a reinforcement as yet—nor do I think they have much prospect of any, worth Speaking of, as I believe they stand very critically with respect to France.

As the Post waits I shall only add my love to my Sister and the family, & Strong assurances of being with the sincerest regard & Love—Yr Most Affecte Brother

Go: Washington

Not only Washington but others wrote about Providence protecting him and saving him for future greatness. Lieutenant Colonel Alexander Hamilton, one of General Washington's aides-de-camp, wrote to Elias Boudinot on July 5 expounding upon Washington's bravery and leadership during the June 28 battle. He pointed out that three of Washington's aides-de-camp were injured during the battle,[41] while remarkably the general emerged unscathed.[42]

My dear Sir,

You will by this time imagine that I have forgotten my promise of writing to you, as I have been so long silent on an occasion, which most people will be fond of celebrating to their friends. The truth is, I have no passion for scribbling and I know you will be at no loss for the fullest information. But that you may not have a right to accuse me of negligence, I will impose upon myself the drugery of saying something about the transactions of the 28th, in which the American arms gained very signal advantages; and might have gained much more signal ones.

Indeed, I can hardly persuade myself to be in good humour with success so far inferior to what we, in all probability should have had, had not the finest opportunity America ever possessed been fooled away by a man, in whom she has placed a large share of the most ill judged confidence. You will have heard enough to know, that I mean General Lee. This man is either a driveler in the business of soldiership or something much worse. To let you fully into the silly and pitiful game he has been playing, I will take the tale up from the beginning; expecting you will consider what I say, as in the most perfect confidence.

When we came to Hopewell Township, The General unluckily called a council of war, the result of which would have done honor to the most honorable society of midwives, and to them only. The purport was, that we should keep at a comfortable distance from the enemy, and keep up a vain parade of annoying them by detachment. In persuance of this idea, a detachment of 1500 men was sent off under General Scot to join the other troops near the enemy's lines. General Lee was primum mobile of this sage plan; and was even opposed to sending so considerable a force. The General, on mature reconsideration of what had been resolved on, determined to persue a different line of conduct at all hazards. With this view, he marched the army the next morning towards Kingston and there made another detachment of 1000 men under General Wayne; and formed all the detached troops into an advanced corps under the command of the Marquis De la fayette. The project was, that this advanced corps should take the first opportunity to attack the enemy's rear on the march, to be supported or covered as circumstances should require by the whole army.

General Lee's conduct with respect to the command of this corps was truly childish. According to the incorrect notions of our army his seniority would have intitled him to the command of the advanced corps; but he in the first instance declined it, in favour of the Marquis. Some of his friends having blamed him for doing it, and Lord Stirling having shown a disposition to interpose his claim, General Lee very inconsistently reasserted his pretensions. The matter was a second time accommodated; General Lee and Lord Stirling agreed to let the Marquis command. General Lee a little time after, recanted again and became very importunate. The General, who had all along observed the greatest candor in the matter, grew tired of such fickle behaviour and ordered the Marquis to proceed.

The enemy in marching from Allen Town had changed their disposition and thrown all their best troops in the rear; this made it necessary, to strike a stroke with propriety, to reinforce the advanced corps. Two brigades were detached for this purpose, and the General, willing to accommodate General Lee, sent him with them to take the command of the whole advanced corps, which rendezvoused the forenoon of the 27th at English Town, consisting of at least 5000 rank & file, most of them select troops. General Lee's orders were, the moment he received intelligence of the enemy's march to persue them & to attack their rear.

This intelligence was received about five oClock the morning of the 28th. and General Lee put his troops in motion accordingly. The main body did the same. The advanced corps came up with the enemys rear a mile or two beyond the court House; I saw the enemy drawn up, and am persuaded there were not a thousand men; their front from different accounts was then ten miles off. However favourable this situation may seem for an attack it was not made; but after changing their position two or three times by retrograde movements our advanced corps got into a general confused retreat and even route would hardly be too strong an expression. Not a word of all this was officially communicated to the General; as we approached the supposed place of action we heard some flying rumours of what had happened in consequence of which the General rode forward and found the troops retiring in the greatest disorder and the enemy pressing upon their rear. I never saw the general to so much advantage. His coolness and firmness were admirable. He instantly took measures for checking the enemy's advance, and giving time for the army, which was very near, to form and make a proper disposition. He then rode back and had the troops formed on a very advantageous piece of ground; in which and in other transactions of the day General Greene

& Lord Stirling rendered very essential service, and did themselves great honor. The sequel is, we beat the enemy and killed and wounded at least a thousand of their best troops. America owes a great deal to General Washington for this day's work; a general route dismay and disgrace would have attended the whole army in any other hands but his. By his own good sense and fortitude he turned the fate of the day. Other officers have great merit in performing their parts well; but he directed the whole with the skill of a Master workman. He did not hug himself at a distance and leave an Arnold to win laurels for him; but by his own presence, he brought order out of confusion, animated his troops and led them to success.

A great number of our officers distinguished themselves this day. General Wayne was always foremost in danger. Col Stewart & Lt Col Ramsay were with him among the first to oppose the enemy. Lt Col Olney at the Head of Varnum's Brigade made the next stand. I was with him, got my horse wounded and myself much hurt by a fall in consequence. Col Livingston behaved very handsomely. Our friend Barber was remarkably active; towards the close of the day, he received a ball through his side—which the doctors think will not be fatal. Col: Silly, Lt Col: Parker were particularly useful on the left—Col Craig, with General Wayne, on the right. The Artillery acquitted themselves most charmingly. I was spectator to Lt Col: Oswalds behaviour, who kept up a gallant fire from some pieces commanded by him, uncovered and unsupported. In short one can hardly name particulars without doing injustice to the rest. The behaviour of the officers and men in general was such as could not easily be surpassed. Our troops, after the first impulse from mismanagement, behaved with more spirit & moved with greater order than the British troops. You know my way of thinking about our army, and that I am not apt to flatter it. I assure you I never was pleased with them before this day.

What part our family acted let others say. I hope you will not suspect me of vanity when I tell you that one of them Fitsgerald, had a slight contusion with a Musket ball, another, Laurens, had a slight contusion also—and his horse killed—a third, Hamilton, had his horse wounded in the first part of the action with a musket ball. If the rest escaped, it is only to be ascribed to better fortune, not more prudence in keeping out of the way. That Congress is not troubled with any messenger-aids to give swords and other pretty toys to, let them ascribe to the good sense of the Commander in Chief, and to a certain turn of thinking in those about him which put them above such shifts.

What think you now of General Lee? You will be ready to join me in condemning him: And yet, I fear a Court Martial will not do it. A certain preconceived and preposterous opinion of his being a very great man will operate much in his favour. Some people are very industrious in making interest for him. Whatever a court Martial may decide, I shall continue to believe and say—his conduct was monstrous and unpardonable.

I am Dr Sir   Yrs. Affecty   *Alex Hamilton*

Brunswick
July 5th. 78

One wing of the army marched this morning towards the North River, another goes tomorrow. The enemy by our last accounts were embarking their baggage. They lie three miles below Middletown. French importunity cannot be resisted. I have given two frenchmen letters to you. I am very serious about Mr. Toussard, and as far as a Majority in some Corps Armands, Pulaskis or such like, would wish you to interest yourself for him. The Marquis De Vienne, I am so far in earnest concerning, that if his pretensions are moderate and he can be gratified I should be glad of it, but I fear they will be pretty high.

While waiting for Congress to reconvene in Philadelphia, Henry Laurens wrote a personal note to General Washington. He exclaimed his approbation of Washington's achievement at the Monmouth battle. In his letter, Laurens acknowledged that Heaven had protected Washington during this crucial confrontation and his name would be revered in posterity.[43]

Dear Sir.   *Philadelphia 7th July 1778*
I have had the honor of presenting to as many Members of Congress as have been convened in this City since the adjournment from York, Your Excellency's

several favors of the 28th & 30th June & 1st Inst: & at their special Instance have caused them to be printed for the information of the public.

I arrived here on Tuesday last, but hitherto have not collected a sufficient number of States to form a Congress, consequently I have received no Commands. Your Excellency will therefore be pleased to accept this as the address of an Individual intended to assure you Sir of my hearty congratulations with my Country Men on the success of the American Arms under Your Excellency's immediate Command in the, late Battle of Monmouth & more particularly of my own happiness in the additional Glory atcheived by Your Excellency in retrieving the honor of these States in the Moment of an alarming dilemma.

It is not my design to attempt encomiums upon Your Excellency, I am as unequal to the task as the Act is unnecessary, Love & respect for Your Excellency is impressed on the Heart of every grateful American, & your Name will be revered by posterity. Our acknowledgements are especially due to Heaven for the preservation of Your Excellency's person necessarily exposed for the Salvation of America to the most imminent danger in the late Action; that the same hand may at all times guide & Shield Your Excellency is the fervent wish of Dear sir Your much obliged & faithful humble servant

Henry Laurens

The Battle of Monmouth Court House was the largest and longest of the American Revolutionary War and the last of the major battles in the northern states. Although there is no accurate casualty count, the Americans reported around three hundred casualties and the British reported about five hundred casualties. Hamilton and Washington wrote of numbers in excess of one thousand British casualties.

At the Battle of Monmouth Court House, General Washington performed heroically, riding from unit to unit in the face of fierce enemy fire, providing guidance and commanding the movements of his army while motivating his troops to hold the line. Although he placed himself in harm's way during this extremely intense firefight, he again survived without an injury. Washington had once again been protected by Providence, and as he believed and his associates predicted, he became one of the most revered leaders of the eighteenth century. As he had assured Martha at the beginning of the war, he did return to her unscathed at the conclusion of the war.

BIBLIOGRAPHY

Ackerman, Bruce. *The Failure of the Founding Fathers: Jefferson, Marshall, and the Rise of Presidential Democracy.* Cambridge: Harvard University Press, Belknap Press, 2005.

Alberts, Robert C. *A Charming Field for an Encounter: The Story of George Washington's Fort Necessity.* Washington: Office of Publications, National Park Service, US Dept. of the Interior, 1975.

Ammon, Harry. *James Monroe, the Quest for National Identity.* Charlottesville: University Press of Virginia, 1990.

Anderson, Fred. *The War That Made America: A Short History of the French and Indian War.* New York: Penguin Press, 2005.

Allen, Steven W. *Founding Fathers: Uncommon Heroes.* Mesa, AZ: Legal Awareness Services, 2003.

Allen, W. B. ed. *George Washington: A Collection.* Indianapolis: Liberty Fund, 1988.

Babits, Lawrence Edward. *A Devil of a Whipping: The Battle of Cowpens.* Chapel Hill: University of North Carolina Press, 1998.

Becker, Carl. *The Eve of the Revolution: A Chronicle of the Breach with England.* United Kingdom: DODO Press, 1918.

Bonk, David. *Trenton and Princeton 1776–1777: Washington Crosses the Delaware.* New York: Osprey Press, 2009.

Bourne, Russell. *Cradle of Violence: How Boston's Waterfront Mobs Ignited the American Revolution*. Hoboken, NJ: John Wiley & Sons, 2006.

Brady, Patricia. *Martha Washington: An American Life*. New York: Viking, 2005.

Broadwater, Jeff. *George Mason, Forgotten Founder*. Chapel Hill: University of North Carolina Press, 2006.

Burgarner, John R. *The Health of the Presidents*. Foreword by Walter M. Floyd. Jefferson, NC: McFarland, 1994.

Burgoyne, Bruce E., trans. *The Trenton Commanders: Johann Gottlieb Rall, George Washington*. Bowie, MD: Heritage Books, 1997.

Chartrand, René. *Monongahela 1754–55: Washington's Defeat, Braddock's Disaster*. Oxford: Osprey, 2004.

Chernov, Ron. *Washington: A Life*. New York: Penguin Press, 2010.

———. *Alexander Hamilton*. New York: Penguin Press, 2004.

Clark, Harrison. *All Cloudless Glory: The Life of George Washington*. Vol. 1, *From Youth to Yorktown*. Washington, DC: Regnery Publishing, 1995.

———. *All Cloudless Glory: The Life of George Washington*. Vol. 2, *Making a Nation*. Washington, DC: Regnery Publishing, 1996.

Clement, Justin. *Philadelphia 1777: Taking the Capital*. Oxford: Osprey, 2007.

Collins, Varnum Lansing, ed. *A Brief Narrative of the Ravages of the British and Hessians at Princeton in 1776–77: A Contemporary Account of the Battles of Trenton and Princeton.* Princeton: The University Library, 1906.

Côté, Richard N. *Strength and Honor: The Life of Dolley Madison.* Mt. Pleasant, SC: Corinthian Books, 2005.

Darlington, Mary C., ed. *History of Colonel Henry Bouquet and the Western Frontiers of Pennsylvania. 1747–1764.* [Pittsburgh]: Privately Printed, 1920.

Davis, Burke. *George Washington and the American Revolution.* New York: Random House, 1975.

Davis, Derek H. *Religion and the Continental Congress: 1774–1789…* New York: Oxford University Press, 2000.

Dearborn, Henry. *Revolutionary War Journals of Henry Dearborn, 1775–1783.* Lloyd Arnold Brown and Howard Henry Peckham, eds. Biographical essay by Hermon Dunlap Smith. Westminster, MD: Heritage Books, 2007.

Dinwiddie, Robert, and R. A. Brock. *The Official Records of Robert Dinwiddie: Lieutenant-Governor of the Colony of Virginia, 1751–1758.* Richmond, VA: Society, 1883.

Duncan, Louis C. *Medical Men in the American Revolution, 1775–1783.* Washington, DC: US Army Medical Department, Office of Medical History, 1931.

Dwyer, William M. *The Day is Ours!: An Inside View of the Battles of Trenton and Princeton, November 1776–January 1777.* New Brunswick: Rutgers University Press, 1998.

Ellis, Joseph J. *American Creation: Triumphs and Tragedies at the Founding of the Republic.* New York: Alfred A. Knopf, 2007.

———. *American Sphinx: The Character of Thomas Jefferson.* New York: Vintage Books, 1998.

———. *First Family: Abigail and John.* New York: Alfred A. Knopf, 2010.

———. *Founding Brothers: The Revolutionary Generation.* New York: Vintage Books, 2000.

———. *His Excellency: George Washington.* New York: Alfred A. Knopf, 2004.

Ferling, John E. *Adams vs. Jefferson: The Tumultuous Election of 1800.* New York: Oxford University Press, 2004.

———. *Almost a Miracle: The American Victory in the War of Independence.* New York: Oxford University Press, 2007.

———. *The Ascent of George Washington: The Hidden Political Genius of an American Icon.* New York: Bloomsbury Press, 2009.

Fischer, David Hackert. *Washington's Crossing.* New York: Oxford University Press, 2006.

Fleming, Thomas. *The Intimate Lives of the Founding Fathers*. New York: HarperCollins, 2009.

—————. *The Perils of Peace: America's Struggle for Survival After Yorktown*. New York: HarperCollins, 2007.

—————. *Washington's Secret War: The Hidden History of Valley Forge*. New York: Smithsonian Books/Collins, 2005.

Forbes, John, and Irene Stewart. *Letters of General John Forbes Relating to the Expedition against Fort Duquesne in 1758*. Compiled from books in the Carnegie Library of Pittsburgh for the Allegheny County Committee, Pennsylvania Society of the Colonial Dames of America. University Park, PA: Pennsylvania State University Press, 2006.

Fowler, William M. *Empires at War: The French and Indian War and the Struggle for North America 1754–1763*. New York: Walker & Company, 2006.

Fritz, Jean. *Traitor, the Case of Benedict Arnold*. New York: Putnam, 1981.

Furstenberg, Francois. *In the Name of the Father: Washington's Legacy, Slavery, and the Making of a Nation*. New York: Penguin Books, 2007.

Gist, Christopher, and William M. Darlington. *Christopher Gist's Journals with Historical, Geographical and Ethnological Notes and Biographies of His Contemporaries*. New York: Published for University Microfilms, Ann Arbor, by Argonaut Press, 1966.

Golway, Terry. *Washington's General: Nathanael Greene and the Triumph of the American Revolution*. New York: H. Holt, 2005.

Gould, Dudley C. *Forgotten Army: The Abandonment of American Revolutionary War Soldiers*. Middleton, CT: Southfarm Press, 2007.

Griffith, Lucille. *The Virginia House of Burgesses, 1750–1774*. University, Ala: University of Alabama Press, 1970.

Griffith, Samuel B. *The War for American Independence: From 1760 to the Surrender at Yorktown in 1781*. Chicago: University of Illinois Press, 2002.

Grizzard, Frank E. *The Ways of Providence: Religion & George Washington*. Charlottesville: Mariner Publishing, 2005.

Henriques, Peter R. *Realistic Visionary: A Portrait of George Washington*. Charlottesville: University of Virginia Press, 2006.

Holton, Woody. *Abigail Adams: [a Life]*. New York: Free Press, 2009.

Horn, James. *A Land as God Made It: Jamestown and the Birth of America*. New York: Basic Books, 2005.

Idzerda, Stanley J., ed. *Lafayette in the Age of the American Revolution: Selected Letters and Papers, 1776–1790*. Vol. 1, *December 7, 1776–March 30, 1778*. Ithaca: Cornell University Press, 1977.

———. *Lafayette in the Age of the American Revolution: Selected Letters and Papers, 1776–1790*. Vol. 2, *April 10, 1778–March 20, 1780*. Ithaca: Cornell University Press, 1979.

Isaacson, Walter. *Benjamin Franklin: An American Life*. New York: Simon & Schuster, 2003.

Kaminski, John P., and Jill Adair McCaughan, eds. *A Great and Good Man: George Washington in the Eyes of His Contemporaries.* Lanham, MD: Rowan & Littlefield, 2007.

Ketchum, Richard M. *The Winter Soldiers: The Battles of Trenton and Princeton.* New York: Henry Holt and Company, 1999.

———. *Decisive Day: The Battle for Bunker Hill.* New York: Henry Holt, 1999.

———. *Saratoga: Turning Point of America's Revolutionary War.* New York: John Macrae/Owl Book, 1999.

———. *Victory at Yorktown: The Campaign That Won the Revolution.* New York: Henry Holt, 2004.

Labunski, Richard E. *James Madison and the Struggle for the Bill of Rights.* Oxford: Oxford University Press, 2006.

Lanning, Michael Lee. *The American Revolution 100: The People, Battles, and Events of the American War for Independence, Ranked by Their Significance.* Naperville, IL: Sourcebooks, 2009.

Lengel, Edward G. *General George Washington: A Military Life.* New York: Random House Trade Paperbacks, 2007.

Longmore, Paul K. *The Invention of George Washington.* Charlottesville: University of Virginia Press, 1999.

Marshall, Peter J., and David B. Manuel. *The Light and the Glory: 1492–1793 Gods Plan for America.* rev. ed. Grand Rapids: Revell, 2009.

Martin, Joseph Plumb, and Thomas Fleming. *A Narrative of a Revolutionary Soldier: Some of the Adventures, Dangers, and Sufferings of Joseph Plumb Martin*. New York: New American Library, 2001.

McCullough, David. *1776*. New York: Simon & Schuster, 2005.

———. *John Adams*. New York: Simon & Schuster, 2001.

McGuire, Thomas J. *The Philadelphia Campaign*. Vol. 1, *Brandywine and the Fall of Philadelphia*. Mechanicsburg, Pa: Stackpole Books, 2006.

———. *The Philadelphia Campaign*. Vol. 2, *Germantown and the Roads to Valley Forge*. Mechanicsburg, Pa: Stackpole Books, 2007.

Meacham, Jon. *American Gospel: God, the Founding Fathers, and the Making of a Nation*. New York: Random House, 2006.

Montross, Lynn. *The Reluctant Rebels; the Story of the Continental Congress, 1774–1789*. New York: Harper, 1950.

Morgan, Edmund S. *Benjamin Franklin*. New Haven: Yale University Press, 2002.

Morpurgo, J. E. *Treason at West Point: The Arnold-André Conspiracy*. New York: Mason/Charter, 1975.

Morrissey, Brendan, and Adam Hook. *Monmouth Courthouse 1778: The Last Great Battle in the North*. Oxford: Osprey, 2004.

Novak, Michael, and Jana Novak. *Washington's GOD: Religion, Liberty, and the Father of our Country*. New York: Basic Books, 2006.

O'Brien, Conor Cruise, and Christopher Hitchens. *First in Peace: How George Washington Set the Course for America*. Cambridge: Da Capa Press, 2009.

Palmer, Dave Richard. *George Washington and Benedict Arnold: A Tale of Two Patriots*. Washington, DC: Regnery Pub., 2006.

Peckham, Howard H., ed. *Sources of American Independence: Selected Manuscripts from Collections of the William L. Clements Library*. Vol. 1. Chicago: University of Chicago Press, 1978.

————. *Sources of American Independence: Selected Manuscripts from Collections of the William L. Clements Library*. Vol. 2. Chicago: University of Chicago Press, 1978.

Philbrick, Nathaniel. *Mayflower: A Story of Courage, Community, and War*. New York: Penguin Books, 2006.

Phillips, Donald T. *On the Wing of Speed: George Washington and the Battle of Yorktown*. New York: iUniverse Star, 2006.

Puls, Mark. *Henry Knox: Visionary General of the American Revolution*. New York: Palgrave Macmillan, 2008.

Rakove, Jack N., and Oscar Handlin. *James Madison and the Creation of the American Republic*. New York: Longman, 2002.

Rhodehamel, John, ed. *George Washington: Writings*. New York: Library of America, 1997.

Rosaler, Maxine. *A Timeline of the First Continental Congress*. New York: Rosen Central, 2004.

Sargent, Winthrop. *A History of an Expedition against Fort Duquesne in 1755: Under Major-General Edward Braddock*. New York: Arno Press, 1971.

Schwartz, Seymour I. *The French and Indian War 1754–1763: The Imperial Struggle for North America*. Edison, NJ: Castle Books, 1994.

Smith, David. *New York 1776: The Continentals' First Battle*. Oxford: Osprey Pub., 2008.

Smith, Samuel Stelle. *The Battle of Monmouth*. Monmouth Beach, NJ: Philip Freneau Press, 1964.

———. *The Battle of Princeton*. Monmouth Beach, NJ: Philip Freneau Press, 1967.

———. *The Battle of Trenton The Battle of Princeton: Two Stories*. Canada: Westholme Publishing, 2009.

Stahr, Walter. *John Jay: Founding Father*. New York: Hambledon and London, 2005.

Stryker, William S. *The Battles of Trenton and Princeton*. Trenton: Old Barracks Association, 2001.

Stryker, William S., and William Starr Myers. *The Battle of Monmouth*. Princeton: Princeton University Press, 1927.

Taylor, Alan. *American Colonies: The Settling of North America*. New York: Penguin Books, 2002.

Thatcher, James. *A Military Journal during The American Revolutionary War, From 1775 To 1783: Describing Interesting Events and Transactions of This Period; with Numerous Historical Facts and Anecdotes, from the Original Manuscript.* 2nd ed. LaVergne, TN, 2009.

Thompson, Mary V. *In the Hands of a Good Providence.* Charlottesville: University of Virginia Press, 2008.

Tomlinson, Everett T. *The Boys of Old Monmouth: A Story of Washington's Campaign in New Jersey in 1778.* Boston, MA: Houghton, Mifflin, 1898.

Tourtellot, Arthur Bernon. *Lexington and Concord.* New York: Norton, 1959.

Washington, George. *The Diaries of George Washington.* Edited by Donald Jackson and Dorothy Twohig. 6 vols. Charlottesville: University of Virginia Press, 1976–79.

———. *The Diaries of George Washington.* Edited by John C. Fitzpatrick. 4 vols. Cranbury, NJ: Scholars Bookshelf, for the Mount Vernon Ladies' Association of the Union, 2005.

———. The *Papers of George Washington, Colonial Series.* Edited by W. W. Abbot and Dorothy Twohig. 10 vols. Charlottesville: University of Virginia Press, 1983–95.

———. *The Papers of George Washington, Confederation Series.* Edited by W. W. Abbot and Dorothy Twohig. 6 vols. Charlottesville: University of Virginia Press, 1992–97.

————. *The Papers of George Washington, Presidential Series.* Edited by W. W. Abbot, Dorothy Twohig and Philander D. Chase. 12 vols. to date. Charlottesville: University of Virginia Press, 1987–.

————. *The Papers of George Washington, Revolutionary War Series.* Edited by W. W. Abbot and Dorothy Twohig. 16 vols. to date. Charlottesville: University of Virginia Press, 1985–.

————. *The Papers of George Washington; Retirement Series.* Edited by W. W. Abbot and Dorothy Twohig. 4 vols. Charlottesville: University of Virginia Press, 1998–99.

Washington, George, and Archer Butler Hulbert. *Washington and the West; Being George Washington's Diary of September, 1784, Kept during His Journey into the Ohio Basin in the Interest of a Commercial Union between the Great Lakes and the Potomac River.* New York: Century, 1905.

Washington, George, Earl Schenck Miers, and Bruce Rogers. *Trial by Wilderness: The Emergence of George Washington as Revealed in His Own Journal, 1753–1754.* Kingsport, TN: Kingsport Press, 1957.

Washington, George, and Edward G. Lengel. *This Glorious Struggle: George Washington's Revolutionary War Letters.* New York: Smithsonian Books/HarperCollins, 2007.

Washington, George, Fred Anderson, and Philander D. Chase. *George Washington Remembers: Reflections on the French and Indian War.* Lanham, MD: Rowman & Littlefield Publishers, 2004.

Washington, George, and Joseph M. Toner. *Journal of Colonel George Washington.* Albany: J. Munsell's Sons, 1893.

Washington, George, and Julius Friedrich Sachse. *Washington's Masonic Correspondence as Found among the Washington Papers in the Library of Congress, Comp. from the Original Records, under the Direction of the Committee on Library of the Grand Lodge of Pennsylvania, with Annotations.* Philadelphia: Press of the New Era Printing Company, 1915.

Washington, Irving. *George Washington: A Biography.* Abridged and edited with an introduction by Charles Neider. Cambridge: Da Capa Press, 1994.

Weems, Mason L. *The Life of Washington.* Edited by Marcus Cunliffe. Cambridge: Harvard University Press, Belknap Press, 1962.

Wood, Gordon S. *Revolutionary Characters: What Made The Founders Different.* New York: Penguin Press, 2006.

Wood, W. J. *Battles of the Revolutionary War 1775–1781: Major Battles and Campaigns.* Introduction by John S. D. Eisenhower. Cambridge: Da Capo Press, 1990.

ENDNOTE ABBREVIATIONS

CGTJ – Christopher Gist's Journals with Historical, Geographical and Ethnological Notes and Biographies of His Contemporaries, Third Journal–1753

GWD – The Diaries of George Washington, Donald Jackson, editor, Dorothy Twohig, associate editor

GWDF – The Diaries of George Washington, edited by John C. Fitzpatrick

GWPCS – The Papers of George Washington Colonial Series

GWPRWS – The Papers of George Washington Revolutionary War Series

GWPCFS – The Papers of George Washington Confederation Series

GWPPS – The Papers of George Washington Presidential Series

LGF – Letters of General John Forbes, Relating to the Expedition against Fort Duquesne in 1758, compiled from books in the Carnegie Library in Pittsburgh

VHS – Collection of the Virginia Historical Society, New Series, Vol. III

The Official Records of Robert Dinwiddie VI:

Lieutenant-Governor of the Colony of Virginia 1751–1758

ENDNOTES

Introduction

1   GWPCS William Fairfax to GW 1:345–346

2   Mason L. Weems, *The Life of Washington*, edited by Marcus Cunliffe, 42

3   Ibid., xxxiv

The Grim King

1   GWD Donald Jackson and Dorothy Twohig, editors 1:9–12

2   GWPCS GW to Ann Fairfax Washington 1:38

3   GWD Donald Jackson and Dorothy Twohig, editors 1:82

4   GWPCS GW to William Fauntleroy 1:49

5   Ibid., GW to William Fairfax, note 3 1:259

6   Ibid., GW to Robert Orme 1:286

7   Ibid., GW to Sarah Cary Fairfax 1:307

8   Ibid., GW to John Augustine Washington 1:310

9   Ibid., Robert Morris to GW 1:315

10   Ibid., GW to John Augustine Washington 1:319

11   Ibid., GW to John Augustine Washington 1:343

12   Ibid., GW to Mary Ball Washington 1:337

13   Ibid., GW to Augustine Washington 1:351–352

14   Ibid., GW to Richard Washington 4:132

15   Ibid., Robert Stewart to Robert Dinwiddie 5:46

16 Ibid., GW to Sarah Cary Fairfax 5:56

17 Ibid., Robert Dinwiddie to Robert Stewart 5:62

18 Ibid., Robert Stewart to John Stanwix 5:63–64

19 Ibid., James Craik to GW 5:64–65

20 Ibid., GW to John Blair 5:82–83

21 Ibid., GW toJohn Blair 5:95

22 Ibid., GW to John Stanwix 5:101–102. He used the phrase "Esculapian tribe" to refer to his doctors who had taken the Aesculpian Oath.

23 Ibid., GW to Francis Fauquier 6:165

24 Ibid., James Craik to Washington 6:170

25 Ibid., GW to Richard Washington 7:54

26 Ibid., GW to Andrew Burnaby 7:59

27 Ibid., GW to Charles Green 7:68–69

28 Ibid., Robert Stewart to GW 7:70–71

29 Ibid., GW to Robert Cary & Co. 7:73

30 Ibid., GW to Richard Washington 7:80

31 Ibid., George William Fairfax to GW 7:95

32 Ibid., GW to Peter Stover 7:97

33 Ibid., Andrew Burnaby to GW 7:98

34 GWD Donald Jackson and Dorothy Twohig, editors 1:295

35 GWPCS GW to Robert Cary & Co. 7:135

36 Ibid., GW to Burwell Bassett 7:147

37 GWPRWS William Shippen to GW 8:158

38 Ibid., GW to William Shippen 8:264

39 Ibid., Alexander Hamilton to Alexander McDougall note 3 8:536

40   Ibid., Tench Tilghman to William Livingston 8:541

41   Ibid., Joseph Reed to GW 8:618

42   GWDF John Fitzpatrick 3:110

43   GWPCFS GW to George Gilpin and John Fitzgerald 4:234

44   Ibid., GW to David Humphreys 4:237

45   Ibid., GW to John Fitzgerald 4:242

46   GWDF John Fitzpatrick 3:116

47   GWPCFS GW to the Society of the Cincinnati 4:316

48   Ibid., James Madison to GW 4:345

49   Ibid., GW to James Madison 4:382–383

50   Ibid., GW to Henry Knox 5:74–75

51   Ibid., Henry Knox to GW 5: 97

52   Ibid., GW to Edmund Randolph 5:113

53   Ibid., GW to Henry Knox 5:120

54   Ibid., GW to Arthur Lee 5:191

55   GWPPS James McHenry to GW note 1 (McVickar) 3:76–77

56   Ibid., James McHenry to GW 3:75–76

57   Ibid., James McHenry to GW note 1 (re GW to James McHenry), 3:77

58   Ibid., GW to Bushrod Washington 3:334

59   Ibid., James Craik to GW 3:529–530

60   Ibid., James McHenry to GW note 1 (re Samuel Bard to Susan Bard), 1, 3:77

61   Ibid., GW to James Craik 4:1

62   GWD Donald Jackson and Dorothy Twohig, editors 6:76

63   GWDF John Fitzpatrick 4:129

64   GWPPS William Jackson to Clement Biddle 5:399–400

65   Journal of William Maclay, 265

66   GWPPS Cyrus Griffen to GW 5:441

67   Ibid., David Stuart to GW 5:458–459

68   Ibid., GW to Henry Hill note 1, 5:389

69   Ibid., GW to Lafayette 5:469

70   Ibid., Henry Lee to GW 5:515

71   Ibid., GW to David Stuart 5:527

72   GWDF John Fitzgerald note 1, 4:320

73   Louis Duncan, *Medical Men in the American Revolution* (1931), 371

74   Joseph J. Ellis, *His Excellency, George Washington,* 12

The Cold was so Extremely Severe

1   GWPCS editorial note 1:57

2   Ibid., Dinwiddie commission to GW to deliver message to the French commandant 1:58

3   *Maryland Gazette* archives March 28, 1754, No. 464 – Dinwiddie's letter to the French commandant

4   GWPCS Dinwiddie's instructions to GW 1:60–61

5   GWD Jackson and Twohig 1:153

6   GWDF John Fitzpatrick 1:43

7   CGTG Christopher Gist's third journal 1753 3:80

8   GWDF John Fitzpatrick, 1:44–45

9   Ibid., 1:47–48

10   Ibid., 1:48

11   Ibid., 1:49

12   Ibid., 1:49

13   Ibid., 1:50

14   Ibid., 1:54

15   Ibid., 1:54

16   Ibid., 1:57

17   Ibid., 1:58–59

18   Ibid., 1:59–61

19   *Maryland Gazette* archives March 7, 1754, No.461 – French commandant's reply to Dinwiddie

20   GWDF John Fitzpatrick 1:61

21   Ibid., 1:62

22   Ibid., 1:62

23   CGTJ Christopher Gist's third journal 1753 3:83–84

24   GWDF John Fitzpatrick 1:63

25   CGTJ Christopher Gist's third journal 1753 3:84

26   GWDF John Fitzpatrick 1:64

27   CGTJ Christopher Gist's third journal 1753 3:84–85

28   GWDF John Fitzgerald 1:64–65

29   CGTJ Christopher Gist's third journal 1753 3:85–86

30   GWDF John Fitzgerald 1:65

31   CGTJ Christopher Gist's third journal 1753 3:86

32   GWDF John Fitzgerald 1:67

33   Ibid., 1:67

Charming Sound

1   GWPCS editorial note 1:63

2   The forks of the Ohio refers to the site where the Allegheny and the Monongahela Rivers join to form the Ohio River and was considered

the gateway to the Ohio Country and is now modern-day Pittsburgh, Pennsylvania.

3   VHS Dinwiddie to William Trent 1:55–56

4   Ibid., Dinwiddie's instructions to GW 1:65

5   Ibid., message of Governor Dinwiddie proroguing the Assembly 1:79

6   Ibid., Dinwiddie's instructions to Fry 1:88–90

7   GWPCS Dinwiddie to GW 1:75–76

8   GWDF John Fitzpatrick, 1:73

9   VHS Dinwiddie to DeLancey 1:117

10   Ibid., Dinwiddie to Hamilton 1:121

11   GWDF John Fitzpatrick 1:73–74

12   VHS Dinwiddie to Glen 1:129

13   GWDF John Fitzpatrick 1:75

14   Ibid., 1:74

15   GWPCS GW to Dinwiddie 1:87

16   VHS Dinwiddie to Fry 1:147

17   GWPCS GW to Dinwiddie 1:93–95

18   GWDF John Fitzpatrick 1:84–85

19   Ibid., 1–85

20   GWPCS GW to Dinwiddie 1:104–106

21   GWDF John Fitzpatrick 1:87

22   Ibid., John Fitzpatrick 1:87

23   Ibid., John Fitzpatrick 1:87

24   Ibid., John Fitzpatrick 1:87–88

25   Ibid., John Fitzpatrick 1:88

26   GWPCS GW to Dinwiddie 1:109–112

27   Ibid., GW to Fry 1:117–118

28   Ibid., GW to John Augustine Washington 1:118

29   GWDF John Fitzpatrick 1:90

30   GWPCS GW to Dinwiddie, note 12, 1:125–126

31   Ibid., Dinwiddie to GW 1:119

32   Ibid., GW to Dinwiddie 1:124

33   Ibid., Dinwiddie to GW 126–127

34   Ibid., Charles Carter to GW 1:128

35   GWDF John Fitzpatrick 1:92

36   GWPCS GW to Dinwiddie 1:129–130

37   Ibid., GW to Dinwiddie 1:135–138

38   Ibid., John Carlyle to GW 1:142

39   Ibid., Sarah Carlyle to GW 1:145

40   VHS Dinwiddie to Hamilton 1:214–215

41   Ibid., Dinwiddie to Sharpe 1:212–213

42   GWPCS Bryan Fairfax to GW 1:147–148

43   GWDF John Fitzpatrick 1:100–101

44   GWPCS minutes of a council of war 1:155–156

45   Ibid., Articles of Capitulation 1:166–167

46   Ibid., William Fairfax to GW 1:173–174 The "brave Dinwiddie
       & Monacatoocha" refers to Chiefs Half-King and Monacatoocha
       since Washington had assigned the Half-King the honorary name of
       Dinwiddie. The letter also refers to Lawrence Washington, George
       Washington's half brother, who had participated along with Captain
       Innes and Captain Clarke in the unsuccessful British attack on the
       Spanish fort at Cartagena in 1741.

47   Ibid., James Innes to GW 1:176 In Colonel Innes's reference to Bell Haven he was referring to Alexandria.

48   Ibid., GW and James McKay's account of the Fort Necessity battle 1:159–161

49   VHS Dinwiddie to Colonel Innes 1:232

50   Ibid., Dinwiddie to the Lords of Trade 1:241–242

51   GWPCS Dinwiddie to GW 1:206–207

52   Ibid., Horatio Sharpe to GW, editorial note, 1:211

53   VHS Dinwiddie to Sir Thomas Robinson 1:355, Lords of Trade 1:365, Earl of Halifax 1:369, Earl Granville 1:372–373, and James Abercromby 1:376

54   GWPCS William Fitzhugh to GW, note 1, 1:224

55   Ibid., William Fitzhugh to GW 1:223–224

56   Ibid., GW to William Fitzhugh 1: 225–227

Some Important Service to the Country

1   VHS Dinwiddie to Sharpe 1:453

2   Ibid., Dinwiddie to William Allen 1:455

3   Ibid., Dinwiddie to Abercromby 1:512

4   GWPCS Orme to GW 1:241

5   Ibid., GW to Orme 1:242–245

6   Ibid., GW to Sarah Cary Fairfax 1:279. Washington mentiod to Sarah Cary Fairfax that he was with General Braddock during the parade review in Alexandria, which was on March 31, 1755.

7   Ibid., GW to Orme 1:246–247

8   Ibid., Orme to GW 1:249

9   Ibid., GW to William Byrd 1:249–251

10   Ibid., GW to William Fairfax 1:257–258

11   Ibid., GW to Sarah Cary Fairfax 1:261

12   Ibid., GW to William Fairfax note 7, 1:264

13   Ibid., GW to William Fairfax 1:262–263

14   Ibid., GW to Lord Thomas Fairfax 1:265

15   Ibid., GW to Lord Thomas Fairfax, note 4 1:266

16   Ibid., GW to John Augustine Washington 1:266–267

17   Ibid., GW to Augustine Washington 1: 271–272

18   Ibid., GW to John Augustine Washington 1:277–278

19   Ibid., Braddock's instructions to GW 1:281

20   Ibid., GW to John Hunter 1:284–285

21   Ibid., GW to Orme 1:286–287

22   Ibid., GW to Orme 1:288

23   Ibid., memorandum 1:282–283

24   Ibid., GW to William Fairfax 1:298–300

25   Ibid., GW to John Augustine Washington 1:310

26   Ibid., GW to John Augustine Washington 1:319

27   Ibid., GW to John Augustine Washington 1:319–320

28   Ibid., GW to John Augustine Washington 1:321

29   Ibid., GW to John Augustine Washington 1:321

30   Ibid., GW to John Augustine Washington 1:322

31   Ibid., GW to John Augustine Washington 1:324

32   VHS Dinwiddie to Innes 2:80

33   Ibid., Dinwiddie to Braddock 2:81–82

34   GWPCS memorandum 1:331

35   Ibid., memorandum, note 4 1:332–333

36 Ibid., GW to Innes 1:334

37 Ibid., GW to Mary Ball Washington 1:336–337

38 Ibid., GW to Dinwiddie 1:339–340

39 Ibid., GW to John Augustine Washington 1:343

40 Ibid., William Fairfax to GW 1:345–346

41 VHS Dinwiddie to GW 2:122–123

42 GWPCS Philip Ludwell to GW 1:356–357

43 Ibid., Warner Lewis to GW 1:358–359

44 Ibid., GW to Warner Lewis 1:360–363

45 VHS commission from Governor Dinwiddie to Colonel George Washington 2:184

46 Samuel Davies, "Religion and Patriotism the Constituents of a Good Soldier," Sermon LXI, 363–387, the quotes are in the footnote on page 370, by the Reverend Drs. Gibbons and Finley, *Sermons on Important Subjects, by the late reverend and pious Samuel Davies, A. M., Sometime President of the College in New Jersey*

47 Samuel Davies later became the president of the College in New Jersey (today's Princeton University).

48 VHS Dinwiddie to the Lords of Trade 2:192–194

Between Two Fires

1 VHS Dinwiddie to Lord Loudoun 2:455–456

2 GWPCS GW to Dinwiddie 3:317

3 Ibid., GW to John Campbell, Earl of Loudoun 4:79–93

4 Ibid., GW to James Cuninghame 4:105–107

5 Ibid., John Stanwix to GW note 1, 4:160

6 VHS Dinwiddie to Lord Loudoun 2:616–617

7 GWPCS Lewis Stephens to GW note 1, 4:417

8   Ibid., GW to Dinwiddie 4:419–421

9   Ibid., GW to John Stanwix 5:9–10

10   Ibid., Dinwiddie to GW 5:19–20

11   Ibid., GW to John Robinson 5:34

12   Ibid., John Robinson to GW 5:43

13   Ibid., Robert Stewart to John Stanwix 5:63

14   Ibid., John Blair to GW note 3, 5:115

15   Ibid., Beverly Robinson to GW note 4, 5:99

16   Ibid., Beverly Robinson to GW note 3, 5:98–99

17   Ibid., GW to Stanwix 5:101–102

18   Ibid., GW to Stanwix 5:117

19   Ibid., John St. Clair to GW 5:133

20   Ibid., GW to John St. Clair 5:148

21   LGF Forbes to William Pitt 13

22   LGF Forbes to William Pitt 18–20

23   GWPCS John St. Clair to GW 5:210–211

24   Ibid., GW to Francis Fauquier 5:219–221

25   LGF Forbes to William Pitt 21–23

26   GWPCS Colonel Henry Bouquet to GW 5:246

27   Ibid., GW to Colonel Henry Bouquet 5:282–283

28   Ibid., Colonel Henry Bouquet to GW 5:286

29   Shade, Robert J., *Forbes Road Love, War and Revenge on the Pennsylvania Frontier*, CreateSpace

30   GWPCS GW to Francis Halkett 5:360–361

31   Ibid., Colonel Henry Bouquet to GW 5:364–365

32   LGF Colonel Henry Bouquet to Amherst 47–48

33 GWPCS GW Francis Fauquier 6:44–45

34 Ibid., Orderly Book, October 13, 1758 note 1, 6:78

35 Ibid., Orderly Book October 16, 1758 6:79

36 Ibid., GW to Henry Bouquet 6:115–116

37 Ibid., Orderly Book November 12, 1758 note 1, 6:122

38 Ibid., Orderly Book November 12, 1758 note 1, 6:122–123

39 Ibid., Orderly Book November 14, 1758 note 1, 6:125–126

40 Ibid., Orderly Book November 12, 1758 note 1, 6:121

41 Ibid., Order Book November 24, 1758 note 4, 6:158

Commander in Chief

1 GWPCS House of Burgesses resolution Feb. 26, 1759 6:192

2 Ibid., GW to John Alton 6:200

3 Ibid., GW to Robert Cary & Co. 6:315–316

4 Ibid., GW to Robert Cary & Co. 6:459–460

5 Ibid., GW to Robert Cary & Co. 7:135–137

6 Ibid., GW to Francis Dandridge 7:395–396

7 Ibid., GW to Robert Cary & Co. 8:85–86

8 Ibid., GW to Robert Cary & Co. 9:271–272

9 Ibid., Thomas Johnson to GW 10:102–103

10 Ibid., GW to Bryan Fairfax 10:154–156

11 Ibid., GW to Thomas Johnston, note 1, 10:143

12 The Quebec Act passed by Parliament in 1774 extended the boundaries of Quebec south to the Ohio and west to the Mississippi. A governor and council were to be appointed to govern this territory.

13 Robert McKenzie was a captain with Washington's Virginia regiment until he received a commission in the British army in 1761.

14   GWPCS Robert McKenzie to GW 10:161

15   Ibid., GW to George William Fairfax 10:367–368

16   GWPRWS GW to Martha Washington 1:3–5

17   Ibid., GW to Martha Washington 1:27

18   Ibid., GW to Samuel Washington 1:134–136

19   Ibid., council of war 2:282

20   Ibid., GW to Nathaniel Woodhull 2:388. In 1911, this manuscript was damaged in the New York State Library fire. The portions within brackets were copied from the letter-book version.

21   Ibid., Henry Knox to GW 2:495–496

22   Ibid., Henry Knox to GW 3:29

23   Ibid., GW to Joseph Reed 3:369–374

24   Ibid., GW to Lord Stirling 3:497–498

25   Ibid., GW's circular letter to Nicholas Cooke, Lord Stirling, Brigadier General William Thompson, and Jonathan Trumbull Sr. 3:543–544

26   Ibid., John Hancock to GW 4:16–17

27   Ibid., General orders, April 14, 1776 4:58–59

28   Ibid., Colonel Henry Knox to GW 4:491

29   Ibid., GW to John Hancock 5:159–160

30   Ibid., GW to John Augustine Washington 5:428–430

31   Ibid., GW to John Hancock 6:4–5

32   Ibid., GW to John Hancock 6:31

33   Ibid., Lieutenant Colonel Robert Hanson Harrison to John Hancock, 6:140–142

34   Henry P. Johnson, *The Campaign of 1776 around New York and Brooklyn*, Project Gutenberg, online reader, 128

35   GWPRWS GW to John Hancock 6:177–178

You Alone Can Defend Us

1 GWPRWS GW to John Hancock 7:96–98

2 Ibid., GW to General Charles Lee 7:133–135

3 Ibid., GW to John Augustine Washington 7:102–106

4 Today Fort Washington is remembered by a plaque at the Manhattan end of the George Washington Bridge. Fort Lee is located on the opposite shore in New Jersey.

5 GWPRWS GW to John Hancock 7:182–183

6 Ibid., GW to General Charles Lee 7:193–195

7 Ibid., GW to General Charles Lee 7:224–225

8 Ibid., GW to John Hancock 7:245

9 Ibid., GW to Colonel Richard Humpton 7:248

10 Ibid., GW to John Hancock 7:273

11 *Journals of the Continental Congress*, dated December 12, 1776, 6:1027

12 *Journals of the Continental Congress*, dated December 27, 1776, 6:1045

13 GWPRWS Major General John Sullivan to GW 7:328

14 Ibid., GW to Lund Washington 7:289–291

15 Ibid., GW to Samuel Washington 7:369–371

16 Ibid., GW to John Hancock 7:382

17 Ibid., Colonel Joseph Reed to GW 7:414–416

18 Hessians were German mercenaries that Great Britain had brought to America to reinforce their forces.

19 GWPRWS Brigadier General Philemon Dickinson to GW 7:427

20 Ibid., general orders for 25 December 1776, 7:434–436

21 *The Diary of Captain Thomas Rodney*, The Historical Society of Delaware 22–23

22 William S. Stryker: *The Battles of Trenton and Princeton*, note 41, 366–367

23 GWPRWS Major George Johnston to Level Powell note 8, 7:459

24 Ibid., GW to John Hancock 7:454–456

25 David Hackett Fischer: *Washington's Crossing*, 289

26 GWPRWS GW to Major General William Heath 7:468

27 Ibid., GW to John Hancock 7:477–478

28 Ten dollars in December 1776 is equal to $290 according to some sources. http://www.wealthvest.com/blog/wade-dokken/the-history-of-what-things-cost-in-america-1776-to-today-247-wall-st-wade-dokken/

29 GWPRWS GW to the commanding officer in Morristown, note 2, 7:491

30 Ibid., GW to the commanding officer at Morristown 7:490–491

31 Ibid., GW to Colonel John Cadwalader and Brigadier General Thomas Mifflin 7:510

32 *The Diary of Captain Thomas Rodney*, The Historical Society of Delaware 32–33

33 William S. Stryker: *The Battles of Trenton and Princeton*, 286–287

34 GWPRWS GW to John Hancock 7:519–523

35 William S. Stryker: *The Battles of Trenton and Princeton*, note 97, 452–456

36 GWPRWS GW to John Hancock 8:9–10

37 Ibid., Bartholomew Dandridge to GW 8:79–80

38 Ibid., GW to John Parke Custis 8:123–124

Providence Which has Never Failed Us

1 Stanley J. Idzerda, editor, *Lafayette in the Age of the American Revolution Selected Letters and Papers, 1776–1790*, 1:92

2 GWPRWS GW to Landon Carter 12:25–26

3 Ibid., GW to John Hancock 11:78

4 Captain Patrick Ferguson invented the breech-loading rifle that could fire six times a minute.

5 De Witt Bailey, PhD: *The British Military Flintlock Rifles 1740–1840*, 48

6 Hammond, *Sullivan Papers*, letter from John Sullivan to Meshech Weare 1:542–547

7 Benjamin Tallmadge, *Memoir of Col. Benjamin Tallmadge, prepared by himself at the request of his children [1858]*, 22–24

8 GWPRWS GW to Henry Laurens 12:683–687

9 Ibid., GW to William Buchanan 13:465–466

10 Ibid., GW to Major General Nathanael Greene 13:514–515

11 Ibid., general orders, headquarters, Valley Forge, Pa., Sunday, March 1, 1778, 14:1–2

12 Ibid., Henry Laurens to GW 14:549

13 Ibid., Henry Laurens to GW, note 3, 14:550

14 Ibid., Major General William Heath to GW 14:580

15 Ibid., GW to Major General Charles Lee 14:585

16 Ibid., GW to Henry Laurens 14:601

17 Ibid., Edmund Pendleton to GW 14:666–667

18 Ibid., from the council of war on May 9,1778 15:83–88

19 Ibid., GW to Major General Nathanael Greene 15:135

20 Ibid., Brigadier General Henry Knox to GW 15:142–143

21 Ibid., general orders May 18 1778 15:150

22 Ibid., general orders May 23,1778 15:194

23 Landon Carter (1710–1778) was a wealthy landowner and served

in the House of Burgesses (1757–1761). He was one of the most prolific writers of his time and a strong supporter of the war for independence from Great Britain.

24   GWPRWS GW to Landon Carter 15:267–269

25   Ibid., GW to John Augustine Washington 15:374–375

26   Ibid., Major General Charles Lee to GW 15:403–405

27   Ibid., GW to Major General Charles Lee 15:406–407

28   Ibid., council of war, Valley Forge, 17 June 1778 15:414–417

29   Ibid., Major General Charles Lee to GW 15:457–458

30   Elias Boudinot was the commissary of prisoners. He had the responsibility of caring for prisoners of both the Continental and British armies.

31   GWPRWS Elias Boudinot to GW 15:433

32   Ibid., general orders June 19, 1778 15:470–471

33   Ibid., council of war 24 June, 1778 15:520–521

34   Ibid., Major General Lafayette to GW 15:528–529

35   Ibid., GW to Major General Lafayette 15:539

36   Ibid., Major General Charles Lee to GW 15:541–542

37   Ibid., GW to Major General Charles Lee 15:556

38   Ibid., GW to Henry Laurens 15:578–579

39   *A Narrative of a Revolutionary Soldier – Some of the Adventures, Dangers, and Sufferings of Joseph Plumb Martin, With an Introduction by Thomas Fleming,* 110–111

40   GWPRWS GW to John Augustine Washington 16:25–26

41   Sons of Liberty Chapter, Revolutionary War historical article, "George Washington's Military Family," "The duties of the Aides-de-Camp were often dangerous. On the field of battle,

they galloped about the battlefield delivering the General's orders or observing the action for him. At the Battle of Monmouth, in 1778, three Aides-de-Camp, Alexander Hamilton, John Fitzgerald, and John Laurens, were all wounded. On more than one occasion the Aides-de-Camp had to gallop through a hail of musket balls to force the utterly fearless Washington to retire to safety." The article can be found on the internet at: http://www.revolutionarywararchives. org/washington-link/153-george-washingtons-military-family

42 *Alexander Hamilton Writings*, contents selected and notes written by Joanne B. Freeman, The Battle of Monmouth Alexander Hamilton to Elias Boudinot, 51–55

43 GWPRWS Henry Laurens to GW 16:35–36